Australia's Foreign Relations

Australia's Foreign Relations

IN THE WORLD OF THE 1990s

Gareth Evans
Bruce Grant

MELBOURNE UNIVERSITY PRESS

First published 1991
First paperback edition 1992
Reprinted 1992
Printed in Australia by
Brown Prior Anderson Pty Ltd, Burwood, Victoria, for
Melbourne University Press, Carlton, Victoria 3053
U.S.A. and Canada: International Specialized Book Services, Inc.,
5602 N.E. Hassalo Street, Portland, Oregon 97213-3640
United Kingdom and Europe: University College London Press,
Gower Street, London WC1E 6BT, UK

National Library of Australia Cataloguing-in-Publication entry

Evans, Gareth, 1944–   .
  Australia's foreign relations in the world of the 1990s.
Bibliography.
Includes index.
ISBN 0 522 84477 4.
ISBN 0 522 84485 5 (pbk.).
1. Australia—Foreign relations—1990–   . I. Grant, Bruce,
1925–   . II. Title.
327.94

To the men and women of the Australian Department of Foreign Affairs and Trade—a very fine career service and an under-appreciated national resource.

Contents

Preface

THIS BOOK is about the kind of foreign policy Australia needs to have if we are to successfully position ourselves, and advance our national interests, in the world of the 1990s.

A geographically remote country of seventeen million people in a world of five and a half billion should not get ideas above its station. But imaginative and effective diplomacy, of which Australia has shown that it is amply capable, can win for us a significant and respected place both in our own Asia Pacific region and in the wider international community. We can and should be able not only to pursue our own interests effectively, but in so doing to make a positive and constructive contribution to a more peaceful and prosperous world.

The world of the 1990s, it is already clear, will be one quite unlike that of any previous decade. The tumultuous events of 1989–91—the collapse of Soviet East Europe, the end of the Cold War, the beginning and end of the Gulf War—produced a great divide from which there is no going back. Any analysis of Australian foreign policy (and we use that term throughout to embrace both foreign policy narrowly defined *and* trade policy, for the two are now inextricably connected) has to have as its starting point the new international environment in which every country is now operating.

We begin Part I with a discussion of that environment. The rest of this Part—on the *dynamics* of Australian foreign policy—deals with the processes and mechanisms by which Australian policy does, or should, adjust to its international setting: how this has been done in the past, how it is being done now, and how it should go on being done as the world continues to change around us. A central theme is that, for all the inherent uncertainties of foreign policy making, and for all the obvious limitations on the capacity of a country like Australia to impose its will upon the world, policy making can and should be an intellectually orderly process. Australia, like any other country, has national interests of its own: they can be defined, and should be pursued. The art of the process is to define national interests rigorously, recognise what is and is not achievable, and set priorities accordingly.

An associated theme of this Part, and indeed of the whole book, is that Australia should not underestimate its capacity to achieve its own national interest objectives, and to do so in a way which benefits the whole international community. Our population size and location mean that we can never, realistically, become a major player on the world stage. But Australia is a significant power in regional terms, economically and otherwise, and does have a wider international profile as a diplomatically active trading nation willing to apply both imagination and energy to the resolution of international problems. It is only on occasion that foreign policy can be proactive: a good deal of the time one is necessarily reacting to events not of one's own making or choosing. But there is no excuse for a country like ours, with the interests we have at stake and with all the assets and resources available to us, just being driven by wind and tide. We can do a very great deal to forge our own international destiny.

Part II—on the *issues* of Australian foreign policy—puts flesh on these bones, subject by subject. It deals with how Australia can contribute to greater global security; how we should work to ensure greater regional security; how we should advance our economic and trade interests; how we should meet our responsibility towards the poorer developing countries; and how we should respond to some of the emerging issues of the new internationalist agenda, including human rights and the environment.

Issues, in international affairs, can never be pursued in isolation from the interests of other countries. Part III of the book—on *relationships*—deals with that traditional staple of diplomacy: getting on with other countries, whether they be neighbours, allies, friends, acquaintances or something less. Diplomats these days understand, rather better than they are often perceived to, that having Good Relations with another country is not an end in itself so much as a means to the end of advancing Australian national interests. Occasions will necessarily arise, for any self-respecting country, when sound policy compels that action be taken which puts a particular relationship under strain; in extreme situations, sound policy may demand that a relationship be broken off entirely. But in all except pathological situations, national interests are likely to be most productively advanced by developing and sustaining relations with other countries based on both professional respect and personal warmth, and a good deal of the conduct of Australian foreign policy, at both ministerial and diplomatic level, involves seeking to do just that.

Our relationships with the rest of the world are described in Part III from the perspective of Australia looking out upon the world. We begin with our neighbours in the South Pacific and South-East Asia; then look further north to Indo-China and North-East Asia; then across the Indian Ocean to South Asia, the Middle East and Africa; and only then to the Americas and Europe. The sequence is deliberate. It is not to denigrate the huge continuing importance to us, economically and otherwise, of our relationships with the United States and the European members of the Western alliance, nor for that matter the huge continuing role in world affairs of the Soviet Union, notwithstanding all its present difficulties: these themes are amply developed in Part II. Rather it reflects a way of looking at the world which we believe is long overdue for a country whose geography and future is that of the Asia Pacific. As we say, Australia's days of perceiving itself, and being perceived by others, as a European outpost—a cultural misfit isolated by its geography—are well and truly over.

When a book of this kind is co-authored by an incumbent Foreign Minister, as Gareth Evans has been since September 1988, some interesting questions arise. One is simply the stylistic conundrum of how best to treat, as we have had to from time to time, the actions, statements or positions taken by him in his ministerial capacity. The most economical solution, and the one we have adopted, was simply to adopt the third-person form.

A second issue was the use of Cabinet and other sensitive source material. While knowledge of this material necessarily indirectly underlies and informs a good many of the policy judgements we have made, and accounts we have given about how particular policies evolved or processes work, we have nowhere directly relied on material not already on the public record. There may be a history, or memoir, to be written in due course about the foreign policy alarums and diversions of the Hawke Government period, but this is not such a book.

A third question is that of partisan special pleading. Certainly, so far as Gareth Evans is concerned, it cannot be expected that this book could be written otherwise than from the perspective of a particular political commitment, and from a particular body of shared ministerial experience. Moreover its co-author is a minister who is proud of the role the Hawke Government has played in carving out a new and respected role for Australia in international affairs, especially in our own Asia Pacific region. But, all that said, both of us have a strong view that it is very much in Australia's interests that foreign policy be made and conducted on as bipartisan a basis as possible, with the absolute minimum of conflicting signals being sent abroad. By and large, in the post-Vietnam years, that has in fact been the case. To the extent that differences persist, we have not sought to accentuate them: our emphasis throughout has been on getting Australian foreign policy right, whoever happens to be in government, and not on castigating the weakness of some current alternative prescriptions. In the Australian political system, there are plenty of other opportunities for that.

An arbitrary cut-off date in a work of this kind is an unhappy necessity. While this book is policy focused and forward looking, and does try to stand back a little from the ebb and flow of daily events in order to look at some of the more enduring themes that will be involved in the conduct of Australian foreign policy throughout the next decade and beyond, there is always the risk when writing about contemporary affairs that the world will change between writing and publication, and one's judgments with them.

That risk was starkly realised with the failed coup in the Soviet Union of 19–21 August 1991. While the revolutionary changes achieved under President Gorbachev themselves remained intact, the coup's overthrow generated a rapid series of further changes, including the dramatic collapse of the Communist Party of the Soviet Union and the assertion of Russian authority by President Yeltsin. These developments, in turn, seemed certain to have a significant impact upon the structure of central government institutions, the Union's longer term viability as a political, military and economic entity, and the status and authority of its constituent republics—as well as upon such larger issues as global and regional power balances and the future political architecture of Europe. But holding the presses long enough to include everything would mean never publishing anything. This book, accordingly, reflects the world as we saw it, and the judgments we were able to make, as at 30 June 1991.

Acknowledgements   No book of this one's scope, size and contemporaneity could be written, at least quickly, without a good deal of assistance, and we are indebted to a great many people—particularly from the Department of Foreign Affairs and Trade—for contributing ideas, information and secretarial and other support. For those officers whom we do not mention by name in what follows, we hope that the book's dedication will be at least partial compensation.

In the first place there were the legions of officers from the Department and AIDAB, not least speech writers Peter Varghese and David Ritchie, who have contributed material to the seventy or so substantial Ministerial speeches and statements over the last three years—addressing most, but by no means all, of the topics here covered—which were the raw clay from which we started to craft. Then there were the individuals—again numbered in legions, and reaching out beyond the foreign service to other Departments, universities, libraries and non-government organisations—who helped us track down specific material along the way. Particularly helpful in this respect were Mal Ferguson and his whole Central Statistics Section, Frank Frost and Brian Martin from the Parliamentary Library Legislative Research Service, and Stewart Firth from Macquarie University who gave invaluable guidance in compiling the bibliographies. A further substantial contribution was made by the dozens of departmental officers, co-ordinated by Bill Farmer, who, in their areas of respective expertise, check-read each chapter as completed for factual errors, possible security sensitivities and egregious errors of judgment—although we of course accept responsibility for such problems as remain.

Books do not produce themselves, and we have some particular debts to acknowledge, within the Department, to Fiona Cousins, whose typing and administrative assistance to Bruce Grant was invaluable, and to Evie Fondum for her epic but ultimately triumphant struggle to produce the Charts. Every author owes a debt to his publisher—as we do in this case to John Iremonger—for the leap of faith involved in committing to a book which may never be completed; the completion of this one was certainly often in doubt with the multiple distractions we faced. Not every author, by contrast, has cause to thank his publisher's editor for anything other than adding a load of new frustrations—but here we had, in Jean Dunn, nothing short of a gem, always sensitive, constructive and thoroughly helpful.

That leaves until late in the list, but absolutely not least, the people in the engine room. We have both derived enormous support from Gareth Evans's ministerial staff, with no-one more crucial to the enterprise than Ellen Rayment with her inexhaustible reserves of energy, efficiency and amiable common sense. Julie Hafner, Fiona Hitchen, Chris Neville and David Chaplin have all been immensely helpful with secretarial and related support; and, on the policy side of the office, Senior Adviser John Dauth, together with Paul Robilliard, David Shires and Keith Scott, each played a major role in contributing ideas and checking information. The whole office worked marvellously together in sustaining a thoroughly professional, and at the same time good-humoured, work environment.

Good staff are not just technically proficient, but give strong personal support especially at times of over-work and stress—and with events unfolding at the pace they have over the last two years, those situations have not been in short supply. But no support can ever replace that of one's own family, and Gareth Evans is particularly grateful to Merran, and his teenagers Caitlin and Eamon, for living as happily as they did with his absence —and, for that matter, his presence—over the many gruelling months it took to get this book finally to press.

We should, finally, acknowledge each other. Gareth Evans was responsible for the overall shape, direction and policy focus of the book, and the initial outlines of each chapter. Bruce Grant then did the long, backbreaking job of compiling the detailed material, and preparing the first drafts of all chapters. The final drafts were produced by Gareth Evans, with some reshaping of material and a good deal of additional writing. The preparation of bibliographies, proof checking and related tasks were carried through by Bruce Grant. We came to the project with rather differing approaches and writing styles, and more than a handful of different policy perspectives and emphases. The mix could have been difficult, but in the event we were able to manage what we think has emerged as a genuinely seamless blend, in which our respective roles were completely complementary. It is for readers to judge whether, in the process, we have managed to say something worthwhile.

Gareth Evans
Bruce Grant

August 1991

Abbreviations

AACM	ASEAN–Australia Consultative Meeting
ABC	Australian Broadcasting Corporation
ACFOA	Australian Council for Overseas Aid
ACIAR	Australian Centre for International Agricultural Research
ACIO	Australian Commerce and Industry Office
AIDAB	Australian International Development Assistance Bureau
AJMC	Australia–Japan Ministerial Committee
ANC	African National Congress
ANZCERTA	Australian New Zealand Closer Economic Relationship Trade Agreement
ANZUS	Security Treaty between Australia, New Zealand and the United States
APEC	Asia Pacific Economic Co-operation
ASEAN	Association of South-East Asian Nations
ASIS	Australian Secret Intelligence Service
Austrade	Australian Trade Commission
BADGE	Business Advisory Group on Europe
BJP	Bharatiya Janata Party (India)
BRA	Bougainville Revolutionary Army
BW	biological weapons
CAAA	Comprehensive Anti-apartheid Act (US)
CANATA	Trade Agreement between the Government of Canada and the Commonwealth of Australia
CAP	Common Agricultural Policy
CARICOM	Caribbean Community
CD	Conference on Disarmament (UN)
CEDAW	Convention on the Elimination of All Forms of Discrimination against Women
CER	Australian New Zealand Closer Economic Relationship Trade Agreement
CERD	Convention on the Elimination of All Forms of Racial Discrimination
CFE	Conventional Armed Forces in Europe Treaty
CFMSA	Committee of Foreign Ministers on Southern Africa
CGDK	Coalition Government of Democratic Kampuchea
CHOGM	Commonwealth Heads of Government Meeting
CHR	Commission on Human Rights
COMEVEN	Group of Three Energy Basin Institute agreement

CONASUR	Southern Cone Agricultural Co-operation Council
CRAMRA	Convention on the Regulation of Antarctic Mineral Resource Activity
'CSCA'	'Conference on Security and Co-operation in Asia'
CSCE	Conference on Security and Co-operation in Europe
'CSCM'	'Conference on Security and Co-operation in the Mediterranean'
CW	chemical weapons
CWC	Chemical Weapons Convention
CWRI	Chemical Weapons Regional Initiative
DIFF	Development Import Finance Facility
DIO	Defence Intelligence Organisation
DK	Democratic Republic of Kampuchea
DPRK	Democratic People's Republic of Korea
DSP	United States Defense Support Program
EAEC	European Atomic Energy Community
EBRD	European Bank of Reconstruction and Development
EC	European Community
ECSC	European Coal and Steel Community
EEA	European Economic Association
EEC	European Economic Community
EFIC	Export Finance and Insurance Corporation
EFTA	European Free Trade Association
EMU	European Monetary Union
EPC	European Political Co-operation
EPG	Eminent Persons Group
EURATOM	European Atomic Energy Community
FAO	Food and Agriculture Organization
FPDA	Five Power Defence Arrangements
G7	Group of Seven
GATT	General Agreement on Tariffs and Trade
GDP	Gross Domestic Product
GNP	Gross National Product
IADS	Integrated Air Defence System
IAEA	International Atomic Energy Agency
IBA	International Bauxite Association
IBRD	International Bank for Reconstruction and Development
ICCPR	International Covenant on Civil and Political Rights
ICESCR	International Covenant on Economic Social and Cultural Rights
ILO	International Labour Organization
IMC	Informal Meeting on Cambodia (Jakarta)
IMF	International Monetary Fund
INF	Intermediate-range nuclear forces
IOC	Indian Ocean Commission

IOMACC	Indian Ocean Marine Affairs Co-operation Council
IOZOP	Indian Ocean Zone of Peace
ISA	International Sugar Agreement
IWA	International Wheat Agreement
JIM	Jakarta Informal Meeting
JMEC	Australia–China Joint Ministerial Economic Commission
KMT	Kuomintang Government of the Republic of China
KPNLF	Khmer Peoples National Liberation Front
LNG	Liquefied Natural Gas
MFP	Multi-Function Polis
MINURSO	Mission for the Referendum in the Western Sahara (UN)
MERCOSUR	Southern Cone Common Market
MTCR	Missile Technology Control Regime
NAFTA	North American Free Trade Agreement
NATO	North Atlantic Treaty Organisation
NGO	Non-Government Organisation
NIEs	Newly Industrialising Economies
NLD	National League of Democracy (Burma)
NPT	Nuclear Non-Proliferation Treaty
NSG	Nuclear Suppliers Group
ODA	Official Development Assistance
OECD	Organization for Economic Co-operation and Development
ONA	Office of National Assessments
ONUCA	Operacion de las Naciones Unidas en Centroamerica
OPEC	Organization of Petroleum Exporting Countries
OPTAD	Organisation for Pacific Trade and Development
PAC	Pan Africanist Congress
PAFTA	Pacific Free Trade Area
PAFTAD	Pacific Trade and Development Conference
PBEC	Pacific Basin Economic Council
PICC	Paris International Conference on Cambodia
PLO	Palestine Liberation Organisation
PMC	Post Ministerial Conference (ASEAN)
PPQ	Possible Parliamentary Question
PRK	People's Republic of Kampuchea
ROK	Republic of Korea
SAARC	South Asian Association for Regional Co-operation
SADCC	Southern Africa Development Co-ordination Conference
SALT	Strategic Arms Limitation Treaty
SAPSA	Special Assistance Program for South Africans
SBS	Special Broadcasting Service
SDI	Strategic Defense Initiative
SEANWFZ	South-East Asia Nuclear Weapons Free Zone
SEATO	South-East Asia Treaty Organisation

SLORC	State Law and Order Restoration Council (Burma)
SNC	Supreme National Council (Cambodia)
SOC	State of Cambodia
SPARTECA	South Pacific Regional Trade and Economic Co-operation Agreement
SPREP	South Pacific Regional Environment Protection Commission
START	Strategic Arms Reduction Treaty
UN	United Nations
UNAVEM	United Nations Angola Verification Mission
UNCED	United Nations Conference on Environment and Development
UNEP	United Nations Environment Programme
UNESCO	United Nations Educational Scientific and Cultural Organization
UNFICYP	United Nations Force in Cyprus
UNFPA	United Nations Population Fund
UNHCR	United Nations High Commissioner for Refugees
UNICEF	United Nations Children's Fund
UNIKOM	United Nations Iraq–Kuwait Observer Mission
UNIIMOG	United Nations Iran–Iraq Military Observer Group
UNTAG	United Nations Transition Assistance Group for Namibia
WEOG	Western Europe and Others Group
WEU	Western European Union
WHO	World Health Organization
WTO	Warsaw Treaty Organisation
ZOPFAN	South-East Asia Zone of Peace Freedom and Neutrality

PART I

DYNAMICS

1

The Changing International Environment

IN INTERNATIONAL AFFAIRS, change is the only constant. Certainly the twentieth century seemed to have had rather more than its quota, even before its last decade began. Two world wars; the arrival of revolutionary communism on the world stage; a massive economic depression creating a crisis for capitalism; fascism and the Holocaust; the advent of nuclear weapons and their deployment in support of an ideological confrontation threatening to end all human history; the sweeping aside of three centuries of European colonialism in Asia and Africa; the emergence of the Asia Pacific region as a dynamic new engine for world economic growth—these make a formidable shortlist in support of the claim that this century has been the most turbulent in recorded history.

But more was to come. In 1989, and the year-and-a-half which followed, the world was turned inside out: Soviet communism collapsed; democratic revolutions swept East Europe; Germany was reunited; the Middle East ignited, but the world combined through the United Nations to quench the flames; and, perhaps most welcome of all to a world long fearing the worst, a white South African government set about dismantling the whole abhorrent apartheid system on which its existence had been premised.

Within a breathtakingly short period, the international landscape seemed comprehensively transformed, more so than at any time since World War I and the Russian Revolution, and perhaps the French Revolution before that. New patterns and shapes began to emerge, and in a way which seemed to guarantee them some durability. But just as no-one predicted the collapse of the East Europe communist states in such dramatic

3

fashion, so no-one can calculate now with certainty the shape of international relations over the next decade and beyond. The course of history is rarely if ever the irresistible working out of forces in obedience to some discoverable law of human affairs; certainly that is the impression of those who have had to make major decisions, usually quickly, in the latter years of this century. Modern men and women have been taught to believe in the rational pursuit of achievable goals. As the twentieth century fades, we must still try to be rational, but we have also learnt that we must be extremely agile.

Australia, like any other country, has to reassess and where necessary reformulate its foreign policy against the backdrop of the world as it now appears. Turbulence never does much to assist clarity of vision, and we can only hope that our perception of what is important and enduring in the new international landscape will stand the test of time. That said, there would appear to be three basic features of that landscape which have emerged in strong relief and which are crucial from an Australian perspective: the end of East–West confrontation; the emergence of a new internationalism in the conduct of nations' affairs; and the economic dynamism of the Asia Pacific region.

THE END OF THE COLD WAR

Three dates have credible claims to be *the* date on which the Cold War ended: 9 November 1989, when the Berlin Wall was breached at the Brandenburg Gate; 19 November 1990, when the Conference on Security and Cooperation in Europe convened in Paris to formally declare that the NATO and Warsaw Pact member states 'are no longer adversaries'; or 31 March 1991, when the military structures of the Warsaw Pact were formally and finally dismantled. The choice is a matter of taste. What matters is that unquestionably we have come to the end of a forty-five year era, one in which East–West confrontation was the central prevailing fact of life not only in European and North Atlantic affairs but in world affairs.

The Cold War began in the closing stages of World War II with the descent, in Churchill's unforgettable phrase, of the 'iron curtain' dividing East from West Europe. Where the armies of the Allies came to a halt after the defeat of Nazi Germany and Fascist Italy, so, on the one side, stood the democracies of West Europe protected by the North Atlantic Treaty Organisation (NATO) and, on the other, the Soviet Union and the communist regimes of East Europe protected by the Warsaw Treaty Organisation (WTO).

The arbitrary division of Europe came to be symbolised by the Berlin Wall, erected in 1961 to crudely and blatantly separate East Germans from West Germans. It was the failure of the Berlin Wall in the northern spring of 1989 to stop East Germans from getting to West Germany (through Hungary and Czechoslovakia) that immediately precipitated the dramatic collapses of communist regimes in East Europe in 1989. But the underlying factor was the knowledge that Soviet military power was—as a result of the absence of political will to support it—no longer available to prop up those regimes, as it had done in Hungary in 1956 and in Czechoslovakia in 1968. The Soviet Union, itself embarking under President Mikhail Gorbachev on a fundamental reshaping of the old communist system, in effect nodded assent to the people massing in the old city squares of East Europe.

The political changes that followed had all the character of a revolution, or the end of a war. They were so rapid and so unpredictable that they could not be associated with the normal process of political change in peacetime, and they transfixed the watching world. Dissident writers and scholars, who had been enemies of the people, suddenly found themselves elevated into positions of power and authority. People who happened to be at a television station on the night that government crumbled found themselves, in the absence of an alternative government, broadcasting their demands to the world as if they had been appointed to do so. It was politics at its most heady and exciting—progress which made the triumph of the trade union movement Solidarity through the earlier 1980s in Poland seem snail-like by comparison.

Yet during the same period, in June 1989, a demonstration of students in Beijing's Tienanmen Square was suppressed with a ruthlessness that shocked the West not only into a retaliatory down-grading of its relations with China, but also into a rethinking of comfortable assumptions about the inevitability of democratic change there. One of the many ironies of the fraught relationship of the two major communist powers is that the reforming zeal of the post-Mao regime in China had spurred the Gorbachev reforms in the Soviet Union, and that Gorbachev's visit to China to symbolise the healing of the generation-old rift had been a factor in sustaining the demonstrators in Tienanmen Square. The surrender of the leading role of the communist parties in East Europe, and to a lesser extent in the Soviet Union, has simply been ideologically—and perhaps just as important, personally—unacceptable to the present generation of Chinese rulers. Fundamental political change there will be longer coming.

While ideology has certainly not disappeared as a motivating force in the affairs of nations—and there will be plenty willing to argue that it still has a key role in sustaining the resistance to change of the remaining Asian communist regimes—it is difficult to refute the suggestion that Marxism-Leninism, at least as an economic system, has comprehensively lost to its capitalist and mixed economy competitors the battle for the hearts and minds of national policy makers. (Whether the triumph of the political ideology of Western liberal democracy over its competitors is quite as comprehensive or complete as Francis Fukuyama claims in his famous 1989 essay, 'The End of History?',[1] it is still too early to tell, but his argument is a compelling one.)

Certainly we have witnessed a decline in the hostility with which communist systems have viewed capitalist systems: perhaps most engagingly illustrated by Vietnam Foreign Minister Nguyen Co Thach's disclosure to Gareth Evans at their 1988 meeting in Hanoi that his favourite bedtime reading was Samuelson's *Economics*! From a global perspective, it is this decline that marked the 1980s and has produced a more positive atmosphere for international relations generally. One reason for it is that each superpower discovered limits to its power: not just in Vietnam and Afghanistan, where they learned that military solutions have limited applications, but also in the crucial matter of economic performance.

In this, the Soviet Union has something in common with the rest of the countries of the communist world. All have been unable to deliver the goods in one important aspect or another. Whether small like Cuba and Laos, or medium-sized like the East Europeans and Vietnam, or large like the Soviet Union and the People's Republic of China, each has had to acknowledge to some degree the utility of private ownership, competition and a market economy. None has yet succeeded in managing the transition, but all—with varying degrees of enthusiasm and competence—are trying.

At the same time, the exemplar of the Western model, the United States, has progressively lost its relative post-War economic dominance. This is not because the Western model has proved wanting but, on the contrary, because it has been skilfully adapted by others who have begun to perform better than the United States—and, not least, because in the years following World War II, the United States had the strategic vision, and generosity, to encourage the economic development of Europe and Japan.

The continuing extent of United States economic power in absolute terms should not be underestimated. Clearly the United States will remain for many years to come the largest national economy, and one critically important to the health of the global economy. The rise of United States international debt and the continuing size of its budget deficits are a cause for concern both domestically and internationally, but the country has an enormous demonstrated capacity for change and renewal. Some similarities have been discerned with the decline of Imperial Britain or Spain, or with France in the 1780s, but it would seem to be just a little premature to write off the United States as another impending victim of 'imperial overstretch'.[2]

However much the United States may be feeling the economic pinch, there is no sign of this translating into any weakening of its military power. Its decisive and extraordinarily effective leadership of the Coalition forces in the Gulf War against Saddam Hussein amply demonstrated that, as nothing else could. There is simply no non-Soviet competitor, in this sense, for the United States's superpower status. Nor does any other country have a comparable *breadth* of authority and influence. Japan is a global economic and financial superpower, but with limited political, cultural or military projection. The European Community, if it ever achieves complete union, would be a potential superpower of comparable dimension—as none of its individual member nations can be—but at this stage it is simply not a comparable political or military unit. Of the other potential claimants to superpower status, China is a vast aggregation of people, but with regional —rather than global—political, cultural and military capacity; and the same is true of India.

However, the continued pre-eminence of the United States in so many respects, when looked at alongside the collapse of the will and capacity of the Soviet Union to exercise the kind of authority it used to before 1989, should not lead us to rush to the conclusion that the bipolar world familiar to us since the end of World War II is now a unipolar one. In a strategic sense, the world is still very much bipolar, in that the main game continues to be the relationship between the two full-scale global nuclear powers, who have stockpiled between them some fifty thousand nuclear warheads, as compared with not much more than one thousand for everyone else combined. There is a one-to-one relationship between them that they do not have with anyone else, and no other power can have with either of them. Even a significant break-up of the present Soviet Union, with a number of its constituent republics going their own way, is unlikely to fundamentally change this equation. Central control of the nuclear armory will, on most assessments, not be significantly dispersed—whether it takes place under the authority of a continuing Union of Soviet Socialist Republics, or of some combination of one or more of the Union's present constituent republics.

The most practical analysis is that for the rest of this century we can expect the United States–Soviet Union bipolar relationship to remain the core of the central strategic balance. But we can also expect that, increasingly, the central strategic balance will not dominate and determine the agenda of international relations as it has in the past. Global security will continue to pivot on the fulcrum of the United States–Soviet military balance and nuclear deterrence, but confrontation will be muted. Co-operation between the United States and the Soviet Union in the resolution of conflict has occurred now in a number of contexts—Cambodia, Afghanistan, Iran–Iraq, Namibia and, most spectacularly and effectively of all, the 1990–91 Gulf crisis. For all the internal uncertainties still looming for the Soviet Union, there is no particular reason to assume that this co-operation cannot continue. Other powers—and the United Nations itself—will play increasingly significant roles in the resolution, or prolongation, of particular conflicts. At the same time, we can expect international economic issues to assume greater importance in the international agenda, as increasing economic interdependence brings new problems in its train.

For more than forty years, strategic and ideological hostility between the United States and the Soviet Union permeated all international life. It threatened nuclear war. It also meant that almost every issue—whether a regional conflict, the role of the United Nations, preferred models of economic development, humane treatment of refugees, or the definition of human rights—became enmeshed in the central contest. The change we are experiencing is that the Soviet Union, which for seventy years asserted the intrinsic superiority of its system and the inevitable conflict with capitalism leading to capitalism's defeat and banishment from the stage of history, has now proclaimed—or at least its currently most influential voices are proclaiming—that its view of the world is no longer dominated by conceptions of class war and capitalism's defeat. Whether global interdependence—a major theme in Gorbachev's public statements—turns out to be a guiding principle of Soviet policy in practice remains to be seen. But the negative, aggressive assumptions with which Moscow previously faced the Western world no longer hold sway.

Naturally, prudence is called for in assessing such dramatic declarations. It was Nikita Krushchev in the 1950s who proclaimed an era of 'coexistence', from which he assumed the Soviet Union would emerge triumphant and the West would be 'buried'. Deeds must match the words. But we must also acknowledge and draw encouragement from the fact there have been deeds in arms control, in human rights, and in regional conflicts.

The consequences are of major significance. It removes the central organising principle of the post-War world, where two armed camps, defined by their adherence to opposing ideologies, confronted each other, and the rest of the world and many of its problems were relegated to a secondary importance. It will increase the chances of resolution of many long-running regional conflicts; give hope for major progress towards arms control and disarmament; and allow the world to turn its attention to other massive and pressing social, economic and political problems. The release of the Soviet Union's strong arm on its internal empire and on East Europe has created its own form of turmoil, but it is turmoil with the prospect of relief, not turmoil at a dead end.

THE NEW INTERNATIONALISM

One of the most striking accompaniments to the end of East–West confrontation has been the re-emergence to centre stage of the United Nations (UN). For all the occasional success enjoyed by the Secretary-General in his conciliatory good-offices role, and for all the utility from time to time of UN peace-keeping operations in supervising and monitoring particular political settlements, the unhappy reality had been that for most of its first forty-five years of existence the United Nations, as a peace-making and peace-enforcing institution, was rendered both sterile and impotent by superpower competition.

From the 1940s to the 1980s many attempts were made to give the United Nations security teeth, and to realise the founders' dream of a new international collective security system which would make impossible any repetition of the horrifying 1930s descent into world war. With the exception of the UN forces in Korea—made possible more by a procedural error of judgment by the Soviet Union than by any superpower co-operation—those attempts failed. The United Nations became more often a forum for confrontation than co-operation in the resolution of conflict. It was placed in an East–West straitjacket. Set-piece debates dragged to inevitably unproductive conclusions: a Security Council veto by one permanent member or another was almost the only certainty when the United Nations was called upon to act.

With the collapse of the Cold War a wholly new atmosphere has emerged. Negotiations over Afghanistan, Cambodia and Namibia, and the settlement of the Iran–Iraq conflict during 1989–90 saw an unprecedented degree of constructive co-operation between the five permanent members. This in turn laid the foundation for the almost superhuman levels of co-operation achieved and sustained throughout the course of the Gulf crisis. From Saddam Hussein's invasion of Kuwait in August 1990, through the imposition and enforcement of economic sanctions, the delivering of a military ultimatum, and the pursuit to successful conclusion of full-scale war in January–February 1991, an extraordinary level of understanding was maintained between the United States and Soviet Union. No real attempt was made by either side to exploit each other's internal difficulties; no attempt was made by the Soviet Union to rally an 'anti-imperialist coalition'; there was no use of the veto in the Security Council. Without all that, unthinkable in the Cold War years, the task of gathering and sustaining international support would have been immeasurably more complicated, and probably in fact beyond practical attainment. As it was, the international response was overwhelming: 38 countries participated directly in the action against Iraq, another 4 (including Germany and Japan) contributed major financial and logistic support, and 144 UN members joined in the General Assembly resolution of 18 December 1990 condemning Iraq.

Is this new momentum sustainable? If the concept of a 'new world order', shorn of its rhetorical overlay, means anything at all, its essential defining characteristic would seem to be co-operation by the major powers in the containment and resolution of conflict under the umbrella of the United Nations and using its institutional processes. Will the emerging pattern of 'Permanent Five' co-operation continue? Was the successful handling of the Gulf crisis simply a product of its own particular circumstances—the particular villainy and obduracy of Saddam Hussein, the threat to world oil prices, accidents of timing—or does it genuinely presage a new era of internationalist solutions to security problems?

It is simply too early to give a definitive answer. Everything depends, in the first instance, on the attitude struck by the Soviet Union and the United States. No-one can be sure, in the present environment of turmoil and fragmentation, that the highly constructive foreign policy orientation of the

Soviet Union under President Gorbachev will continue indefinitely. And for all its conspicuous success in working through UN processes in the Gulf crisis, and much greater commitment to UN principles evident in President Bush as compared to almost any of his predecessors, it cannot be assumed that the United States will routinely see its national interests being advanced by multilateral diplomacy through the United Nations. Certainly it has to be acknowledged, given present world realities, that an effective UN collective security system depends heavily on United States commitment. Collective security action simply could not be mounted, or even credibly threatened, without United States support.

Moreover, the sustaining of a new internationalist momentum in security matters is not wholly dependent on the superpowers alone. They, and the Permanent Five members, will need to take into account the mood of the rest of the United Nations membership. Richer countries among them are going to be cautious about the financial implications of major new peace-keeping or peace-enforcement commitments. And smaller countries are becoming aware of the political and economic effects upon them of Security Council resolutions in which they have no part, and are beginning to express concerns that great power co-operation, if not handled sensitively, may develop—as one country put it recently—into a 'great power directorate'. But all that said, a new mood of optimism about the future does generally prevail. There are few policy makers around the world who believe that the new prominence of the United Nations in peace and security matters—and the demonstrated willingness of the major powers to work within this framework—is anything other than a beneficial and important new development in world affairs. At the very least, any country contemplating aggression must now take very much into account the possibility that a United Nations system of effective sanctions, backed by a UN-authorised international military coalition, can again be mounted.

While developments on the security front have been the most striking recent manifestation of a new internationalist mood, they are certainly not the only one. Elsewhere within the United Nations system a quite dramatic change of atmosphere has been evident since 1989. The Forty-Fourth and Forty-Fifth Sessions of the UN General Assembly have been widely remarked as being among the most harmonious and co-operative on record, with major progress on issues such as the environment, human rights, drugs and even the reform and rationalisation of the United Nations administrative system itself. The familiar developed–developing country voting blocs acted less cohesively, and with more regard to consensus. Similarly, the 1991 Session of the United Nations Commission on Human Rights—more often than not the scene of bitter controversy and recrimination, with North–South cultural differences looming large—was regarded as very successfully advancing a more recent trend toward moderation, co-operation and consensus. Country-specific resolutions were adopted for such sensitive areas as Iran, Cuba and Burma, and a number of new monitoring mechanisms were set up.

These atmospheric developments are partly attributable to flow-on effects from the end of the Cold War, but they appear to owe rather more to an emerging world-wide recognition that a great many problems can be dealt with effectively only by co-operation on a multilateral, and in some cases global, scale. To familiar and established topics in this category like refugees, famine, debt and the control of nuclear weapons have now been added issues such as major environmental problems, AIDS, narcotics and terrorism.

Undoubtedly the most prominent recent addition to the new internationalist agenda has been the environment. While from the 1970s environmental protection became an important part of the domestic political programs of many nations—particularly Western developed nations —it was not perceived as having an urgent international dimension. Other issues—non-alignment, the new international economic order, disarmament and decolonisation—all had a higher priority. The environment was generally regarded as a domestic issue or, at most, a worthwhile but minor aspect of international co-operation. The 1980s saw a significant shift in both perceptions and priorities. In Europe and North America, ecological problems like acid rain served to highlight the trans-national aspects of environmental threats. The scientific evidence on trends like global warming began to accumulate. The push of the financial markets and communications technologies were drawing all countries—developed and developing alike—closer together and making them more aware of their common interests and inescapable links. Particularly in Western developed countries, an active and articulate Green movement was gaining strength and demanding that environmental protection be built into both national and international strategies.

By 1987 the Brundtland Commission on Environment and Development —with a membership drawn from across the regional, economic and political spectrum—captured both the direction and driving rationale of this new trend with its seminal report on *Our Common Future*.[3] The Brundtland Report signalled that environmental issues were on the global agenda to stay, and since then hardly an international meeting has not repeatedly underlined the urgency of common action—to save our common future. In less than a decade, protection of the global environment has emerged as perhaps the most pressing issue facing the world. The greenhouse effect, the ozone layer, the future of tropical rainforests, have all become part of the established lexicon of international diplomacy.

If there is an emerging 'one world' vision among nations around the globe it is not that which inspired in the past the proponents of world government, but rather one based on an appreciation of environmental interdependence, combined with a recognition of the inexorable logic of science and technology, and financial markets. Modern communications and information systems mean that information is more rapidly and widely dispersed, and instantly available on a global basis, than would have been conceivable to earlier generations. Entrepreneurial and professional skills have become internationally mobile. And capital has become extraordinarily mobile: every day in 1990, for example, some $600 billion of foreign currency was being traded by speculators in the markets of Tokyo, London and New York, compared with an *annual* trade between the United States and Japan of $200 billion.[4] Globalisation in all these senses is here to stay.

Insulation from the competitive pressures of the international marketplace is becoming harder and harder for any single country to sustain. It is gradually coming to be appreciated that breaking down such remaining barriers as stand in the way of economic interdependence is a matter of intelligent self-interest; that it is against all experience, as well as all theory, to yearn after autarky in a world increasingly interconnected. That appreciation lay behind the initiation of the eighth—or 'Uruguay'—Round of multilateral trade negotiations in 1986, which encompassed a much more wide-ranging agenda (including, for example, agriculture and services) than any previous attempt at international trade liberalisation. But while economic inward-thinking may be as old-fashioned as trench warfare, protectionist sentiment dies hard in even the most advanced industrial societies. At the time of writing, the Uruguay Round—its duration already extended by six months—had not concluded, and a good deal of hard negotiation lay ahead.

The process of globalisation, in its translation into particular policy areas, will not be without its fits and starts. Not only protectionist sentiment, but deep-seated ethnic and regional loyalties and the like, will go on cutting across the logic of interdependence and co-operation. But globalisation is unquestionably now a primary factor for change in international affairs, generating its own new issues on the international agenda as well as a greater capacity to solve them. The challenge for the international community, and for foreign policy makers, is to develop and implement co-operative strategies to tackle systematically the big problems that do remain: the problem of peace and security for those millions who are threatened by continuing conflict, and the problems of over-population, hunger, debt and environmental degradation that threaten yet more hundreds of millions of people.

ASIA PACIFIC DYNAMISM

The emergence of the Asia Pacific region as the most economically dynamic in the world is a development of great international significance, not least for Australia. Since the end of the Vietnam War, its growth has been phenomenal. Moreover, its vitality has been outward-looking. Its dependence on trade has been very high, and it has so far resisted the temptation to try to form any kind of defensive economic bloc. While the tendency towards regionalism in other parts of the world is likely to encourage ever greater internal co-operation within the Asia Pacific region, it is difficult to imagine its habit of mind remaining other than open to the outside world.

The centre of gravity of world production shifted from the Atlantic to the Pacific in the 1980s. The Asia Pacific region as a whole, including North America, generates more than one-third of the world's trade, and is likely in the course of the 1990s to create more than half the world's economic output. Per capita incomes are growing quickly, and in countries like Singapore and Hong Kong already rival the lower income European countries. The region's economic importance to Australia is obvious: more than half our exports and nearly half our imports are directed to or sourced from our western Pacific neighbours. Seven of Australia's ten largest markets can be found there. About a quarter of the total foreign investment in Australia has come from the western Pacific region, and almost one-fifth of Australia's total investment overseas is located there.

The region is politically, culturally and militarily diverse, indeed so diverse as to scarcely qualify being described as a 'region'. It really only defines itself by a process of exclusion: it is not the American hemisphere, nor Europe, nor Africa, nor the Middle East. It can itself be sub-divided into regions such as North-East Asia, South-East Asia and the South Pacific. About its only common focus is the Pacific Ocean—although even that fails to hold if one chooses to define the region as including South Asia. The region has its share of military conflict, territorial disputes and political disagreements, most obviously in relation to the Korean Peninsula, Cambodia, the four islands contested by Japan and the Soviet Union, and—if one extends the focus to the sub-continent—Kashmir, with the Spratly Islands (contested variously by six nations) having the potential to join this list at almost any time. But, in contrast with Europe, it is not dominated by or made up of military blocs, although there are a number of significant bilateral links, most importantly those between the United States and, respectively, Japan, South Korea, the Philippines and Australia.

Generally the elements of economic dynamism, openness and diversity lend a strongly pragmatic flavour to the region. The desire for growth and prosperity is the most compelling and significant force in almost every individual country, and economic aspirations constitute the primary dynamic of both internal and external policies. The hope for the region, in security terms, is that there will be a maturing consensus that economic development is more important than building military strength, and that security is best guaranteed by working in co-operation and increasing cross-links of interdependence rather than by building armouries.

Australia's interests manifestly lie in encouraging such a view. They also lie in maintaining the open nature of the Asia Pacific region, economically, strategically, politically and culturally, and in securing an accepted place for ourselves within the region not as an outsider but as a nation among nations.

2

The Evolution of
an Independent
Foreign Policy

AUSTRALIAN FOREIGN POLICY has been slow evolving. There were no revolutionary jolts of self-consciousness, and Australians clung to a British Imperial view of the world rather longer than might have been expected of the brash and nationalistic people who created a nation for themselves in 1901. A factor in this may have been that the twentieth century, which they entered with high hopes, turned out to be a tough training ground for an essentially fearful people. In spite of their appearance of confidence, Australians at that time were just that. They were frightened that the turmoil might unseat Britain and install some other hegemonic European power in Australia's neck of the woods or, even more unpalatable although less likely, that the Europeans would lose control altogether and allow Australia to be overwhelmed by 'Asiatic hordes'.

The proposition can be stated today with rhetorical licence because it seems fanciful. At the opening of the twentieth century, however, it seemed entirely realistic. The shape of world politics was determined by who won and lost in Europe. The United States was dominant in its particular hemisphere, but still uncertain of its role beyond. Japan was emerging as a modern nation-state, soon to demonstrate unexpectedly its naval supremacy over Tsarist Russia, and Imperial China was breaking up. While these developments seemed vaguely threatening from Australia's point of view, our immediate neighbourhood was under the control of Britain and the other European colonial powers, and it was in the cockpit of Europe that the relative strengths of those powers—and their attitude to emergent Asia—would be decided. The evolution of Australian foreign policy needs to be assessed against a background in Australian politics of persistent anxiety about a threat from Asia: sometimes vague and undifferentiated, sometimes specific, but always there. Other issues surface from time to time, but an enduring theme is how Australians could best come to terms with the region in which, for better or for worse, they were destined to live.

FROM 1788 TO NATIONHOOD

British settlement in Australia was established twelve years after the American colonies revolted successfully against the British and one year before the most cataclysmic event of the eighteenth century, the French Revolution. The outside world made little impression, however, on the gaol at Sydney Cove, which was overwhelmed in the early years by the novelty of its surroundings and preoccupied with its own internal social order and survival. Thirty years after settlement, in 1819, the non-Aboriginal population of New South Wales was just 26 026 and that of Van Diemen's Land (Tasmania) 4270; it is estimated that about three-quarters were convicts or the children of convicts. (By mid-century the total Australian population was still only around 400 000; it trebled in the gold-rush decade of the 1850s, and by Federation was 3.77 million.)

Early decisions, such as occupying Norfolk Island, navigating Bass Strait and circumnavigating the Australian continent involved official extensions of the Sydney settlement. In 1803–04, to forestall the French, settlements were established at Port Phillip in Victoria (temporarily) and Hobart. In 1810, Napoleon ordered the Governor of Mauritius to 'take' the colony at Sydney, but—in one of the more significant, albeit less well known, turning points of Australian history—he declined.

By the 1850s, two foreign policy impulses that were to become common for almost a century could be detected. One was the effort by self-made Australians to get to the source of authority in London, as a way of influencing the direction of the colony. The example was set by John Macarthur who, sent by Governor King to England as an army officer in 1802 to face court martial, convinced the Secretary of State, Earl Camden, that New South Wales could grow fine wool to compete with Spain and the German states, and was granted ten thousand acres south-west of Sydney to try his luck.

The other impulse was to help Britain win its wars. In 1854, when Britain went to war with Russia in the Crimea, there was a rush in Sydney and Melbourne to volunteer. However, this was also the year of the Eureka stockade, and when news of the military reverses in the Russian winter reached Australia the local press had a field day with the aristocratic incompetence of the English governing classes. As democracy and nationalism developed, so it appeared did anti-British sentiment, but this did not prevent an outpouring of sympathy—and the despatch of 750 troops by New South Wales—to support the rescue of General Gordon from Khartoum in 1885. Despite the controversial nature of the Boer War (1899–1902) the Australian colonies sent eight battalions to help the British.

The first hints of defiance of the British in foreign policy show in Australian attitudes to the South Pacific. In 1883 Queensland, nervous about Germany's intentions, tried to annex New Guinea and was blocked by Britain. A year later, Germany claimed north-east New Guinea and the Bismarck Archipelago. In 1886 Britain and Germany agreed on the demarcation of their spheres of influence in New Guinea and associated island groups. In the same year the Victorian Government expressed its concern over Britain's failure to force France to withdraw troops from the New Hebrides.

While no single voice can be said to express the growing national sentiment of the late nineteenth century in Australia, that of Sir Henry Parkes in presenting the argument for Federation at the 1890 conference in Melbourne possibly comes closest. He pointed out that Australia's population was nearly four million, that its per capita average private wealth was greater than enjoyed by the inhabitants of Europe, the United Kingdom and the United States, and that in other respects, such as economic and political development, it was entitled to nationhood. He argued that Australia, not the European powers, should be 'mistress of the Southern Seas' and that, if the Australian colonies had been able to speak with a single voice in 1883, New Guinea would 'have belonged to' Australia. He looked to a future in which the Australian Governor-General 'would be able to hold a court that would be as attractive as that of the monarchs of the old world'. Nevertheless, the British Imperial idea remained so powerful at this time, when indeed the British Empire was at its zenith, that his preferred future for Australia was within an enlarged empire that would carry 'our language, our laws, our social habits, our literature, our great stores of science, to all parts of the habitable globe'.[1]

As nationhood dawned, a divided loyalty seems to have settled in the minds of many Australian nationalists, both wanting and not wanting British power, being unable themselves to do anything to prevent the Germans or the French from occupying territory close at hand yet prepared to answer the bugle call to arms in Khartoum or South Africa. The origins of Australia's thwarted nationalism in the twentieth century can thus be seen at the end of the nineteenth century. The beginning of a tradition of inflated rhetoric is also apparent. The warnings against Chinese and other 'Asiatics' (on the grounds that they were diligent and clever, while asserting at the same time that the Australians could beat any man on earth in fair competition)[2] were typical of the ambivalent rhetoric that created the White Australia policy.

TO THE OUTBREAK OF WORLD WAR II

Australia had one quick victory after Federation in 1901. The colony of Papua was transferred to it by London over the period 1902–06. Japan's naval victory over the Russians in the war of 1904–05 made the new nation more than ever sensitive to sea-power: the United States's 'Great White Fleet' visited Australia in 1908 and the Royal Australian Navy was established in 1910. When World War I (1914–18) arrived, however, it was Australian money and manpower that Andrew Fisher pledged in support of the British Empire 'to our last man and our last shilling'.[3]

The exploits of the Australian 'digger' fighting the Germans on the battlefields of Belgium and France, and especially in the fatal expedition against the Turks at Gallipoli in 1915, have created the legend that Australia became a nation during World War I. The reckless bravery of these young men, many of them from the Australian bush, suggested that Australia had come of age in the sense that its manhood did not flinch when faced with the experienced soldiers of Europe. While the legend has inspired generations of poets and artists—and politicians—its bearing on the reality of Australian nationhood is romantic in the extreme. When the Australian soldiers returned to civilian life they discovered that the Australian nation had very little control over its destiny, as it had had little control over the decision to land at Gallipoli. Its security was assumed to depend on the British navy continuing to rule the waves; its economy was enmeshed with Britain's; and in foreign policy, despite Prime Minister William Morris Hughes thumping the table at Versailles in 1919 (and being successful to the extent that Australia received a mandate over German New Guinea), Australia was still a daughter of Empire.

Moreover, the gallantry of the Australian soldier and the patriotic fervour with which the war was fought by Australia barely concealed dissension within Australian society. Such dissension had existed from the Crimean War onwards, and would again, after unity between government and people in World War II, during the war in Vietnam. Irish-Australians and the Catholic Church, both influential in the trade union movement and the Australian Labor Party, were less than enthusiastic about the British Empire and opposed to sending Australian troops across the world essentially to fight for Britain. It was largely their opposition which influenced Australians to reject conscription for military service in two separate referendums during World War I.

There were some perceived legal inhibitions to Australia's capacity to make decisions about foreign policy. Although the Constitution of 1901 listed 'external affairs' as a legislative power to be exercised under Section 51 by the new Federal government, this was construed by governments to mean little more than that the Commonwealth, rather than the States, had the responsibility of implementing British government decisions. Not until

1923 were the Dominions permitted to conclude treaties and agreements with foreign powers, and not until the 1931 Statute of Westminster did the British Parliament relinquish its power to make laws binding the Commonwealth government. But steps were not taken by Australia to formally adopt the Statute of Westminster until 1942, which shows how little the governments of that time valued—either symbolically or practically—such freedom as it gave them. Formal legal restraints were not in themselves the reason for Australian foreign policy subservience.

It is a mark of Australia's relaxed attitude to foreign policy that early foreign ministers—to the extent that the job was held other than by the prime minister of the day—were neither politically notable nor especially active. In 1916 Hughes abolished the Department of External Affairs —such as it then was (being responsible mainly for immigration and territories)—and it was not until 1932 that a post-War Minister for External Affairs was appointed who was not Prime Minister. The Department was re-established in 1921 on a very small scale (operating as, in effect, a branch of the Prime Minister's Department), and it was not until 1935 that a fully fledged foreign office was established. Only in 1940 were the first 'foreign' diplomatic posts (that is, outside Britain, where our Australian High Commission had been set up in 1910) established in Washington, Tokyo and Ottawa. And this last initiative was, obviously, sparked by the shock of war. Robert Gordon Menzies, as Prime Minister in 1939, had the ironic distinction of announcing the new legations. He said:

> Little given as I am to encouraging the exaggerated ideas of Dominion independence and separatism which exist in some minds, I have become convinced that, in the Pacific, Australia must regard herself as a principal providing herself with her own information and maintaining her own diplomatic contacts with foreign powers.[4]

The irony is that Menzies had persistently opposed separate legations for many years (on the grounds of Imperial unity), but inherited the decision after the death of Lyons.

The slow growth of a professional service in Australia contrasts with the experience of Canada, South Africa and Ireland. The reason is perhaps not far to seek. In the case of Canada, which opened a legation in Washington in 1927, the strong French component and closeness to the United States, as well as remoteness from the far-flung Imperial possessions, gave Ottawa a less intense relationship with London. In the case of South Africa, the internal struggle for power between the Afrikaans-speaking Dutch and the English-speaking British and others, which erupted in the Boer War, remained throughout the twentieth century and, the issue of apartheid apart, obviously conditioned attitudes of successive South African governments towards London, the Empire and its successor the British Commonwealth. In particular, the Boers learned that they had to become utterly self-reliant in defence. South Africa had embassies in Washington, Rome and The

Hague by 1929. In the case of Ireland, the combination of hostility and proximity to Britain made a flexible foreign policy a high priority.

Australia was remote from Britain and yet unable to see an alternative to being British. The period from 1901 to 1939 is thus characterised not by the evolution of an Australian foreign policy, but by Australian sensitivity about being—or rather, about *not* being—consulted by the British. Australians were sceptical at times of Britain's desire or ability to look after Australia's interests. But the sentiment of kith and kin; the fact that Australia was protected by the British fleet, not the Royal Australian Navy; that the bulk of Australia's trade was with Britain; that the greater part of investment in Australia was British; that Australian children learned everything from British textbooks and, when they grew up, became British subjects and travelled on British passports—all this meant that most Australians felt they *were* British, and thought it quite natural that their diplomacy should be conducted on their behalf by British officials.

Australia's preoccupation with Imperial and then Commonwealth links was reinforced by strong prime ministerial interest in external affairs. To some extent this was a mutually sustaining equation. London responded to the demand for consultation by nominating the most authoritative Australian figure, the prime minister, as the consultant. In turn, the prime minister's personal interest was a factor in preventing the development of a foreign policy supported by a professional department. Stanley Melbourne Bruce as High Commissioner in London (1933–45) offered a counterweight to the dominance of prime ministers during this period, but Bruce had, of course, been a prime minister himself.

Australia took some initiatives in the field of trade. A trade representative was sent to China in 1921 (withdrawn in 1925) and to Singapore in 1922 (also withdrawn in 1925). In 1929 an official Australian commercial representative was appointed to Canada. In 1934 J. G. Latham, the Minister for External Affairs, headed a mission to Asia and in 1935 Trade Commissioners were appointed to China, Japan and the Netherlands East Indies. Australia had several disagreements with the United States on economic issues during the 1930s, including the large adverse trade balance with the United States, Washington's tariff policies, Pan American landing rights in Australia, and the cost of cabling North America.

In commercial diplomacy Australia showed some natural skills and tenacity. Australia gave as good as it received in some of the exchanges with the British, as in the negotiations for the Ottawa Conference of 1932. Yet the framework of Ottawa reinforced the dependence on Britain as it was intended to bolster a system of Imperial preference in the hope of helping the British unemployed. In 1936, Australia directed trade away from United States and Japanese imports in favour of British manufacturers, in accordance with the terms of Ottawa (but, faced with American and Japanese retaliation, rapidly backed down).

When the Washington Naval Limitation Agreement (established in 1922 to control naval rearmament in the Pacific) lapsed in 1936, Prime Minister Lyons floated the idea of a Pacific non-aggression pact, but Australia had neither the resources nor the influence to follow the idea through. Australia supported Neville Chamberlain's appeasement of Hitler, culminating in the Munich Agreement of 1938. During the debate on Munich, Menzies, then Attorney-General, put the view he was to maintain throughout his prime ministership: 'I have always believed . . . that the British Empire exercises its greatest influence in the world . . . when it speaks with one concerted voice'. It was 'suicidal' for a Dominion to formulate its own foreign policy. Australia wished to be in a position to 'say useful things at the right time' to the United Kingdom for consideration in determining Empire policy as a whole. The attitude in the Munich debate of John Curtin, Leader of the Labor Opposition, has been described as isolationist, but it reflected Labor's opposition to Australian soldiers being recruited for battlefields abroad. The best service Australia could render the British Empire, Curtin said, was to manage Australia effectively and be able to rely upon itself in an emergency.[5]

Menzies led a fact-finding mission to Germany in 1938 before becoming Prime Minister on Lyons's death in 1939. His choice of words announcing Australia's declaration of war on Germany has become a touchstone of the Imperial idea: '. . . it is my melancholy duty to inform you officially', he said in a radio broadcast to the Australian people on 3 September 1939, 'that in consequence of a persistence by Germany in her invasion of Poland, Great Britain has declared war upon her and that as a result, Australia is also at war'.[6] The implication that because Britain was at war so, automatically, was Australia dogged Menzies's later career, but at the time it seemed perfectly natural.

Australian leaders showed in the period from 1901 to the outbreak of World War II that they were interested in the world outside Australia, especially on issues such as immigration, regional security and relations with Japan and the United States. They were prepared to differ with the British, but in an effort to influence Imperial or British policy, not to create an Australian foreign policy.[7] The Australian nationalism of the 1890s was still awaiting its expression in the Australian nation-state when war brought home to all Australians how precarious our dependence on British power had become.

FROM WORLD WAR II TO 1972

The importance of World War II in the evolution of an Australian foreign policy is that the Japanese overwhelmed the colonial powers in Australia's neighbourhood, including the British; struck at Australia itself, by bombing Darwin, Broome and even penetrating Sydney Harbour; and were turned back by the Americans. For the first time, the Australian continent was actually under fire, the attacker was the long-heralded

Asiatic foe, and we were rescued not by the Imperial British but by the republican Americans. This was a half-turning point in Australian history. It was only a half-turn, because we turned from one protector to another. However, in the process we shed some illusions and learned some lessons.

Coming to power in October 1941, just two months before the Japanese attack on the United States base at Pearl Harbor and four months before Darwin was bombed, John Curtin, on 27 December 1941, made his famous declaration which annoyed both Menzies and Churchill (and Roosevelt as well,[8] although this has been less widely appreciated): 'I make it quite clear that Australia looks to America, free of any pangs as to our traditional links or kinship with the United Kingdom'.[9] The new Government then set about bringing back Australian troops to defend, literally, the Australian continent.

One of the curiosities of Australian history is that we developed a martial tradition without contemplating the essential art of self-defence. This martial tradition was the result of expeditionary valour—in Africa, the Middle East, Europe and Asia, alongside first the British and then the Americans. Australian men and women served bravely in many foreign theatres of war, creating legends about themselves and their country. But from the point of view of responsible nationhood, there were at least two problems with this form of national gallantry. The first was that Australia did not itself determine whether to make the commitment of military force. This decision was made for many years by the British and assumed automatically by Australia to be in our interest simply because we needed Britain's protection. Anything that weakened Britain weakened us. Moreover, as we were a long way from Britain and would not be completely confident of British will or capacity to defend us, our instantaneous commitment was a form of insurance, a reminder of our loyalty. Secondly, because of the attachment to Empire and the glamour of events abroad of great consequence, Australians distinguished between military service at home and abroad in a way that made self-defence seem derisory. The soldier who stayed home was a 'chocolate' soldier, not a real soldier. So Australia's inability to defend itself was transformed into a negative moral judgment about 'defensive' defence.

World War II changed the perception of the 'choco' and turned Australia's defence thinking away from Europe (and the life-line of Empire through the Middle East) towards South-East Asia. The fall of Singapore and the bombing of Darwin brought home to Australians that it was in their own part of the world that their future had to be secured. This became the first priority of Australian foreign policy, the origins of 'forward defence'. It was also the source of the great debates in the 1950s and 1960s—between those who urged self-reliance for Australia, even to the point of acquiring nuclear weapons; those who called for a neutral Australia, non-aligned and armed only for self-defence; those who believed Australia should have regional defence arrangements without the external powers; and those who supported what became for a time official policy, namely regional defence with the external powers, especially the United States. Australia in 1954 joined with Britain, France, New Zealand, Pakistan, Thailand and the Philippines, as well as the United States, in the South-East Asia Treaty Organisation (SEATO).

The security of South-East Asia was the core concern after World War II. However, Australia was pulled in other directions by events and personalities. It drew on a fresh source of immigration from war-torn Europe. It was drawn into the prolonged struggle by the newly proclaimed Indonesian government against the Dutch. It initiated the Colombo Plan in 1950, which was a modest version for Asia of the Marshall Plan for Europe. As the price for accepting a softer peace treaty with Japan than it wanted, it gained in 1951—with New Zealand—the ANZUS treaty with the United States that became the cornerstone of Australian security policy. It committed ground forces in defence of South Korea against North Korea (1950–53).

The personalities of Herbert Vere Evatt as Foreign Minister (1941–49) and Leader of the Opposition (1951–60) and R. G. Menzies as Prime Minister (1949–66) are dominant during this period. Each was impatient with the finer detail of foreign policy; each was committed to a grander role for Australia in world affairs than the security of South-East Asia. Evatt fought for the rights of small nations in the United Nations, rendering again in another era Woodrow Wilson's refrain of popular self-determination, and in recognition was elected President of the United Nations General Assembly in 1948. While he was careful to protect Australia's security interests in Asia, he placed great faith in the United Nations, and Australia's role in it, as an agent of social and economic reform and a guarantor of international peace. Menzies placed his faith in those he called 'our great and powerful friends',[10] namely the United Kingdom and the United States. The role he saw for Australia was that of a bridge in the Asia Pacific region between those two Atlantic powers.

The Cold War shaped Australian politics and foreign policy for two decades. On the one hand, there was intense debate and increasing diplomatic activity. Australian diplomats (Plimsoll, Tange, Waller, McIntyre, Shann, Renouf, Critchley, Shaw and the like) were now senior and experienced enough to have a sense of an emerging Australian foreign policy and the ability to implement it. On the other hand, the political atmosphere of the time was so fraught with global consequences, so caught up with the desire to be loyal to wider interests than the national interest of Australia, that not much was done except in the margin. Australia steered a course somewhere between the United Kingdom and the United States on the Suez Crisis and China; somewhere between the United Kingdom and Indonesia on Malaysia; and somewhere between the Dutch and the Americans on West Irian.

The Suez Crisis in 1956 was especially significant because it marked a notch in the decline of Britain in Australia's estimation. This had been arrested since the fall of Singapore by a variety of factors, including Britain's heroic fight against Nazi Germany in Europe, the excitement generated by the new welfare state introduced by the Attlee Government, the accession of a young Queen, and the Cold War itself. When President Nasser of Egypt nationalised the Suez canal, he brought to the surface issues that could not be resolved for Australians simply by the force of moral and political support for Britain or for the State of Israel. There was the issue of law: although the Suez Canal Company was technically an Egyptian company, it had been operating since 1888 under a concession which required it to maintain the canal for international use. There was the issue of trade: the canal had become a vital link between the European industrial states and their global markets, and the Arab oil-producing states. And there was the issue of superpower politics: the fear in the United States that siding with Israel against Egypt would offer the Soviet Union an opportunity to align itself with Arab nationalism.

In Australia, the rift between Britain and the United States was especially agonising. For Menzies, British prestige was an important consideration, part of Australia's own national interest:

> It is apparently not fashionable to speak of prestige. Yet the fact remains that world peace and the efficacy of the United Nations Charter alike require that the British Commonwealth and, in particular, its greatest and most experienced member, the United Kingdom, should retain power, prestige and moral influence.[11]

Again later:

> So far as Australia is concerned, I need hardly say that an open Canal is essential to British prosperity, and that a closed Canal could mean mass unemployment in Great Britain, a financial collapse there, a grievous blow at the central power of our Commonwealth, and the crippling of our greatest market and our greatest supplier.[12]

Although the public was divided, and some of Menzies's colleagues (in particular Lord Casey) took the American view and felt vindicated when finally the Americans voted with the majority of the United Nations against the British, the French and the Israelis, Menzies's dominance of Cabinet meant that Australia was effectively on the losing side over Suez. Our association with Britain, and with Israel, was somewhat weakened as a result.

When Australians reflected on their national interest, divorced from the emotional persuasion of their Prime Minister's rhetoric, they found that the Canal was not as important as had at first seemed. Larger tankers were built for the Cape route, Australian trade with Britain was in any case declining and Australian exports became more competitive in the Persian Gulf and on the east coast of Africa while the Canal remained closed. Most of

Australia's oil imports at that time came from Arab states sympathetic to Egypt and from Indonesia. In addition, Australia's wheat sales to Egypt were growing. Finally, of course, the security issues were beginning to focus for Australia on South-East Asia, and there were some far-sighted enough to see that Britain's failed Suez venture of 1956 was an indicator of a general retrenchment that brought the withdrawal of British forces 'east of Suez' in the 1960s.

The Vietnam War brought more ambiguities to an end. The slow (and on Menzies's part grudging) transference of commitment by Australia from Britain to the United States quickened when Menzies was replaced by Harold Holt and, in Washington, John Kennedy was replaced by Lyndon Johnson. The concept of 'forward defence' had been explained by Menzies in 1955 as follows:

> The simple English of this matter is that with our vast territory and our small population we cannot survive a surging Communist challenge from abroad except by the co-operation of powerful friends, including in particular the United Kingdom and the United States. Similarly, it is unbelievable that any responsible Australian should fail to see that if the battle against Communism is to be an effective one it must be as forward of Australia as possible . . . If Malaya is vital to our defence, more vital, properly understood, than some point on the Australian coast, then we must make Malayan defence in a real sense our business.[13]

In short, Australia's forward defence made sense only if we were able to rely on our great and powerful friends to maintain the forward position. Australia still needed a protector over its forces abroad, and the corollary of forward defence was the need to ensure that either British or American forces were actually committed on the ground. In Vietnam, the British were not so committed but the Americans were.

The Vietnam War (1965–75) dominated Australian politics and foreign policy for a decade. A generation of young Australians learned about the world through its pitiless lens. A generation of older Australians were bitterly divided over it. The failure of American, Australian and other allied arms to bring the desired political result in Vietnam was one reason for the collapse of the conservative coalition in Australia and the election in 1972 of the first Labor Government for twenty-three years.

AFTER 1972

It is obviously not true to say that the Whitlam era (1972–75) represents something entirely new in the way of a distinctively Australian foreign policy. Many had tried before to strike a distinctive Australian note in their attitude to the outside world. Hughes had certainly tried; Bruce in London had some instinct for it; Curtin was vigorously nationalistic when needed; Evatt was provocatively independent; and, in their different ways, Spender, Casey and Hasluck as Foreign Ministers, and Gorton as Prime Minister, had an Australian quality in their outlook on the world. However, the Whitlam period provided a watershed. It divided the prolonged obeisance of Menzies to the idea of Imperial unity, and the transference of many of the emotions and attitudes of loyalty to the United States during the period of the Cold War, from the emergence of the kind of Australian foreign policy that we now take for granted.

When Edward Gough Whitlam came to power in 1972, Australians were still struggling with the notion that a loyal ally of the United States could not also have an independent foreign policy. Of course no nation, not even the superpowers with their numerous commitments, can have an entirely independent policy. But Australia in 1972 faced something more prosaic: the assumption that Australia would be endangering its security if it did not accept the role of loyal ally of the United States in this part of the world. Whitlam, with twenty-three pent-up years of conservative rule to break through, finally shrugged this off. The Whitlam Government declared, and acted on, the assumption that Australia had its own interests and could make its own assessment of what they were. Being an ally of the United States did not mean, in other words, being subservient to the interests of the United States.

Whitlam also broke through the cynical political arrangement by which the Democratic Labor Party had kept in power, through the second preferences of its voters, a series of coalition governments which knew they would never lose DLP support so long as they pitched their electioneering to the lowest common anti-communist denominator. Thus for nearly two decades, defence and foreign policy had been in the forefront of controversy, and always debated in a political or ideological context.

Particular stress was placed on Australian policy development in the Asia Pacific region. Again this was not new. Harold Holt in his short-lived prime ministership had stressed the potential of the region to Australia. As far back as the mid-1950s Australia had recognised that its special trading relationship with Britain was doomed and had turned to Japan. The Whitlam Government, however, made a breakthrough in relations with China and in renouncing the military adventure in Vietnam. These two decisions gave the impression of an entirely new form of engagement by Australia in Asia, and to a degree this was true.

Whitlam was determined to show that his Government was not isolationist just because it was unsympathetic to military intervention in Asia. On the day he was sworn in as Prime Minister he said:

> The change of government provides a new opportunity for us to reassess the whole range of Australian foreign policies and attitudes ... Our thinking is towards a more independent Australian stance in international affairs, an Australia which will be less militarily orientated and not open to suggestions of racism; an Australia which will enjoy a growing standing as a distinctive, tolerant, cooperative and well-regarded nation, not only in the Asia and Pacific region, but in the world at large.[14]

Before very long, Australia had recognised China, North Vietnam, East Germany and North Korea; withdrawn our military from Vietnam and our aid from Cambodia; stopped wheat sales to Southern Rhodesia; provided some indirect aid to South African liberation movements; and arraigned France in the International Court of Justice for its nuclear tests in the South Pacific. Australia was also busy during Whitlam's prime ministership in contracting cultural agreements with the countries of Asia and the Pacific; removing racial discrimination from immigration procedures (non-European immigration had begun in 1966); increasing development assistance; bringing Papua New Guinea to independence; re-establishing sympathetic relations with Third World countries in the United Nations and elsewhere (in 1974 Australia attended as an observer at the Non-Aligned Movement Conference); and opening up the Australian market, especially to textile, footwear and clothing imports from the region.

One controversial area was the decision (subsequently revoked by the Fraser Government) to accord *de jure* recognition of the incorporation of Estonia, Latvia and Lithuania into the Soviet Union. Another was Australia's relationship with Indonesia, with whose leadership Whitlam developed a close rapport. In the dying days of his Government in 1975, as the constitutional crisis wracked Australia, Indonesia invaded East Timor after a change of government in Portugal had released several political movements in the colony, vying respectively for independence or integration with Indonesia. The swift Indonesian action was an embarrassment to the Whitlam Government, and remained for many years a source of tension in both Indonesian–Australian relations and Australian domestic politics.

The Whitlam Government dramatically revitalised the Australian political landscape, both externally and internally. But it was a meteorite, short and dramatic, rather than a star, stable and lasting. When it fell in 1975 it had shattered the pattern of Australian politics and Cold War thinking about foreign policy in Australia, but the Government had not been long enough in office to establish a new pattern. In particular, it had not tackled the essential task of self-reliance in defence. Until Australia grasped this nettle, the alliance with the United States would always offer itself to Australian governments as a simple, and cheap, way of apparently securing Australia.

Perhaps influenced by the divisive circumstances of its assumption of office, the Fraser Government (1975–83) did not set about reversing the Whitlam Government's foreign policy initiatives. Often it retained the policy while changing the motivation, so that good relations with China and a concern for the Third World, for example, became part of an anti-Soviet strategy more in keeping with Fraser's conservative constituency. It was constrained in South-East Asia by the United States's withdrawal of interest as a consequence of the defeat in Vietnam. Fraser acknowledged the significance of the Asia Pacific region without dramatising it, as Whitlam had done, and without placing the same degree of systematic stress, especially on its economic significance, as has the Hawke Government. However, Fraser's Foreign Minister, Andrew Peacock, maintained good relations with the ASEAN states, Papua New Guinea and the Third World generally, performing something of the same corrective to Fraser's leadership as had R. G. Casey (1951–1960) to Menzies's prime ministership.

Fraser was nationalistic at times. He described as 'an unfriendly act' the United States government's decision to support the Dillingham Corporation's claim for compensation following the termination of sand-mining on Fraser Island.[15] He had differences with the United States over multilateral tariff negotiations and Washington's pressure for another airline carrier across the Pacific; and he was sometimes cautious, as shown by a long delay in approving the use by B52 bombers of Darwin as a transit base. Yet he was also impetuous, as in his statement after the Russian invasion of Afghanistan that '. . . the world is facing probably its most dangerous international crisis since World War II'.[16] His rivalry with his Foreign Minister, Andrew Peacock, meant that the Department of Foreign Affairs did not play its normal role in foreign policy formulation, and perhaps accounts also for the emphasis he placed on the Commonwealth, the natural arena for prime ministers. Japan was not dealt with adequately by either Fraser or Peacock, being left to J. D. Anthony as Deputy Prime Minister and Minister for Trade.

In 1976, early in his prime ministership, Fraser made a visit to China during which he evidently made an abortive attempt to interest the Chinese in a four-power (China, Japan, the United States and Australia) treaty of some kind directed against the Soviet Union. A serious test, which the Fraser Government handled well, came with the arrival of the Vietnamese 'boat people' in Australia—the first landing in Darwin in 1976 and the peak being reached in 1979 with the escalation of conflict in Indo-China. In 1978 the Soviet–Vietnam treaty of friendship was signed, and Vietnam invaded Cambodia. In 1979 China attacked Vietnam (and, incidentally, the Soviet Union invaded Afghanistan, the Shah of Iran was overthrown and war broke out between Iran and Iraq). It was a period of turmoil, in which the boat people represented a threateningly new kind of refugee for Australia to deal with: not the inmate of a distant camp whose credentials could be exhaustively checked before being admitted to Australia, but a live human being washed up on an Australian shore (after drifting south through the archipelago of South-East Asia and sometimes being prodded in Australia's direction). The Fraser Government both met Australia's obligations as a signatory of the United Nations Convention on Refugees and managed to calm popular fears.

Overall, the foreign policy keynote of Fraser's prime ministership was suspicion of the Soviet Union. But he deserves to be remembered for his strong and very genuine commitment—very much against the instincts of the coalition parties—to racial equality, especially in opposition to apartheid in South Africa. A degree of continuity was maintained with the new themes struck by Whitlam, but Fraser's foreign policy was too greatly influenced by his personal passions and whims to develop in any rational and comprehensive way.

The Hawke Government was elected to office in March 1983 and, at the time of writing, is in its fourth successive term, a quite unprecedented tenure for the Australian Labor Party. With Bob Hawke's strong personal commitment to external policy matters, a prevailing feature of his prime ministership, priorities were quickly established: firm and clear support for the alliance with the United States, coupled with initiatives on disarmament; an economic focus on the Asia Pacific region; diplomatic effort to resolve the deadlock on a peace settlement in Indo-China; the intensification of pressure against apartheid in South Africa; and strong support for the role of the United Nations. The unambiguous policy on the alliance with the United States helped Australia through a difficult period when American 'NCND' policy—to neither confirm nor deny the presence of nuclear weapons on its warships—led to the withdrawal of New Zealand from the ANZUS Treaty. Australia retained bilateral arrangements with both New Zealand and the United States which minimised the damaging effects of New Zealand's strong stand. On nuclear disarmament and arms control, Australia became very active and vocal both regionally and on the world scene, taking the position that our hosting various space-defence facilities jointly with the United States should be regarded not as inhibiting our speaking out on global disarmament issues, but as helping establish our credentials for doing so.

A conceptual watershed in Australian foreign policy occurred in March 1987 with the tabling by the Minister for Defence, Kim Beazley, of the White Paper on *The Defence of Australia*. Based upon a review by Paul Dibb a year earlier and supported by subsequent Budget decisions, this spelt out a coherent policy of defence self-reliance, involving a strategy of defence in depth based upon early detection, long-range sea and air strike capability, highly mobile ground forces, and the joint operation of communications and intelligence facilities with the United States. And it did so in a way which enabled the simultaneous achievement, or advancement, of four fundamental objectives: independent defence of Australian territory; promotion of regional security and stability; capacity to meet alliance obligations; and contribution to global strategic security. While no country can ever have a totally independent foreign policy, unless it wishes to live in isolation from other nations or in a state of perpetual conflict with them, Australian foreign policy had suffered from a particularly restrictive dependency—that its first task was to attract the protective attention of great and powerful friends. The intellectual breakthrough was to establish that self-reliance was possible in most of the circumstances likely to confront

Australia, short of major war. In other words, in most of the contingencies with which Australia might be faced in going about our daily business, we could look after ourselves.

This new confidence in our defence capability liberated Australian foreign policy. Australian foreign ministers are freer to think about their responsibilities more systematically, and more intricately, than ever before. It is possible now to contemplate an approach to foreign policy decision-making which involves, not the writing of manuals on how to get one's foot in the door of a protector's office, but rather the case by case weighing and balancing of national interests, and opportunities for influence, across a complex and variegated field. In short, the evolution in our defence and strategic thinking has put into sharp relief the reality that Australia's interests are many and varied, and that to promote these interests we need policies that are equally multi-dimensional.

Bill Hayden's period as Foreign Minister (1983–88) was one of the most fertile and active on record. His displacement by Bob Hawke as Labor leader just before the 1983 election led to persistent speculation about differences of approach between them, especially over issues on which Hawke was known to have strong views, such as support for Israel and the alliance with the United States. But whatever tension there may have been between them, it did not inhibit Australian foreign policy developing a new maturity during this period, especially in respect of Australia's contribution to global security through the United States alliance. It was Hayden who thought through, and within the Labor Party fought through, the controversy surrounding Australia's hosting of the joint facilities, and who gave Australia a voice in the international debate on nuclear deterrence and disarmament which came to a head during Ronald Reagan's presidency. When he visited Moscow in 1984, it had been twenty years since an Australian foreign minister had visited the Soviet Union.

On issues of human rights and Third World development Hayden revived many of the themes of the Whitlam years, and Australian diplomacy in these areas became very active. The Hayden period was also characterised by intense activity in pursuit of a peaceful settlement in Cambodia. Hayden visited Vietnam and Laos in 1983 and 1985 and Vietnamese Foreign Minister Thach came to Australia in 1984, as did Prince Sihanouk in 1985. Australia took several initiatives to break the deadlock, including the concept of a Pol Pot war crimes tribunal: they did not succeed in resolving the conflict, but they were important contributions to the evolution of a solution. And it was under Hayden in 1987 that the long-overdue amalgamation of the Departments of Foreign Affairs and Trade was finally consummated.

Gareth Evans, who became Minister for Foreign Affairs and Trade in September 1988, has been a beneficiary of this evolving Australian foreign policy. In particular, the effect of the Defence White Paper and the departmental amalgamation has been to create a base for Australian foreign policy and its implementation which has in turn created the potential for a foreign policy of new freedom and new relevance.

The profound and dramatic changes now shaking the world have put every nation's foreign policy to the test, including Australia's. If Australia did not have an independent foreign policy by now, we would have needed to find one in a hurry. The highly activist, high-profile foreign policy in which Australia has engaged in recent times—with initiatives such as the Cairns Group, Asia Pacific Economic Co-operation (APEC), the United Nations peace plan for Cambodia, the campaign for protecting the Antarctic environment, the early participation in the military response to Iraq, and the diplomatic assault on chemical weapons—has surprised some observers, but it is really no more than should have been expected. The changing world and our changing region are a challenge to Australia, to be met primarily from our own resources and according to our own needs.

3

Elements in Foreign Policy Making

DECISIONS IN FOREIGN POLICY are by their nature complex, involving always at least one other country and sometimes scores, very often several different subject areas, and almost invariably matters over which the government making the decision does not have full control. Moreover, foreign policy problems also have a habit of arriving in a less than orderly sequence, and as often as not out of clear blue skies. Some strategies and initiatives can be developed in a measured and systematic way, but the opportunity for proactive planning arises much more rarely than does the need for a reactive response to events not of one's making or choosing.

In this kind of environment, if one is going to exercise careful, consistent judgment, thinking effectively both in reaction to events and in anticipation of them—and foreign ministers and their advisers have to do this day in and day out, with events tumbling headlong around them—then there is really no alternative to having a clear-headed appreciation of what one wants to achieve, and what one is likely to be able to achieve, and to allocate scarce resources of time and energy accordingly. At least there is no alternative if one wants to avoid a foreign policy characterised by incoherence, inanity or both—the kind, for example, which pursues Good Relations with another country as an end in itself without assessment of whether Australian interests are thereby being advanced; or the kind which devotes resources to the pursuit of interests in inverse proportion to the prospect of achieving them. No-one can anticipate, in the complex, uncertain and changing world in which we now live, every kind of foreign policy issue which may arise. But one can sort out principles and priorities in advance: it *is* possible to disentangle, in a reasonably orderly way, the kind of intellectual process necessary if those issues are to be addressed in a way that maximises Australia's interests.

Australian foreign policy makers clearly do not have the luxury of stepping back from the flow of events. Change has not yet run its course, and however well we may have done in recent years in elevating our standing as a concerned, constructive and innovative member of the regional and world community, we simply cannot linger on past achievements. In international affairs, as in the domestic economy, Australia cannot afford the mentality of the plodder or the recluse. Responding effectively to change means keeping our wits about us—in anticipating the currents of change, in reacting to events as they occur, and above all else in being constantly alert to new opportunities for influence in the protection and advancement of Australian national interests.

NATIONAL INTERESTS

The starting point in making decisions about foreign policy is necessarily the concept of national interest. It is a truism that *all* foreign policy is, or should be, directed at the protection and advancement of the national interest. But the elements that make up the national interest, and our capacity to advance it, are not necessarily self-evident at all. They require definition, elaboration and thinking through. We believe it is helpful to group Australian interests in three broad categories: geo-political or strategic interests; economic and trade interests; and the national interest in being, and being seen to be, a good international citizen. The scope of the first two categories is fairly obvious, the third probably less so.

Our overriding geo-political or strategic interest is the defence of Australian sovereignty and political independence. That has both a regional and a global dimension. As to the first, we do have a direct interest in ensuring that the countries around us remain peaceful, stable and well-disposed, or at least neutrally disposed, toward us. The region of primary Australian security interests, in foreign policy terms, is essentially identical to that identified in the 1987 Defence White Paper. It comprises the combination of an inner 'area of direct military interest' (which includes Australia's territories and proximate ocean areas, Indonesia, Papua New Guinea, New Zealand and other nearby countries of the South West Pacific) and a larger 'area of primary strategic interest' covering the eastern Indian Ocean, and the rest of South-East Asia and the South West Pacific).[1] But there is a close interaction between what happens in these countries, and others in our region more broadly defined—namely the countries of North-East Asia, Indo-China and South Asia.

At the global level, Australia's most obvious interest, which we share with everyone else, is the avoidance of nuclear war. As Gareth Evans said in his first address as Foreign Minister to the United Nations General Assembly on 4 October 1988:

> Nuclear disarmament and arms control are not matters exclusively for those great powers which currently possess nuclear weapons. For if there is a nuclear conflict, it is not just the peoples of the nuclear weapon states who will suffer. The peoples of the world will be devastated. As the potential victims of nuclear catastrophe, the people of all nations have the right to demand real progress and the eventual elimination of nuclear weapons. They have the right to demand that the nuclear arms race not take new forms, including its spread into outer space.

Global and regional security concerns also overlap. It has long been the case that the global balance of power has impacted, for better or worse, on regional conflicts. A series of such conflicts after World War II in Asia, Africa, the Middle East and elsewhere, defined as part of the grand ideological struggle, were intractable test cases which neither side could afford to lose. It is now the case, by contrast—with the constraints of the Cold War and the encouraging experience of the Gulf War behind us—that the evolution of a genuine system of international collective security, of the kind envisaged by the founders of the United Nations, is no longer unthinkable. We do now have the possibility of global resources being mobilised to resolve regional problems. Achieving this kind of overlap between global and regional security concerns, with the United Nations playing a central role in both, is very much in Australia's interests to pursue.

In the economic and trade sphere our overriding interest, as a commodity producer with growing exports in services and both value-added and high-technology manufactures, is in trying to secure a free and liberal international trading regime. We need a stable, rational and equitable system that allows us reasonable market access, but all too often the international trading environment diverges from this model, restricted by tariffs, non-tariff protective measures, competition from subsidised exports, so-called 'voluntary' restraint arrangements, or straight-out political influence. Our stake in a secure international economic environment also encompasses international banking, investment and technology flows, our transport links and communications—and the whole complex web of bilateral and multilateral arrangements that variously help or hinder them.

The third group of national interests involves being, and being seen to be, a good international citizen. Global environment problems like the ozone layer require global solutions: so do international health problems like AIDS, or the international narcotics trade, or unregulated population flows, or a number of other phenomena sometimes referred to as 'non-military threats to security'. Australia has a role to play in all these areas, just as in other fields of international action such as decolonisation, peace-keeping, and the whole arms control agenda.

In a sense, these are what Hedley Bull used to call 'purposes beyond ourselves',[2] but it is not just a matter of disinterested altruism. In the first place, this kind of agenda involves an extension into our foreign relations of the basic values of the Australian community—values which are at the core of our sense of self and which a democratic community expects its government to pursue. It *is* proper, if for no other reason than to maintain our own sense of worth in pursuing ends that are inherently valuable, to seek improved standards world-wide in human rights and equal opportunity; to work for an end to apartheid in South Africa and racial intolerance everywhere else; to seek to crush the drug trade; to solve the world-wide problem of refugees; to assist through substantial aid programs the economic and social development of those countries struggling with debt, poverty or national calamity. In the longer term, the evolution of just and tolerant societies brings its own international returns—in higher standards of international behaviour, and in the contribution that internal stability makes to international stability and peace.

In the second place, there are some more direct returns that flow to a country that takes seriously its international citizenship obligations. Although there may be occasions when taking a principled stand carries costs for us, an international reputation as a good citizen tends to enhance any country's overall standing in the world, and will at times prove helpful in pursuing other international interests, including commercial ones. Idealism and realism need not be competing objectives in foreign policy, but getting the blend right is never simple.

OPPORTUNITIES FOR INFLUENCE

It is one thing to define and clarify foreign policy interests in this way, but quite another to advance them. Interests, in the real world, are not the same as influence. In turn, influence is not necessarily quickly or easily measured. It involves assessing, in the first place, the country's potential or prima facie capacity for exercising influence in pursuing a particular interest—the assets it can deploy. On the other side of the ledger are the various constraints, internal and external, that in practice stand in the way of that capacity being applied. Actual opportunities for influence in pursuing an interest are, in the diplomatic marketplace, what is left over when capacities are discounted by constraints.

On the face of it, our capacity to exercise any real influence on matters of global (as distinct from regional) war, peace and disarmament is so limited that any attempt to exert it would be quixotic. But our hosting of the joint facilities—especially Pine Gap and Nurrungar with their unique intelligence gathering, arms control and disarmament verification, and early warning functions—strengthens our capacity to regularly put views at the highest level to the United States administration. That, together with the thought and effort that has gone into developing and articulating arms control strategies, and the highly visible role we have played in multilateral forums in promoting nuclear non-proliferation and other disarmament objectives (for example, the outlawing of chemical weapons) has made us highly respected interlocutors on these subjects, not only in Washington, but in Moscow, Beijing and around the globe. Certainly, we have nothing like the clout of the main nuclear players at the table, but nobody could argue, given the nature of the issues involved, that the game is not worth the candle.

Conversely, our influence may be rather less than it appears at first sight. Take Fiji, after the military coups in 1987.[3] Australia has significant strategic and security reasons, quite apart from human rights value preferences, for wishing to see a stable, prosperous and racially harmonious Fiji. And by any objective measure we bring solid assets to the bilateral relationship. Australia is far-and-away Fiji's largest economic partner. We have the largest military capacity of all countries of the South Pacific region. We have an extensive network of people-to-people links, through tourism, business, education and official visits, and a long history of working together in the Commonwealth and South Pacific Forum.

But there are constraints which prevented the full utilisation of these assets. There was never any question of deploying our military capacity, not just because nobody ever asked us to, but because the situation demanded a political, not a military solution. No major group sought the continued application of economic sanctions, official or unofficial. And nobody reacted very warmly to the notion of using aid funds, whether regular or supplementary, by way of either carrot or stick. Our oral encouragement to those advocating the resumption of constitutional democracy and Western liberal values was at best of marginal utility. The very characteristics that may seem influential—our disproportionate size, wealth, state of political and economic development, and liberal democratic tradition—make it easy in these situations to paint us as uncomprehending, domineering and patronising, however carefully we may tread.

Another very significant constraint upon Australia's response was the reaction of its Pacific island neighbours, whether Melanesian, Micronesian or Polynesian. Very few appreciated, let alone applauded, the military means by which Fiji's indigenous nationalism asserted itself, but it was simply not the case that the political end thus achieved was perceived as wholly unacceptable. In an environment where Australia has identified its interests in its relationship with its South Pacific neighbours as best served by a strategy of 'constructive commitment'—involving a spirit of partnership rather than dominance, mutual respect for sovereignty and national individuality, and the development of shared perceptions of regional strategic and security interests—it would be self-defeating to ride roughshod over that kind of reaction.

In the conduct of trade and economic relations, Australia can lay claim to several advantages such as a relatively high per capita GDP, an impressive standard of education, and a well-developed communications system. While our manpower base remains small, we have a huge stock of sought-after resources, a sophisticated industrial and technological base gradually emerging from several lifetimes of protective sheltering, and an increasing willingness to take our economic chances domestically and internationally in a free-market environment. But, particularly in the arena of multilateral trade negotiations, these assets do not of themselves give us any particular influence. Since Australia is only one—and not among the biggest—participant in such negotiations, we cannot depend solely on our own advocacy to secure a successful outcome.

The most effective way of coping with this gap between what Australia wanted and had the capacity to achieve, was judged to lie in building a coalition of allies: a group of agricultural traders that could become a real 'third force' in international negotiations with the United States and the European Community. In 1986, under John Dawkins as Trade Minister, the Government set about tying together an extraordinarily disparate coalition of Latin Americans, East Europeans, South-East Asians and old Commonwealth countries: the Cairns Group. While the current Uruguay Round of multilateral trade negotiations has yet to run its course, there is no question but that the Cairns Group has been outstandingly successful in keeping agricultural issues at the forefront of the international trade liberalisation agenda—and in keeping the other major players honest.[4]

In pursuing good international citizenship objectives, the asset that matters most is credibility, and here we start with a reasonably strong asset base. It includes a strong internal tradition of liberal democracy; a very strong record of commitment to multilateral institutions and codes (symbolised early on by Dr H. V. Evatt's passionate devotion to the United Nations and in particular to the Universal Declaration of Human Rights adopted by the General Assembly during his Presidency in 1948); a leading role in the international campaign against apartheid, an important and legitimate touchstone of moral credibility in most of the developing world; and a long-standing willingness to accept the resettlement of more than our fair share of the world's refugees, particularly those from our own region. All of this helps us to get results when pursuing good citizenship causes, whether it be the commutation of death sentences passed on Buddhist monks in Vietnam, the development of a regional consensus behind a new international Chemical Weapons Convention, or the promotion of a complete ban on mining and oil drilling in the Antarctic.

But here, as elsewhere, there are constraints. For a start, one has to be acutely conscious of the likely impact of a given initiative, particularly in human-rights related matters where the life or health of individuals may be concerned, and that is not always easy to assess. The object of these initiatives, which is not always appreciated, must be not to satisfy a domestic constituency or some other perceived political imperative, but to get positive—and not counter-productive—results. Another important constraint is that our opportunity to influence events depends, in this area more than anywhere else, on keeping our domestic house absolutely in order. Our ability to secure advances in the areas of human rights, refugees or development assistance rests on our being, and continuing to be seen to be, a liberal democracy with a solid record at home; a country which articulates and applies human rights and similar principles with absolute consistency and impartiality; a country which not only talks about aid but delivers it. We will not achieve much if in our national policies on Aboriginal affairs, immigration or the like we are seen to be indulging in double standards. Hypocrites are not merely disliked, in international relations as elsewhere. If they are our size, they are ignored.

SETTING AUSTRALIAN PRIORITIES

In this untidy world, with a cacophony of claims for attention but a limited pool of resources to satisfy them, the effective political management of foreign affairs depends not just on being able to recognise opportunities for influence, but also on developing and constantly refining priorities. Priorities, in turn, define themselves as those policy areas where a major interest coincides with at least some opportunity to influence its achievement. There is not much point in devoting major resources to the inherently important but immovable—or, on the other hand, the attainable but inherently trivial.

Given the fluid international environment and the particular evolution of Australian foreign policy, we would identify the four major priorities of Australian foreign policy in this order: maintaining a positive security and strategic environment in our own region; contributing to the best of our capacity to global security; pursuing trade, investment and economic co-operation; and making a realistic contribution to the cause of good international citizenship. These headings do not exhaust the whole content of Australian foreign policy. Innumerable issues arise that require Australia to take positions of one kind or another—for example the Palestinian issue—and it is again important that we have a broad conceptual framework, based on Australian interests, within which to address them. But not every one can sensibly be regarded as a high priority issue for Australia.

Regional Security   Maintaining our physical integrity and sovereignty must necessarily be our first foreign policy priority, as it is for any country. And for Australian diplomacy that means, above all else, acting to maintain a positive security and strategic environment in our own region—defined for this purpose, as we have said, to mean essentially the South Pacific and South-East Asia, but with linkages that need to be discussed with North-East Asia, Indo-China and with the Indian Ocean and South Asia, as well.

The most effective approach to regional security is a multi-dimensional one, in which all the components of Australia's network of relations in the region—military and politico-military capability, diplomacy, economic links, assistance with development and so-called 'non-military threats', and the exchange of people and ideas—work together to help shape a favourable security environment. This approach necessarily involves a particular effort being made to maintain a harmonious set of individual relationships with our regional neighbours. In successive chapters in Part III we discuss how we should shape those relationships with the countries of the South Pacific within a policy framework of 'constructive commitment', emphasising partnership rather than dominance; how we should approach the even more complex question of our relationships with Indonesia and the other countries of South-East Asia within a suggested policy framework of 'comprehensive engagement'; and how we should build our relationships with the countries of North-East Asia, Indo-China and South Asia.

In our discussion of Australia's regional security, we perhaps place less emphasis than has been traditional in works of this kind on Australia's alliance with the United States. This is not because we do not value both it and the wider United States military role within the region. On the contrary, we are conscious that while our defence policy is one of self-reliance, it is self-reliance within an alliance framework. Quite apart from such deterrent value as the ANZUS Treaty has, that alliance is crucial to our capability in terms of the access it gives to United States intelligence, technology, re-supply and training. Moreover, there is far more to our alliance with the United States than ANZUS and the bilateral defence relationship. But it is important that some of the misconceptions and unrealistic expectations that have grown up around the ANZUS Treaty be stripped away. The existence of that relationship does not absolve us from the responsibility to think and act for ourselves, and to pull our full weight in our own protection. Australia does not these days claim a 'special' relationship with the United States, or with anyone else: nor should we, for such claims in the past have too often been an excuse for not having an *Australian* foreign policy.

Global Security There can be no doubting that Australia's future would be put as much at risk by a global security catastrophe as by a regional one. The only question is whether Australia is realistically capable of contributing to the avoidance of such a catastrophe, and whether we should be devoting priority resources to that task. It is not quixotic for Australia to seek to play an active role in these issues, at least in a selective and focused way. We already play a particularly significant global role in our hosting of the joint space-defence facilities at Pine Gap and Nurrungar, and in certain areas of the disarmament agenda. We cannot upstage the superpowers when it comes to nuclear arms reduction but we can, as an active and respected middle power, play a leading role in the multilateral diplomacy needed to implement a ban, for example, on chemical weapons. And in an environment where the United Nations is once again beginning to play the central role originally envisaged for it in both global and regional security issues, Australia can turn to advantage its long-standing and acknowledged commitment to, and expertise in, United Nations diplomacy.

Trade, Investment and Economic Co-operation   With the amalgamation of the former Departments of Foreign Affairs and of Trade into a single entity in 1987, the artificial distinction between trade policy and foreign policy—increasingly impossible to sustain in an international environment where economics and politics are at least as intertwined as they are domestically—was, not before time, abandoned. Australia became much better placed to mobilise its international political influence in support of our international economic objectives, namely to safeguard Australian markets and expand economic opportunities for Australian industry; and to create a perception of Australia as an attractive place in which to invest, and of the Australian Government as a partner with which to co-operate at governmental level. Our capacity to target and penetrate export markets was further enhanced by the decision in 1991 to relocate Austrade—the Australian government's external trade promotion arm—within the Foreign Affairs and Trade portfolio, in the process integrating its activities more closely with those of Australian diplomatic missions abroad.

Australian trade performance depends, in addition, on the impact of domestic economic policy on international competitiveness; the role of entrepreneurial efficiency, energy and imagination; and international price movements beyond the capacity of any government, let alone business, to influence. But in the difficult balance-of-payments circumstances that Australia will continue to confront for the foreseeable future, there can be few higher external policy priorities than trade policy.

Good International Citizenship   The new internationalist agenda—of issues which had been largely regarded as either internal matters or nobody's business, but are now seen as requiring international co-operation if they are to be successfully tackled—has expanded so rapidly that even the most determined good international citizen would have difficulty in giving priority attention to them all. Australia must continue to play a positive and constructive role across the whole range of issues now the subject of multilateral diplomacy—including refugee care and resettlement, terrorism, the drug trade, international health issues, Third World debt and the like. But it is clear that to be most effective we should concentrate our resources in the areas in which, as a result of our established profile, expertise, complementary policy objectives or some other relevant factor, we have a particularly useful contribution to make.

Thus Australian policy emphasis is being placed on three areas: development co-operation, human rights and the environment. Australia's

development co-operation program, quite apart from its inherent humanitarian objectives, is squarely linked with other regional policy objectives, especially in relation to Papua New Guinea and the South Pacific. Human rights is not only an area which is inherently worthwhile pursuing for a country with our strongly held values—albeit not without its practical diplomatic difficulties—but also one in which Australia has built up a particular international record in recent years which it would be unfortunate not to use to continuing advantage. Environment questions are simply too pre-eminently important, given the condition of the planet's resources, for any country these days not to give priority to them. From the vast range of such questions now squarely in the international spotlight, Australia has focused resources on two in particular—climate and the Antarctic.

REALISM AND IDEALISM IN INTERNATIONAL RELATIONSHIPS

The conduct of foreign affairs is about responding realistically to the world as we find it. We have to have trade relations with many regimes of which we disapprove. We have to have working relations with many forms of government we think less than ideal. We have to balance questions of international morality against the 'pragmatic acceptance of irreversible fact'.[5] We sometimes have to operate a multi-track policy, sending two or more signals at once: the luxury of absolutism is very rarely available to the practitioners of this profession.

The case for realism in public affairs has been put by some distinguished practitioners. One was Abraham Lincoln in 1862, when urged to make the liberation of slaves the standard of his Civil War policy:

> If there be those who would not save the Union unless they could at the same time destroy slavery, I do not agree with them. My paramount object in this struggle is to save the Union, and is not either to save or destroy slavery. If I could save the Union without freeing any slave I would do it, and if I could save it by freeing all the slaves, I would do it . . . I have here stated my purpose according to my view of official duty; and I intend no modification of my oft-expressed personal wish that all men everywhere could be free.[6]

Machiavelli, a more familiar realist, was brisker:

> . . . how we live is so far removed from how we ought to live, that he who abandons what is done for what ought to be done, will rather learn to bring about his own ruin than his preservation.[7]

But the case for idealism, in international as in domestic affairs, can also be put strongly. The world cannot be changed overnight, but it can be changed—gradually—for the better. Nation states and peoples should be allowed to develop their own distinctive capacity and individual personality. Their systems of government and economic management should not be such as to deny fundamental political, economic or social rights to their own peoples. Those great liberating ideas of recent decades—racial equality in the 1960s; sexual equality in the 1970s; protection of the environment in the 1980s—all have their place in international affairs. The rules of international behaviour should not be different from those governing every other kind of human behaviour.

We are idealistic because it is the nature of men and women who live by the precepts of democracy to believe that they can change the world for the better. But in Australia's case there are some additional special reasons. Established as we were as a gaol for the discards of British society, and with a significant proportion of our present population derived from those fleeing persecution or seeking a better life, at least part of the national psyche is profoundly committed to notions of reform and improvement. And being the size and weight that we are, it is in Australia's national interest that the world should be governed by principles of justice, equality, talent and achievement, rather than status and power.

Certainly there is no sense in biting off arguments needlessly, especially in our own regional neighbourhood. And as a government, we should seek to encourage Australian community and media understanding of the values of our neighbours, respect for their unique ways of living, and appreciation of the very real sensitivities of other countries with different cultural traditions—as well as an understanding of the importance of our relations with the region. But while it should be accepted that all the societies in our region have their own distinctive characteristics and values, at the same time we do not believe we should be trapped into embracing crude cultural relativism. Australia should make no apology for raising human rights and related issues, and expecting others to acknowledge the integrity of our values, such as freedom of the media. Making our views known, quietly and courteously, is far from condescension or interference in another country's internal affairs. It is simply projecting a set of values that the international community is increasingly coming to accept as universally applicable standards for the treatment of its citizens; and indeed, a set of values that Australians expect their governments to advance internationally.

In the practical management of these matters, as always in international relations, almost as much depends on how things are done as upon what is done. Strident and aggressive condemnation of what to us is unconscionable behaviour may be good for domestic morale—and may sometimes be the right note to strike for maximum effect, especially when accompanied by an international chorus. But more often than not, quite apart from any risk to other aspects of the relationship, this kind of approach will be counter-productive in that it will generate a wounded, defensive reaction more likely to reinforce than undermine the behaviour pattern in question.

Australia has been possibly the most active country in the world in recent years in making bilateral representations on human rights matters—460 of them in 1990, in 82 countries—sometimes publicly, when we judged it not counter-productive, but usually more quietly. There is simply no evidence that that particular policy has in itself ever prejudiced the achievement of Australian policy objectives, in relation to trade or anything else. Of course we must take into account the full range of Australia's national interests when deciding how to approach a particular human rights issue—but the choice is not whether to act, but how to act.

In a sense the dichotomy between realism and idealism is a false one. Whether the context is human rights, the environment, or any other of the good international citizenship issues which so often raise this apparent dilemma, the issue is one of means and ends. The ends remain clear, but it is a matter of tempering what we want to achieve with what we can deliver, and at what cost.

4

The Politics of Foreign Policy

ONE CANNOT PRESUME to define a role for Australian foreign policy in the 1990s, or any other decade, without understanding the dynamics, and the limitations, of the institutional processes which in practice have to be employed to develop and apply that policy. Who, then, does what, and how, in the making and implementation of Australian foreign policy?

It is convenient to distinguish three distinct dimensions in which foreign policy operates: we focus on the first in this chapter, and on the second and third in the next. First is the political: the role of the foreign minister and the formidable cast of domestic actors, from the prime minister down, who may become involved in influencing, advising or directing him. Second is the professional diplomatic service: its role, despite massive changes to the context in which diplomacy has traditionally been practised, is and will remain as important as it has ever been. Third is public diplomacy, sometimes called 'second track' diplomacy[1] to distinguish it from more traditional government-to-government dealings: its objective is essentially to shape attitudes in other countries in a way which is favourable to Australian national interests.

FOREIGN POLICY IN THE CABINET

Not since the Vietnam War has foreign policy dominated domestic political debate as it routinely did in the 1950s and 1960s. But while foreign policy issues no longer make or break governments, they do continue to take centre stage with great frequency, particularly in the very fluid international environment which has prevailed since 1989. Perceptions of how governments handle them contribute a good deal to making or breaking their image of managerial competence and sense of national direction. Australian governments have become ever more conscious that, for all the competence of the diplomatic service and the value of its advice, foreign policy is not something that can just be left to the professionals. Ministers are held politically responsible for the product, and they are becoming ever more closely involved in its day-to-day formulation and presentation.

The product of the policy formulation process in foreign affairs is a little unusual. In domestic policy areas it is more often than not a piece of legislation, a new program supported by budgetary appropriation, or an announced process for reconciling competing claims or interests. In foreign affairs, by contrast, the product is usually just a statement of Australian government position: whether we support or oppose, applaud or deplore, this or that development; whether we will make this or that representation in support of some Australian interest; whether we will seek to persuade this or that group of countries to accept this or that new idea. The closest analogy in domestic affairs is probably with matters within the constitutional competence of the States rather than the Commonwealth, where the Commonwealth government has to advance its preferred positions by persuasion rather than simply exercise authority.

The forms that a statement of foreign policy might take vary enormously. It could be a ministerial speech or statement, inside or outside Parliament; a ministerial answer to a parliamentary question; a ministerial letter to a counterpart, colleague, lobby group or constituent; a ministerial response to a question from the media; a lower-key statement or response from a departmental or ministerial spokesperson; a cabled voting instruction for our diplomatic representatives in the United Nations General Assembly or some other multilateral forum; a cabled instruction to a mission abroad for a message to be delivered to a host government; or, most formally of all, an instrument of accession to an international treaty to which Australia is to become a party.

A good deal of foreign policy product, as thus defined, must necessarily be made on the run by the two ministers immediately responsible for the administration of the Foreign Affairs and Trade portfolio—the Minister for Foreign Affairs and Trade, and the Minister for Trade and Overseas Development (in the Hawke Government both with Cabinet rank, but with the former having overall co-ordinating responsibility for the portfolio, and the latter having primary carriage of trade policy and development assistance). In the rush of events, only a handful of matters will lend themselves to full-scale Cabinet or Cabinet Committee deliberation on the basis of prior-circulated formal submissions. In recent years, Budget deliberations aside, the average has been about a dozen a year, including such topics as our overall relations with Indonesia, China, Taiwan and Papua New Guinea, or Australian negotiating positions for Antarctic or other environment-related conventions. Sometimes the issue can be dealt with 'under the line' in Cabinet, i.e. without formal submission but on the basis of prior prime ministerial agreement that it will be raised. Several developments during the Gulf crisis, for example, were dealt with in this way.

Rather more often, consultations with other ministers on particular current issues occur outside a formal Cabinet framework, and are limited to those ministers immediately concerned. For example, the Minister for Defence would be consulted on a matter affecting arms exports; the Minister for Immigration, Local Government and Ethnic Affairs on a question of refugee policy; the Minister for Arts, Sport, Environment, Tourism and Territories, and probably Primary Industries and Energy as well, on a point arising in a climate convention negotiation; the Minister for Transport and Communications on a question of aviation links; the Minister for Employment, Education and Training on overseas student policy; the Treasurer on a question affecting the policy of international financial institutions like the World Bank or Asian Development Bank; the Minister for Industry, Technology and Commerce on a particular question of bilateral trade access; and so on. Almost every minister in the government has an interest, at any given time, in some matter or other passing across the desk of the two portfolio ministers.

A good deal of this consultation is in fact carried out beforehand by officers of the respective departments, communicating either formally through interdepartmental committees or correspondence, or more informally over the telephone. If this departmental consultative process is to alleviate pressures on ministers, rather than add to them, it is crucial that it be conducted in a co-operative rather than unduly competitive spirit. One of the more encouraging developments in the Canberra bureaucracy in recent years has been the emergence of just that, not least as between traditional rivals like Foreign Affairs and Defence. The December 1989 Ministerial Statement on *Australia's Regional Security*[2] was an excellent demonstration of how productive that co-operation could be.

Most of the remaining pieces are picked up by contact between the staff of the respective ministerial offices. Direct contact between ministers themselves on various contentious issues may as a result be limited in an average week to half-a-dozen or less such communications. Of course there has to be almost continuous contact between the two foreign affairs portfolio ministers themselves, and their respective offices, to ensure effective co-ordination. Day-to-day departmental processes—including, for example, the sending of a duplicate 'information' copy of all substantive departmental submissions to the non-action minister, and daily co-ordination of 'PPQ' (Possible Parliamentary Questions) briefings—ensure in practice that each knows what the other is doing, and that so far as practicable there is discussion and agreement within the portfolio before positions are taken on particularly sensitive issues. For each minister to have a clear idea of what the other is doing is also crucial in ensuring policy continuity on those many occasions when one is formally acting for the other during the latter's absence overseas.

The most crucial of all co-ordination tasks for any government is the relationship between the foreign minister and the prime minister.[3] While there is a prime ministerial directive that the Minister for Foreign Affairs and Trade (assisted by the Minister for Trade and Overseas Development) has 'prime responsibility for external affairs and for ensuring a coherent and consistent approach to the conduct of Australia's international relations',[4] designed to ensure that other ministers and departments with external interests work through a single channel, that primary responsibility is in fact subject to the role the prime minister himself chooses to play.

Australian prime ministers have almost invariably taken a major personal interest in foreign affairs. Changes in world politics and global communications have resulted in them showing more rather than less interest and, as a practical matter, foreign ministers no less than any other ministers take their cue from the prime minister of the day. In recent times, the Asia Pacific Economic Cooperation proposal, the campaign to ban mining and oil drilling in Antarctica, and Australia's Chemical Weapons Regional Initiative are three important and high-profile examples of foreign policy initiatives in which the Prime Minister was unequivocally the prime mover, with the Foreign Minister playing a subsequent implementation role.

There is no reason in practice why these institutional realities should generate any particular stress. They certainly have not during Gareth Evans's time as Foreign Minister, not least because a great deal of effort has been put into both day-to-day consultation and longer-term policy co-ordination. The main focus of the day-to-day effort has been to ensure that neither the Prime Minister nor the Foreign Minister springs surprises on each other—that each can go into the Parliament or face an impromptu 'doorstop' media conference knowing what the other is likely to be saying about the current issue of the day; and that any significant policy initiative that either is inclined to float has been the subject of prior discussion.

Most of this consultation occurs at the ministerial staff level, with both ministers' senior advisers constantly moving between each other's offices (which happen to be more or less adjacent to each other in the Executive Wing of the Parliament House building), with a good deal of communication also occurring between officers of the respective departments of Prime Minister and Cabinet and of Foreign Affairs and Trade. Whenever necessary, this is supplemented by direct discussion between the Prime Minister and Foreign Minister, usually brief and focused on the problem immediately in hand. In a rapidly moving situation like the Gulf crisis, such discussions might take place twice or more a day; otherwise, their frequency might average less than once a week.

The present Prime Minister and Foreign Minister have also found it helpful to sit down together every few months for lengthier periods—two or three hours or more—to work through the current state of play on a number of issues, to explore the room that may exist for new policy movement, to identify issues on which it may be appropriate to bring forward submissions to Cabinet, to discuss possible visits and generally to probe each other's thinking on Australia's foreign policy agenda. In one such meeting early in 1991, for example, they worked through a list of topics including (apart from the then-current Gulf crisis) Papua New Guinea, Malaysia, Australia—New Zealand—United States relations, Indonesia, South Africa, China, Taiwan, and the Soviet Union. Consultative processes of this kind do ensure that any shades of difference in philosophical approach or initial inclination are worked through in a way that not only avoids domestic political difficulties but, more importantly in foreign affairs terms, avoids sending confusing or conflicting signals to other governments.

INFLUENCES ON POLICY MAKERS

Inputs to the foreign policy making process obviously come from a variety of sources other than ministers themselves. The policy advice of the Department of Foreign Affairs and Trade itself is crucial, based as it is on a combination of the accumulated experience and expertise of its officers; extensive reporting of facts and opinion from relevant posts; representations received from other governments, through posts and the Canberra diplomatic corps; and detailed consultations with other relevant departments and agencies of government. If the concept of a 'departmental view'—as something with a life of its own, known about and reported as such—has less currency than it used to, that is more a matter of the significantly more active role now played by governments and ministers personally in the formulation of policy than of any lessening respect for the quality of performance of the department.

In the case of the Australian Labor Party in government—whatever may be the situation with the Liberal and National Parties—the views of the Parliamentary Party as expressed through its weekly Caucus meeting, or the deliberations of its Foreign Affairs, Defence and Trade Committee, must also be closely taken into account by ministers. In recent times most sensitive issues have been talked through in extensive committee briefing sessions, and divisive set-piece debates avoided. But the Party room remains an important channel through which at least one stream of community sentiment on foreign policy issues makes its views clearly known. The regular State and biennial National conferences of the Party are other such channels, the latter being particularly important because its platform resolutions are formally binding on a Labor government. Although throughout the 1970s and 1980s issues like the Australia—United States joint facilities, East Timor and Indo-China have been hardy perennials, the experience has generally been that frank and open debate produces a large measure of consensus between the extreme idealists, extreme pragmatists and those—including most ministers—in between. At the June 1991 Centenary National Conference, that consensus extended, remarkably, to all but one of the twenty-five policy resolutions debated.[5]

The Parliament itself plays a not unimportant role in foreign policy development, partly through the probing that goes on in daily question time (the present Foreign Minister, for example, answered a total of 375 questions without notice in the Senate directed to him in that capacity in his first two-and-a-half-years in the job) and partly, although less frequently, in the set-piece debates that occur in the two chambers, but much more substantively through the work of the parliamentary committees. The Joint Committee on Foreign Affairs, Defence and Trade, first established in 1952, has produced nearly fifty substantial reports on almost every aspect of Australia's foreign relations, most recently on Third World debt, and on Papua New Guinea; and its Senate standing committee counterpart produced sixteen such reports between 1973 and the end of 1990, most recently on Perestroika and its implications for Australia—Soviet Union relations, and on the trade and security dimensions of Australia—India relations. Quite apart from the hearings and visits associated with their reports, meetings of these committees are often the occasion for briefings by ministers and others on current issues, and this helps sustain what is largely these days a genuinely non-partisan approach to the conduct of Australian foreign policy. A somewhat less nonpartisan atmosphere prevails at one other set of parliamentary committee hearings at which foreign policy issues are often canvassed, the twice-yearly Senate Estimates Committees. Although notionally the occasion for scrutiny of departmental expenditure and administration only, they sometimes become the occasion for an all-purpose policy discussion.

Set-piece foreign affairs debates in the parliamentary chambers are less frequent than they used to be, particularly those based on wide-ranging ministerial statements. It used to be considered appropriate for a minister of foreign affairs, after a journey abroad, to report to the Parliament. While this was a proper acknowledgement of the importance of Parliament, it was also a quaint reflection of an Australian belief that events 'overseas' required especially deliberate and even sombre attention. Foreign ministers' travels today are so frequent and so business-like that it would be an imposition on Parliament to burden members with accounts of them. Gareth Evans, for example, made in his first two-and-a-half years in office 24 separate visits totalling 306 days, to 67 countries (or 108 countries if one includes return visits). Occasionally a ministerial statement to Parliament is warranted, but it is more likely to be an account of a development of importance to Australian foreign policy—such as, in 1990, an analysis of the current negotiations in the Cambodian peace process or an explanation of the Government's position at a critical stage of the Gulf crisis—rather than a description of developments in which Australian foreign policy has no significant input, even when these developments may be significant in themselves. There is just not the time, even if there were the interest, in Parliament for the *tours d'horizon* with which Australian foreign ministers once sought to impress their colleagues and the media. In turn, Opposition and other party spokespersons tend now to offer advice on foreign policy issues through direct communications to the media, in the guise of questions without notice at parliamentary question times, and through the parliamentary committee system.

Governments, in foreign affairs as elsewhere, also derive a significant amount of advice, both solicited and unsolicited, from outside the structures of government, party and Parliament. In the development assistance and trade policy areas, a good deal of this involves formal advisory groups such as the Trade Development Council, the Trade Negotiations Advisory Group, the Consultative Development Committee, and the Commodities Trade Advisory Group. Similar bodies in the mainstream foreign affairs area include the National Consultative Committee on Peace and Disarmament, and the 'public diplomacy' bodies like the Australia–Japan Foundation. The most formidable external lobbyists—certainly the noisiest, especially around Budget time—are the non-government aid organisations like the Australian Council for Overseas Aid (ACFOA) and its member bodies, but there is a considerable cast of pressure groups active on issues across the whole portfolio range. Academic writing on international relations perhaps has not been as prolific or as influential in Australia as in some other countries, but that seems gradually to be changing. An effort is now being made to tap that body of expertise with a series of brain-storming seminars on emerging policy issues recently organised by the Department of Foreign Affairs and Trade, under ministerial chairmanship, to which both academics and a wide range of participants from other departments and agencies have been invited.

THE ROLE OF THE MEDIA

The media in Australia is both a vehicle reflecting foreign policy outcomes and a source of input to that process. In its reflective—or reporting—role, the media certainly places great demands on government. World events, by definition, occur around the clock, irrespective of edition times or of television or radio news slots, and today's foreign minister has to be prepared to respond to questions at all times and on a wide range of subjects. One active media week for the present Foreign Minister in the latter part of 1990 included, for example, several morning 'doorstop' sessions about Australian hostages in Iraq; half-a-dozen short television and radio interviews on the Gulf crisis; a forty-five minute recorded interview with a crusading television journalist making a documentary on the disposal of chemical weapons on Johnston Atoll (about four minutes of which was used in the final product); participation in a recorded program for ABC radio on the issues involved in a Cambodian peace settlement; an interview on government policy generally with a senior press gallery journalist, partly on a background and partly on an on-the-record basis; and an interview with Radio Australia generating material for some current affairs programs beamed to the South Pacific and Asia Pacific regions. The Gulf crisis may have made this period particularly intense, but even with that issue taken out, the load is indicative of that carried week after week. And there is probably even less room for slips of the tongue in foreign relations than in domestic politics!

The pressure on ministers for 'doorstop' interviews and participation in talk-back programs means that very often complex issues have to be dealt with in a simple, often superficial, way. There are many opportunities, nonetheless, to redress the balance, for example by ministerial and departmental backgrounding of editors and senior writers in State capitals as well as Canberra; by regular ministerial and departmental briefing sessions with business leaders; and by speeches, articles and substantial interviews—not to mention books.

A good many issues are generated by the media itself. If a newspaper publishes an article critical of a foreign government or leader to which that government responds, an official Australian comment may be required. The foreign minister would need to decide whether this comment should be associated with a public announcement or be limited to an official response in confidence to the foreign government. If an Australian film or television program is considered offensive to a foreign government, official reassurances may have to be given that no offence was intended by the Australian government, and the explanation given—not for the first time —that such matters are beyond the capacity, not to mention the will, of the government in our system to deal with. Successive Australian governments have taken the view that they cannot be responsible for what the Australian media says, but they nevertheless make an effort to keep the media fully briefed, in the hope that a well-informed media—which among other things better understands the implications of its actions—is less likely to cause at least inadvertent offence.

The overall record of the Australian media in foreign affairs matters is mixed. The routine coverage of international affairs in newspapers that would regard themselves as serious is less detailed and informative, and their editorial discussion possibly less sophisticated, than that provided by comparable European and American papers. But across the whole range of print and electronic outlets, Australia is probably better served than most countries in the quantity and quality of its day-in, day-out foreign affairs coverage and in the range and depth of the editorial and feature-page attention given to foreign policy issues. Certainly in radio, the Australian Broadcasting Corporation (ABC) provides a cover of international affairs that is just about as good as anywhere in the world, and in television the publicly funded Special Broadcasting Service (SBS) provides—again with the ABC—very substantial foreign news and analysis. The legacy of the English language still makes Britain and the United States preferred locations for overseas media offices and the purchase of material, especially in television, but the cultural cringe is becoming less obvious: ever more, and more sophisticated, resources are being committed by media organisations to the Asia Pacific region.

While the Australian public is, on balance, relatively well served for routine reporting and analysis, this is less obviously the case when it comes to the exercise of news judgment about major stories, particularly when Australia itself is involved. Any ripple on the surface of diplomatic relations with any country—whatever the context and whatever the justification from the point of view of Australian national interests—is likely to be characterised as a 'diplomatic row' reflecting adversely on the conduct of Australian diplomacy, whose job it is to maintain Good Relations.[6] At the same time—and the inconsistency is rarely remarked—Australian foreign ministers are routinely berated for not being aggressively objectionable enough on matters like self-determination for East Timor or human rights in China. If we are not rowing, we must be kowtowing.[7]

The extent to which foreign ministers uniquely suffer from the Australian media lash should not be exaggerated: an all-pervasive scepticism about the motives and performance of those in high places is a distinctive national habit. But it is perhaps more difficult in foreign affairs than in most other areas of government to consistently marry responsible with accessible journalism. The nature of the subject matter works against it: the ever-changing agenda of issues, the complexity so often of the relevant facts, and the need so often to take into account many conflicting factors in reaching a balanced judgment about Australian national interests. It is not a matter of the media never getting things right: of course it very often does. And, equally obviously, it is valuable for governments to have to work in a society where an active and critical media makes its own discoveries and delivers its own judgments. But in foreign affairs, however much media interest impacts on ministerial work programs, it is simply not wise for governments to make policy in response to a media-driven agenda.

THE LIFE OF A FOREIGN MINISTER

The multiple pressures on ministers generally, and foreign ministers in particular, are better understood than they used to be, but are no less burdensome for that. The travel commitments impose an immense burden of their own, but personal contact is as important an element in ministerial diplomacy as ever, particularly in our own region, and the ever-growing multilateral agenda generates more and more occasions demanding a ministerial presence. Moreover, the days are long gone when a few days of meetings, speeches and conference commitments could be balanced by a few more days of gently paced recreational travel: the demands both at home and abroad make that impossible.

For example, in one three-week period in February 1991, the present Foreign Minister—whose family home is in Melbourne—followed a week of speaking engagements in Sydney, and of Cabinet, Party Executive and a dozen or so meetings with officials and visitors in Canberra, with a twenty-four hour weekend visit to Bali to attend, with his Indonesian counterpart, the inaugural meeting of the Timor Gap Treaty Ministerial Council. He returned from that to spend a week in Parliament, with a full round of Cabinet, Caucus and another ten or so meetings with visiting dignitaries, resident ambassadors, business groups and the like, to depart then on Thursday afternoon for London for a day-long meeting of the Commonwealth Committee of Foreign Ministers on Southern Africa, with another day of bilateral and preparatory calls. He was back in Australia by early Monday morning, after flying another twenty-four hours, to face another full parliamentary week, this time involving some fifteen ministerial meetings, requiring preparation of their own, in addition to Cabinet and Caucus—not to mention four Senate question times. That week concluded with the hosting and chairing of a full-scale meeting, on Thursday and Friday, of the annual Australia–Papua New Guinea Ministerial Forum. Home at midnight on Friday, he was back in Sydney to address an international conference on Sunday night, with another week in Canberra to follow . . .

While in a more normal period, overseas travel commitments might be four or five weeks apart, rather than a single week, there is really no such thing *as* a normal period in foreign affairs. During this particular period the Gulf crisis was also at its height, and all the media and other demands flowing from that had to be accommodated. Moreover the paper—what British ministers call 'doing the boxes'—never stops flowing. In a given year—to take an average of departmental figures for the last three—the foreign minister has to sign some two thousand items of more or less routine correspondence; read and digest about seven hundred 'information' submissions, some of considerable length and complexity; and deal with some twelve hundred other submissions requiring substantive consideration and decision of some kind—whether it be a new policy strategy, a voting position in the United Nations, the appointment of an ambassador, the terms of a reply to a ministerial counterpart, the text of a statement or whatever. In addition there are a myriad matters, not in the shape of formal submissions, originated by the Department or by other ministers or parliamentary colleagues or whoever, which nonetheless require ministerial attention. There are speeches to prepare—a major one perhaps every two or three weeks, and a number of minor ones in between. And there are the daily cables to read, seven days a week—culled of the trivial and pre-sorted by the minister's staff, but still amounting to an average for reading by him of 150 each day, and rather more than that when a major crisis is running.

It all adds up to a workload of some sixteen hours a day, six days a week. That could no doubt be less if the foreign minister were to read less, see fewer people, make fewer speeches, travel less, initiate less policy, sign less correspondence personally, and generally be prepared to delegate more from the political to the departmental level. But in the present fast-moving international and regional environment, with Australia needing to have a very clear idea of how it can ensure a place in that world which will maximise our interests, there is no justification for giving the task of advancing those interests anything less than maximum effort.

5

The Practice of Foreign Policy

IN A WELL-FUNCTIONING SYSTEM, and Australia's has been that in recent years, the role of the Department of Foreign Affairs and Trade precisely complements that of its ministers. The ministers, and the government of which they are part, are there to give policy leadership—but they can only do so on the basis of good advice, for the provision of which they must necessarily depend largely on the Department. The international standing and reputation of Australia and its government depend very significantly on the quality of the performance of its representatives abroad, at conferences and in smaller face-to-face settings, and that quality has to be evident in both the ministers and the professional diplomats. Credibility and reputation, at home and abroad, also depend significantly on the quality of administrative performance, whether in delivering aid dollars, running an efficient passport system, handling the consular problems of distressed Australians abroad, or simply answering correspondence in a timely and helpful fashion: here ministers have to depend almost wholly on the Department.

In assessing Australia's needs in relation to the professional management of its foreign policy, it is important to be aware of a number of factors which impact particularly upon us. They were well identified by Stuart Harris in his 1986 *Review of Australia's Overseas Representation*[1], along the following lines. First, there is a need to avoid dependence on the assessments, advice and help of allies and associates, whose interests in any situation may be different, and who will be perfectly capable of indifference or worse to Australian concerns. Secondly, there is a need to build resources to cope effectively with the rapidly growing internationalist agenda in which we have legitimate interests. Thirdly, Australia's highly multicultural community has generated a need to maintain links with a number of countries with which we might otherwise have only limited contact. Fourthly, there is the fact that:

> perhaps most important, and possibly unique to Australia . . . although geographically isolated and a long way from its markets, Australia lives increasingly closely with neighbours with cultures, traditions and languages which are largely alien to it. It shares no tradition or history with the countries of its region to provide a common and widespread understanding of cultures, values and social systems. While other Western countries may not need a deep understanding of these societies, it is vital to Australia's national interest that it is able to analyse in depth their processes of cultural and social change and of nation-building.[2]

The point is made that this factor works both ways, and that in addition to Australia seeking understanding of its neighbours, we have to direct much more effort to explaining Australia to its neighbours.

STRUCTURE OF THE DIPLOMATIC SERVICE

Within Australia, the Department of Foreign Affairs and Trade has a central office in Canberra comprising ten major divisions—three 'geographic', four 'functional' and three 'corporate' in character—and two small unattached branches. The Australian International Development Assistance Bureau (AIDAB) is an autonomous body within the Department, reporting directly to the ministers. So too, following a decision announced in March 1991, is the statutory trade promotion body, the Australian Trade Commission (Austrade). In addition to their overseas representation, all three bodies—the Department, AIDAB and Austrade—have a network of regional offices in State capitals. The basic organisational structure—together with information on staff numbers and budgetary appropriations—is summarised in Chart 1. It should be noted that the Australian Secret Intelligence Service (ASIS) is also responsible to and under the control of the Minister for Foreign Affairs and Trade—but, other than its budget ($21.1 million in 1990/91), its structure and activities are not a matter of public record.[3]

Although the Department attracts distinctively high-level applicants for its annual trainee intake, it in no sense operates as a separate service, with a career structure protected against lateral appointments within the government service or from outside. There has been in recent years a significant leavening of some of the more stereotypical older-style diplomatic traditions within the Department, especially since the comprehensive integration of the former Department of Trade with Foreign Affairs after 1987. The amalgamated Department has a very wide-ranging set of talents and experience available to it, and is becoming ever more adaptable to the needs, and demands, of the fluid new era in international relations in which Australia is striving to find a place—although there is still more distance to travel.

Australia had, as at 30 June 1991, a total of 103 overseas missions, spread over 98 cities in 73 separate countries. Of these missions, 88 were Embassies, High Commissions or Consulates managed by the Department of Foreign Affairs and Trade; 13 were Consulates or Offices managed by Austrade; and 2 (Edinburgh and Manchester) were Offices managed by the Department of Immigration, Local Government and Ethnic Affairs. In addition to the posts wholly managed by Austrade, there was an Austrade presence in 51 other posts managed by the Department (see Chart 2). These arrangements are not static. In any year, two or three Department posts might be closed and a similar number of new posts opened, reflecting both budgetary constraints and new priorities: for example in 1990/91, Algiers and Lusaka were replaced by Berlin and Prague. Austrade arrangements are similarly dynamic. Following a major review of the balance of the organisation's overseas representation, it was anticipated that in 1991/92 four North American Offices would close (in San Francisco, Chicago, Miami and Vancouver) and at least three others open elsewhere (in Surabaya, Hanoi and Guangdong)[4].

The character—and size—of the Foreign Affairs missions vary enormously. In mid-1991 there were 51 Embassies and 24 High Commissions ('High Commission' being simply the terminology adopted for embassies located in Commonwealth countries). Five of the Embassies were multilateral, co-located in each case with other Australian posts in the city in question, namely the United Nations posts in New York and Geneva; the General Agreement on Trade and Tariffs (GATT) and Disarmament posts also in Geneva; and the Organisation of Economic Co-operation and Development (OECD) post in Paris. The largest of these missions, Washington, had 43 Australia-based personnel working for the Department; the smallest, Nauru, just 2. In many cases, moreover, the Head of Mission in a post is accredited as Ambassador or High Commissioner to one or more other countries, usually in the same region, where Australia does not have a resident mission, and this can add enormously to both the variety and volume of the post's workload: for example, the Australian High Commissioner in Jamaica is accredited to 11 other Caribbean countries. In all, while Australia has resident missions in 73 countries, accreditation arrangements of this kind exist with another 66 countries.

In addition to the High Commissions and Embassies there were, in mid-1991, 17 Consulates and Consulates-General managed either by the Department or Austrade, ranging again from very large and busy posts like Hong Kong to almost nominal presences. Yet another layer of representation—not recorded on Chart 2—is provided by Honorary Consuls, established in seven cities since 1989, but with that number expected to double by the end of 1991: they play a role that has been long found useful by other countries, particularly those around Australia's size.

It is not only the Department of Foreign Affairs and Trade and the other agencies so far mentioned who maintain representatives abroad. Defence, Treasury and many others have officers placed within the posts described, and on other assignments. In all, in mid-1991, fully 18 government departments and agencies together maintained a total of 1311 Australian staff abroad: of these, Australia-based Foreign Affairs, AIDAB and Austrade staff numbered 971. In addition, locally engaged staff numbered 2460. The trend has been towards streamlining rather than expanding Australia's representation abroad: in recent years the number of Australia-based staff has declined (from 1534 in 1975) and that of locally engaged staff even more.

The overseas posts operated by the Department of Foreign Affairs and Trade absorb, excluding AIDAB and Austrade, about two-thirds of the Department's total operating budget: their cost in 1990/91 was $205.6 million. The pressure is continually on to cut back this representation further, and to justify why we need such an extensive, and expensive, body of representatives. What, it is still asked, do diplomats actually *do*? Stuart Harris put the familiar question succinctly:

> It is a common argument that changes in the world have reduced the need for overseas representation through resident missions. Developments in communications, it is suggested, reduce needs for resident representation because of speedy alternative sources of information. Telephones, it is argued, enable Ministers or home-based officials to discuss and negotiate directly, by-passing in-place foreign representatives, and easy plane travel enables Ministers or expert officials to replace Ambassadors in much international negotiation, reducing their independence of action and, perhaps, the need for local representatives at all.[5]

His answer, with which we strongly agree, is that diplomats do so much these days that we need, if anything, more of them, not fewer. The international agenda, for both bilateral and—especially—multilateral matters, is expanding dramatically in both range and complexity, and in respect of every part of it there is as much need as ever in Australia for traditional overseas post reporting. Information has to be gathered and assessed by someone, and there is no substitute for continuous on-the-ground contact to pull together shifts in attitudes and policies, and to develop the kind of person-to-person understandings on which those analyses have to be based. Equally, there has to be reciprocal communication in relation to that agenda: representations have to be made to host governments, arguments put, and the task of influencing assiduously pursued. And then there is the actual bargaining process where matters have to be negotiated: very little of this can be done effectively on the telephone, or on a fly-in fly-out basis.

Even though involvement of ministers and home-based officials in the day-to-day practice of diplomacy has increased enormously in recent times, thereby relieving overseas representatives of some functions and some of the demands upon them for independent action, it needs to be appreciated that plane travel can add to, as much as relieve, the local representatives' load. Harris gives the example of Bangkok, which now experiences some five to six hundred Australian ministerial, parliamentary and senior official visits annually, all of which place a servicing load on the post. He also points to the downside associated with dramatic improvements in communications technology: 'The speed and intensity of media reporting has intensified rather than replaced the need for overseas representatives to explain, verify, elaborate, assess, interpret or refute media reports'.[6]

The conjunction of rapid domestic and world changes, and the acceptance by Australians that we have to make our own way in a more competitive environment, is a good time to reassess our diplomatic capabilities and potential. The first step is to set aside the stereotypes of both diplomats and diplomacy that tend to cloud the real issues. It is a tribute to the persistence of myths in the public imagination that the Australian media—and some politicians—still feel disposed to speak of diplomacy in terms of striped pants and the cocktail circuit. In this they are occasionally assisted by the nostalgic memoirs of former Australian diplomats. But the fact is that just about the only valuable survivor of Australian diplomacy's association with tradition is the concept of a professional service.

What Australia needs—and is now getting—are men and women who do not expect a career in diplomacy to provide them with an existence separate from other careers that make up the world of affairs. Abroad, they must be skilled at gathering information and conveying it accurately and succinctly, at negotiation and public persuasion. At home, they must work effectively not only with the Canberra diplomatic corps (dealing with whom has many similarities to the work of diplomacy abroad), but also within the Department and within the Canberra bureaucracy—appreciating that even the best policy advice is ineffective if one is unable to marshal support for it. Recent public service reforms—including the identification of corporate goals, the introduction of program budgeting, and much greater devolution of managerial responsibility—have all given an emphasis to management skills, without which any Australian diplomat of the future will be at a disadvantage.

It is prudent to assume further reduction in the size of the Australian public sector and continuing constraints on government expenditure. However, in foreign affairs, the prospect is for greater Australian involvement and, as there is little scope for privatisation in the operation of this particular department of state, this means an increased demand on government. Two cultural changes are required for the seemingly impossible task to be accomplished of doing more with less. One is public recognition that Australian diplomats abroad have important work to perform—and are not embalmed in a sybaritic, duty-free lifestyle that inoculates them against the rigours of life at home. It has been a ritual to call for the closing of posts abroad as an economy measure when the need is, if anything, for more posts, and certainly for more, rather than fewer, professional diplomats on the ground.

The other cultural change needed is one of organisational culture within the Australian bureaucracy and specifically within the Department of Foreign Affairs and Trade. The point has been made that while the industrial age was built on the division of labour, the post-industrial age will be built on the integration of labour, and this means especially the integration of management skills and policy skills. The assumption that in some way the Australian public service should provide a haven of welfare and tenure and the maintenance of skills and attitudes that are not in demand elsewhere no longer has any legitimacy—if it ever did. Certainly the demands on the Department of Foreign Affairs and Trade, and Australia's diplomatic personnel, are the demands of a very real world indeed.

DIPLOMACY BILATERAL AND MULTILATERAL

The role of the overseas diplomatic representative varies considerably depending upon whether the post is bilateral or multilateral in character. So far as bilateral diplomacy is concerned, a good account of just what does happen in such a post was given recently by the Australian Ambassador to Japan, Rawdon Dalrymple:[7] the Tokyo experience here described is readily translatable elsewhere.

First, there is the business of ceremony, formalities and attention-paying. Probably the most derided, and misunderstood, aspect of diplomatic activity, this is nonetheless of very considerable importance, especially in formal and highly structured societies like Japan. It involves, in the Japanese context, laying the foundation for a relationship of mutual respect and substance through the formalities associated with visits at prime ministerial and ministerial levels, careful attention to the forms as well as content, prior consultation over a range of areas, and simply paying attention to political and business leaders and the senior members of the bureaucracy who deal with matters of concern to Australia.

Secondly, there is the promotion and support of Australia's economic interests. Part of that has involved pursuing the Australian government's multilateral agenda, especially our commitment to GATT and the Uruguay Round, and encouraging the Japanese to do likewise. But the main emphasis is on bilateral matters. The government has been significantly involved over the years—although less so in this deregulatory era—in minerals and energy export through the operation of export controls; participation in project start-up negotiations (e.g. the North-West Shelf Liquefied Natural

Gas (LNG) project); and support for industry consultative bodies (like the tripartite Western Australian Iron Ore Industry Consultative Council). All this has a Tokyo Embassy as well as a Canberra dimension to it. Agricultural exports have involved intense diplomatic activity in securing market opening—as for beef—and seeking reductions in other forms of protection through the relaxation of plant and animal quarantine restrictions (such as presently inhibit the export of fruit and vegetables and dairy products) and of food import controls (such as exist in particular for rice and sugar). Fisheries matters involve almost constant representational activity, particularly in the context of driftnet fishing and the conservation of the southern blue fin tuna resource.

The Embassy also works closely with Austrade in trade promotion activity seeking to expand and diversify our exports of manufacturers and services; in encouraging investment, not least through constantly explaining the very limited policy impediment the Australian government places in its way; in developing and formalising science and technology co-operation agreements; in the ongoing effort to develop and implement the Multi-Function Polis concept, which brings together a number of economic issues including investment and science and technology co-operation; and in continuing to encourage tourism, through a variety of information and promotional efforts and, not least, the efficient issuing, through the mission, of about 450 000 visas each year.

Thirdly, there is the diverse range of other specifically focused activity relating to traditional 'political' matters, to cultural and educational exchanges, information provision and public diplomacy generally. The political agenda is steadily growing and diversifying as the Australia–Japan relationship becomes less one-dimensionally trade based, more focused on the potential for region-wide co-operation, and generally more mature. An interesting recent development has been the dialogue, in which the embassy has played a significant part, on regional security issues—including both specific problems like Cambodia, and the more general question of the evolving strategic balance and role to be played in the Asia Pacific region by the various global and regional powers.

Multilateral diplomacy has its own distinctive character. The working environment is the conference room and the corridor; the interests that have to be taken into account extend across the whole spectrum of Australia's relationships, with decisions rarely if ever being able to be made on calculations of their effect on relations with one country alone; and the diplomacy involved, based on an endless search for compromise that does not destroy substance, is painstakingly, often agonizingly, slow. There are three sets of multilateral forums in which Australia is especially active: the United Nations, the Commonwealth, and the South Pacific Forum and Commission. Outside these, multilateral activities are also conducted in groups like the Antarctic Treaty Parties, the Australia Group (established to develop informal constraints on the export of chemical weapons precursors), the Non-Aligned Movement (to which Australia is accredited as a 'guest'), and in the growing number of specific-purpose conferences.

More of the world's states are represented at the United Nations —presently 159 of them—than in any other diplomatic meeting place. Australia was one of its fifty founding members in 1945. All of the UN member states sit in the General Assembly, while there are varying membership criteria for the subsidiary bodies created from time to time by the Assembly (e.g. the forty-member Conference on Disarmament) and for the Organization's other 'principal organs'—the Security Council, the Economic and Social Council (and the commissions created under it, including the Commission on Human Rights), the Trusteeship Council and the International Court of Justice. Most United Nations member states, including Australia, are also involved in some or all of the funds and programs within the system (including the Development Programme (UNDP), the Children's Fund (UNICEF), the High Commissioner for Refugees (UNHCR), the Population Fund (UNFPA) and the World Food Programme), as well as in the sixteen independent specialised agencies associated with the United Nations (including the Educational Scientific and Cultural Organization (UNESCO), the Food and Agricultural Organization (FAO), the International Bank for Reconstruction and Development (IBRD or 'World Bank'), the International Monetary Fund (IMF), the International Labour Organization (ILO), and the World Health Organization (WHO)), and the two 'related' organisations (the General Agreement on Trade and Tariffs (GATT) and the International Atomic Energy Agency (IAEA)).

The United Nations system offers Australia an important set of forums for participating in the resolution of problems bearing on our national interests across an extraordinary diversity of fields. For most individual countries, including ourselves, progress in this respect can only be made by coalition-building. Although voting blocs are less rigid than they used to be, Australia's starting point is our membership of the Western Europe and Others Group (WEOG). This may be somewhat at odds with our present preoccupation with forging links with our own region, but it is a hard mould to break out of, particularly in the context of seeking election to the Security Council (on which we have been represented four times, in the years 1946/47, 1956/57, 1973/74 and 1985/86) or other bodies within the system where executive or other membership rotates.

Australia—along with a number of other countries—has had a long-standing concern with the managerial and budgetary efficiency of the United Nations system, and we keep our membership of various agencies under regular review. But we have overwhelmingly maintained the judgment that was so articulately stated by Dr H. V. Evatt, who became President of the Third General Assembly in 1948, when he said of the United Nations:

it is the best presently available instrument, both for avoiding the supreme and ultimate catastrophe of a third world war, waged with all-destroying weapons, and also for establishing an international order which should and can assure to mankind security against poverty, unemployment, ignorance, famine and disease.[8]

There is no doubt that Australia's standing at the United Nations has improved since the 1960s and early 1970s, when we were still inclined to temporise or prevaricate on issues of racism and to be defensive on regional questions such as independence for Papua New Guinea and our military alliance with the United States. It is not unreasonable to claim that Australia is now generally perceived as a responsible, tolerant, multicultural society, willing to take our share of international responsibilities, and a country wholly committed to making the United Nations system work effectively.

The Commonwealth is a free association of sovereign independent States, numbering fifty in mid-1991, whose only common link is that they were once former dependencies, of one kind or another, of Britain. It has no charter, treaty or constitution. It manifests itself in a series of programs for co-operation, consultation and mutual assistance, co-ordinated by the Secretariat in London; in two-yearly meetings of Commonwealth Heads of Government, and irregular meetings of other ministers in particular subject areas; in specific consultative bodies like the Commonwealth Trade Union Council and Parliamentary Association; and in the four-yearly Commonwealth Games. Functional co-operation has been increasing in recent years in areas such as the environment, drug trafficking, education, technical and scientific co-operation, women and development, cultural exchanges, and election monitoring.

The Commonwealth's highest-profile political role, and the one in which Australia has been most intensively engaged, has been in relation to African affairs. The pressure maintained by the Commonwealth on its former member, South Africa, has been a reference point for the whole international community on apartheid—with, in recent years, the Commonwealth Eminent Persons Group and subsequently the Commonwealth Committee of Foreign Ministers on Southern Africa being the focal points for the co-ordination of this activity.

Generally speaking, Australia's multilateral diplomatic activity through the Commonwealth is not as extensive, demanding or significant as our involvement in the United Nations system. But it does provide a valuable further opportunity for contact and coalition-building with a number of countries in our own region or who share common interests or both, and in this sense is helpful to Australia in advancing its own interests. And it does enable us to take part in a collaborative effort which manifestly generates a number of international benefits.

The South Pacific Forum and South Pacific Commission are smaller forums still, but enormously important to their individual Pacific island member states, and quite centrally important to the whole pattern of trade, aid and diplomacy in this region. The South Pacific Commission, an initiative of H. V. Evatt established under the 'Canberra Agreement' in 1947 by the then metropolitan powers in the region (Australia, France, the Netherlands, New Zealand, United Kingdom and United States), is essentially a development and technical assistance agency, with an advisory and consultative role in such fields as marine resources, rural management and community and education services. Based in Noumea, and with major meetings annually, the Commission has since 1983 changed its character by giving full and equal membership to the independent island governments in the region: in mid-1991 there were twenty-seven members. Australia is strongly committed to the Commission, and presently contributes one-third of its annual core budget of (in 1990/91) $9.1 million, with significant voluntary additional contributions beyond that.

The South Pacific Forum, formed in 1971, currently has fifteen members and a permanent secretariat based in Suva: its annual budget in 1991 was $10.5 million, which Australia supported to the extent of some $3.6 million. Confined in its membership to the independent states of the region, it is as such the premium body for multilateral diplomacy within the region. Its annual Heads of Government meetings range over an agenda which has included in recent years nuclear testing, driftnet fishing, New Caledonia, climate change, economic co-operation and chemical weapons destruction at Johnston Atoll, with the negotiation of the South Pacific Nuclear Free Zone Treaty being perhaps its most internationally visible achievement. Post-Forum dialogue arrangements with major countries having an interest in the South Pacific (currently the United States, France, United Kingdom, Japan, China and the European Community) are a recent innovation which can only help bring the issues confronting the region to a more influential international audience. The Forum and its Secretariat also embrace other significant regional institutional structures, notably the University of the South Pacific and the Forum Fisheries Agency; the latter has been playing an increasingly important and sophisticated role in developing and protecting the island countries' overwhelmingly important economic resource.

DIPLOMATS AS POLICY INSTRUMENTS

One of the perennial questions that arises in foreign policy, which it is as appropriate to treat here as anywhere else, is how the presence or absence of diplomats in another country should itself be used as a means of expressing approval or disapproval. In traditional diplomatic practice, the strongest expression of disapproval was refusal to recognise a new government, or the severing of diplomatic relations with an existing one. A lesser step was to withdraw not the whole staff but just the head of mission, leaving it in the hands of a chargé d'affaires. A lesser step still was to withdraw the ambassador temporarily 'for consultations'. To what extent can or should these practices be employed today?

The most sustained example of non-recognition by Australia was that of the communist regime in China, which came to power in 1949 and was not recognised until 1973. Examples of breaks in relations include the following: in 1953 Moscow recalled its ambassador and all embassy staff from Canberra and ejected the entire Australian embassy staff from Moscow following the defection of Vladimir Petrov; in 1956 Egypt broke diplomatic relations with Australia over our support of the military intervention of Britain and France in the Suez Canal; and in 1975 the Democratic Peoples' Republic of Korea—apparently misreading Australian voting intentions on some Korean issues in the United Nations—unceremoniously withdrew its representatives from Canberra, and expelled ours from Pyongyang. Australia withdrew its ambassador to Chile in 1973, after the assassination of President Salvador Allende; and, more recently, its high commissioner to Suva, after a military coup toppled the elected government of Timoci Bavadra in 1987.

Over recent years, however, there has been a significant shift in international thinking on these matters, which Australia has now followed. In January 1988 the government decided to abandon the policy of recognising or withholding recognition of foreign governments and instead to recognise only states. This followed a review by the Department of Foreign Affairs and Trade which established that the clarity of a policy of recognising or not a particular government was more than offset by the difficulty of maintaining consular, commercial and other activities in a country whose government Australia did not recognise. In addition, recognition of a new regime was persistently interpreted by the Australian public as approval, in circumstances where it often constituted nothing of the kind.

Australia's change of policy followed a similar change by Britain in 1980. The British decided not to accord formal recognition to governments, but rather to determine the nature of regimes that came to power unconstitutionally according to an assessment of whether they controlled the territory of the state concerned and seemed likely to continue to do so. The new Australian policy brought us closer to the new United Kingdom practice, and that of the United States, West Germany, France, Belgium and several Latin countries, although the ASEAN countries, New Zealand and Ireland among others still follow the practice of recognising governments.

It is likely that, in any single year, several changes of government will occur with varying degrees of constitutionality. The black-and-white options of recognition or non-recognition are blunt instruments in what is often an evolving situation. They do not allow for flexibility in determining at what level and in what area of business official contact with the regime is maintained. The advantage of not recognising a particular government is that it becomes a matter to be determined from the degree and extent of dealings with it whether it is being treated as *the* 'government' of the state or not. When factions are competing for power and one replaces another, it becomes a matter of inference, from the nature of the dealings with each faction which is to be regarded as being the government.

In changing its recognition policy, the Australian government paid particular attention to its experience in Afghanistan, Cambodia and Fiji. In Afghanistan, Australia had not recognised the Najibullah government, which had excluded us from normal diplomatic dealings, in particular with consular relations, in a complex developing situation. In Cambodia, where three factions comprised the resistance to the Hun Sen government (and from one of which, the Khmer Rouge, Australia had withdrawn recognition when it was in power in Phnom Penh) the new policy enabled us to deal with officials of all the factions without inferring that any of them had a claim to be accepted as the representative of Cambodia. In Fiji, Australia had not recognised any government after the coup of May 1987. When the High Commissioner was recalled, the rest of the staff remained in Suva; when Fiji withdrew from the Commonwealth, we replaced our departed High Commissioner with an Ambassador, without recognising the government with which he had to deal, as this occurred after the policy change by Australia in favour of recognising states rather than governments.

Issues will still arise about the territorial sovereignty of states—e.g. the Baltic or Yugoslav republics—but these will be much less frequent than the issue of which government rightfully represents the state. By recognising the state, Australia is now less likely to feel compelled to withdraw an ambassador or a high commissioner to indicate disapproval of the manner in which a government has taken power. It can still do so, but the need is less imperative. This has a practical benefit. Many of Australia's diplomatic missions are small and the withdrawal of the head of mission can leave the rest of the staff overburdened with consular and other activities which are likely to increase during a crisis (for example, evacuation of Australian nationals), and perhaps unable to provide political representation at a sufficiently influential level to satisfy the requirements of the government in Canberra. Similarly, the quality of assessment and advice from the post could be diminished by the absence of a head of mission. In addition, if Australia's official activities are to be adjusted, or even perhaps in some cases terminated (for example, defence co-operation or development assistance), management of the changes could require sensitive handling at the post.

None of this change of practice means that it is no longer possible to express unmistakable disapproval of a government or its policy in circumstances where that is appropriate. It is always possible to announce a substantial policy change in bilateral relations. This was the course Australia adopted, for example, to show disapproval of the Chinese government's suppression of demonstrators in Beijing in June 1989. We did not break relations, nor did we withdraw our ambassador. Rather we announced that we would not continue our previously close relationship: government-to-government contact was reduced to a minimum in a number of identified ways, and several official high-level visits were cancelled. On the other hand, it was also announced that we intended to keep open other lines of people-to-people access and communication, by which we would indicate continuing support for economic liberalisation and political reform. In response to evolving circumstances, both within China and in terms of the reaction of like-minded countries elsewhere, this policy was subsequently modified in January 1990 and remaining political and economic restrictions were lifted after a further review a year later, in February 1991. The point about this policy response was that it was subtle and graduated, in a way that the blunt instrument of non-recognition could not have been. Moreover, it was both more effective and more workable than the lesser step of ambassadorial withdrawal would have been.

There will always be room for argument as to just how far Australia can go, in the management of its international relations, in usefully and sensibly pursuing principled or idealistic policy objectives. But at least the practical instruments are now more readily available for those choices to be made on a more finely tuned basis than was possible in the past.

PUBLIC DIPLOMACY

Professional diplomats—and ministers—are not the only people engaged in practising diplomacy. There is an important further dimension to the working of Australian foreign policy—involving the practice of 'public' diplomacy—where they constitute only a small proportion of a very much larger cast of players, both inside and outside government.

All diplomacy is an exercise in persuasion and influence. Public diplomacy differs from the more traditional kind only in its methodology and in terms of whom it sets out to influence and persuade. Whereas traditional diplomacy seeks directly to influence the influential, public diplomacy not only reaches to the decision-makers and opinion-formers, but also casts its net much wider, beyond the influential few to the 'uninvolved' many. Public diplomacy is, of course, not new. The ancient Greeks' penchant for the study of rhetoric was in part aimed at putting a convincing case to neighbouring states and their peoples. In modern times, libraries, exhibitions and films have all become well tested delivery systems for public diplomacy. Its starting premise is that familiarity, far from breeding contempt, can in international relations be a spur to broad-based links between nations. We need to be concerned about what other nations think of us for the good reason that the images which others carry of us influence their attitudes towards us—not only in a general sense, but also with regard to our security requirements, to our goods and services, to our appeal as a place to invest in, to migrate to, to visit and so on.

There is no single approach to public diplomacy. How you approach it and what tools you use depend on your objectives and audience. Public diplomacy is sometimes divided into hard-edged information programs and the more subtle appeals of cultural diplomacy. Yet such distinctions are neither precise nor particularly useful. Many information programs have a cultural component, and many cultural programs are designed to inform. Moreover, the distinction ignores the fundamental requirement for public diplomacy to be implemented in a co-ordinated way, carefully calibrated to the needs and interests of the target audience.

A more useful approach is to look at public diplomacy in terms of the purposes it, in all its various manifestations, is designed to serve. In the first place, there is its role in persuading particular individuals or target groups of the validity of an Australian point of view on a particular issue. In extreme cases, such as wartime, this can take the form of hard-sell propaganda. But normally it is a question of persuasively putting a case: convincing the United States Congress, for example, that export subsidies which may be aimed at the European Community have also caused real damage to efficient Australian farmers; assisting Sydney's overseas campaign to stage the Olympic Games in the year 2000; launching a targeted promotional campaign in Japan which emphasises the quality of Australian products; briefing journalists in the ASEAN countries about the objectives of Australia's initiative on Asia Pacific Economic Co-operation; making and placing on overseas television a program about the merits of preserving Antarctica as a nature wilderness and land of science, designed to help create a political climate of support in that country for this diplomatic initiative.

Secondly, there is the role of public diplomacy in persuading particular groups or individuals to adopt a generally positive attitude towards us, for example through visitor programs, the exchange of parliamentary delegations, or the provision of scholarships for future community leaders to study in Australia. The establishment, as part of cultural programs, of Australian studies centres designed to encourage students to seek places in Australia also comes broadly within this aspect of public diplomacy.

Thirdly, there is the role of public diplomacy in persuading the general community in another country to adopt a generally positive attitude to Australia by projecting a familiar, benign and constructive image of our country. The means chosen may be essentially symbolic, such as providing ceremonial gifts, or quite indirect, such as encouraging the distribution of Australian television soap operas on the basis that, implausible as this may seem to some Australians, exposure to the life and loves of sunlit Melbourne suburbia does constitute an effective form of subliminal foreign policy advertising. Its driving assumption is that communities in other countries are likely to respond positively to overtures from, or initiate contact with, those they understand, and less likely to so act in relation to those countries about whom they neither know, nor care. All this can be extremely important when it comes to decisions to invest in Australia, or buy holiday travel or educational services here.

Image projection is particularly relevant to Australia's relations with Asia, where cultural, religious and social differences are wide. Most contacts in the broad area of cultural relations fall into this category, as do the general information programs carried out by Australian embassies. Image projection of this kind derives from many sources. The television series *Return to Eden*, for instance, has had an enormous following in Indonesia and undoubtedly helps to shape the image of Australia held by many ordinary Indonesians, although its distribution was the result of a commercial initiative rather than any particular government intervention. Similarly, the huge success overseas of films like *Crocodile Dundee* and books like *The Thornbirds*—and serials like *Neighbours*—do have an effect on the way in which Australia is perceived in other countries.

Radio Australia plays a particularly important role in informing the region about Australia. For many it is probably their only link with Australia. Here, as elsewhere in public diplomacy, credibility is crucial to success, and Radio Australia's independence from government control is the touchstone of its credibility. Were Radio Australia to be seen as a tool of the Australian government, its credibility in Asia and beyond would be diminished. Even though its broadcasts sometimes create difficulties for official bilateral relations, Australia's overall and long-term interests are better served by a Radio Australia which is valued for its independence, and for the window which it opens on to Australian society, than by a broadcaster of government propaganda.

Public diplomacy programs are a prominent part of the foreign policies of several countries, especially the superpowers, the Europeans and—in Asia —China and India. Institutions like the British Council, the Goethe Institute, Alliance Francaise and the United States Information Service are active throughout the world and operate with budgets that run to several hundred million dollars. Australia, by contrast, has until recently placed little emphasis on public diplomacy. There are probably several reasons for this. Unlike, say, Germany after World War II, we have not had a reputation to rebuild. Unlike the two superpowers, we have not seen the same need to indulge in the great propaganda campaigns which were the public face of the Cold War. Unlike Britain and France, we do not see ourselves as the standard bearers of a great culture or language with—as the French say —a *mission civilisatrice*. Indeed over the years there has been in Australia a certain ambiguity about the meaning of Australian culture, at least as regards its suitability for export. We have as a community also been ambivalent towards 'high culture', and about how it should relate to popular culture, in creating an Australian national identity.

Our neglect of public diplomacy has no doubt also reflected scepticism about its measurable returns. People can understand the openly persuasive role of public diplomacy, or the value of trade promotions or scholarships.

But other aspects—image projection, general facilitation and so on—are vulnerable to the barbs of the sceptic. It is not always obvious how the means match the ends, or indeed whether the programs deliver the goods at all. This will always be a conceptual problem with public diplomacy because it is usually a long-term process in which results are not easy to measure. However, as a country dependent on international trade; as a nation committed to a close and constructive involvement in the culturally diverse Asia Pacific; and as a community with a distinctive national identity, engaged in a form of niche marketing in a rapidly changing world, public diplomacy is beginning to play an important role in helping to advance Australia's many international interests, and needs to play an every more substantial role in the future.

To the extent that a large part of public diplomacy is about reducing cultural distance, making Australia better known abroad, and ourselves knowing more about the nations with which we must trade and live, public diplomacy is more relevant to our relations with Asia than with any other region. Asia, after all, is where we live and must learn the business of normal neighbourhood civility. Our position in this neighbourhood is, however, quite distinct, even by the standards of an area of great diversity. The cultures, traditions and languages of our nearest neighbours are very different from ours.

It must be acknowledged that Australia continues to have something of an image problem in Asia. While there are a number of positive elements to our image—and our recent high-profile diplomacy in relation to APEC and Cambodia has been helpful in reinforcing and developing them—there are still a number of negatives: perceptions of us as having a one-dimensional economy, poor industrial relations performance and, still, an immigration policy tainted with racism. That these perceptions lack substance is less important than the fact that they are still widely held, and do impinge on our interests in the region.

We also face the separate but related problem that the peoples of Asia know very little about us and our society. The polls summarised in the Garnaut Report on community perceptions of Australia in North-East Asia reveal huge gaps in popular perceptions of Australia.[9] The problem here is not that we have an unfavourable image but that, to the extent that we impinge at all on the consciousness of ordinary North-East Asians, it is in terms of a collage of simple images: Australia as a land of open spaces, exotic flora and fauna, an exporter of commodities—and a good place to relax. We are not seen as having any kind of economic dynamism, nor are we perceived as a country with intellectual and cultural achievements in our own right.

At one level little can be done about this, in that there is an autonomous development of community attitudes which will take place regardless of what is done in public diplomacy. This is the reality of global communications. Nor is this sort of one dimensional portrayal of Australia at the popular level necessarily harmful to our interests in all cases. In the case of tourism, it is probably a plus. At the same time, a more complex and rounded image of Australia than currently exists would greatly help us to build the sort of multidimensional relations in Asia that we seek. For example, encouraging television stations in Asia to screen *Beyond 2000* can help present Australia as a technologically advanced country with a depth of scientific talent.

In the financial year 1990/91, the Department of Foreign Affairs and Trade spent around $8 million dollars on public diplomacy, world-wide. This figure does not include some substantial items like government publications, AIDAB-funded scholarships, or expenditure on such projects as trade pavilions, all of which could arguably also be counted as public diplomacy. By far the largest portion of the public diplomacy budget is spent in Asia. Of the four bilateral councils which have been established to foster cultural and other non-government links, three cover Asian countries: Indonesia, China and Japan. The other is New Zealand. The Australia–Indonesia Institute, which was established only in 1989, has put in train an imaginative work program targeted towards the 'young and influential'. It is also paying particular attention to the media and to exchanges in such fields as the law, teacher-education and sport. The Australia–China Council, established in May 1978, has done a great deal to expand relations between the two countries in many fields. It has kept open people-to-people links at a time when it is vital that China not turn inward. The Australia–Japan Foundation has since 1974 also made a valuable contribution towards improving our knowledge of Japan, and Japan's of us.

Expanding public diplomacy is not simply a question of resources, important though funding always is. It is also a matter of improved co-ordination, a sharper focus, a more sophisticated definition of objectives and a more rigorous means of evaluation. The decision finally to bring the former Australian Overseas Information Service—which has had several homes over the years—into the amalgamated Department of Foreign Affairs and Trade was an important step. So was the more recent decision to create a new Public Affairs Division within the Department which brings together the various information and cultural components of our public diplomacy.

A potentially more important decision still was the creation in June 1990 of the Australia Abroad Council (AAC) to advise the Minister for Foreign Affairs and Trade on means of giving greater drive and direction to projecting Australia overseas. At present a wide range of organisations and individuals help shape Australia's image abroad. The intention in establishing the Council was to better harness and focus this activity. It includes the heads and chief executive officers of twenty-two bodies, including the four bilateral councils mentioned above, the Australia Council, the Australian Tourist Commission, Austrade, Radio Australia and Qantas, as well as relevant Commonwealth and State government departments.

Between them these organisations have what can be characterised as public diplomacy budgets of at least scores and probably hundreds of millions of dollars. Mobilizing at least some of these resources in a more specifically targeted and focused way, particularly if the private sector can be brought into the process as well, can only advance Australia's national interest.

Relations between nations are not the exclusive preserve of governments. There are a whole range of contacts, through travel, business, the arts, professional associations, service clubs, and community action groups which occur without any government involvement. These contacts add extra texture and depth to our bilateral relations, and they inevitably contribute to community perceptions abroad about what kind of nation we are.

Foreign policy, like all policy in a democracy, should be the product of a dialogue between the government and the community. Public diplomacy is not just about what we do overseas. It is also about engaging the Australian community to better understand our policies and objectives, and about helping Australians—through language teaching, a wider range of cultural contacts, a better informed media and the like—better to understand the world around us: not just informing others about Australia, but also informing Australia about others.

Public diplomacy of this sort should not be seen first as the government educating the community. It is a two-way process. Sensible government means drawing on the resources of the community. Government benefits from new ideas, and from informed community debate about foreign and trade policy issues. Discussion in the universities, at conferences, in seminars can all help pave the way for new policy approaches. Government often is not in a position publicly to advocate novel, adventurous or controversial ideas. Community groups are, and they can play a useful role in preparing the ground for changes in policy, and for easing governments gently into new approaches.

Indeed, the key to successful public diplomacy is its adoption of democratic processes. While its objective may be a specific, perceived national interest, its method depends very largely on enlisting resources of debate and discussion and the varied opinions and diverse talents of a community. It will not succeed if a government seeks to manipulate or control what is done internationally outside the government area. Public diplomacy is not about tethering community groups to the government's foreign policy agenda. Above all, it is not about creating front organisations. It is a response to the reality that multidimensional relationships with countries and their peoples cannot be built by governments alone: it must also embrace the exchange, at a wholly non-governmental level, of people and ideas.

PART II

ISSUES

6

The Search for Global Security

AUSTRALIA'S INTEREST in avoiding a global conflagration is as self-evident as that of any other country. The question to be addressed here is what, if anything, a country of our size and authority can contribute to avoiding it.

The problem is still a real one, despite the relief and optimism that has come with the end of the Cold War. There are still two nuclear superpowers, possessing between them an estimated 50 000 nuclear warheads—30 000 for the Soviet Union and 20 000 for the United States—with a destructive capacity of 16 000 megatons, enough to reproduce Hiroshima 1 200 000 times over. Disarmament talks have a long way to go even to begin to make an impression on these stockpiles. And for all the confidence that President Gorbachev had engendered in the West, nobody can predict with any certainty what the future course of the Soviet Union will be, politically or militarily.

Three other countries—France, the United Kingdom and China—are acknowledged nuclear powers, with some 1200 nuclear warheads between them; at least three other countries have present nuclear weapons manufacturing capability, and half-a-dozen more have the potential to become proliferators within the short to medium term. In the event of a breakup of the Soviet Union, a theoretical risk of still greater proliferation—by existing component republics—is clearly present, but most analysts are presently assuming that the Soviet nuclear arsenal will continue to be centrally controlled by Russia if not the Soviet Union.

Moreover, even if the nuclear arsenals were somehow able to be taken out of the security equation, by their elimination or neutralisation, this century has already had experience enough of world wars fought with conventional weapons—or, in the case of the gas attacks of World War I, with non-nuclear weapons of mass destruction—to know that the risk of global-scale conflict, and global-scale casualties, has not disappeared. The habits of millenia do not change so quickly. Indeed it is a widely held view, given obvious credence by the aggression of Saddam Hussein against Kuwait, that the end of the Cold War has, if anything, introduced a new period of destabilisation into world affairs. Regionally powerful countries long held in check by their superpower patrons may be inclined to shrug off the leash and engage in some military adventurism of their own, with wider consequences that might be presently quite unforeseeable. Certainly no one can credibly assert that the decline in tensions and automatic confrontation between the United States and the Soviet Union will automatically result in stability, order'and an absence of conflict in the world.

Perhaps the one change of analytical consequence that the end of the Cold War has brought is a blurring of the distinction between global and regional security issues. For most of the last forty-five years, it is not an excessive caricature to say that global security strategy involved planning how to avoid a nuclear holocaust between the superpowers, while regional security problems were everything else. Now the prospect of that kind of global conflict seems reduced, but the prospect of bigger, nastier, more frequent and generally less restrained regional conflicts may be greater: global conflicts can from unrestrained regional conflicts grow. And some regional powers have, or are capable of acquiring, so much military power that it may in fact take a global response to stop them. Iraq is a country of less than nineteen million people, just over Australia's size, but in 1990 it had one million men under arms; a definite chemical weapons armoury, possible biological weapons capability, and a fast-approaching nuclear weapons capability; 5500 tanks and 500 aircraft; and generally all the readiness to wage war that defence expenditure over ten years of some US$50 billion on arms purchases, and some US$200 billion overall, could buy. Increasingly, then, it seems that how the world as a whole shows itself capable of reacting to regional conflict is becoming the litmus test for both regional security *and* global security.

If these are the dimensions of the global security problem that still confronts us, what can Australia do to help solve it? We suggest that first, we continue to play an active and committed role within the Western alliance; secondly, we continue to play an active and committed role in arms control and disarmament, particularly in issues like chemical weapons where, as a middle power with a strong track record both on this issue and in multilateral diplomacy generally, we can make a difference; and thirdly, we put all our weight and effort into supporting the peace-making, peace-keeping and peace enforcement roles of the United Nations. The international reaction to Iraq's aggression in 1990–91 has to be affirmed as a precedent, not dismissed as an aberration.

AUSTRALIA'S ROLE IN THE WESTERN ALLIANCE

As host to several joint Australian–United States facilities which assist Washington in maintaining the central strategic balance with Moscow, Australia has been drawn into the issues of global security, arms control and disarmament almost from the beginning of the nuclear age. The facility at North West Cape was established in June 1963, Pine Gap in December 1966, and Nurrungar in November 1969.

The station at North West Cape provides very low frequency radio communication with submarines, uniquely in the Indian Ocean and parts of the western Pacific, and on a back-up basis for the northern Pacific. Pine Gap is a satellite ground station, collecting intelligence data in support of the national security of both Australia and the United States, and which contributes importantly to the verification of arms control and disarmament agreements (including INF, SALT and START). Nurrungar is a ground station used for controlling satellites in the United States Defense Support Program (DSP), which give ballistic missile early warning—longer than other systems—and other information relating to missile launches, surveillance and the detonation of nuclear weapons.[1]

There has been, not altogether surprisingly, fierce controversy in Australia over these facilities, particularly the latter two.[2] Unfortunately, when Australia made the initial decision to host the United States facilities, the political temper of the times was both divisive and superficial on the great issues of nuclear war. The facilities were shrouded in secrecy; the Australian public was not informed about their function and in consequence speculated wildly. Governments of the 1960s seemed so grateful to the United States for having chosen Australia as the site of these facilities that they failed to negotiate terms which properly acknowledged Australia's sovereignty. So, coupled with the understandable anxiety of Australians about nuclear war and the seemingly obvious fact that, by hosting these facilities, Australia was increasing the likelihood that it would be physically involved in an exchange of nuclear weapons, the politics of the time did not do much to assist rational public debate.

But over time the terms of this debate have shifted. In the first place, it has come to be better appreciated—with both the Chernobyl reactor disaster in 1986, and the continuing scientific debate about the possibility of a 'nuclear winter' contributing to public understanding in this respect—that no country can insulate itself from the horrors of nuclear war. Defence Minister Kim Beazley put the point well in 1988:

The plain fact is that Australia's geographic remoteness from the parts of the world where the largest concentrations of military force exist, and where the major military engagements would probably be fought if nuclear war ever broke out, offers little protection against the hazards of nuclear war. Regardless of whether Australia itself were subjected to direct attack in a nuclear war, we would inevitably experience major or possibly even catastrophic economic, medical, ecological, security and cultural consequences, along with any other countries that might survive the holocaust. Avoidance of nuclear war is the fundamental and most important Australian defence interest. There is, of course, no way of knowing in advance what would be the detailed effects of a nuclear war between the US and USSR. It is not necessarily the case, for example, that either side would use all of its nuclear weapons in such a conflict. Nor is it certain that either side would seek the extinction of the other. What is clear, however, is that there can be no guarantee that nuclear war, should it ever occur, would be controllable, and there can be no confidence either that the human species would survive it.[3]

Secondly, it has come to be much better appreciated that the best way of ensuring that nuclear weapons will never in fact be used is to maximise the knowledge that each side has of the other's capability and intentions, and to minimise the uncertainty. Intelligence systems, early warning systems, arms control verification systems and effective communications systems are all, from this perspective, part of the process not of waging war but of guaranteeing peace. For example the DSP, of which the Nurrungar facility is such an important component, makes it effectively impossible for the Soviet Union, for all its numerical advantage in the possession of nuclear warheads, to disarm the United States in a surprise first strike: this constitutes an overwhelming disincentive for the Soviet Union, and gives the United States confidence that it will never be tempted to mount such an attack. This technical contribution to stable deterrence has in turn generated its own confidence-building mechanisms. Recognising the logic of transparency, the superpowers have become more and more willing to disclose their destructive capacities and strategic intentions. Alongside the huge industry that makes nuclear weapons and their delivery systems, another industry has grown up which monitors the systems and devises control regimes and inspection mechanisms with the intention of making each side's real capacity well and truly visible to the other.

All this has transformed the debate in Australia. It has shifted attention from the danger which Australia faces from hosting the facilities to the opportunity, and indeed the moral obligation, which Australia has to discharge its responsibilities to prevent nuclear war. Moreover, by hosting the facilities, which are themselves such an important part of the mechanism of rational transparency, Australia has acquired the right to a voice on the purposes for which they are used. We have entered the nuclear age not just as a fearful bystander but as an active participant in the search for global security.

Australia's alliance with the United States, not only through ANZUS but more generally, provides the core of our role in the Western alliance system. But we also have working intelligence-exchange arrangements with the United States, United Kingdom, Canada and New Zealand (with whom we are also bilaterally linked through ANZUS) which are long-standing and provide connections with other Western countries.[4] Within the Asian region, our close links with the United States and its close links with Japan provide Australia and Japan with mutual global and regional perspectives. We are seen respectively as the northern and southern anchors of the Western alliance in the western Pacific rim.

The Western alliance has served the world well in the years since World War II as has, in a sense, the West and East bloc alliance system generally. Whether we find it comfortable to acknowledge it or not, the maintenance of two enormously powerful blocs, facing each other across Europe and the North Atlantic since 1945, did operate to prevent the threat of global warfare from being realised. The opposing alliances did create a balance, with their huge arsenals of nuclear weapons constituting a terrifying but effective mutual deterrent, and with that balance becoming more stable over time as transparency grew. The alliances also created a certain discipline which prevented tensions from boiling over as might have occurred in their absence. In this sense, too, NATO—and in its own way the Warsaw Pact—were both stabilising factors in international relations. With NATO, genuine common interests amongst the membership, and acceptance of American leadership, maintained that essential element of a stable alliance, namely unity of purpose. The case of the Warsaw Pact was more ambiguous, in the sense that it was imposed by one member on the others. It lacked the essential cement so obvious in NATO—agreement on common political values—and it was no coincidence that, when the moving power behind the Warsaw Pact made clear it could not and would not impose its will on them, the Pact disintegrated because it had nothing left to hold it together.

But if stability has been the main advantage of the post-War system, it has been stability at a price. In the first place, there has been the enormous price of the ever-spiralling arms race generated by the Cold War: hundreds of billions of dollars of resources which could have been put to other use. Both sides built higher and higher walls of more and more sophisticated offensive and defensive weaponry, short-changing the demands of economic development both within their own frontiers and in other countries around the world.

And, secondly, there was the price paid in negating the collective security functions of the United Nations. A number of attempts were made to give substance to the United Nations's security role, but with the fortuitous exception of Korea, and a handful of other much smaller and less controversial peace-keeping operations, the strait-jacket of East–West confrontation meant that, so long as the Cold War lasted, those attempts conspicuously and comprehensively failed. Much of the East–West tension contained in Europe was unleashed elsewhere in regional conflicts, often of terrifying intensity. Sometimes stoked by the opposing alliances and sometimes amounting to proxy wars, these conflicts stimulated endless human misery—which the United Nations was created to seek to alleviate. If there are any still yearning for the certainties of the Cold War era, they would do well to reflect that the benefits of stability were distributed far from equally.

The third price paid has simply been psychological: living with the knowledge, as the world has had to now for nearly two generations, that miscalculation of one kind or another by political leaders could result in the annihilation of all humanity. And for all the apparently guaranteed strategic stability of the present balance between the nuclear superpowers, the prospect of miscalculation can never be ruled out. This is why, for example, President Reagan's Strategic Defense Initiative (SDI), announced in 1983, generated so much international concern, and why Australia has not endorsed it. Whatever the attractions, at first sight, in the development of a system that really would amount to a comprehensively effective defence against ballistic missiles (and the success of Patriot anti-missile missiles in defending Israel and Saudi Arabia against SCUD attacks during the Gulf War will undoubtedly reinforce that perception), the unhappy truth of the matter is that even the prospect of SDI succeeding to the extent proposed would—unless its success were able to be achieved absolutely simultaneously on both sides—collapse the whole logic of the present deterrent system. The undefended side would simply have to rely on the moral integrity of the other not to use the advantage it would gain from breaking the deterrent equation. Nuclear deterrence has, until now, prevented a recurrence of global war: but it is an inherently fragile form of protection.

For all these reasons, the intellectual search for a credible alternative to the post-War balance of fear as a means of sustaining global security has continued throughout the Cold War period. And now, with the end of the Cold War, it has at last some prospect of realisation. A whole new approach to guaranteeing global security *is* emerging. East–West strategic competition is no longer the touchstone of international relations; co-operation is replacing confrontation as the leitmotif. Significant new arms control and disarmament measures are coming to fruition, with each building upon the last and the pace accelerating. The vicious circle of the nuclear arms race is breaking: for the first time in the nuclear age, we have the prospect of replacing a vicious circle with a virtuous circle, where confidence builds on itself, co-operation extends and security is strengthened.

All this represents the coming of age of a concept which seemed visionary, maybe even fantastical, when it was first articulated by a group of statesmen from many continents under the leadership of the late Swedish Prime Minister, Olof Palme, in 1982.[5] This is the concept of 'common security', sometimes also called 'co-operative security'. The central idea is that lasting security does not lie in an upwards spiral of arms development, fuelled by mutual suspicion, but in a commitment to joint survival, to taking into account the legitimate security anxieties of others, to building step-by-step military confidence between nations, to working to maximise the degree of interdependence between nations: in short, to achieving security with others, not against them. The basis of 'common security' is that every nation is entitled to share in it. Its beginnings can be glimpsed in the common desire of nuclear adversaries to share information relevant to maintaining stable deterrence. The two major military alliances in Europe, NATO and the Warsaw Pact, have fulfilled a diplomatic and organisation role in bringing about, within the framework of the Conference on Security and Co-operation in Europe (CSCE), reductions in force levels and a generally relaxed atmosphere in which political changes, including the reunification of Germany, has proceeded.

Nothing in the idea of common security implies passivity or appeasement in the face of a security threat. It does not involve emasculating our military forces, nor removing our capability to respond to a direct threat to our nation or, as was the case in the Gulf, a threat to the international security framework. (The corollary to *common* security is in fact *collective* security: while common security is both the objective, and also a way of describing the confidence-building process by which that objective may be peacefully attained, collective security is the ultimate guarantee that that process will not be blown off course by the aggressive behaviour of individual states, or that if it is, the international reaction will be swift.) Common security implies an understanding, rather, that while each country has to responsibly assess and meet its own legitimate security needs, it also has to avoid—to the extent possible—generating, through its own actions, security anxieties and military reactions on the part of other countries. As confidence builds in this way, the upwards spiral of arms competition can rapidly be translated into the downwards spiral of arms reduction that we now see well under way in Europe and the North Atlantic, with enormously favourable consequences for the peace of the world.

What has been and what will be the role of alliances in all of this? On the face of it, it might be thought that alliances have outlived their usefulness; that in the emerging world of common security, backed—hopefully—by a reliable system of collective security, everyone can have confidence that security will be maintained without the need for elaborate, competing and balancing international power blocs. But it would be naive to make that assumption for a long time yet. Even if the Cold War is over, and new forums like the Conference on Security and Co-operation in Europe— embracing both the NATO and Warsaw Pact countries and others as well —are operating more constructively than anyone could have believed possible even two years ago, the global security millenium has not yet arrived. Until we are very much closer to achieving a world in which threats to global security are wholly eliminated, alliances will go on playing important roles in international relations in a number of respects.

The first is as a driving mechanism to keep the process of confidence building, and common security building, moving forward. The NATO and Warsaw Pact alliances may not have been themselves the main driving forces toward the end of the Cold War: the stimulus for that came from the imminent economic collapse of the Soviet superpower under the weight of its own internal contradictions. But they have been very important in the management of the transition. It requires a good deal of confidence to move from an upwardly spiralling arms race to a downwardly spiralling process of arms reduction, and the existing alliance networks were crucial to the superpowers having that sense of confidence. The Warsaw Pact provided the Soviet Union with a formal security structure which enabled it to allay some of its security concerns while beginning the business of domestic reform. And during the months of the rapid departure of the East Europeans from Soviet tutelage, the Pact—the retention of which the Soviets seemed to regard as more important than almost anything else—provided a form of cover within which the Soviet Union could establish understandings with NATO about the shape of the new Europe and, essentially, its own security. NATO was always inherently stronger than the Warsaw Pact, and the West in any event has had nothing like the same agony of self-doubt as the new security order in Europe has started falling into place, but it is worth acknowledging the institutional role that NATO has played in co-ordinating and advancing the Western response. In the process NATO has been visibly undergoing a transition, by no means yet complete, from a military alliance—against a clearly perceived military threat—to a more political organisation, albeit one with a continuing military defence role and some new military-related roles, for example in arms control verification. But an alliance NATO remains, and it is as an alliance that it is helping construct the new security architecture.

The second role that alliances can and will play for a long time yet in the global context is as a fail-safe mechanism. History almost certainly has some aces up her sleeve. Conflict still persists at the regional level, and some of it has explosive potential globally. We still cannot be confident that all is for the best in the best of all possible worlds. In particular, we still live in a world where, for all the change in atmosphere and for all the disarmament progress that has already been made, there are still in existence over 50 000 nuclear warheads. And they have a horrifying destructive capacity, equivalent to 3.3 tonnes of TNT for every one of the five-and-a-half billion men, women and children on earth. With arsenals like this still in existence and their elimination a long way off, and with all the uncertainty that presently prevails about the future course of events in the Soviet Union, quite apart from those countries with nuclear proliferation potential, it is not an unnecessary luxury, but a necessity, to stay on one's guard. It is in this context that, for example, satellite ground stations with unique early warning and verification functions—of the kind that Australia provides in its joint facilities with the United States in Central Australia—will go on being important for a long time yet.

The third important role of alliances is in contributing to the maintenance of regional security in a new environment where the traditionally restraining leash of superpower patrons has eased and, as a result, the prospects are now greater both for conflict breaking out, and for its massive escalation when it does.

A fourth, and not unrelated role, particularly for the Western alliance, is helping to ensure that collective security works, whether the aggression in question is well-confined regionally or has potentially global consequences. While the Soviet Union and China co-operated throughout the United Nations Security Council's handling of the Gulf crisis, it was the United States and its NATO allies who unequivocally took the lead in mobilising the international response. The Soviet Union's capacity to exert any kind of international leadership for the foreseeable future has been seriously eroded by its internal problems; China is likely to remain as cautious as it has always been about a proactive role; and the countries of the Non-Aligned Movement have neither the unity nor ultimately the authority to play a really major role. In these circumstances, it seems likely that any international response to serious problems in the short to medium term will again need to be led by the Western alliance. It is very much to be hoped—and this is a theme to which we return later in this chapter—that this occurs within a United Nations framework.

AUSTRALIA'S ROLE IN ARMS CONTROL AND DISARMAMENT

The decade of the 1980s was a roller-coaster ride for disarmament and arms control. It began simply with the United States concerned about its window of vulnerability, and East–West relations at their lowest ebb since the Cuban missile crisis. It ended in jubilation with the Berlin Wall breached, solid progress on nuclear and conventional disarmament in Europe, and the promise of even better things to come. Along the way, arms control between the two superpowers evolved from a channel of communications grudgingly kept open, to the flagship of a new more co-operative era. The pace of superpower negotiation has flagged a little since, with internal upheavals in the Soviet Union, but in the aftermath of the Gulf War the political will in the international community generally to consolidate and build upon the progress achieved to date has probably never been greater.

Australia has long taken the view that the great issues of arms control and disarmament cannot be left just to the superpowers to resolve. While we have regularly, in ministerial and officials talks with the United States in particular, advocated the active pursuit of negotiations between the major powers, our most strenuous efforts in a global security context have necessarily been focused on multilateral forums—the United Nations General Assembly; the various review conferences associated with the Nuclear Non-Proliferation Treaty and other major existing treaties; and the sole negotiating forum within the United Nations system for arms control agreements, the forty-member Conference on Disarmament (CD) in Geneva, of which we became a member in 1979.[6]

Through the 1980s our involvement and influence in the CD has grown markedly, especially since the new Labor Government took the decision in 1983, reconfirmed in 1988, to appoint a full-time Ambassador for Disarmament based in Geneva. Australia's profile in relation to the whole range of multilateral disarmament issues, both nuclear and non-nuclear, and our input to the work of the CD, have been quite disproportionate to our size as a nation or standing as a military power. We are now one of the handful of most active countries in the world in pursuing these issues.

Nuclear Testing   The Australian Government does not—and should not —accept nuclear deterrence as a permanent condition. We should continue to work, as we have, to achieve stable deterrence at progressively lower levels of nuclear arsenals; to avoid vertical proliferation of weapons among the existing nuclear weapon states; to prevent the horizontal spread of nuclear weapons to other states; and, related to all these objectives, to achieve a comprehensive ban on nuclear testing.

A nuclear-test ban has been sought for over thirty years. A universally adhered-to treaty would help inhibit the spread of nuclear weapons by making it impossible to test nuclear explosive devices. It would also prevent the development of new weapons and the improvement of existing ones by the nuclear-weapons states. In the late 1950s and again in the late 1970s the world came tantalisingly close to concluding a test ban. In the last decade, progress has been frustratingly elusive, although some moves have been made—with Australia's strong support and involvement—to initiate an international seismological monitoring network, which would play a crucial role in the verification and enforcement of such a ban. Recently the issue has at least come back to something approximating centre stage in Geneva with the re-establishment in the CD, after a lapse of seven years, of an Ad Hoc Committee on a Nuclear Test Ban. Australia, moreover, continues to be—with New Zealand—the joint prime-mover of an annual resolution in the United Nations General Assembly in support of the urgent need for a comprehensive test ban, notwithstanding the considerably less than enthusiastic response this continues to generate from Washington and Paris.

Nuclear Weapons Free Zones   Consistently with Australia's attitude towards nuclear testing, we have supported the creation of nuclear weapons free zones, and played a leading role in the negotiation in particular of the South Pacific Nuclear Free Zone Treaty (or Treaty of Rarotonga) which came into force in 1986, and which prohibits the testing, production, acquisition, possession or stationing of nuclear weapons within the region. But although the Treaty does not affect the transit through the zone—including port visits—of ships or aircraft carrying nuclear weapons, an accommodation to the realities both of strategic necessity and our alliance relationships, it has not won the support of the United States or the United Kingdom (or, less surprisingly given its continued nuclear testing program at Mururoa Atoll, France). The United States has supported nuclear free zones in the past—in the context, for example, of Latin America, with the 1967 Treaty of Tlatelolco, and the Antarctic Treaty of 1959—and has expressed willingness to do so in the context of the post-Gulf War Middle East. The only apparent reason for its lack of support here, apart perhaps from some fear that the non-nuclear disease might prove catching in areas more strategically significant for the United States, is the continued lack of participation in the Treaty by one of the states important to its effective observance, namely France.

While Australia has given in-principle support for other nuclear weapons free zones in our own larger region, in the context both of the Indian Ocean and South East Asia, a number of factors arise to make these policy issues more complex than was the case with the South Pacific. In the case of the Indian Ocean Zone of Peace (IOZOP), Australia would wish to secure transit rights for the United States, for the same reason as in the South Pacific. However, as there are already putative nuclear weapons states in the area, in addition to the United States military presence on Diego Garcia, the problem of providing a nuclear free zone involves more dimensions than merely resolving the issue of transit. This is one reason why discussions over the IOZOP have been proceeding without notable success since 1971. In the case of the proposed South-East Asia Nuclear Weapons Free Zone (SEANWFZ), which has been formally on the ASEAN agenda since 1983, there is presently far from a consensus within the region, let alone outside it, that a treaty along Rarotonga lines is workable here.

Nuclear Non-Proliferation We have had, of course, no similar problems with the United States, or any of our other Western alliance partners, with our support for the Nuclear Non-Proliferation Treaty (NPT) of 1968, which by mid-1991 had 144 adherents. This has been the single most effective and widely supported international arms control agreement in existence: without it we would by now be facing a world with perhaps twenty or thirty nuclear weapons states.

Helping keep that treaty both alive and effective, including encouraging stand-out countries (both nuclear, namely China and France, and 'threshold', like India and Pakistan) to adhere to it, has been and should remain one of the highest priority tasks for Australian diplomacy. Australia, through its then Ambassador for Disarmament, Richard Butler, did in fact play a crucial role—by last minute mediation between Iran and Iraq—in securing agreement on a final document at the Third Review Conference for the Treaty in 1985 (thus avoiding the fate of the Second Conference, the failure of which had begun to call into question the NPT's future). We were unable to repeat the performance at the Fourth Review Conference in 1990, but did succeed there in getting an agreed commitment during negotiations to require 'fullscope' safeguards as a condition for the future supply of nuclear materials, equipment and technology.[7] Diplomatic attention is now focused on the 1995 Review Conference, which must make a decision to renew the Treaty at the end of its initial twenty-five year period.

It is perhaps worth noting that the NPT has featured prominently not only in foreign policy but also in domestic political debate in recent years, because of the way in which its existence has related to the mining and export of Australian uranium. This follows from the 'bargain' inherent in the terms of the Treaty and which is an important basis for its acceptance by developing countries—namely that in return for renouncing nuclear weapons, non-nuclear weapons states are to receive assistance in obtaining the benefits of the peaceful uses of nuclear energy. Australia's supply of uranium to NPT member states is thus in partial fulfilment of our own reciprocal obligations under the Treaty in this respect.

The international safeguards system administered by the Vienna-based International Atomic Energy Agency (IAEA) is the second pillar of the nuclear non-proliferation regime. Australia has been a strong supporter of the IAEA and a member of its Board of Governors since its inception in 1957. The IAEA's safeguards inspection system provides essential assurances that safeguarded nuclear material and facilities are not being diverted from peaceful to military or explosive purposes. Without the assurances offered by the NPT and IAEA safeguards, there would be precious few barriers to proliferation, and distrust of nuclear intentions would feed regional security problems around the world. Without these assurances, nuclear trade and co-operation would dwindle. It is of central importance to the continued effectiveness of the NPT that the IAEA has the resources, both human and financial, to carry out its international legal responsibilities in the application of safeguards. Maintaining support for the IAEA and the credibility and effectiveness of its safeguards should remain an important objective of Australian diplomacy.

Export controls on nuclear material, equipment and technology are the third crucial element in preventing nuclear proliferation. Australia is a member of the Zangger (NPT Suppliers) Committee established in 1970 (as an informal but active group, limited to NPT parties, to determine conditions governing the export of nuclear materials and equipment) and the Nuclear Suppliers Group (NSG). The latter was established in 1975, with the initial participation of seven nuclear exporters, in response to heightened concern about the inadequacy of controls over nuclear trade following India's explosion of a nuclear device in May 1974. The NSG Guidelines, a set of principles and conditions applying to the transfer of nuclear materials, equipment and technology, were first published in February 1978. Australia also adhered to the Guidelines at that time. Membership of the NSG now stands at twenty-six. In March 1991 the NSG decided to extend the existing Guidelines to control exports of nuclear 'dual-use' items, and to intensify efforts to win new adherents to the them among emerging supplier countries.

Chemical Weapons The outstanding example of the sort of role Australia can play in multilateral disarmament issues is the effort we have been making, for some years now, in relation to the abolition of chemical weapons (CW). In the more than seventy years since chemical weapons were first used in the trenches of Europe—including, on a large scale, against Australian soldiers—three generations of government leaders and diplomats have sought, with an urgency that has ebbed and flowed, to ensure that these peculiarly horrifying instruments of death are never again used. For twenty years, and particularly since the mid-1980s, when the issue arose starkly again in the Middle East, the Geneva Conference on Disarmament has been wrestling into shape a draft text for a comprehensive Chemical Weapons Convention (CWC), which would ban absolutely and for all time the manufacture, possession and use of all such weapons. The length of the task has been partly a function of the difficulty, not uncommon in multilateral diplomacy, of translating a generalised political will into the necessary practical will to devote enough resources and high attention to conclude the task. It has also been a product of the immense complexity of devising a control regime that will, without undue intrusion, enable the necessary regulation not only of government action but also of the world's chemical industry.

During 1991 Australia increased its efforts towards the early conclusion of the CWC in the atmosphere of a re-emergence of public awareness and concern about the possible use of chemical weapons during the Gulf crisis. A major element in this was support for the early convening of a meeting of the Conference on Disarmament at ministerial level to resolve outstanding issues. At the same time the United States, through major announcements by President Bush, pledged itself to early conclusion of the CWC.

Australia has become very closely involved in the whole issue at a number of levels, quite apart from our close participation in the continuing technical negotiations in Geneva (recently as Western Group Co-ordinator) and our own continuing efforts to accelerate those negotiations by higher-level political involvement. Least well known is possibly our role in convening the so-called 'Australia Group' which has developed as follows. In April 1984 a number of Western governments, including Australia, imposed controls on the export of a number of chemicals used in the manufacture of chemical weapons. They had acted in response to the findings of the special investigatory mission (on which Australia was represented) sent by the United Nations Secretary General that chemical weapons had been used in the Iran–Iraq War. These controls, however, were not uniform either in scope or application, and it soon became apparent that attempts were being made to circumvent them. This led Australia to propose, in April 1985, that those countries which had imposed such controls might meet in order to examine the scope for harmonising the measures taken individually and enhancing co-operation. Accordingly, the first meeting of what subsequently became known as the Australia Group took place in Brussels in June 1985. All agreed there was benefit in continuing this process, and meetings of the Group—attended by representatives of twenty OECD chemical-exporting countries and the European Community, are now held on a roughly biannual basis in the Australian embassy in Paris.

Australia Group meetings are informal, with no set rules of procedure. The controls agreed on by meetings of the Group are applied on a national basis. The effectiveness of the system cannot be established in an absolute manner, but it has raised the cost of acquiring an offensive CW capability by drying up sources and diverting the delivery routes of CW proliferators. It may, therefore, have delayed the programs of countries seeking to acquire CW by forcing then into alternative and less efficient routes.

It should also be mentioned that while the work of the Group has concentrated on harmonising national export controls on precursor chemicals, and restraining the supply of equipment which could be used for CW production, it has also produced an agreed approach to dealing with the potential diversion of biotechnology to biological weapons (BW) programs. This involves the adoption of warning guidelines on biological agents and equipment, to be used to sensitise industry, academic institutions and others to what may possibly be BW-related enquiries.

One clear result of the Australia Group's activity has been to raise the awareness of the chemical industry about the risks of involuntary association with chemical weapons. Australia, at the personal suggestion of United States Secretary of State Baker, built upon this background to host in 1989 in Canberra a highly publicised international conference, the Government—Industry Conference Against Chemical Weapons, which was attended by representatives of sixty-six countries and the world's chemical industry. The achievement of that Conference was to produce the first collective statement by the world's industry of its commitment to assist governments in bringing about a total ban on chemical weapons through a comprehensive Chemical Weapons Convention; an extensive dialogue between governments and industry on detailed technical issues relating both to the conclusion and implementation of the CWC; a renewed expression of commitment by governments to conclude and implement a comprehensive CWC at the earliest date; and the establishment by Australia of a National Secretariat to plan for the implementation of the CWC, as an administrative model for possible emulation internationally.

Again, in its Chemical Weapons Regional Initiative (CWRI) launched by the Prime Minister in 1988, Australia has hosted a series of seminars, and organised a workshop and trial inspection for officials from twenty-two regional governments and the South Pacific Forum Secretariat. They have been designed to help produce a better understanding of the complexity of the issues involved in bringing the CWC to finality and subsequently implementing it, and to help produce, as a result, the basis for speedy regional adherence to its terms. This approach is, again, beginning to be picked up as a model appropriate for emulation in other regions of the world.

Conventional Weapons   The Gulf crisis of 1990–91 showed up in stark relief how, for all its efforts in recent years to deal with the problem of weapons of mass destruction (nuclear, chemical and biological) and to prevent the international arms race taking alarming new directions (for example into outer space) the international community has conspicuously failed to come to grips with the proliferation of massive amounts of offensive conventional weaponry. This is an issue on which a sustained focus will be necessary—and not only in the regional context of the Middle East—not least as the end of the Cold War and the agreement on Conventional Armed Forces in Europe (CFE) have resulted in the greater availability of such material in markets elsewhere.

Australia is, and will need to continue to be, an active participant in the growing exchange between countries on this problem—in particular through our representation on the United Nations Expert Group on Conventional Arms Transfers, which has been focusing particularly on increasing the transparency of such transfers and the creation in this respect of a United Nations Register of Arms Transfers. It will also be a matter of ensuring that defence exports in which we are involved are not only sensitive to Australia's own foreign policy concerns, but also take place in accordance with best international practice.

During 1990 Australia adhered to the Missile Technology Control Regime (MTCR). This is not a treaty but a 'regime' involving a set of export guidelines established in 1987 by the Group of Seven (United States, United Kingdom, France, Germany, Italy, Japan and Canada), these being the major suppliers of missile technology besides the Soviet Union and China. Since early 1990 another seven European nations have joined, along with Australia and New Zealand. The MTCR aims to control the proliferation of missile technology which could be used for the delivery of weapons of mass destruction, focusing particularly on missiles capable of carrying nuclear warheads. Australia made clear that our participation reflected our concern about the proliferation of missile technology regardless of the type of warhead carried, a concern which has become even more widely felt internationally since the Gulf War.

SECURING PEACE THROUGH THE UNITED NATIONS

The first Article of Chapter 1 of the Charter of the United Nations states that the first purpose of the United Nations is:

> To maintain international peace and security, and to that end: to take effective collective measures for the prevention and removal of threats to the peace, and for the suppression of acts of aggression or other breaches of the peace, and to bring about by peaceful means, and in conformity with the principles of justice and international law, adjustment or settlement of international disputes or situations which might lead to a breach of the peace.

Although the Charter does not spell this out so explicitly, four separate dimensions to the United Nations's role in relation to peace and security have evolved over the decades. All have been strongly supported by Australia in the past, and all remain absolutely crucial for the future. Disarmament and arms control is one: multilateral negotiations in UN forums have had only limited success to date, but one simply cannot envisage collective security working effectively in a world where there is a continued proliferation of weapons of mass destruction, and indeed conventional weapons, on the scale we have seen in recent years. The other dimensions of the UN role can be described respectively as peace-making, peace-keeping and peace-enforcement.

In the Past   The United Nations, through the Secretary-General, Security Council and to some extent General Assembly, has always been able to contribute something to the prevention or resolution of conflict through the forty-five years of its history. But perceptions of its ability to deliver in any more comprehensive a way on the expectations raised by its first Charter objective have been through a long cycle of optimism, through pessimism, to now a considerable degree of renewed optimism.

For the first two decades or so of its existence, the United Nations was constantly at the forefront of international political issues, but its performance in security matters was at best very mixed. Most political leaders—and certainly the leaders of the United States and the Soviet Union—used its forum for major speeches. The question of membership rights, and especially the seemingly interminable issue of the admission of the People's Republic of China, was always on the agenda. The perpetual conflict between Israel and its Arab neighbours, the future of Hanoi and neutral Laos and Cambodia, Indonesia's campaign to take West New Guinea from the Netherlands, the emancipation of colonial territories in Africa —issues such as these kept the United Nations in the public eye, tending to overshadow the social, economic and cultural work that the specialised agencies were undertaking to eliminate poverty, hunger and ignorance.

But the United Nations's collective security role created tension from the outset between the combatants of the Cold War. With each of the five permanent members of the Security Council—China, France, the United Kingdom, United States and Soviet Union—having the right of veto, their agreement to act was practically impossible to obtain. When North Korea attacked South Korea in 1950, the Security Council did promptly recommend that members should put armed forces at the disposal of an American commander-in-chief, the Soviet delegate being absent from that meeting in protest against China's seat being occupied by Taiwan. But when the Soviet representative later returned and vetoed further action, the locus of action switched to the General Assembly, where the United States successfully sponsored the 'Uniting for Peace' resolution, (which provided for immediate consideration by the Assembly of a threat to the peace, with a view to recommending collective measures 'if the Security Council, because of lack of unanimity of the permanent members, fails to exercise its primary responsibility').

This established the pattern until the 1960s—the USSR relentlessly blocking action in the Security Council by using its veto and the United States, more adept at marshalling voter support, using the General Assembly. The influx of new members, especially from Africa, eventually eroded United States support in the Assembly, but by then the United Nations had established a string of commitments, by juggling the focus of its peace-keeping authority between the Security Council, the General Assembly and the office of the Secretary-General. The United Nations interventions in the Suez Canal in 1956 and in the Congo in 1960 were dramatic examples.

The early years of the United Nations were thus a confusing mixture of hope and idealism, on the one hand, and the most cynical display of power politics on the other. Both superpowers sought to use the United Nations for their own interests, as leaders of two powerful military blocs, and to seek the favours of the emerging group of non-aligned nations from Asia, Africa and Latin America. Both superpowers sought to manipulate the United Nations machinery, often clumsily, as the machinery was brand new. They both savagely attacked the first Secretary-General, Trygve Lie (1946–53) from Norway, when at different times he disagreed with them. The Soviet Union was a persistent and at times unrestrained critic of the second Secretary-General, Dag Hammarskjold (1953–61) from Sweden, especially when he took an initiative on behalf of the United Nations in Africa in the early 1960s: it was on a night flight to the Belgian Congo in 1961 that Hammarskjold's aircraft crashed, killing him. The choices of U Thant (1961–71) from Burma, and of Kurt Waldheim (1972–81) from Austria, were intended to avoid appointments of independent activists who might upset the superpowers, and the decline in authority of the United Nations in the 1970s and early 1980s owed at least something to that change in direction. The appointment of Javier Perez de Cuellar from Peru in 1981 has been associated with a somewhat more active Secretariat, but it is only with the ending of East–West confrontation and the Cold War itself in the last years of the decade that there has been any real cause for renewed optimism about the efficacy of the United Nations's peace and security role.

The flexibility and agility of the United Nations in its early stormy days can be seen with hindsight to have been the result of a creative tension between several forces: the major powers, especially the superpowers, whose authority outside the United Nations was greater than their influence within; the flood of new, often small, nations whose influence in the world depended on bonding together within the United Nations; and the organisation itself, especially the office of Secretary-General, which saw itself partly as trail-blazer for a better world, and partly as an international civil service acting for the most part without clear instructions from its political masters. These forces ceased to stimulate each other in the latter 1970s and early 1980s, and the United Nations entered a period of low activity and low esteem. One reason was that the superpowers ceased to give the UN forum the importance of earlier years. The hardening of relations between the United States and the Soviet Union during the Brezhnev–Reagan period, with a consequential build-up of military might, was a clear signal that debate at the United Nations had become an irrelevant exercise.

It took President Gorbachev to initially break that mould, and the Gulf crisis of 1990–91 to consolidate what looked like, at least from the vantage point of mid-1991, the foundations of a new order. We have already suggested in Chapter 1 (perhaps a little prosaically for some tastes) that, if the concept of a 'new world order' means anything at all, its essential defining characteristic would seem to be co-operation by the major powers in the containment and resolution of conflict under the umbrella of the United Nations and using its institutional processes. What, then, is this likely to mean in practice?[8]

Peace-enforcement   The conduct of the Gulf crisis represented a triumphant reaffirmation of the United Nations's collective security role, so clearly envisaged for it by its founders but so long in limbo. Whether this role is likely to be respected in the future depends essentially on two factors: the willingness of the United States and other permanent five members to go down this path again, and the nature of the conflicts likely to arise.

For the first question, there is no doubt that the position taken by the United States will be crucial. Its supporters hope that the United States will act through the Security Council but fear that it will not (lapsing either into inaction or unilateral action); its detractors fear that it will indeed act, but in order to impose on the United Nations its own agenda. The fact is that without the United States there can be no United Nations role in collective security. That is for both procedural and practical reasons: the dominance of the permanent five is, of course, written into the Charter and collective security action requires at least the tacit assent of each of them, but in any case the reality of present world power dictates that UN collective security action could not be mounted or even credibly threatened without the support of the United States military. The United Nations is not a supranational government; it is a mechanism through which governments agree to act together, and the dominance of the United States in decisions on the Gulf crisis merely reflects its current dominance in world affairs. It will be difficult, however, for the United States to pick and choose, from the perspective of its own national interests, between those conflicts it will bring to the United Nations and those it will deal with unilaterally. This is not really a long-term option: if the United States bypasses the United Nations on a series of issues, the system of UN collective security will lose all credibility, and co-operation—which has to be not assumed but nurtured, as it was in the Gulf crisis—will simply not be available when the United States does decide that it is time to turn to the United Nations. An enlightened view of self-interest would, from this perspective, be one that maintained and nourished the UN system.

As to the likelihood of the kinds of conflict arising which will stimulate UN peace-enforcement action in the future, it has to be acknowledged that the Gulf circumstances were exceptional, albeit a textbook case of what the founders had in mind. The UN Charter was written so as retrospectively to avert World War II, and in Saddam Hussein the United Nations found a 1930s-type aggressor: the aggression was unprovoked, across recognised boundaries and by a national army invading and occupying the territory of another member state—and in a region, moreover, engaging the vital interests of great powers. Such a conjunction is unlikely to occur again soon. Most disputes in which the United Nations is asked to intervene have a strong element of purely internal conflict, perhaps of an ethnic or religious nature, perhaps with one or both factions aligned with outside powers; they often have long-standing root causes overlaid by many years of retaliation and response and claim and counterclaim; rarely does one of the parties have a monopoly of right on its side behind which the international community can unite. But obviously a system of collective security, to be worth the name, must be universal in its application, and if Saddam-style aggression recurs elsewhere—even in a region of less strategic or economic importance—and the international community does not respond through the United Nations with the same forthrightness, the cynics will have been vindicated.

If the United Nations does again respond to such a situation—and there is no present basis to doubt that it will—it is likely that the pattern of response will be similar to the Gulf crisis. Sanctions will continue to be the first line of response, and if they fail—or, as with Iraq, are reasonably judged to be unlikely to bring success within any manageable time frame—something along the lines of Security Council Resolution 678, authorising military action by member states, is likely again to be the model, rather than reliance on Articles 42 and 43 of the Charter, which envisage the creation of a command structure by the United Nations itself. There will be undoubtedly much UN debate in the next few years about the operations of the Military Staff Committee (established by Article 47) and the establishment of future UN commands, but nothing that happened in the Gulf War is likely to make the United States (or any of the other permanent members) more willing to commit the fate of their forces to some form of multilateral command. It is quite likely that sufficient progress will be made so that any future operation can be conducted under the UN flag but, as in Korea, the major contributor will have the final say.

The most important consideration in all of this, and one that should govern the conduct of Australia's UN diplomacy, is that even if such enforcement action does not occur for many years, this does not reduce the importance of building a collective security system. The example of the Gulf crisis—and the possibility that such a UN authorised international coalition, or at least a system of effective sanctions, can again be mounted —must now be taken into account by any country contemplating aggression. The more the system is elaborated, the greater the commitment countries give to it, the greater the expressed readiness to support it by physical measures, the more likely is a system of deterrence based on United Nations collective security likely to work.

Peace-keeping Situations like Namibia and Cambodia are more likely than the Gulf to set the pattern of future United Nations action. In the absence of clear-cut aggression, what may well emerge is a form of peace-making activity that falls somewhere between 'good offices' on one end of the spectrum and enforcement action on the other. The final settlement of a dispute will be through negotiation and agreement among the parties to it, but they will be negotiating under various forms of pressure and inducement from the United States and other permanent members of the Security Council. Such settlements will often contain a peace-keeping component.

Peace-keeping operations, defined as the non-forceful use of soldiers as a catalyst for peace (usually by the separation of combatants as a confidence-building measure) were not originally envisaged in the Charter. They are generally seen as an improvisation of the Cold War, when the enforcement provisions of the Charter could not be activated because of differences among the permanent members. While there is some truth in this, peace-keeping operations could be mounted only in circumstances where there was in fact sufficient consensus among the permanent members for a conflict to be brought to a halt—and usually in situations where enforcement action was impractical because neither side was clearly the aggressor. Thus although peace-keeping operations are a product of the Cold War, they are designed precisely for the sort of circumstances which are likely to occur more often in the post-Cold War era, and thus we are likely to see more rather than less of them. The trend is already evident: six new peace-keeping operations of different kinds—UNIIMOG (UN Iran-Iraq Military Observer Group), UNAVEM (UN Angola Verification Mission), UNTAG (UN Transition Assistance Group—for Namibia), ONUCA (Operacion de las Naciones Unidas en Centroamerica), UNIKOM (UN Iraq-Kuwait Observer Mission) and MINURSO (UN Mission for the Referendum in the Western Sahara)—were launched in 1988–91, as against sixteen over the previous forty years. The 1988 Nobel Peace Prize was won, and deserved to be, by the UN peace-keeping forces.

In this environment, Australia will need to develop a somewhat more purposeful policy towards Australian participation in peace-keeping operations if we are to play an effective part in the UN peace and security system. Our image of our role in peace-keeping is heavily influenced by our recent participation in UNTAG in Namibia, but it has to be acknowledged that the personnel we supplied on that occasion comprised almost a third of the total we have supplied in forty-two years: in fact, only one peace-keeper in 250 has been Australian. This is a very small proportion when it is remembered that the permanent five members, with minor exceptions, do not contribute personnel to peace-keeping operations. A further third of the peace-keepers we have provided are the police in the United Nations Force in Cyprus (UNFICYP), so our proportion of military personnel is considerably smaller even than one in 250. The professionalism and competence of our personnel; the fact that we have been a consistent, if small contributor; our recent contribution to UNTAG and MINURSO; and our willingness to play a major peace-keeping role in Cambodia have maintained for us a standing higher than these numbers would suggest. But our standing in future will depend increasingly on our willingness to do more.

Peace-making In the new climate it would be logical to anticipate a greatly expanded role for the United Nations in preventive diplomacy, or peace-making. The part that it should be able to play in the resolution of conflict, before it escalates out of control, has long been understood. Insofar as conflict is caused by ignorance of the factual situation or of the motives of rival states, or by mutual misunderstanding, the United Nations can act to bring the parties to a common appreciation of the facts and of each other's intentions. Insofar as it is caused by angry and emotional reaction to specific problems, the United Nations can act through discussion and delay to institute a cooling-off period. Insofar as it is caused by a lack of imagination in finding original solutions to difficult bilateral problems, the United Nations as an outside party may be able to identify pacific outcomes that the parties directly and intimately involved cannot see unaided. Insofar as it is caused by the ambition of individual leaders, UN peace-making can utilise the spotlight of global public opinion to press for more reasonable attitudes. Insofar as conflicts are perpetuated by the unwillingness of the parties to back down and make concessions to one another, UN peace-makers can be impartial third parties to whom concessions can more easily be made. And insofar as conflict is created by irreconcilable national inter-ests, the United Nations can at least interpose itself between the parties until such time as those differences do not have the sort of priority that impels nations towards armed conflict, or until longer-term solutions are found.

However obviously more desirable it is to prevent an armed conflict than to mop up after it, it is nonetheless likely that the United Nations will expand its role in this area only gradually. It is only logical that the United Nations take the initiative in bringing together the parties to an inter-national disagreement while it remains peaceful, and attempt to broker a settlement between them. It is even more logical that in doing so it should apply the now well understood principles of conflict resolution, and have available to it the professional and other resources needed to apply those principles in practice. But these ideas are regarded with much suspicion by many member states. This is especially so since many conflicts have an internal component. Smaller member states are concerned that there will be infringement of their (often newly won) independence and sovereignty or, worse still, an imposition of solutions they do not like. Israel is not alone in its lack of affection for multilateral diplomacy. All states, not only the smaller ones, are cautious about an expansion of the influence of the UN bureaucracy.

Nevertheless the United Nations has already demonstrated its prepared-ness to extend the previously accepted limits regarding the role it should play in the internal affairs of countries. Important, albeit small, steps were taken in this regard with UN Security Council Resolutions 687 (dealing, among other things, with practical measures to reduce Iraq's military capa-bilities) and 688 (on assistance to minority groups in Iraq). In effect these resolutions juxtaposed the traditional notion of national sovereignty with over-riding international humanitarian purposes. Australia responded positively to both resolutions. We provided experts to the UN Special Commission established pursuant to 687 to oversee the destruction of Iraq's weapons of mass destruction and its missiles, with a senior officer of the Department of Foreign Affairs and Trade in fact being appointed to head the Special Commission's Working Group on Chemical Weapons. And we contributed seventy-five Australian Defence Force personnel to support the international relief effort for Kurdish refugees in Turkey and Northern Iraq.

It can be expected that the Secretary-General will only very slowly be able to expand the Secretariat's information-gathering capacity, and that there will be considerable opposition to the establishment of permanent structures for peace-making or for further extensions of the kind of intrus-ive action thought justified after the Gulf War. But these developments do need to be pursued. The capacity, for example, for the United Nations to be aware of dangerous local build-ups in armaments, and to step in to counsel and warn the parties, is an important element in the development of an effective collective security system. And there is a case for arguing that, despite the sensitivities involved, the United Nations should have a right to play a role in the internal affairs of countries if the tensions they generate are likely to spill over into international conflict or create disasters demanding international action. Certainly Australia should not be among those always prepared to wait for the climate to be right for settlement of a dispute. We should rather be prepared, as has been the case in recent years, to continually encourage the United Nations and interested countries to produce confidence-building measures among the parties to ensure that the right climate in fact develops.

7

Security in
the Asia Pacific
Region

AUSTRALIA'S 'REGION' in security terms is, in the first instance, the South Pacific, South-East Asia and the eastern reaches of the
Indian Ocean. This was what the Defence Minister in his 1987 White Paper
described as our 'area of primary strategic interest'[1] It was also the primary
focus of the Foreign Minister's December 1989 Parliamentary Statement on
Australia's Regional Security, which remains the most substantial official
statement of the regional security perspective we adopt here.[2] But there is a
close linkage between what happens in these areas and in other parts of the
broader Asia Pacific region, and any discussion of security in our region
needs to look as well at developments in North-East Asia, Indo-China and
South Asia.

An underlying theme of the discussion which follows is that it would be
very much to the advantage of Australia, and the region, to develop a perception and understanding of the common security interests we share in
this broader region. It is not an easy perception to grasp that there could be
any common interests in a region as diverse and disparate as this, with its
many different cultures, histories and sources of conflict. But there is no
reason why the principles of common security we have outlined—in a
nutshell, that security is best achieved with others, not against them—
should not be as applicable in the Asia Pacific region as anywhere else in
the world. There is a considerable degree of uncertainty right around our
region about its strategic future, but that uncertainty should lead us not to
retreat into a defensive intellectual shell, but rather to think positively and

creatively about how developments might be influenced in a favourable direction.

THE REGIONAL SECURITY OUTLOOK

The international order crafted in the aftermath of World War II and sustained through the Cold War is now drawing to an end, in the Asia Pacific region as well as in Europe. The flow-on effects of this period of transition are, in the Asia Pacific region as elsewhere, far from clear. It *is* clear that the equations of power in Europe and the Pacific are changing as the roles and capabilities of the two superpowers change, and the United States and Soviet Union are joined by the European Community, Japan, China and India as major global influences. All these trends—and others such as economic globalisation—are likely to have implications for regional security.

In the first place, it would be wise not to assume that the United States will continue to maintain its present level of security activity in this part of the world, in particular in South-East Asia. The United States will want to continue to protect its major strategic interest in maritime passage through the region; and its persistence in renegotiating the Philippines Bases Agreement (although the havoc wrought by the eruption of Mt Pinatubo in June 1991 added an entirely new dimension to those negotiations), and in developing modest facilities in Singapore, suggests that it certainly wishes to maintain some military presence in the region. But with the decline in ideological competition and other global and regional developments, United States attention to the region may well become increasingly less geopolitical and more oriented to its major economic interests. Against this background, governments have become if anything more conscious of the benefits of a US strategic presence in the region, in the time-honoured manner of appreciating someone's company only when he or she is about to leave. A benign US presence—one which preserves the status quo, acting (in Defence Secretary Dick Cheney's phrase) as a 'balancing wheel'—is now seen to be in the interests of almost everyone.

Asia has been through its twentieth century upheavals and revolutions and is now preoccupied with economic development, in which the United States has an important role, not just as a major economic power but as a strategic influence for stability. The United States defence budget has not grown in real terms in the last four years and it is likely that Congressional pressure on the military budget will, over time, force cuts in the United States presence in Asia. It has been Australia's position that if these cuts have to be made—say in the US forces committed to Japan and South Korea, or in the Philippines—they should be gradual, predictable, subject to review and generally staged in such a way as to allow others to adjust and therefore preserve a stable political environment.

The military investment of the Soviet Union in the region has grown during the 1970s and 1980s, but mainly in the deployment of army divisions on the border with China, and in tactical aircraft based in Siberia. The Soviet Pacific Fleet, although it does not match—here or elsewhere—United States naval capability, is the largest of the four Soviet fleets. But the Soviet navy's strategic role traditionally has been to operate as an extension of land-based defences and to support ground force operations, and its capacity for power projection—certainly as far south as Australia—remains limited. Generally, the Soviet Union has not been able to turn its more substantial military commitment in Asia to its economic or political advantage. Hopes of Japanese investment in the development of Siberia and the Soviet Far East have come to little, with Japan suspicious of the Soviet Union's intentions and likely to remain so until the issue is finally resolved of the northern territories taken by the Soviet Union after World War II. With the exception of India to some extent, and (although less so recently) Vietnam, the Soviet Union has had little success in building its influence, and its parlous economic circumstances will continue to be an impediment to any improvement of its standing in the region.

If the superpowers reduce or merely maintain their defence levels, the three main resident powers will loom larger, creating the prospect of five powers jostling for position in the Asia Pacific region. Japan's economic strength is well-established fact, but its military capability is not so well known. Pegged by public policy at just on 1 per cent of GNP (compared with around 3 per cent for Australia and 6 per cent for the United States), Japan's defence expenditure is nevertheless now the third largest in the world, because of the size of Japan's economy, and has been growing annually at the high rate of about 6 per cent. While restricted, again by public policy, to protecting sea lines of communication for a radius of one thousand nautical miles from Tokyo (agreed with the US as a defence-sharing initiative in the early 1980s) it polices those lines with very sophisticated forces. However, even with a defence budget that could reach US$50 billion by the end of the century at present growth rates, Japan could not defend itself against an all-out attack by the Soviet Union. Also, as presently constituted, Japan's forces lack a strategic strike capacity and power projection. They are geared to operate in tandem with United States forces, and the United States–Japan Security Treaty continues to underpin both Japanese security and that of North Asia generally.

It has been the preference of most countries in the region—including Australia—that Japan's defence posture remain in its present essentially defensive form, with any quantitative increase in its commitment taking the form of a greater contribution towards the cost of the United States presence in the country (presently involving some 50 000 personnel) rather than a greater share of overall military responsibility. Such a preference should not be regarded as either patronising or paranoid: from Australia's perspective, it would be wholly desirable if *every* country in the region were to adopt an essentially defensive strategy, with limited power projection capabilities. None of this is to say that Japan should not be steadily drawn into a much more substantial dialogue on defence and security issues with its neighbours than has been the case in the past: we believe it should. And, controversial as this may have been domestically and in some parts of the region during the Gulf crisis, we believe that there is no good reason in principle why Japan should not in future contribute to United Nations peace and security operations, wherever these may occur.

More damage was done to China's international reputation on the night of 3–4 June 1989 than by any event since the Cultural Revolution began in the late 1960s. The political cost of using repression to stay in power—after developing expectations about being embarked on a wholly different course—was all the greater because it came at the moment that the Soviet Union and China agreed, after thirty years, to bury the hatchet, and just before the East European communist governments were successively to tumble, having considered—and had the Soviet Union reject for them—the Tienanmen option. Unlike Japan, China is a nuclear power in its own right, dependent neither on the United States nor the Soviet Union. It was friendly with the Soviet Union until the late 1950s but, when the Vietnam war ended in America's humiliation and the Soviet Union became Hanoi's patron, China deliberately moved closer to the United States, a position which became harder to sustain after 1989.

Yet the internal uncertainties of China after June 1989, while hardly welcome, have not done much to change the overall regional security outlook. China was concerned to show externally that it had not become the threatening presence that so many who lived in its shadow had assumed it to be during the Cold War period. Its relatively civilised discourse with Taiwan continued. The return to normal relations with Indonesia was undisturbed. Its positive, if cautious, attitude to a comprehensive settlement in Cambodia seemed unaffected. It became for a time more shrill, and generally more hard-nosed, towards the British in the negotiations over Hong Kong, but nevertheless conceded some points on legislative representation by Hong Kong after 1997. In the Spratly Islands dispute it had already shown that it was prepared to use force, but a naval or military build-up was not apparent. It did renew the sale of its ballistic missiles, notably to the Middle East, but was then co-operative in the Security Council's conduct of the Gulf crisis (albeit by way of abstention rather than support for crucial resolutions).

China's influence in the Asia Pacific region will always be weighty. The size and powerful strategic location of the country; its huge population; the spread of 'overseas Chinese' with continuing emotional links to the ancestral homeland; its economic potential; its determination not to allow Vietnam to exert hegemony over Indo-China; its more general determination, since the communists seized power in 1949, to count for something in world affairs (including its support in the past for communist insurgencies within the region): all these make China a factor in any strategic consideration of the region. Especially near at hand, in circumstances where its army can be used (as in Korea and Vietnam), China has never been reluctant to teach a recalcitrant a lesson when appropriate circumstances arose. Nor has it been slow in acting to defend its claimed borders (as with India in 1962) or to resist what it claims to be the undermining of its sovereign authority within its own territory (as, over the years, with Tibet). But it has not in the past been an aggressive power outside these generally limited contexts, and there is no reason to assume that it will become one. Certainly its military posture is land-based, and essentially defensive, with the Soviet Union still seen as its most immediate strategic threat. Most of the Chinese navy is suited only to coastal operations, and its airforce is also primarily defensive.

India is the most underrated of the likely great powers of the 1990s. It has a huge population—with what is already estimated to be a middle class of close to one hundred million people—which is likely to outstrip China's by the year 2010. It has a substantial land mass, an increasingly educated population and a developed manufacturing industrial sector. It already has very significant military capabilities—as the fourth largest force in the world in manpower, with an increasingly effective naval force—which makes it unquestionably the predominant power in South Asia. India would like to be granted more international recognition than it has traditionally received—especially as compared with China. Developing a formidable military capability is a time-honoured way of earning that. But there can be no suggestion that India's capability has been developed to date for other than legitimate purposes. The country is self-reliant in defence: with a developing satellite and missile capability, and its nuclear technology, India is certainly capable of defending itself against practically all comers. Its capacity to project power into South-East Asia and the Indian Ocean is considerable, but that should be understood as a function of the assets needed to protect a 7500 kilometre coastline and to guard against possible threats from the north, rather than constituting anything that should be perceived as a direct security threat to Australia or its neighbours. To the extent that South-East Asians sometimes express concern about India's capability, they also do so about Japan and China. All that said, there is virtue, here as elsewhere, in dialogue—both bilaterally and on a regional basis—to ensure that misperceptions or misunderstandings do not develop. Australia has begun in recent times a quite successful series of exchanges with India in this respect, and it is obviously important that this should continue.

The security picture in Australia's most immediate neighbourhood, South-East Asia, is relatively favourable, with most of the countries in the region, for all their various internal problems, more likely than not to continue down the path of nation building based upon participation in the global economic system and a generally pro-Western foreign policy outlook. Indo-China has been something of an exception, but even here there are ever-growing signs of a more outward-looking economic orientation. While the dominant security concern of most South-East Asian countries was for years internal, focusing especially on communist subversion, it is the case now that with growing political stability and trade and economic co-operation high on the agenda, several countries have begun to define their national interests more broadly, recognising in particular the importance of maritime areas for exploiting resources.

Corresponding changes in force structures are becoming evident: Thailand and Indonesia have improved their naval capabilities with additional frigates; Malaysia is upgrading its helicopter and strike aircraft; Singapore has acquired advanced, early-warning aircraft; Thailand and Indonesia and Singapore are purchasing F-16 aircraft. Australia regards these changes as appropriate and expected, no more than we have ourselves put in place in adjusting our capacity to protect our national interests in changing circumstances. Certainly there is no basis for us being over-awed by them, given that the pattern of Australian defence expenditure has been in recent years roughly equivalent to that of all the ASEAN countries combined—not surprisingly, given the size of the continent and coastline we have to be able to defend against a variety of contingencies, and also given the need to substantially reshape our force structure in accordance with the new conceptual framework of defence self-reliance articulated in the 1987 White Paper.

The security outlook for the South Pacific is different again. A number of the island nations confront economic, environmental, cultural and demographic pressures which will place increasing strain on their political systems. In view of its crucial strategic location for us, the course of Papua New Guinea's development will have a particular significance for Australia's security, requiring a sustained and sensitive Australian policy response. The South Pacific region as a whole is unlikely to pose major strategic problems for Australia over the next ten years or so. Neither of the superpowers, nor any of the major Asian powers, is seeking a substantial role there. But there is a possibility that we will see over this period, in some of the island nations, a renewal or a continuation of the political tensions which have been evident over the last few years.

Overall, the easing of the adversary relationship between the United States and the Soviet Union is obviously welcome in our region, as it is elsewhere, even if it means some reshaping of the strategic map. India, China and Japan are militarily capable of projecting power to take up any particular local slack in United States–Soviet Union relations which could create tension. However, they have been so capable for decades: the Asia Pacific region has always had a multipolar character. If Vietnam, Indonesia, and for that matter Australia itself are added to the list of players with some capacity for independent action, the range and variety of interacting and intersecting interests is considerable. While the overall prospects for our regional security environment are positive, there are also uncertainties, and undoubtedly surprises, in store for us. For Australia, the essential fact is that we are dealing with a more fluid and complex region, requiring a range of Australian responses.

The main trouble spots are well known: the Korean Peninsula; India–Pakistan relations, especially in Kashmir; the continuing civil war in Cambodia; the American bases in the Philippines, as both a stabilising factor in the region and to some extent a destabilising factor politically in the Philippines itself; rivalry between China, Vietnam and others in the Spratlys; the hand-over of Hong Kong to China; Chinese relations with Taiwan; the Bougainville secession issue. While these neuralgic points in the Asia Pacific's sub-regions have in most cases a significant course of deterioration to undergo before they approach the stage of open conflict of region-wide significance, none of them can be ignored, and prevention is always going to be better than any possible cure. Here as elsewhere, these issues need to be discussed continually in bilateral talks, and on other appropriate occasions. Australia's responsibility, like that of every other country in the region, is to contribute positively and constructively to that dialogue and to act in a variety of other ways to help build the kind of links between nations that commit them to avoiding conflict, not promoting it.

DEFENCE SELF-RELIANCE

In recent years Australia has conducted its search for security on the unfamiliar basis that no immediate threat to our national integrity could be identified. The effect was a little like the calm that descends on a patient after a fever. From the end of World War II until 1975, when the collapse of the fatal Vietnam enterprise was at last plain for all to see—it had been apparent to defence planners earlier—public perceptions of security in Australia were inflamed with xenophobia and the helpless conviction that the continent was indefensible by Australians alone. A kind of gravity theory seemed to prevail: what was up there sooner or later had to come down here. In the calmer atmosphere induced by assurances of no immediate threat, the public was forced, like the defence planners, to ask fundamental questions about security rather than urgent questions about imaginable dangers. From that moment the search for a lasting security policy for Australia began.

It is relatively easy, however costly or politically restrictive, to plan a nation's defence against an immediate and identifiable enemy. When there is no identified enemy and no immediate threat, the task becomes more elaborate, calling for both flexibility in response (to a wide range of possible threats) and consistency in approach (based on the long-term process of developing an appropriate force structure and its associated skills). In the past, Australia's armed forces had been seen as an adjunct to much larger American forces. The argument which continued into the 1980s for the maintenance of an Australian aircraft carrier, essentially as an integral part of an American force structure, makes the point. The search for a more self-reliant Australian defence capability—the ability to defend Australia from within its own resources—had to begin from the bottom, the irreducible minimum that Australians needed to protect, rather than from the top, the threat of a major conflict in which our ally the United States would be involved.

This irreducible minimum was, of course, the Australian continent and its territories. It was necessary to define, first, the enduring features of Australia's strategic landscape; its geography and environment; the nation's industrial capacity; the size and distribution of its population and from where the physical threats to the national territory were likely to come. When Australia's defence needs are examined in this way, a striking feature of our situation emerges immediately. The population and infrastructure are concentrated in the south, while the north is underdeveloped, vulnerable to the approach of any likely hostile conventional force (which would be from or through the archipelago of South-East Asia or the island seas to our north-east) and isolated from the south. The defence of Sydney or Melbourne or Canberra may have to be conducted three thousand kilometres away, and across the full width of the continent: in the combined forces exercise Kangaroo 89, for example, the area tested itself extended some three thousand kilometres, from Pilbara in the west to Cape York in the east.

These realities were once used to support the assumptions that Australia lacked the population, the armed forces and the industrial capacity to provide anything approaching an adequate defence of the whole continent. One response was to assume that the northern half of Australia was indefensible and should be used as a kind of buffer of wasteland between southern Australia and a likely aggressor. Another was to look for outside assistance. Another was to locate Australian forces beyond our shores as a trip-wire, as it were, against an approaching enemy. But the assumptions on which these responses were based are no longer tenable. For a start, Australia's population has grown with migration, skills are more varied, and defence industries are more efficient. New technology, especially intelligence and surveillance capabilities, including Australia's own over-the-horizon radar, has reduced somewhat the daunting scope of the task of defending Australia's north. And today's armed services, although still rivals for individual treatment when the defence budget is allocated, have learned that modern defence requires flexibility of response and interoperability of all services. Applied to Australia's situation, this has meant now thinking in terms of defence-in-depth, in which Australia would choose, depending on the circumstances, at which level its armed forces would engage an aggressor.

A further important change in conceptual thinking, clearly reflected in the Dibb Report of 1986[3] and the 1987 Defence White Paper based on it, was the emphasis on fully understanding Australia's strategic environment, and the conclusion based on that analysis that it was not likely to change in unmanageable ways. 'Worst case scenario' is a valid method of testing defence capability, but it needs to be contained within a realistic framework. Subjective assessment of individual countries' motivations, including the possibility of irrational behaviour, can lead to a position where a response is designed to meet every conceivable need and is unable to meet any of them properly. When this is linked to the demands and interests of a global ally like the United States, the inadequacies of an Australian capability are emphasised. When however, the enduring features of Australia's particular security assets and liabilities are given prominence, on the presumption that it is the duty of Australians, not someone else, to take the first steps in defending their country, it was found possible to make a realistic match between threats and contingencies on the one hand and an improved Australian capability on the other.

Since Australia's decision that self-reliance is militarily realistic and affordable—an approach that will no doubt be continued by all future Australian governments (albeit not without the usual arguments from year to year as to what they should be actually spending)—Australia's national defence capacity has become itself a factor in our assessment of security conditions outside the national territory. This is because the kind of military capacity that Australia needs in order to be self-reliant can also be projected to meet an adversary well forward in the sea and air approaches to northern Australia. Australia may have dispensed with an aircraft carrier, but it is maintaining long-range strike aircraft, such as the F111, and building submarines and frigates as part of its strategy of defence-in-depth. This has had to be explained to our neighbours, especially Indonesia. But it has not created any problems. A strong program of reciprocal visits and consultations has continued with Indonesia, and there has been, if anything, a reinforcement of the extensive defence relationship already existing with Malaysia and Singapore under the Five Power Defence Arrangements. A new climate of thinking is slowly emerging in the region around the concept of a community of shared strategic interests.

Self-reliance does not necessarily mean complete self-sufficiency. Australia remains a military ally of the United States, and our self-reliant military posture is based on an appreciation of the asset that alliance represents: ours is self-reliance within an alliance framework. The alliance is important to Australia in that the United States enjoys strategic superiority in the Asia Pacific region, based on the forward deployment of its naval and air forces, and to that extent the alliance has a deterrent value against potential aggressors. In addition, it provides logistical and technical, including intelligence, benefits for Australia without which our self-reliant posture would be less convincing. Former Defence Minister, Kim Beazley, made the general point well in a comment on the Gulf crisis:

> It is much easier, it has to be said, to uphold one's territorial integrity if one has managed to resist one's would-be attacker at the borders, and to a considerable extent nations these days require a self-reliant capability in order to be able to do it. Prudent nations advance their self-reliant capability, firstly, by establishing it and, secondly, by having friendships. Alliances are not irrelevant to a strategy of self-reliance. They are not irrelevant to ourselves; they are not irrelevant to the Saudis; and they were not irrelevant to the Kuwaitis. Alliances are important and they are worthwhile keeping intact.[4]

There is no doubt that the balance between alliance commitment and defence self-reliance is well understood, and appreciated, by our major alliance partner. The United States has recently described its defence relationships in the Asia Pacific area as being based on the principle of 'co-operative vigilance', in which there is a 'network of balanced security concerns to which each nation contributes to the full measure of its capability'.[5] Clearly the major emphasis here is on the need for more financial responsibility-sharing by Japan and the Republic of Korea, in a post-Cold War environment where there is budgetary pressure on the United States to reduce its regional commitments. But this nevertheless describes a United States approach to the region's security with which Australia is, and should remain, entirely comfortable.

A MULTI-DIMENSIONAL POLICY FOR AUSTRALIA

For all its importance, military capability is just one among many instruments of an effective national security policy. Security in a regional context is best guaranteed when military capability is backed by effective diplomacy and trade and other contacts—building up a set of relationships, and networks of interdependence, that will minimise the likelihood of conflict ever breaking out. The most effective regional security policy for Australia, from this point of view, is a multi-dimensional policy, one in which *all* the components of Australia's network of relations in the region—military and politico-military capability; diplomacy; economic links; assistance with development and so-called 'non-military threats'; and the exchange of people and ideas —work together to help shape a security environment which is favourable to Australia's interests. This was the theme of the Ministerial Statement of December 1989: while it has been the subject of a good deal of comment and discussion since,[6] the essential elements of that theme, and its continuing relevance to the conduct of Australian foreign policy in the 1990s, have not been in any way seriously challenged.

The first policy dimension identified in the Statement is the acquisition and maintenance—in line with current defence policy—of a military capability designed to deter, and if necessary defeat, aggression against our territory or maritime jurisdiction. This capability, based on the principles of self-reliance and defence-in-depth, can be seen as relevant not only to the defence of Australia, but also to the security of the region as a whole. Australia's possession of significant but non-aggressive military power contributes to the strategic stability of our neighbouring regions by providing a 'secure south' for South-East Asian countries, and a 'secure west' for South Pacific nations.

Secondly, Australia can use its military assets and presence in the region to help foster the gradual development of a regional security community based on a sense of shared security interests: this is usually described as the exercise of politico-military capability. We should not be embarrassed about using the military capability we possess, with prudence and sensitivity, to advance both Australia's and the common security of the region through such avenues as defence co-operation programs, and military assistance in disaster relief and fisheries surveillance and the like. We need in this respect to face up to the difficult question of the extent to which we should be able, and prepared, to use military force in pursuit of security interests going beyond the defence of Australian territory, for example to assist an elected government to resist a coup, noting that this is an issue which arises in the South Pacific rather than the South-East Asia context. The use of military force may conceivably be appropriate in unusual and extreme circumstances, but such a decision can only be made on a case-by-case basis, bearing in mind certain cumulative criteria.[7] The Ministerial Statement explicitly rejects any notion of Australia claiming the role of regional arbiter of political legitimacy or moral acceptability.

Another way in which we can build a shared sense of security interests in the region is through participating in, and contributing to the development of, regional security arrangements. The Five Power Defence Arrangements (FPDA) are the only functioning regional security arrangement of which Australia is a member. They have involved us working together with Malaysia, Singapore, the United Kingdom and New Zealand since 1971, with their main operational manifestation these days being the Integrated Air Defence System (IADS). The Ministerial Statement makes the point that it would be sensible for Australia to work—in a low key and gradual way, given the sensitivities potentially involved—towards the establishment of complementary kinds of defence co-operation with Indonesia and Thailand. Perhaps it would also make sense, although this moves into larger and more sensitive diplomatic questions still, for Australia to encourage the evolution over time of some more formal collective security arrangement for the whole region.

Thirdly, Australia should use traditional diplomatic skills of persuasion to manage tensions and frictions, to ensure that small problems stay small, and to achieve accommodations of interests with mutual benefit. Diplomacy should also extend beyond the region itself to dialogue on regional security issues with those external actors capable of exercising influence within the region.

Fourthly, trade and investment is important in creating more substantial and mutually beneficial links, especially in South-East Asia where economic complementarities offer a great deal of scope for expansion. Australia needs to devote a level of effort and resources to our economic relationship with this part of the region greater even than its current relative importance might otherwise justify, bearing in mind that, here as elsewhere, our success will depend primarily on the success of our efforts to restructure the Australian economy into a strong and internationally competitive entity.

Nations which trade together do not always stay together. But extensive economic linkages create mutual interests which can work to restrain any resort to military conflict. The Asia Pacific Economic Co-operation process, notwithstanding its exclusively economic focus and broader membership (extending as it does across the Pacific to the United States and Canada), is an example of how new connections can be built up in the region. The Timor Gap Treaty with Indonesia, signed in 1990, is an example of a non-military solution to a problem that historically has often led to conflict—a disputed boundary involving prized resources.

Fifthly, development assistance programs can contribute to our national security interests in the region in a variety of ways: promoting economic and social development; reducing the political disaffection caused by economic deprivation; creating further economic linkages with Australia; and encouraging perceptions of Australia as a sensitive, practical and technologically competent neighbour.

Sixthly, Australia can demonstrate its neighbourly credentials by assisting regional countries with so-called 'non-military threats' such as environmental degradation, AIDS, narcotics trafficking and unregulated population flows, including the problem of refugees.

Finally, there is scope for a great deal more to be done in the area of exchanges of people and ideas to reduce the cultural distance between Australia and the region, and to overcome the significant image problem we still tend to have. Mutual understanding, like all of the other strands in this multi-dimensional approach, is no guarantee of peace. But mutual ignorance is a greater risk, and 'public' diplomacy—seeking to get our message across through various non-governmental channels—has an important role to play in countering it.

The essential point is that, instead of seeing the security of the region essentially in military terms and acting accordingly, as Australia did for so many years—looking out nervously, behaving defensively and turning anxiously to Britain and the United States for reinforcement—the only possible and sensible course for Australia to take is to engage *with* its region in the most direct possible way. We should utilise all the many dimensions of our external policies in an informed, co-ordinated and vigorous way to help shape a welcoming regional environment. In so doing we will give ourselves the best possible chance of safeguarding our national security into the next century.

BUILDING A SECURE REGIONAL FUTURE

It clearly follows from the multi-dimensional approach we have urged that if every country in the region were to deal with every other country in the way suggested—focusing on building a complex web of relationships extending across the whole range of government-to-government and people-to-people activity—the region would eventually become a rather more integrated, mutually understanding and generally secure place. While the capacity of any one country to influence how others behave is necessarily limited, Australia does have a role in helping to build a more secure regional future.

Part of that role is simply to encourage broader acceptance of the idea that the best security policy is multi-dimensional, not just pursued militarily. But it is also a matter of thinking afresh about the specifically military and political dimensions of security policy and encouraging our regional neighbours to do likewise. Prime Minister Bob Hawke has described Australia's contribution to developing a new regional security system in terms of laying four corner-stones: first, support for the United Nations as the supreme international guarantor of peace and security; secondly, support for the continued engagement of the United States in the security affairs of the western Pacific; thirdly, support for the development of regional co-operation and dialogue on security matters; and fourthly, continued development of Australia's defence force both as the final guarantor of our own security and also as a contributor—through the FPDA and other co-operative programs—to the security of the region as a whole.[8]

The newest, and ultimately perhaps most important, of these themes is the emphasis on developing a more systematic process of dialogue between nations in the region on security matters. What is involved here is dialogue to reduce the possibility of misapprehension that is so large an element of friction between nations; dialogue so that we can come to share perceptions as the strategic landscape changes around us; dialogue so that we can assure others, and be reassured ourselves in turn, about the role of military forces; dialogue that can be used to reach out to former adversaries as well as to strengthen existing links with friends; and dialogue that can be used to build up a co-operative capacity to tackle jointly regional issues such as the security of sea lanes.

This kind of approach has a little more substance and bite—and a little more potential for controversy[9]—than might at first sight be apparent. This became evident from the debate which followed some remarks made at the ASEAN Post Ministerial Conference in Jakarta in July 1990 by Gareth Evans (and also to some extent by the then Canadian Foreign Minister Joe

Clark). The suggestion was made that if such processes of dialogue were to get under way, and if they were successful in enhancing confidence and developing new patterns of co-operation among various groups of countries in the region, then at some stage there might evolve a more formal structure—perhaps a 'Conference on Security and Co-operation in Asia' ('CSCA') along the lines of the Conference on Security and Co-operation in Europe (CSCE) established in Helsinki in 1975.

Obviously, as was acknowledged at the time, there are no simple comparisons to be drawn between the Europe–North Atlantic theatre and the Asia Pacific region. The Helsinki CSCE process—designed to focus equally on three 'baskets' of issues: military security, economic co-operation and human rights—might in practice prove absolutely non-transferable. Asia *is* a diverse and non-homogeneous region with little of the common diplomatic tradition or the sense of common cultural identity, with its strong focus on individualism, that is so evident in Europe. There are many different issues of contention and many different 'fronts', unlike Europe with its overriding East–West conflict. The Asia Pacific region is itself a conglomerate of regions. Conflict between India and Pakistan over Kashmir is distant in both space and political sensitivities from the conflict between Japan and the Soviet Union over the northern territories, or that between China and Vietnam over the Spratly Islands, or from that between the two Koreas. Even when a degree of cohesion is achieved within one part of the whole, there are limits to its reach. ASEAN, for example, may have achieved significant progress in broad economic and political co-operation since its establishment in 1967, but there has been little if any agreement about how to give content to the objective of a 'Zone of Peace, Freedom and Neutrality' (ZOPFAN) adopted in the Kuala Lumpur Declaration in 1971. Also distinguishing the Asian region from the European is that while there has been no systematic Cold War conflict, neither has there been a political collapse of the communist system in Asia comparable with that in Eastern Europe, or even in the Soviet Union.

Moreover, while there is a Western alliance system operating in the western Pacific rim, it functions quite differently from that in Europe. Unlike the NATO system, the Western alliance in our region operates through a series of essentially bilateral alliances: the United States–Australian alliance (including, but not limited to, the ANZUS Treaty), and the United States defence arrangements with Japan, the Republic of Korea, the Philippines and so on. There are no peak councils, like NATO and the Warsaw Pact, to manage changes. All these considerations mean that, if the idea of a 'CSCA' has any application, it is not so much as an institutional prescription, but as a metaphor for a process of dialogue and mutual confidence-building—leading to the gradual development of a sense of regional community, based in turn on a sense of shared security interests.

As unexceptionable as this aspiration might be thought to be, there are some who have taken exception to it. There is one school of regional policy-makers, for example, who subscribe to the view that any approach to regional security in the Asia Pacific that does not focus wholly on the maintenance of traditional Western alliance discipline, on keeping a distance from non-Western peace initiatives, and on resistance to the blandishments of Scandinavian heresies about 'common security', is destined to slip quickly down the slope and over the precipice of unacceptable policy concessions. The touchstone of this kind of concern has always been naval arms control. This is a particularly sensitive subject for the United States, not only in the Pacific but worldwide: it is said, not wholly in jest, that the first of the US arms control negotiators' ten commandments is that 'If it floats it's non-negotiable'. The concern here is that any move down the track of dialogue, confidence-building measures, transparency and all the rest, is inevitably destined to generate pressure, sooner or later, for unacceptable naval limitation measures.

A more relaxed view is that much is to be gained and nothing much at all risked by the kind of dialogue and processes envisaged. The argument is that security is enhanced by reducing heat and introducing light into exchanges between traditional adversaries, and that greater degrees of transparency can be introduced into military arrangements, and confidence-building measures like joint exercises devised, without stepping over predetermined lines, let alone falling down slopes and over precipices. Central to this view is that traditional alliance relationships are not so much ends in themselves as means to the end of greater security.

We certainly take the view that the Western alliance is likely to remain crucial to global stability into the indefinite future, and we have already indicated that we share the widespread view in the Asia Pacific about the regional utility of the United States presence as a 'balancing wheel'. In this region, even more than in Europe, countries need the reassurance of these established alliances as they face up to new policy questions. And the need for fail-safe mechanisms is even greater in Asia than in Europe, because of the many questions and apprehensions that an uncontrolled movement to multipolarity would otherwise generate. But it is perfectly possible here, as it was in Europe, to employ that alliance mechanism in a co-operative rather than a confrontational way while the new dynamics of the post-Cold War world are working themselves out. Doing so may well advance rather than hinder the very security cause the alliance was originally designed to promote.

In our judgment the situation does call, in the Asia Pacific region as in Europe, for a 'common security' approach, with countries working in various ways, largely informally, to build multi-dimensional linkages of mutual benefit and interdependence—economic, political and strategic—between old adversaries as well as between old friends. In the early stages, a sub-regional building-block approach to security dialogue may be more effective than a region-wide approach. Australia's own interests are in the first instance focused on contributing to such dialogue around South-East

Asia and the South Pacific, but, given the innumerable linkages between us, we also have an immense interest in security dialogue in North-East Asia and the North Pacific. There is no prestige in over-reaching ourselves, or enthusiastically pursuing ideas—particularly for formalised institutional structures—that simply have no support. But the idea of a more systematic commitment to security dialogue throughout the region, after many years in which just about the only such dialogue was that of the deaf, appears to be an idea whose time has come.[10]

The very nature of the Asia Pacific region, and especially its recent economic successes, make it an ideal arena for new thinking about security. The unsuccessful history of defence arrangements in Asia promoted by the Soviet Union and the United States in the 1950s—which helped generate the momentum creating the Non-Aligned Movement at Bandung, in Indonesia, in 1955—are a reminder that power is not only widely dispersed, but also of different qualities. The United States is primarily a sea power, the Soviet Union a land power, and Japan an economic power. The two other major regional powers, India and China, are each developing a full range of attributes, but do not themselves tend to meet—except at rarefied altitudes in the Himalayas. If there is any underlying unity in the Asia Pacific region, it may prove to be much more easily realisable in the short to medium term not through politics or defence, but through economics. The essential process registering this fact is an Australian initiative, the Asia Pacific Economic Co-operation (APEC) process. And it is to economic issues—regional as well as global and bilateral—that we now turn.

8

Trade and Investment Imperatives

IN INTERNATIONAL AFFAIRS, economics and politics are now as intertwined as they always have been in domestic affairs. Trade policy issues are more prominent on the international stage than they ever have been, and at the same time more complex thanks to the ever-growing numbers of issues and actors on that stage. To some extent the combative emotions applied to strategic and political issues during the Cold War decades are now being applied to economic issues, as witness the United States–European Community duelling over farm policy, and escalating United States anxieties about Japan. Maybe, as Clausewitz might have put it, 'economics is the continuation of war by other means'.[1]

Australia has had to come sharply to grips with this reality over the last decade. Our standard of living—leading the world in per capita GNP terms at the turn of the century, now ranking eighteenth[2]—has always depended on our being a trading nation. But we are a trading nation that has been finding it increasingly difficult to trade: while absolute volumes and values have continued to grow, our share of global trade has slipped from 2.6 per cent in 1953 to just 1.3 per cent in 1989; our ranking as an exporter has dropped from sixth in 1948 to nineteenth in 1989 (and from seventh to nineteenth in overall trade terms); we have not succeeded, despite our First World status, in diversifying our export economy away from its Third World commodity base; and we have been struggling with recurringly adverse trade balances and persistent current account deficits, perhaps not surprisingly when one discovers that 'Australia is the only industrialised country that has not increased its proportion of merchandise exports to

GDP during the last thirty years'.[3] If Australia is to maintain its prosperity, and take into the twenty-first century the high standards to which we have become accustomed, then all these trends simply have to be arrested.

There are a number of levels at which this has to occur. International policy is crucial. Australia has been disadvantaged, and continues to be, by the innumerable barriers and distortions that inhibit the free access of our goods and services to overseas markets, and our interests do lie over-whelmingly in the achievement of a freer international trading environment. A very great deal of our diplomatic energy, at both ministerial and official levels, now goes into multilateral and bilateral efforts to achieve just that. The integration that was achieved in 1987 of the former Trade portfolio—the preserve of highly protectionist Country Party ministers for most of the post-War years—into a merged Department of Foreign Affairs and Trade has guaranteed external policy coherence within a squarely global outlook. It has also enabled us, by cross-fertilising the considerable expertise and experience of former trade and foreign affairs specialists, to develop an extremely strong diplomatic profile in these areas. This has been evidenced not least by the continued effectiveness of the Cairns Group, and our successful initiation of the Asia Pacific Economic Co-operation (APEC) process.

However, all the access opportunities that may be won by diplomacy will avail us naught unless the Australian economy is competitive enough to take advantage of them: the domestic economic policy required to achieve this is the second necessary level of response. Building a competitive Australia is, in fact, exactly what domestic policy has been about for most of the last decade. Nothing less than the modernisation of the Australian economy has been required: freeing it of excessive regulation, including the financial regulation which had inhibited the inflow of international capital; recasting its tax structure; reshaping the labour market; stimulating higher education performance, skills training and a new emphasis on research and development and technology uptake; forcing fundamental micro-economic reform, especially in the transport and communications sectors; and, above all else, pressuring Australian industry to make competitive investments—in effect, to get competitive or get out—by the steady dismantling of Australia's own protective barriers.

As a result of a series of such measures, culminating in the industry policy announcements of March 1991,[4] Australia's general level of tariff assistance will be reduced to a general rate of 5 per cent by 1996 (with special provisions, albeit themselves at reduced rates, retained only for the motor vehicle and textile, clothing and footwear industries), while the average nominal rate of assistance will fall to 3 per cent, and the average effective rate to 5 per cent, by the end of the decade.[5] The new tariff rates are negligible by international standards, and their significance is even more apparent when it is appreciated that Australia has never been, and will not be now, a country that has relied extensively on *non*-tariff protective barriers, whether in the form of quantitative restrictions, 'voluntary' restraint arrangements, manifestly excessive quarantine and safety requirements or anything else. Australia's assault on tariff protection, which had been an abiding feature of our economy since Federation, will not only be of manifest benefit to the country's long-suffering consumers and primary producers as it simultaneously blasts a long-overdue competitive wind through Australian industry, but will also ensure that we approach all our international economic policy negotiations with the cleanest possible policy hands. It would be naive, in an imperfect world, to embark on such policy changes for this reason alone, but where those changes have their own independent rationale, clean hands are a useful fringe benefit.

Governments cannot do the whole job. Positive outcomes depend on the business community responding to policy stimuli not only rationally, but energetically. Trade opportunities, and trade- and income-generating investment opportunities, have to be chased. Australian business has not been reluctant to do this in the past in Europe and North America, but—mainstream commodities suppliers apart—there has been much more caution about penetrating their own neighbouring region. That is changing: during the second half of 1990, Australia's exports to the ASEAN economies exceeded those to the European Community. But it is not changing fast enough. The need is for the development not only of a general 'export culture' in Australia[6] but for one specifically focused on the trade and investment opportunities in our own region. Austrade, the Government's trade promotion arm, has a particularly important role to play in encouragement and facilitation, and the 1991 changes in its structure and mode of operation—designed among other things to focus more effort on our own region and less on Europe and North America—should be very helpful.

GLOBAL TRADE POLICY

As the 1990s commence, the future of the whole international trading system is delicately poised.[7] Despite all the efforts after World War II to put in place through the General Agreement on Tariffs and Trade a system of multilateral trade arrangements that would commit the world to the steady implementation of free trade principles; despite all the positive impact that GATT rules have had in the manufacturing areas where they have been allowed to operate (helping multiply the volume of world trade nine times in the period 1946–85); and despite all the effort that has gone into making the Uruguay Round of multilateral trade negotiations, which commenced in 1986, a vehicle for a major new liberalising leap forward, it is not at all clear that this momentum will be sustained.

The trend in recent years has been in many ways otherwise. Protectionist sentiment in the United States, fuelled by a long series of massive trade deficits and a fear, in particular, of Japan's economic muscle in manufacturing and Europe's in agriculture, is as politically powerful as it has ever been. Governments—not only in the United States—have become more and more tempted by the lure of 'managed' trade. The growth of export subsidies, the proliferation of non-tariff barriers and voluntary restraint arrangements, the encouragement of counter-trade, and the growth of resort to bilateral deals and remedies rather than multilateral principles, all testify to a ground swell not easy to resist. The United States–Canada Free Trade Agreement, in effect from 1 January 1989, was in its own way almost as significant as the breach of the Berlin Wall. It signalled a major modification of United States commitment to the multilateral system and a shift away from its previous avoidance of bilateral preferential agreements. Moreover, an extension of the agreement to Mexico is now being considered, mirroring the steady expansion of the European Community's membership and scope.

Australia simply has to resist any trends away from multilateralism. The GATT is the only comprehensive body of widely respected rules governing international trade. Based on the principles of non-discrimination, transparency and consensus, it offers a measure of protection to medium-sized trading countries like Australia with relatively little economic clout. Given the composition and direction of Australia's trade, and our market size and influence, it is doubtful in the extreme that we could hope to gain better access and general trading conditions through bilateral negotiations and preferential trade blocs than we can through the GATT multilateral framework.

The Cairns Group Australia has, accordingly, been actively engaged across the whole range of issues under negotiation in the Uruguay Round —in fifteen negotiating groups in all, including such matters as textiles, intellectual property and services. But, here as elsewhere, resources and effort have to be concentrated if a country our size is to have a realistic impact. The particular issue we have chosen is agriculture, and the vehicle we have chosen is the Cairns Group of Fair Traders in Agriculture. On any view the exercise has been a valuable one.

The genesis of the Group lay in agriculture's second-class status within the GATT system. The Uruguay Round is the eighth since GATT began, but the first in which this sector has been on the negotiating table in a way which offers real prospect of achieving significant liberalisation. Over the last twenty years, subsidisation of exports and increasing protection of major markets has cut a swathe through the trade of efficient agricultural exporters. The European Community's Common Agricultural Policy (CAP) has moved food production from deficit to surplus in a wide range of agricultural products—sugar, wheat, butter, poultry, cheese, beef, veal and pork. Mountains—almost literally—of stockpiled surpluses accumulated in Europe, and a new European Community export strategy emerged, based on subsidising consumers outside Europe and especially in the Third

World. The United States, in a policy of fighting fire with fire, openly subsidised in 1983 a substantial sale of surplus wheat to Egypt, which had been traditionally supplied by Europe. The practice spread and, while maintaining its free market rhetoric, the United States signalled with the introduction of the Export Enhancement Program (EEP) that it would target the traditional markets of other major subsidised agricultural exporters. By the later 1980s a full-scale subsidy war was being waged, and countries like Australia—not targets, but caught in the crossfire—were being badly hit. Not helping any of this was the continuation of Japan's and Korea's well-known habit of making support payments to agricultural producers, especially rice farmers.

In response to all this Australia, under Trade Minister John Dawkins, conceived the idea of forming a lobby of exporters to act as a third force, in a corner of its own between the United States and the European Community. The Group came together for the first time at ministerial level at Cairns in August 1986. It has fourteen member nations, spanning five continents: Argentina, Brazil, Chile, Colombia and Uruguay from Latin America; Indonesia, Malaysia, Thailand and the Philippines from Asia; Australia, New Zealand and Fiji; Canada; and Hungary. Each country has a highly competitive, export-oriented and for the most part lightly protected agricultural sector. Australia's is the second lowest protected (after New Zealand) in the OECD, and one of the lowest in the world. Between them they represented (in 1986–87) 26 per cent by value of world agricultural exports, as compared with the United States's 14 per cent and the European Community's 31 per cent.

The significance of the Cairns Group is that it represented a departure in the negotiating process of GATT, which had previously been dominated by the major industrial countries which founded it, especially the United States. Seven earlier rounds of negotiations (between 1947 and 1979) had failed to deal with the fact that behind the espousal of liberal market principles for which GATT became known, the advanced industrial states were protecting their less competitive farm sectors from international competition and from the domestic consequences of their manufacturing success. As chairman of the Cairns Group, Australia took the lead in putting on the table proposals to wean the industrial countries, especially the states of the European Community, away from the subsidy system they had followed (from their point of view successfully) for four decades. The basic demand —which came to be supported by the United States—was for significant movement in all three contested areas of agricultural policy: export subsidies, import access and internal support. In crude bargaining terms, the Cairns Group made reform of agricultural trade the price for its agreement on other items on the Uruguay Round agenda, although in practice it took a constructive attitude to those negotiations.

At the time of writing the jury is still out on whether the Cairns Group will succeed in its Uruguay Round objectives. But from Australia's point of view it certainly has represented a creative and effective diplomatic innovation, a very successful example of the kind of coalition building in which middle-sized nations have to engage if they are to have their voices heard. Members of the Group were strange bedfellows from all points of view other than their interest in agricultural trade. They came from both sides of the East–West and North–South divides and represented nearly every region of the world. Some of them, like Australia and Canada, were middle-ranking in economic and diplomatic status, but most were developing countries. To bring such a disparate group together, to hold it together for more than four years and to lead it through the difficult negotiations of the Uruguay Round was a diplomatic exercise of a kind with which Australia was not familiar. In the past we had tended, in trade policy as in our political diplomacy, to look for the satisfaction of our demands within our alliance relationships—for example by using our good relations in Washington to gain access to the American market. But the situation facing Australia, and the other Cairns Group agricultural exporters, had by the 1980s become too critical for a diplomacy of nuances.

If Uruguay Fails If the Uruguay Round does eventually break down, or concludes with an agreement that is utterly insubstantial, some very difficult policy questions will be thrown up for Australia, as for the rest of the trading world. The trend toward managed trade and bilateralism, and regional preferential agreements of one kind or another—having the effect in practice of undermining basic GATT principles—will almost certainly gather accelerated momentum. If this happens, some very delicate questions will be thrown up about the best longer term course for Australia to follow. In particular we will have to consider very carefully the pros and cons of entering into one or more formalised free trade agreements of our own.

In the past a number of options for bilateral or regional free trade agreements have been floated, including association with the United States, Japan and even the European Community. Other proposals vary from arrangements with Korea to the extension of the Australian New Zealand Closer Economic Relationship Trade Agreement (ANZCERTA) to include Canada or other countries in South-East Asia. In practice, preferential trade agreements can have quite different effects. Whether an economy gains or loses by entering them turns partly on whether they result in additional market access and security for those exports which it produces efficiently. On the import side, it depends heavily on whether the principal effect is to replace inefficient domestic production by more efficient supplies from a partner (trade creation) or to displace cheaper imports from third countries by more expensive imports from within the arrangement (trade diversion). A range of other effects, including the potential for economies of scale, gains from increased specialisation, and increased competition, also need to be considered. Free trade agreements (or customs unions, the most extreme form of such agreements) can bring benefits by addressing other barriers to efficiency, including investment laws, business regulation and customs procedures.

Within Australia, these kinds of arrangements may have acquired some attractiveness as a result of the success of ANZCERTA. However, a number of special factors apply in this case. For example, trade diversion effects have been limited by the broader process of trade liberalisation in both Australia and New Zealand, and the agreement has not caused major trade relations problems with other countries. Adjustment costs for Australia have been small, reflecting our position as the larger economy in the arrangements, broad similarities in the cost structure of Australian and New Zealand industry, transitional arrangements applying to key sectors, and the fact that much trans-Tasman trade was already free of restrictions.

The case for entering into such agreements with other countries may be much weaker, although it would be premature to offer any concluded judgement at this stage without taking into account all the factors that might apply following a Uruguay Round breakdown. Australia's small market suggests that we would have extremely limited bargaining power in negotiating bilateral agreements with major trading partners (the United States, Japan and the European Community), with this making it difficult to achieve substantial improvements in access in areas, especially agriculture, of principal interest to us. In addition, tariffs on manufactures imports by those countries are low to start with. On the other side of the equation, Australia would find it politically difficult to accord the United States, Japan or the European Community preferential access in those key areas of manufacturing industry, such as motor vehicles, which will continue to require a degree of protection even after the present tariff reforms have run their course. Moreover, trade agreements with any one economy could result in trade relations difficulties with the others. An important consideration in all these calculations would be what other major economies were doing at the same time. A United States–Japan free trade agreement, for example, could pose a significant threat of trade diversion affecting Australia's exports, including for key agricultural products like beef. If such a proposal looked likely to gain momentum, Australia would certainly need to examine, for example, whether we ourselves should then seek to join the association.

A broader regional free trade agreement involving the western Pacific, or larger Asia Pacific region, is another theoretical possibility, and preferable in principle to bilateral arrangements. But it would prove extremely difficult to negotiate such an arrangement in the Asia Pacific region, given political and cultural differences, economic disparities and the number of economies involved. These factors made even the development of APEC, to this point a much looser association than that contemplated here, a task of extreme sensitivity.

The crucial point about all these options, bilateral or regional, is that they are manifestly less attractive than a genuinely free and open international trading system of the kind that GATT members are pledged to support, and to which Australia is, and should remain, wholly intellectually committed. None of them should be even contemplated except in an environment where the existing multilateral disciplines, and the commitment of the parties concerned to the multilateral trading system, have weakened to the point of breakdown. Our primary focus should continue to be on avoiding that breakdown, and APEC is an important means to that end.

REGIONAL ECONOMIC CO-OPERATION

Asia Pacific Economic Co-operation (APEC) is an Australian initiative which illustrates not only another aspect of the economic imperative driving Australian diplomacy, but also our commitment to becoming a fully fledged partner of our neighbouring countries. It is also a useful study of Australian leadership in coalition-building. Despite some early reticence on the part of the ASEAN states, APEC has developed into a serious attempt to work at regional co-operation on a project-by-project basis, as well as being an important continuing focus of support for the principles of trade liberalisation.

The APEC concept was launched by Prime Minister Bob Hawke in a speech in Seoul in January 1989 calling for more effective economic co-operation in the Asia Pacific region, and for inter-governmental dialogue aimed at identifying and advancing, across a broad front, common economic interests. It was greeted at the outset with a little scepticism in some quarters, being seen—wrongly—as floating the idea of a trading bloc, and as a warning shot across the bows of the European Community (and for that matter the United States, which was not mentioned in the original speech) if there was failure to respond to pressure for more sympathetic access and subsidy policies. Some saw it as a fall-back option for Australia in the event that the GATT talks collapsed. But the roots of the initiative lay deeper, essentially in Australia's appreciation of the economic potential of the Asia Pacific region. It was that perception, accompanied by some energetic diplomacy, that came to capture the imagination of the other countries in the region. Within ten months it took a very practical form, with the initial meeting in Canberra in November 1989 of twenty-six trade, industry and foreign affairs ministers from the twelve major trading nations in the Asia Pacific region: the United States, Canada, Japan, Republic of Korea, the six ASEAN countries, Australia and New Zealand.

By the late 1980s the world had become well aware of what those in the region itself had long been conscious: that the Asia Pacific in general, and the western Pacific rim in particular, was the fastest growing and most economically dynamic region in the world. In 1988, the year before APEC began, the major economies there were recording an average GDP growth of about 7 per cent, and an export growth of 14.5 per cent. In less than three decades the production in North-East Asia alone had expanded from something less than one-quarter of that of North America's to one-quarter of that of the world.[8] The Pacific, no longer the Atlantic, was the centre of gravity in world production. These achievements reflected several factors: relative political stability, hard working and increasingly well-educated work forces, high rates of savings and investment, sound economic management, and a crucial willingness to undertake rapid structural change. The successful economies have also displayed great skill in taking advantage of the relatively open post-War international economic order—and the huge demand generated by United States consumerism in the 1970s and early 1980s—by pursuing export-oriented industrial strategies. The result has been a region whose trading instincts are outward-looking, and which is probably the most committed of all regions to trade liberalisation. The economies of the region have also become increasingly linked. As a process of 'shifting complementarities' works its way through the region, the pattern of regional trade and investment, the direction of technology flows, and inter-linkages in sectors such as tourism, have all combined to produce a regional economic map criss-crossed with the ties of interdependence.

Dynamism and interdependence of this order have not been without problems and tensions. These tensions partly reflect the major trading imbalances between the United States, on the one hand, and Japan and some of the 'NIEs' (Newly Industrialising Economies, i.e. South Korea, Hong Kong, Taiwan and Singapore) on the other. There has been a tendency in the United States to ascribe a good measure of these imbalances to unfair trading practices, including virtually closed markets for some industries. As a result, protectionist sentiment in the United States has grown, as evidenced by some aspects of the 1988 Trade Law and the consequent use by the administration of that law's Super 301 'crowbar' provision to open up markets.

Against this background of dynamic regional growth, growing regional interdependence, and the emergence of trade tensions, the Australian initiative was launched. Its objective was to help promote conditions in which the dynamism of the region could be sustained over the next decade and beyond. Our own stake in that outcome was clear. More than half of our exports and over 40 per cent of our imports are directed to or sourced from our western Pacific neighbours. Seven of Australia's ten largest markets can be found there. About a quarter of the total foreign investment in Australia has come from the western Pacific region, and almost one-fifth of Australia's total investment overseas is located there.

The idea of better and more structured regional economic co-operation has, of course, been around for some time. In the 1960s, partly in response to the development of the European Community, proposals emerged for a Pacific Free Trade Area (PAFTA)—like that from Professor Kojima in 1965, involving in the first instance Japan, the United States, Canada, Australia and New Zealand. Ideas for an Organisation for Pacific Trade and Development (OPTAD), along the lines of the OECD, were also actively discussed in the late 1960s and subsequently: the most widely disseminated version of this proposal involved fourteen identified market economies of the region meeting regularly at ministerial level to discuss studies prepared by a small secretariat, and a number of functioning task forces.

In 1967 came the formation of the Association of South-East Asian Nations (ASEAN), with its commitment to regional co-operation and development. Also in that year, largely at the initiative of Japanese businessmen, the Pacific Basin Economic Council (PBEC) was established to bring business representative in the region together, and this forum still meets annually in different cities around the Pacific. The following year saw the first Pacific Trade and Development Conference (PAFTAD).

The process gathered momentum in the 1970s and 1980s. The Pacific Economic Co-operation Conference (PECC) grew out of a seminar at the Australian National University in 1980, initiated and sponsored by the then Japanese Prime Minister Ohira and Australian Prime Minister Fraser. PECC, with its tripartite structure bringing together government, business and academics, has gone on to become an important vehicle for informal regional dialogue. Former Korean President Chun proposed in 1982 an economic summit for the region. In 1983, Australian Prime Minister Hawke proposed, in an early anticipation of his 1989 initiative, that regional countries meet to discuss proposals then circulating for a new round of multilateral trade negotiations. The following year, ASEAN put in place its dialogue process thereby substantially strengthening intergovernmental consultations in the region.

The pace then quickened considerably. Former Japanese Prime Minister Nakasone called in May 1988 for a Pacific forum for economic and cultural co-operation, directed to promoting economic, cultural and general informational exchange, described at the time as a 'Pacific OECD'. In July 1988, former United States Secretary of State Shultz floated the idea of intergovernmental exchanges on sectoral/structural policies (for example transportation and education), in association with the establishment of a 'Pacific Basin Forum'. In December 1988, United States Senator Bill Bradley proposed a Pacific Coalition on Trade and Development to encompass eight Pacific countries (United States, Canada, Mexico, Japan, Republic of Korea, Philippines, Thailand and Australia) whose initial tasks would include, for example, achieving a consensus position on agricultural trade to present to GATT, and establishing mechanisms to reduce yen–dollar exchange rate volatility, as well as to review developing country debt.

Early in 1989 Senator Alan Cranston introduced into the United States Congress a resolution calling for a permanent Pacific Basin Forum, whose main feature would be an annual summit of the US President and other leaders of 'nations bordering the Pacific Ocean', whose objectives would be not only to encourage free trade and economic development, but 'to reduce military tensions'. United States Secretary of State Baker's speech to the Asia Society in New York on 26 June 1989 supported what he described as a new mechanism for multilateral co-operation in the region, embodying the principle of 'creative responsibility sharing' and encompassing a wide array of issues, extending from trade and economic affairs to such matters as cultural exchange and the protection of the Pacific region's natural resources.

All these initiatives and ideas helped to pave the way for a new chapter in the evolving process of Asia Pacific economic co-operation. The coming together of a number of factors—regional interlinkages, a crucial round of multilateral trade negotiations, the growing self-confidence of ASEAN, declining East–West tensions, and a recognition that the Pacific had outpaced the Atlantic in economic terms—combined to make Asia Pacific economic co-operation an idea whose time, at last, had come.

The transition from prime ministerial speech in Seoul to ministerial-level meeting in Canberra was neither automatic nor painless. It involved countless rounds of senior official and bilateral ministerial consultations, with an emphasis throughout on exploration and consensus rather than prescription and pressure. Australia had to respond on the one hand to the need for the United States and Japan to be major players in the process, but on the other to sensitivities about the tendency of the two economic superpowers to set the agenda. And we had to be acutely sensitive to the desire of ASEAN not to be subsumed, and institutionally overwhelmed, in a wider regional process.

Australia approached the initial meeting with five specific practical objectives in mind for regional co-operation: to strengthen the individual and collective capacities of regional countries for analysis and policy formulation; to examine ways of further liberalising trade within the region, in a non-discriminatory manner as against the rest of the world; to alleviate future trade problems of regional countries by providing an opportunity to anticipate and discuss differences sensibly and openly; to strengthen the ability to project—and protect—regional interests in wider economic forums and negotiations, including in the first instance the Uruguay Round; and to develop co-operative projects in specific sectors where wider regional consultation could bring benefits not just to individual economies but to the region's general economic performance.

These suggestions as to what might be achieved fitted comfortably with regional concerns. They avoided the rhetoric of nationalism and 'blocism', and placed the emphasis on communications, avoiding institutional bureaucracy and getting results from discovering mutuality of interests. In the event, all these objectives were supported at the November 1989 meeting. Some of the flavour is captured by the following statement of 'principles of Asia Pacific Economic Co-operation' agreed by consensus and included in the Australian Foreign Minister's concluding statement from the chair:

- The objective of enhanced Asia Pacific Economic Co-operation is to sustain the growth and development of the region, and in this way, to contribute to the growth and development of the world economy;

- co-operation should recognise the diversity of the region, including differing social and economic systems and current levels of development;

- co-operation should involve a commitment to open dialogue and consensus, with equal respect for the views of all participants;

- co-operation should be based on non-formal consultative exchanges of views among Asia Pacific economies;

- co-operation should focus on those economic areas where there is scope to advance common interests and achieve mutual benefits;

- consistent with the interests of Asia Pacific economies, co-operation should be directed at strengthening the open multilateral trading system: it should not involve the formation of a trading bloc;

- co-operation should aim to strengthen the gains from interdependence, both for the region and the world economy, including by encouraging the flow of goods, services, capital and technology;

- co-operation should complement and draw upon, rather than detract from, existing organisations in the region, including formal intergovernmental bodies such as ASEAN and less formal consultative bodies like the Pacific Economic Co-operation Conference (PECC); and

- participation by Asia Pacific economies should be assessed in the light of the strength of economic linkages with the region, and may be extended in future on the basis of consensus on the part of all participants.[9]

The initial ministerial meeting was followed by a second in Singapore in 1990, with the third scheduled in Seoul for late 1991, and further meetings in Thailand in 1992 and the United States in 1993 to follow. A series of senior officials meetings had been held to follow up and plan ahead, with the atmospherics of these meetings becoming, by all accounts, steadily more relaxed and constructive. APEC trade ministers had met separately, in the specific context of the Uruguay Round. Ten specific work projects were underway, on a wide variety of subjects: review of trade and investment data; trade promotion programs and mechanisms; investment and technology transfer; human resources development; regional energy co-operation; marine resource conservation; telecommunications; fisheries; transportation; and tourism. Specific attention was being focused, at officials working group level, on just what might be involved in the concept of non-discriminatory regional trade liberalisation, and how this might be made to work consistently with GATT principles but short of the creation of a regional free trade area on the North American model or customs union on the European model. No particular progress had been made in developing a formal secretariat—that rotated with the chairmanship of the following ministerial meeting—and APEC was still being described as 'process' rather than as an 'institution'. But that suited the mood of the participants, the great majority of whom, including Australia, were well content to let these things evolve naturally rather than forcing the pace.

On the question of expanded participation, discussions were under way with China, Hong Kong and Taiwan. APEC participants were generally agreed that these were all significant economies which met the criterion of strong economic linkage with the other countries of the region, and that the only real question was whether a mutually acceptable formula could be found to accommodate their different constitutional statuses. A Malaysian proposal in late 1990 for an 'East Asian Economic Grouping' appeared to some at first sight (rather as had Prime Minister Hawke's original speech) to be a proposal for a defensive economic bloc—as such cutting across, and having the potential to undermine, the APEC concept. But by mid-1991 it seemed to be evolving into a proposal just for a further layer of consultative process which, while arguably unnecessary, could nonetheless fit reasonably comfortably within, or alongside, the APEC framework.

It has become apparent that APEC is here to stay, and that it will continue to steadily grow in substance and importance, but with its impact being evolutionary rather than revolutionary. Certainly its achievements are not yet spectacular, and there are some—particularly in the business community—still wondering what the fuss is about. But few involved in government (and conscious of the tortuous and painstaking process inherent in reaching multilateral consensus on any issue of real substance) have been in any doubt of the significance of what has occurred. Nor has anyone doubted the significance, for Australia's future in the region, of our being so centrally a part of it.

BILATERAL ECONOMIC RELATIONS

While the high ground of trade diplomacy is occupied by multilateral and regional issues, Australia is also extremely active, as we have to be, in bilateral economic relations. We had in 1991 bilateral trade agreements with over thirty countries and we are continuously negotiating or modifying a variety of investment, double taxation and science and technology arrangements. In this respect, Australia has tended to concentrate on established markets in Europe and the United States, and on both established and growing markets in the Asia Pacific region. But we have begun lately to increase the scope and coverage of our bilateral agreements and to look for partners elsewhere, notably in Latin America and East Europe but also in the Mediterranean region, South Asia and Africa.

There is no easy way to describe what is involved in bilateral economic diplomacy other than on a country-by-country basis. We earlier gave the example of Japan in this regard in describing just what it is that diplomats do for their country while abroad. Further examples abound. In the case of the United States, for example, one could refer to lobbying on the trade and farm bills, and Export Enhancement Programme (EEP) in particular; to the argument about voluntary restraint arrangements in respect of steel and beef; to the endless efforts made, including initiating a GATT challenge, to secure market access for sugar; to beating off, at both official and the highest ministerial levels, US anxiety about denial of access—allegedly on trade discrimination, but actually on health grounds—of a few thousand dollars worth of chewing tobacco; beating off further arguments about Australian local-content rules constituting a discriminatory denial of United States film and television production access; or fighting for secure access to US markets through the courts, for uranium, or through the bureaucracy, for unwrought zinc. Or one could refer, in the case of Canada, to such matters as the continuing controversy over the application of the Canada–Australia Trade Agreement (CANATA) to imports of Australian canned fruit, following the prejudice to those imports by the United States–Canada Free Trade Agreement, and attempts at the prime ministerial level to find a way through the impasse. Or one could mention, again, the hugely important negotiation between Australia and Indonesia culminating in the Timor Gap Treaty.

In the case of the centrally planned economies, or what is left of them these days, bilateral economic relations can involve many aspects of what, elsewhere, would be matters purely for the private sector: concluding export–import negotiations, implementing commodity agreements, chasing payments for purchases and the like. Certainly in these countries the line between trade policy and trade promotion, a little blurred at the best of times (which is one reason for the decision to integrate Austrade into the Foreign Affairs and Trade portfolio), becomes almost wholly indistinguishable. At the same time, it is acknowledged that these days, even in the most robust capitalist economies, there is a need for Australian diplomats to be actively engaged at least in general economic promotion activity on behalf of their country: giving speeches and briefings, attending seminars, talking to the press about Australian economic opportunities and the scope for their bilateral development and so on. Australian official representatives do have a potentially valuable profile, one that nowadays simply has to be employed. In the rush of international business, the shy tend to be overlooked.

In all this activity, ministers are now, here as elsewhere, playing more active roles, as compared with officials, than may once have been the case. It seems necessary, if Australia's profile is to be maintained in this highly attention-competitive environment, that this practice be continued. In this respect it is perhaps worth mentioning that when it comes to dealing with bilateral economic matters overseas, the roles of the two foreign affairs portfolio ministers are practically indistinguishable. While the Minister for Trade and Overseas Development has the primary responsibility for such matters, he will on any bilateral visit take the opportunity to work through an agenda of non-economic foreign affairs matters. Similarly, the Minister for Foreign Affairs and Trade invariably takes the opportunity on his overseas visits to call on his trade and industry counterparts to advance the current economic agenda. The present Foreign Minister, for example, has fond memories of tipping a large carton of candy-coated chocolate balls into the cheerfully outstretched arms of the Thai Minister for Trade and his staff in the course of making a pitch for the reduction of tariff barriers operating against imports of Australian confectionery. By such exercises—along with, it must be acknowledged, a few others—are multi-billion dollar external deficits eventually turned round.

9

Development Assistance Responsibilities

IN A WORLD WHERE fourteen million children still die in developing countries each year before the age of five, and where eight hundred million people still go to bed each night constantly, chronically hungry, there can be no argument about the humanitarian obligation of richer nations to go on helping the poorer. Australia may have been sliding a little down the comparative per capita income charts in recent decades, but there is no doubt that we remain among the wealthiest few countries in the world.

But development assistance also makes good foreign policy sense. Australia and New Zealand are unique amongst OECD nations in that we are located amongst developing countries. A good many of these have political and economic institutional structures which are still fragile, and their internal stability is often threatened by the very demands of having to deal with poverty. We have a basic stake, in terms of Australia's national interests, in their stability and successful development. Giving aid should not, from this perspective, be seen as an act of charity: it is much better described as an exercise in development co-operation undertaken in pursuit of serious political and economic objectives which are shared by developing countries and ourselves.

How much of their GNPs countries like Australia should be contributing in Official Development Assistance (ODA) will go on being a subject for argument, both domestically and internationally. The countries and multilateral programs to which it should be directed, the forms it should take, how it should be administered and the values that should be taken into account in determining how it should be delivered, are all legitimate subjects for debate. But on the threshold question of whether we should have a development co-operation program at all, there should be no need for debate.

It is important that this perspective be maintained by policy-makers, because concern about the North–South divide—the gulf between developed and developing nations—is much less intellectually and politically fashionable than it used to be. The distinction has crumpled at the edges, with a number of 'South' members—conspicuously the Republic of Korea, Taiwan, Singapore and Hong Kong—now enjoying higher incomes and living standards than do parts of the North. This change is recognised in Australia's decision in 1991 to phase out developing country tariff preferences from the four economies mentioned. The status of the East Europe economies—with aspirations to the North, but with plenty of South characteristics about them—has added further to the confusion. And even when there is no confusion about countries' South status, there is a problem about continuing attraction. The decline of East–West ideological confrontation has led to the courtship of the Third World losing a lot of its fascination. Winning the hearts and minds of the millions emerging from centuries of colonial rule was as much as anything else an exercise in denying those hearts and minds, and the strategic and political assets that went with them, to the other side. The later 1980s have seen, moreover, a virtual collapse of private banking flows to developing countries. The industrialised countries have been turning their backs because they can invest more profitably elsewhere, and because they had their fingers burned in the 1980s when credit was advanced on imprudently easy terms after the spectacular growth rates in the Third World in the 1970s.

The emphasis these days tends to be on robust self-help prescriptions. Certainly there is a case for those developing countries whose agricultural markets have been hurt by the United States–European Community subsidy war not just seeking compensatory aid flows, or further trade-distorting concessions elsewhere, but rather joining in an aggressive political fight-back of their own, as has been happening through the Cairns Group. And certainly there is a case for the International Monetary Fund (IMF) and the international development banks demanding a greater degree of discipline in economic and public sector management, and a more substantial effort in mobilising internal resources for growth, than has often been present in the past. But there still has to be compassion, and an understanding of the art of the possible. If, for example, an escalating debt problem has necessitated a very tight austerity program, then it has to be appreciated that this will make it very difficult for that country to meet the traditional local cost component of its aid program. Unless donors become more generous in this respect, a vicious circle will set in whereby programs are retarded that would have led to economic growth and thus better enable the country to meet the debt obligation contributing to the original problem.

Above all else, the sheer magnitude of the continuing developing world poverty problem has to be appreciated by the developed world. One billion people—nearly one in five of the world's population, and about one in three of the developing world's—live in absolute poverty, waking up each morning worrying not about what to eat, but whether they will eat at all. Moreover, contrary to popular assumption, that poverty is concentrated not in Africa but in our own hemisphere. About half the developing world's poor—520 million—live in South Asia, mainly in India and Bangladesh, while a further 280 million live in East Asia, mainly in China. These people are especially concentrated in rural areas with high population densities. In fact, only about 180 million of the world's poor live in Sub-Saharan Africa: here again, the poor are mostly found in rural areas. In Africa, as in South Asia, about half the population lives in poverty; elsewhere in the developing world, the proportion is closer to 20 per cent.

At first glance, the countries of the South Pacific may seem to have escaped the problems of absolute poverty. Yet pockets of real need exist in the South Pacific as well. Papua New Guinea, Vanuatu and Western Samoa are not widely regarded as nations with this kind of problem, but their social indicators reveal areas of real concern. In these countries, *five* or more of every hundred children born die before reaching the age of one. The comparable figure for Australia is *one* in every hundred. Average life expectancy in Papua New Guinea is only fifty-four years—about the same as it was in England in Shakespeare's time. Today in Australia, by contrast, we can expect to live to around seventy-six years of age. If justification is needed for Australia continuing a substantial aid program, focused as ours is on our Asian and Pacific neighbours, these figures alone would provide it.

ALTRUISM AND SELF-INTEREST

Over the years, through changes of government and changes of fashion in thinking about foreign aid, Australia has been a serious participant in the formulation of aid policy and programs at all levels—bilateral, regional and multilateral. Three distinct objectives now underlie our development co-operation program.

First and foremost, Australia's aid effort is founded on the commitment of the Australian population to basic humanitarian concerns—the desire to help alleviate poverty, hunger and suffering wherever it occurs. Within that humanitarian framework the primary objective of Australian aid is to promote growth and economic development in developing countries. Economic growth is the surest long-term means of reducing and ultimately eradicating poverty in any given country, as well as freeing-up aid funds for application to more pressing cases of human disadvantage elsewhere.

Secondly, we have a general foreign policy objective to advance or re-inforce Australian political, strategic and related objectives, provided always that the activities carried out within the aid program are consistent with development goals. A third main objective is commercial: as far as possible, Australian aid activities overseas should be carried out by Aus-tralians, using Australian goods and services. Some people are, naturally, suspicious of what they regard as so-called 'commercialisation' of the aid program. But in practical terms, it is quite straight forward: Australian wheat (rather than wheat from anywhere else) being used in our food aid program; Australian education institutions being involved in our scholar-ship programs for overseas students; and Australian consultants tendering for Australian aid projects in places like Indonesia, the Philippines and Thailand.

It is not a matter of there being a distinction between 'idealistic' (i.e. 'humanitarian') motivation on the one hand, and 'realistic' (i.e. foreign policy and commercial) motivation on the other, and the aid program somehow having to somehow balance the two. The point is rather that our overseas aid expenditure is *both* altruistic *and* in our own interests, and is capable of being looked at from both these perspectives. All Australia's aid, to qualify for the description of 'Official Development Assistance' (ODA) under international accounting rules, has to be altruistic: alleviating pov-erty and distress, promoting development or both. Equally, all Australian aid can be seen as promoting one or more very direct and very real Aus-tralian interests—whether those interests be traditional geo-political and strategic foreign policy interests, trade and economic interests, or simply Australia's reputational interests in being, and being seen to be, a good international citizen. What is important is that these altruistic and self-interested perspectives can readily complement each other. It is perfectly possible to provide high quality aid which promotes equitable economic development while at the same time generating benefits for Australia.

These hard-headed but realistic perspectives were very largely injected into the Australian aid program, along with a good deal else, by the Jackson Committee Report in 1984.[1] Before the Jackson Report, discussions about Australian aid tended to have an air of cloying idealism, dangerously close to the politics of the warm inner glow. Noble and well meant as this was, it was not in itself persuasive enough to justify to the sceptical Australian taxpayer the expenditure of hundreds of millions of dollars. It is still hard to extract the necessary hundreds of millions of dollars each year in the budgetary process—the figure for 1990/91 was in fact $1.3 billion—but at least the debate each year now has a strongly practical air about it.

The Jackson Report was the most thorough review of Australia's over-seas aid program ever undertaken. Indeed, it was one of the most thorough reviews of any bilateral aid program undertaken in any country since World War II. Its recommendations were extensive. They ranged from the objectives and motivations underlying the aid program, to detailed aid management issues. The Government accepted the general thrust of Jackson's recommendations and an ambitious program of reform was then implemented, as a result of which Australia now has a better focused, higher quality aid program than ever before.[2]

The Jackson Committee called for a clear statement of aid objectives; a sharper regional focus and sectoral concentration; reforms in aid management, including a move to country programming; and improved administration and professionalism in the aid agency, the Australian International Development Assistance Bureau (AIDAB). Surprisingly, perhaps, recognition of the need for a clear statement of objectives for Australia's aid was a major step forward, because it injected sensible realism into our foreign aid policy. Throughout most of the 1970s, the official rhetoric in Australia surrounding aid had emphasised humanitarian reasons. The Jackson Committee acknowledged, quite openly, that aid is provided for certain self-interested reasons as well. The opening chapter of the report discussed in detail the foreign policy and commercial objectives that, in addition to humanitarian goals, underpin aid programs in all Western countries. Thus the current 'trilogy' of objectives was publicly established.

Jackson's call for a sharper regional focus was welcome too. The aim was to counter tendencies towards fragmentation of the aid program. All bilateral aid programs in all donor countries run this risk. Fragmentation tends to occur when lobby groups press for 'just a small amount' of aid to be provided for their favourite activities. At the same time, there is often pressure for more and more countries to be fitted, somehow, into the existing aid vote. The Jackson Committee thought that the Australian aid program was too fragmented and proposed a range of measures which would focus the regional impact of Australian aid. The Committee argued that those countries of greatest importance to Australia should be given greatest priority. This meant continuing our special relationship with Papua New Guinea and maintaining Australia's role as a major donor in the South Pacific. The Committee also recognised the political and economic importance to Australia of nearby Asian countries.

The call for the introduction of a so-called 'country programming' approach was at the heart of Jackson's recommendations for improving the effectiveness of aid. Traditionally, Australian aid to particular countries had been provided in an *ad hoc* way. Different forms of aid—project aid, food aid, scholarships, scientific co-operation, multilateral aid and so on—had all been provided more or less independently of each other. Jackson recommended the development of 'country programs' to provide a coherent approach in each country. An increased sectoral focus, emphasising aid in those areas in which Australia is best able to help, was also identified as a main element in the country programming approach.

Improved management of the aid program was seen by Jackson as underpinning the whole approach towards improved aid quality. This encompassed not only country programming, and a number of other changes to make aid delivery less 'clerical' and more 'professional', but also recommendations on the suitability of various forms of aid. For instance, the Jackson Committee recommended a continued steady reduction in the level of budget support to Papua New Guinea. The question of both the overall volume, and the form, of aid to Papua New Guinea has been a controversial aspect of the Australian aid program. The Jackson Committee observed that no other country gives such a large proportion of its aid program to just one country. It recommended a steady reduction in the overall level of aid to Papua New Guinea and a shift away from budget support towards project aid, both to reduce overall Papua New Guinean dependence on Australia and to enable a better targeting (from Australia's point of view as well as Papua New Guinea's) of the assistance that did still flow.

Overall, the Jackson recommendations combined an emphasis on quality in aid administration with an equally strong emphasis on realism, in terms both of the nature of the program delivered and its stated objectives. The Jackson Committee very well understood the domestic political imperative, which no doubt will be a continuing one, of having a rationale for the aid program that could withstand the endless cry, particularly in hard economic times, of the 'charity begins at home' lobby.

THE QUANTITY OF ASSISTANCE

Australian development assistance policy issues have had to be resolved in recent years against a background of constraints in the volume of aid funds, brought about by a very tough budgetary climate generally and the perceived need for aid to take its share of overall cuts in public expenditure. The Official Development Assistance/Gross National Product (ODA/GNP) ratio fell from a 1980s peak of 0.51 per cent in 1983/84 to a low of 0.33 per cent in 1989/90. However it is worth noting that the fall in the ratio is partly a product of the rapid growth experienced in GNP in the late 1980s. The dollar allocations which have served to maintain the aid vote in real terms over the last three financial years would have looked significantly more respectable in ODA/GNP ratio terms had our economy not been growing to the extent it has. (Equally, with lower economic growth than originally expected occurring in 1990/91, the ratio for that financial year moved back to 0.35 per cent). And, looked at from the perspective of the last two decades, not just the last few years, despite all the fluctuations that have occurred Australia's aid vote has not merely been maintained but has in fact increased by around 10 per cent in real terms.

Although our ODA/GNP ratio is, like that of most countries, much lower than the world leaders in development assistance—Norway at 1.09 per cent and the Netherlands at 0.98 per cent—it compares favourably with such wealthy OECD members as the United States at 0.20 per cent and the

United Kingdom at 0.28 per cent, and continues to hover around the OECD average of 0.35 per cent. It is also in a sense understated in the OECD rankings, because our contribution to refugee resettlement, which is not counted as ODA, has been much higher in proportion to population than that of any other OECD member. Nevertheless, it has to be acknowledged that the aid budget has certainly not increased in recent years, and did suffer a significant decline in one year in particular—1986/87—from which its recovery has been extremely difficult.

The Australian community has mixed feelings about the provision of hundreds of millions of dollars for overseas aid. A recent survey of Australians' attitudes to overseas aid sponsored by AIDAB suggests that while there continues to be understanding and support for Australia providing overseas aid, there is not strong support for spending more on aid. At the national election in 1990 the Opposition parties proposed a cut of $100 million in the aid budget as part of their 'National Economic Action Plan'. If implemented, this would—on growth estimates at the time—have reduced Australia's ODA/GNP ratio in 1990/91 to just 0.28 per cent.

Australia's aid budget in 1990/91 was, in the event, $1266.8 million, or 0.35 per cent of our estimated GNP. Australia is still ultimately committed to meeting the agreed international ODA target of 0.7 per cent of our GDP, and to an interim goal of 0.4 per cent. But it has to be acknowledged as a practical matter that it is going to be very difficult for any Australian government to do very much more than simply hold the value of the budget from year to year in real terms.

The problem is a world-wide one. Flows of foreign aid from the First World to the Third were running at about US$50 billion as we entered the 1990s, with no expectation of any significant increase. This may sound, at face value, like a huge amount of money. But some other comparisons put the figure into perspective. In the first place, for every one dollar spent on foreign aid worldwide, twenty dollars are spent on defence. Secondly, the contribution that developed countries make in aid flows is only half the amount by which developed country protectionism reduces developing country national incomes. Thirdly, the sum total of foreign aid received by developing countries is only enough to fund about 10 per cent of their investment needs, leaving the balance to be funded from internal resources. A fourth telling point of reference is that the United States budget deficit in 1989/90 was itself three times the amount of the world's foreign aid total. In short, compared with the scale of the needs of the developing countries, and what developed countries are prepared to spend elsewhere, foreign aid volumes are, at best, modest.

The distribution of the Australian aid budget is shown in Chart 7. The allocation of Australian aid shows a clear foreign policy preference for Papua New Guinea, the South Pacific and South-East Asia, especially Indonesia. Country programs in South Asia, the Indian Ocean area, Southern Africa and the Middle East have a lower priority. When cuts have to be made in the aid budget, foreign policy priorities can be persuasive, so that the first pressure usually comes on international and community programs, such as food aid or refugee support or the work of non-government organisations (NGOs) or the Australian Centre for International Agricultural Research (ACIAR). As in most foreign policy decisions, aid issues have to be resolved by weighing all relevant considerations at the time. Where cuts can never, however, realistically be made is in Australian contributions to the international financial institutions, including in particular the World Bank and the Asian Development Bank, of whose multilateral programs we are strong supporters. The need to give priority to these commitments, in situations where draw-downs on earlier promises amounting to $100 million or more may occur without much prior warning, has created a number of additional pressures on both the overall amount and internal allocation of the aid vote in recent years.

Within regions of foreign policy priority there are further decisions to be made based on internal priorities. For example, in the Indian Ocean area it was decided in 1989 on foreign policy grounds to inject more substance into our relations with India. This involved a sharp increase in our aid of $35 million over three years, which was accommodated in the budget by reductions in the allocation to Africa. On the other hand, total Australian aid to the Indian Ocean island states had grown from $5.3 million in 1986/87 to $10 million in 1989/90. The aid was mainly in the form of commodities assistance, food aid, training and staffing assistance, with two small projects (health in Mauritius and airport development in the Maldives). The other main recipient was the Seychelles. The developmental and humanitarian needs of these small and fragile states are self-evident, but from Australia's point of view the growth of the programs would depend to an extent on an assessment of the strategic significance of these Indian Ocean countries, and whether our political ties with them needed to be fostered.

The most lively recurring debate about the distribution of Australian funds has involved the Development Import Finance Facility (DIFF). Introduced in the mid-1980s, this is a 'mixed credit' facility providing an aid grant combined with export finance under the Export Finance and Insurance Corporation (EFIC). Funding under this program is tied to the procurement of Australian goods and services and is designed to assist Australians to compete in commercial bids for development projects abroad. DIFF support is limited to developmentally worthwhile projects in the public sector, excluding defence-related projects, luxury goods, consumer durables and raw bulk commodities. In theory it is applicable to all worthwhile projects in any developing country, but in practice countries with a GNP per capita greater than US$2500 have been excluded. It has been used especially in countries where other donor governments are active in providing soft loans—China, India, Burma, Indonesia, Malaysia, Thailand, the Philippines, Pakistan and Sri Lanka.

The facility proved so popular, with so many applications queueing in the pipeline, that the Australian Government decided in September 1989 to restrain it. A ceiling of $100 million was imposed for 1990/91, to be maintained thereafter in real terms. No more than 10 per cent of any year's DIFF allocation can be expended outside South Asia, South-East Asia, China and the South Pacific (including Papua New Guinea). No more than 40 per cent of any year's DIFF appropriation can be spent in any one country. The view was taken that unless limits and defined objectives were placed on DIFF funding, scarce aid funds would have been diverted from projects with a high development priority towards more commercially attractive proposals not necessarily of the highest developmental value. The issue is not commercial success, which is desirable in itself, but the scarcity of aid funds.

Asian countries have been the principal recipients of mixed credit financing. About two-thirds of the funds have gone to Asia, in particular to growth economies such as China, Thailand, Indonesia and India, all of whom have embarked on major infrastructure programs. By comparison with most other bilateral donors and multilateral agencies, only a small share of Australian aid is targeted at economic infrastructure, yet it became necessary, if Australia was to compete in the Asia Pacific region, to provide concessional finance for such projects.

So far, the evidence shows that DIFF-financed projects have been of no less development value than grant aid. However, the balance of mixed credits within total aid flows is causing concern. Although the cost of maintaining mixed credit programs is increasing, most recent OECD data indicates that, while aid budgets are relatively static, tied aid and associated financing is expanding. It seems that due to the cost of concessionary programs, some donors are shifting their aid resources from the least developed countries and offering mixed credits to middle developing countries that are credit-worthy and are pursuing infrastructure development. It is possible that developments in East Europe will encourage Japanese, Canadian and especially European donors to switch some of their subsidised credit lines away from Asia, reducing the pressure on Australia. However, the issue seems unlikely to be resolved easily, despite our persistent appeals to the OECD, along with several other countries, to tighten the use of officially supported export credits, at least by placing more restrictions on the projects which can be supported in this way.

It is a fact that without mixed credits Australian companies would stand little chance of winning international competitive tenders in the important area of infrastructure development. It is also a fact that getting Australian firms to invest or trade in the Asia Pacific region in preference to Europe and the United States has been, for cultural reasons, a slow process. Support in the form of concessionary credits (not available for exports to Europe, the United States or New Zealand) is therefore an incentive for Australian companies to engage in the Asia Pacific region. However, the impact on the current account, the exchange rate and the cost of resources of what amounts to a subsidy has to be assessed in the context of Australia's overall economic reform priorities. DIFF is not bad aid, but it is not a cheap form of industry assistance.

THE QUALITY OF ASSISTANCE

In almost all areas of the aid program, the quality of Australian aid has improved markedly during the 1980s. The goals of the program are clearer, implementation of aid in the field is better, and the administration of the program is much tighter. All of these improvements reflect the recommendations of the Jackson Report.

AIDAB is now a much more professional organisation. Its staff have a wide range of expertise. AIDAB has a strong professional development program and it has a better capacity for evaluation and risk management. It now has a comprehensive information technology system which has significantly enhanced the administration of many parts of the aid program. These improvements have resulted in some increase in the proportion of administrative expenditure as a share of total aid. This has been money well spent. Just as there is no such thing as a free lunch, improvements in the quality of aid do not come free of charge. Even after these changes, administrative costs still represent only 2.4 per cent of the total aid budget, a comparatively low amount compared with many other aid agencies.

The emphasis on 'harder' economic issues in the Jackson Report was a very healthy development. For one thing, it focused attention on the central truth that in the long run, the most effective anti-poverty device ever discovered is sustained economic growth. For another, it has encouraged everyone interested in aid in Australia to see the broad context of aid, trade and development into which any aid program must fit. For instance, by providing aid in areas in which Australia itself is an efficient and effective producer, we can maximise the developmental impact of our aid, satisfying our altruistic inclination—but at the same time generate trade spin-offs for Australian firms, a more self-interested perspective. Rural development projects provide a good example. Australia has particular expertise in agricultural and rural development. Through our rural development projects, firms can introduce their products and expertise to overseas markets. At the same time, rural development projects directly benefit the poor in developing countries.

There is now, again following the Jackson Report, a much stronger emphasis on matching areas of our own expertise with recipient needs. The vehicle for much of this has been the move to program management and program budgeting in administering the aid program. Country programming has now become well established. This approach is based on the preparation of aid strategies for individual countries. Recipient countries are involved in the development of these strategies to ensure that their interests are fully taken into account. The aim is to deliver forms of aid which are most suitable to the needs of the recipient country, and which at the same time best reflect Australia's capacity to assist.

Complementing the country programming approach is a sharper focus on the countries of the Asia and Pacific regions. Country programs are now well established for all major Asian and Pacific recipient countries. In particular, our aid relationship with Papua New Guinea has matured and broadened considerably since the Jackson Report. Australia signed in May 1989 a comprehensive Treaty on Development Co-operation with Papua New Guinea, which spells out the principles that will guide the implementation of our development co-operation activities with Papua New Guinea. Both governments agree on the need to reduce Papua New Guinea's reliance on budget support. Under the Treaty, budget support will remain at its current level until 1992/93, but at the same time programmed aid activities are being increased. In the longer term it is expected that budget support will phase out entirely.

A particular issue in assessing the quality of any country's aid program is how it handles the question of poverty alleviation (other than in the context of direct transfers for emergency, refugee and disaster assistance, for which provision will always, unhappily, have to be separately made). In practice, Australia's approach here is broadly consistent with the international consensus on anti-poverty strategies. That consensus is based primarily on the promotion of economic growth; effective targeting, assisted by the participation of the poor themselves in the development process; and the achievement of environmentally sustainable outcomes. Attention to all these elements is necessary to ensure a comprehensive, and sensitive, approach to poverty alleviation.

The promotion of economic growth helps to eliminate the structural factors that keep people poor. They include, for example, inadequate physical infrastructure, low levels of human resource development, and weak government institutions. These considerations are at the heart of many of our country and sector programs. Good examples include the major river improvement and irrigation project at Bah Bolon in North Sumatra, or the Integrated Rural Development project in Northern Samar in the Philippines.

Another example is a steel bridging project which we are supporting in Indonesia. This project shows how infrastructure projects, while not necessarily providing immediate and direct benefits to poor people, can have important indirect effects on poverty. Improved road transport in Indonesia is crucial for growth, because better roads mean that farmers have better access to markets. Reliable studies have shown that the new and improved bridges provided by Australia have reduced travel times, led to lower bus fares, opened up markets for farmers, and increased labour mobility. All of these things have brought substantial benefits for millions of ordinary people in Java—and in other parts of Indonesia as well. And the Australian steel industry has not done too badly either.

The second element in the anti-poverty strategy is the emphasis on participation by the poor in the development process through specifically targeted projects. This is often more easily said than done. Nevertheless, it is important because, first, experience demonstrates that development programs are likely to fail unless there is good community involvement in their design, and secondly, it hardly makes sense to talk about effective development unless there is a human resource development dimension involved, with the people who are affected being genuinely involved in the development process.

One example of this approach in practice is the Australian Rural Water and Sanitation Supply project on the island of Lombok in Indonesia. In 1985 AIDAB began the first phase of a $3 million rural water supply and sanitation project in central Lombok. To ensure a sense of ownership of the facilities, community participation was actively encouraged in the project. Indonesian community organisers, trained and supervised by an Indonesian non-government organisation, lived in rural areas to help villagers plan the installation of new water facilities. A health education scheme was an integral part of the project as well. The Lombok project was a success. Safe drinking water was supplied to about 100 000 people. Improved sanitation and bathing facilities were built with the full involvement of people in village areas. This project is a good example of how 'bottom up' development co-operation can work. As a result of the original success, the project has been carried through to a second phase. It is expected that similar facilities will be provided to around 160 000 people in other parts of Lombok.

Effective targeting is important for poverty alleviation other than in the context of specific projects. It means greater provision of basic health care, primary education assistance and community development projects; and also a greater relative concentration of aid on low income and least developed countries and to poor groups within recipient countries.

Both economic growth and effective targeting must be complemented by a third element, an environmentally sustainable approach to development. In Papua New Guinea and Indonesia in particular the Australian aid program is now working closely to the principle of sustainability. In Papua New Guinea, we are giving strong support to the management and conservation of forests through the implementation of the Tropical Forestry Action Plan. And in Indonesia, a new water supply and sanitation project will bring Lombok-style community approaches to all of West Nusa Tenggara, helping overcome environmental degradation caused by the disposal of human wastes. It will also curb the loss of water which is currently being wasted or illegally tapped. If environmentally sustainable development is to be achieved, there are few more important elements in poverty alleviation strategy than bringing population growth under control. Family planning programs will, and should, rank increasingly high in Australia's development co-operation priorities.

The issue of poverty takes us back to the beginning of the story of Australia's overseas aid program. It has always been based on the presumption that poverty benefits no-one and, although this justification of an aid program is too diffuse to be effective in answering critics who want precise and measurable benefits for Australia and Australians, it nevertheless remains at the core of what Australian development assistance is all about.

It is not difficult to present quantifiable benefits. Australia's trade with developing countries—the recipients of our aid—is greatly in our favour. Aid can be shown to promote economic growth and political stability. It assists exports by exposing them to new market opportunities. The use of Australian goods and services helps countries to become familiar with Australian goods. But these benefits would not justify the expenditure of more than $1 billion a year to assist Australian industry (when Federal budget assistance to industry already amounts to over $2 billion), if there were not also another objective. This objective is to continue to fight against poverty in the world, for the same ultimate reason that governments fight against poverty within national borders—that it diminishes us all as human beings.

10

The New Internationalist Agenda

THERE IS NOTHING NEW about either nationalism or internationalism as such. For as long as nation-states have existed, their right to independence and freedom of action without interference has been sturdily asserted. And for just as long has been urged the need to seek a community of interests between nations, and to find co-operative solutions to common problems.

On the great issues of war and peace, security and survival, the pendulum has swung over the centuries, and over the decades of this century, back and forth between extremes of confidence and pessimism about the possibility of internationalist solutions to competing nationalist aspirations. Taking an historical perspective never does much for one's confidence in the permanence of anything. But a strong internationalist sentiment is currently running on these issues, and the world is entitled to be a little more optimistic than it has been for some time about the prospects for global security.

On issues at the other end of the emotional spectrum, a degree of solid internationalism has always prevailed. Nations, by and large, have been very good at working out between themselves ground-rules to govern the sending of letters and making of telephone calls, the protection of diplomats and migratory birds, the passage of ships and aircraft and all the rest of the stuff of which everyday life is made. The great bulk of international law has to do with these kinds of matters, as has the mass of treaties, arrangements, agreements and understandings in which that law is sourced, and the diplomacy on which these instruments in turn are based.

What *is* new is the emergence over just the last few years of a whole group of previously neglected issues for which internationalist solutions are actively being sought—issues, moreover, which for the most part generate quite strong feelings, and are not readily susceptible to straightforward technical negotiation and settlement. Some of these issues—like terrorism, the trade in narcotics, and the spread of AIDS—are perhaps best regarded, disconcertingly but realistically, as latter twentieth century examples of the traditional 'everyday life' agenda of the international lawyers. Another problem, of unregulated population flows, particularly from Indo-China, is proving to be extremely complex and difficult, as well as politically volatile in the countries most immediately concerned, but seems capable of resolution eventually by a combination of diplomatic negotiation and the easing of the political and economic pressures pushing people to seek refugee status.

The liveliest of all the new issues, and the most resource-intensive in current diplomacy, are human rights and the environment. Human rights is not of course a new issue at all, if one has regard to the international lip-service paid it over the generations. The novelty lies in the way in which the rhetoric of concern is now being translated into action, both in multilateral forums—not only within the United Nations, but in bodies such as the CSCE—and, increasingly, in bilateral relations. The environment, by contrast, is very much a new issue, both in terms of public and political consciousness and the willingness of the international community to start accepting responsibility for it.

Australia has always taken its international responsibilities very seriously. Partly, perhaps, because of the British legal tradition to which we are heir, we have regarded the international instruments to which we adhere as committing us to more than just good intentions. Once we subscribe to a treaty we abide by its requirements in every detail—which sometimes makes us slower in committing ourselves in the first place than some countries whose legal cultures are a little more relaxed in this respect. We similarly take pains to observe to the full the rules of customary international law. We are one of the few countries to have adopted the compulsory jurisdiction of the International Court of Justice without reservations. This has not been without its costs. It has meant, for example, that we have become embroiled in litigation with Nauru (about compensation for the mining of phosphate) which the United Kingdom and New Zealand, who joined us in extracting it, have been able to avoid, and with Portugal (about the status of East Timor) which Indonesia has been able to avoid. We have a long tradition of protest against abuses of human rights, whether they occur in our region or elsewhere. And we have criticised foreign states, including close allies, when we have seen the international legal order violated or put under stress, even when this has not involved Australia as a party principal. For example, Australia did not support the United States in voting on United Nations resolutions critical of the United

States invasion of Grenada in 1982, and of the US refusal, in November 1988 to give Yasser Arafat access to the United Nations as required under the Headquarters Agreement.

We have taken these positions simply because we regard the international legal order, for all its inherent weaknesses, as an essential element in relations between states. It provides a framework for promoting peace, order and predictability in international relations; for promoting co-operation between nations and the resolution of common problems; and for setting new and higher standards of both international and national behaviour. Being a good international citizen is not a soft option in a hard-headed world of competitive interests—the foreign policy equivalent of Boy Scout good deeds. It is a realistic acceptance of the fact that no nation can always act simply, and unilaterally, in pursuit of its interests in a world that is increasingly interdependent. And as a liberal democracy, and a nation with neither the military capability nor the desire to impose its will on its neighbours, Australia has a particular interest in the development of an international civil society.

ADVANCING HUMAN RIGHTS

Philosophers, lawyers, politicians and diplomats have grappled with definitions of human rights for centuries, and there are almost as many claimants to recognition and protection as human rights as there are social, economic, political and philosophical interests and values capable of pursuit. Some argue that human rights embrace such things as the right to clean air, good health, or to live in peace—and in one sense of course they are right. But such an approach—embracing as it does almost the whole content of human endeavour—tends to empty the concept of human rights of all but its rhetorical content, whether one is talking in a domestic or international context. If we are going to make respect for human rights one of the touchstones of good international citizenship, we have to do better than that.

A more manageable approach is to focus on those rights of an essentially civil and political character which the international community has agreed, by enshrining them in international instruments, are universal in character; which reflect an international consensus on the worth of the human person; and which depend for their existence not so much on the mobilisation of large financial resources, which may be beyond the capacity of the country in question, but simply upon the willingness of authority to accept and recognise them. These kinds of rights are what the original signatories of the United Nations Charter had foremost in mind when they reaffirmed their 'faith in fundamental human rights, in the dignity and worth of the human person, in the equal rights of men and women'. And these are the rights that were given pre-eminence in the Universal Declaration of Human Rights of 1948. It specifically recognised—among others—the right to liberty and security of the person; fair trial; freedom from torture and cruel punishment; freedom of expression and participation in the political process; freedom from discrimination on grounds of race, sex or national origin; and freedom of religion. The well-springs of these rights may vary according to political tradition, culture, religion and the like, but there is at least more-or-less universal agreement that these *are* rights, and ought to be respected and protected as such. As one of the delegates is said to have wryly noted when the Universal Declaration of Human Rights was adopted: 'We agree about the rights but on condition that no-one asks us why'.

Even if that question can be avoided, another has to be confronted. Why should governments bother to pursue these rights in the international arena, given that such issues are always likely to be sensitive in the country the subject of attention, and that even their successful pursuit is likely to be marginal to one's own country's strategic, political and economic interests? One answer is that for a country like Australia, human rights policy involves an extension into our foreign relations of the basic values of the Australian community: values at the core of our sense of self, which a democratic community expects its government to pursue. Another is simply that governments like ours believe that a moral obligation is its own justification, and that a commitment to good international citizenship demands no less than acting to help secure universal adherence to universal rights.

But the pursuit of human rights in this way need not be entirely selfless. An international reputation as a good international citizen on these issues probably can be helpful to a country in pursuing its other international interests. But, more importantly, there is a real sense in which by embracing the cause of those who have been denied their rights, we also guard and reinforce the nature of those rights themselves. The historical record shows clearly enough that rights not defended are rights easily lost. More generally, in the longer term the evolution of just and tolerant societies brings its own international returns: in higher standards of international behaviour, and in the contribution that internal stability makes to international stability and peace.

The Multilateral Agenda   In this field, Australia's objectives have been threefold: to encourage adherence to existing human rights instruments; to ensure the effective operation of monitoring machinery; and to expand the body of human rights treaties in specific areas.

We use our participation in multilateral forums, like the Commission on Human Rights and the Third Committee of the United Nations General Assembly, to lend support to the foundation stones of international human rights standards: the Universal Declaration of Human Rights; the International Covenant on Civil and Political Rights (ICCPR); the International Covenant on Economic, Social and Cultural Rights (ICESCR); the

Convention on the Elimination of All Forms of Racial Discrimination (CERD); the Convention on the Elimination of All Forms of Discrimination against Women (CEDAW); the Covenant on the Rights of the Child; the Convention against Torture and other Cruel, Inhuman or Degrading Treatment or Punishment; and Convention 111 of the International Labour Organisation covering discrimination in employment. Australia is a party to all these treaties—our record of adherence is good by any international standard, and certainly better than that of the United States, which has ratified neither the ICCPR or the ICESCR—and we encourage countries that have not yet ratified them to do so.

The only aspect of our treaty record where Australia is at all vulnerable to criticism concerns our signature of optional protocols. In October 1990 we did accede to the Second Optional Protocol to the ICCPR, committing ourselves to outlawing the death penalty, a subject on which Australia has long campaigned internationally. But our signature of the First Optional Protocol remains outstanding: this provides for the recognition by states parties of the competence of the Human Rights Committee to accept complaints from individuals of the country concerned alleging violation of their rights under ICCPR. Our failure to sign puts us in rather limited like-minded Western company. We also lag behind most Western countries in our failure to make a similar jurisdictional declaration under the optional provisions of the Racial Discrimination Convention. Our only answer to such criticisms has been the vagaries of the Australian federal system. Despite the matter being under formal consideration for several years, a number of State governments have failed to accept the need for adherence, and no Commonwealth government to date has been inclined to override them, although there are no technical—as distinct from political—reasons to inhibit this. It is certainly strongly arguable that the time is long overdue for Australia's house to be put in order in this respect. The matter was again under active consideration in Canberra in mid-1991, and the signs were then good that it would be.

Australia takes seriously our obligations to report to the international community on our implementation of those agreements to which we adhere. The machinery for monitoring adherence to international human rights agreements not only serves to verify that commitments are being kept, but also has an important role in establishing the principle that nations are accountable for their human rights performance. Certainly, in our own national reports we seek, as we must continue to do, to meet the highest standards of international accountability. The same is true for the special investigative machinery that operates under the auspices of the Geneva-based Commission on Human Rights (CHR). The appointment of rapporteurs to investigate alleged human rights violations in particular countries is a means of bringing these violations to the attention of the international community. If the country concerned is prepared to co-operate, and there has been an increasing willingness to do so in recent times, the institution of the rapporteur can also help to open up a constructive dialogue on the scope of the problem and on steps to improve the situation.

Bilateral Representations   In terms of bilateral human rights representations, Australia is probably more active than any other country in the world. In 1990 alone, Australia raised 460 new human rights cases with eighty-two countries, as well as pursuing cases first raised in earlier periods. Our representations covered the plight not only of individuals but also of groups, in some cases involving scores of people. A detailed register of these representations has been maintained by the Department of Foreign Affairs and Trade since 1987: a total of 1441 cases were raised over the period July 1987 to December 1990. Over three-quarters of these cases were first brought to the Government's attention through a unique arrangement involving the Amnesty International Parliamentary Group, which includes senators and members of the House of Representatives drawn from all political parties. Other cases were brought to the Government's attention by Australian diplomatic posts, media reports or representations from within the Australian community by individuals or non-government organisations.

In developing and implementing an international human rights strategy of the kind that Australia has been so actively pursuing, it is crucial that we keep a clear head and do not lose sight of basic objectives. Whether one is driven by a sense of moral imperative or anything else, what matters is ensuring that human rights are observed: it is not making the gesture that counts, but getting results—improving the human rights situation on the ground for individuals and groups. The need to ensure that our activities are productive and not counter-productive for the people we are trying to help is, and must continue to be, a constant theme of Australian human rights policy in action. Bearing these considerations in mind, there are a number of aspects of the way in which Australia has gone about its bilateral representations that need to be understood.

First and most important, the representations are consistent and non-discriminatory. Australia has not cut our human rights representations to suit the cloth of bilateral political or commercial relations. Among the countries we have approached on human rights issues are close allies (the United States), important trading partners (China, Iran) and regional neighbours (Indonesia, Malaysia, the Philippines, Fiji). Ours is not a selective approach.

Secondly, the government has paid close attention to getting its facts right. Whether our representations over the years have covered refuseniks in the Soviet Union, Ba'hais in Iran, Tamils in Sri Lanka, dissident journalists in Africa, or East Timorese in Indonesia, they have been made on the basis of the best available information. Australian missions overseas are an important source of information, as are reports from credible human rights organisations like Amnesty International. And where the situation is confused or our information is deficient, we will often seek clarification or additional information from the government concerned. Overwhelmingly Australia's representations have not begun by accusing the government in question of responsibility for the alleged violation: rather it has been a matter of seeking clarification on a credible report which, if correct, would be a cause for concern.

Thirdly, Australia's concerns have been firmly based on standards and rights which the international community accepts as having universal application, and which are obligations under the United Nations Charter and other international instruments. In some very limited respects—most notably in relation to the death penalty, which is the subject only of the Second Optional Protocol to the ICCPR and does not strictly satisfy this criterion—we have gone a little further than this. We do so on the basis that there is broadly evident cross-cultural support for the claim of right in question, and that it is only a matter of time before it gains full international recognition.

One has to recognise, nonetheless, that many of the intellectual assumptions underlying current international civil and political human rights standards are of European cultural origin, and that much of the friction and misunderstanding which sometimes characterise international debates on human rights reflect the differences between liberal democracies, on the one hand, and countries where individual rights have no strong foundation in the national culture, on the other. It is obviously important to appreciate the cultural and social context from which other nations assess questions of individual rights, although there is a big difference between understanding and endorsing. If we judge that certain rights are fundamental and universal, then there is an obligation on us to defend those rights. After all, we are not dealing here with rights that exist only within a particular cultural context, but with those which are, overwhelmingly, enshrined in the Universal Declaration of Human Rights and in widely ratified, legally binding covenants and conventions. There is no culture that does not value human dignity and no country which seriously suggests that the Universal Declaration does not apply to it. We do the victims of injustice no good to dress their tormentors in the respectable garb of cultural relativism.

The last feature of our bilateral representations worth recording is that Australia does not, and should not, shrink from having the tables turned. Some countries to which we make representations have reacted with accusations that Australia is itself a human rights violator, most notably with regard to the treatment of Australian Aboriginal (and Islander) people. In such circumstances, we readily admit the past wrongs done to the Aboriginal people and acknowledge that much more remains to be done, in practice, before Aboriginal Australians can truly be said to be equal participants in the Australian community. At the same time, we point to the absolute equality of the Aboriginal people in law, and the many practical measures taken by governments, now and over many years, to redress the situation. Indeed, we have found that our willingness to discuss the plight of Aboriginal Australians becomes a useful step towards a dialogue on the position of minority groups in other countries.

These four features—consistency, attention to detail, a focus on universal rights, and a willingness to respond to criticisms directed at us—combine to give Australia's human rights policy a basic credibility. They also combine, importantly, to minimise—if not entirely remove—the danger of hostile backlash when we make human rights representations. In making such representations, whether at ministerial or official level, it is extremely helpful to be able to make the point that the country in question is not being singled out, and that we are trying to apply universal values consistently, repeatedly and without double standards.

None of this is to suggest that Australia's human rights policy involves the uncomplicated application of high principle irrespective of the consequences. There are obviously times when we have to make choices about how best to handle a human rights issue in order to be effective and protect our national interests at the same time. With careful handling, human rights policies need not conflict with the short-term needs of other policies to achieve political, defence, trade, investment, tourism, and other objectives, and it is our judgment that to date they have not.

Australia is not one of those countries that abandons its human rights concerns in the face of commercial opportunity. A case in point was our decision to make available an Australian expert to take part in the United Nations investigation into allegations, subsequently proven, of Iraqi use of chemical weapons against Iran. Several other countries which were approached declined, in large part out of concern for their intensive commercial relations with Iraq. We participated, notwithstanding our own significant trade links with Iraq, and those links continued (at least up until the sanctions imposed following Iraq's invasion of Kuwait in August 1990).

Certainly bilateral human rights representations have, from time to time, met with resistance and sometimes hostility on the part of individual interlocutors, especially when the country concerned is not accustomed to receiving human rights representations. But despite such reactions by individual officials, there has been no identifiable instance where a country has retaliated in economic or other unrelated areas to human rights criticisms. Indeed, in some cases, such as the Philippines and Turkey, initial hostility has been followed by real co-operation on individual cases. And in other cases (like Vietnam, Indonesia, Peru and China) we have been able to establish a dialogue on human rights issues which is, by all accounts of the experience of other countries, unique.

All efforts in support of human rights entail fine judgments about how best to achieve results—which is the yardstick by which our endeavours must ultimately be measured. We must make a judgment, for example, about how public our efforts should be. There are occasions, for example in relation to Burma, when measured public criticism of oppressive regimes has had its place. But more often, repeated quiet entreaties—grinding away at an administration—are more effective. It is clear that grandstanding can be very counter-productive. At best, it draws attention to an issue but with virtually no prospect of achieving improvements. At worst, it can lead to a hardening of attitudes, and even execution of the victims—as happened not long ago with ill-judged public comments by some Western governments on the human rights plight of particular individuals in Iran and Ethiopia.

Judgments are also required on the difficult questions of what actions, additional to representations and humanitarian appeals, ought to be pursued in support of our human rights policy. For instance, if we are considering placing a trade embargo against a country, we must first ask ourselves what will be achieved by it. In most cases, we have come to the view that trade embargoes or other punitive measures are not an effective way to bring about human rights reforms. They tend to be very blunt instruments. In many instances the capacity to influence events is greater, the more diverse the bilateral relationship. South Africa has been an exception, simply because apartheid is so far beyond the moral pale; because there have been so very few other avenues of persuasion; and because the (now vindicated) judgment of the Australian government has been that mandatory economic sanctions—and particularly financial sanctions—would prove to be effective.

Another important question is the relationship between aid and human rights. This issue has been addressed in some detail, although not entirely consistently, in two recent reports by the Parliamentary Joint Committee on Foreign Affairs, Defence and Trade—on Australia's Aid Program, and on Australia's Relations with the South Pacific, respectively.[1] Aid has an obviously important role to play in improving human rights in the broadest sense of the term, i.e. when economic, social and cultural values and interests are taken into account. And human rights considerations ought to be taken into account when formulating aid programs, not least in determining how effective aid delivery is likely to be in the country in question, given prevailing political, social and economic conditions. But experience has shown that it is not necessarily helpful to try to directly link—as some advocate—the level of Australian aid to the recipient's human rights performance in any obvious carrot-and-stick fashion.

We should never lose sight of the fundamental point that our primary objective in both aid policy and human rights policy is to improve the situation on the ground for the ordinary citizen. There have been occasions —such as in Fiji after the coups, in China after the Beijing massacre and in Burma—when a temporary suspension of aid, in tandem with other strategies, can be used to signal concerns about human rights abuses. The only way one can really approach these delicate and complex situations is not by trying to lay down ground-rules in advance, but on a case-by-case basis. Such an approach takes into account all the circumstances of a particular situation and does not serve to make the plight of ordinary people worse, but at the same time takes advantage of opportunities as they arise to encourage recipient governments to desist from human rights abuses.

It is a reasonable conclusion to date that on these various matters of judgment and approach Australia has made the right calls. One can certainly point to some results. Of all the bilateral representations we received, on average, responses to nearly 20 per cent of them. It is difficult to precisely assess success rates, but it is calculated that, on average again, there has been some form of positive result in 10 to 15 per cent of all cases raised. This includes, for example, advice that a detainee has been released, or an assurance that steps are being taken to ensure that the human rights of an individual are being protected. We do not of course claim sole credit for all these successes, such as they are, in that many of the individual cases were also the subject of representations by other countries.

For all the dramatic change in the international environment in recent times, we are still a long way from the advent of a world, foreshadowed in the preamble to the Universal Declaration of Human Rights, in which all human beings shall enjoy freedom of speech and belief, and their life and personal liberty. But if the quest is a long one, perhaps a never-ending one, we should not lose sight of the progress that has been made. In the forty years since the Universal Declaration was penned, we have seen its high ideals accepted as fundamental truths by the majority of the world's governments. And from that base, the international community has gone on to forge other weapons—other standard-setting instruments—which reinforce that irrefutable assertion set out in the first article of the Universal Declaration: that all human beings are born free and equal in dignity and rights.

Successive Australian governments have played an honourable part in this process. The Hawke Government has been committed to keeping Australia at the forefront of international efforts to safeguard human rights. The duties of good international citizenship are and must remain a high priority of our foreign policy so long as we take seriously our obligations to guarantee human rights at home and defend them abroad.

PROTECTING THE GLOBAL ENVIRONMENT

While the curriculum of foreign policy is often revised and updated, it is rare for a major new subject to be added to it. But in what seems like a very short time, protection of the global environment has emerged as one of the most pressing issues facing the world. The greenhouse effect, protection of the ozone layer, the future of tropical rainforests, the protection of Antarctica, and the sustainable development of fishing resources have all become part of the lexicon of international diplomacy. An increasing number of nations now recognise that international co-operation on the environment warrants at least as much attention and effort as other endeavours—like arms control and disarmament—directed at maintaining global security.

Concern over the environment was apparent in the 1960s and early 1970s over issues like population growth and air pollution, while focus on the conservation of energy became acute for a time after the quadrupling of oil prices by the Organisation of Petroleum Exporting Countries (OPEC) in 1973. The United Nations Environment Programme (UNEP), with its headquarters in Nairobi, was established in 1972 after a conference on the human environment called by the United Nations on the initiative of Sweden. But the mood of the early 1980s was one of absorption in issues of profit and growth, and it was not until towards the end of the decade that environmental issues successfully clawed themselves back on to the inter-national agenda.

Several developments in the second half of the 1980s brought the issues squarely before governments and their advisers. First, several dramatic reports were widely publicised. A conference in Villach in 1985 drew attention to the greenhouse effect and examined strategies to cope with global warming and the prospect of changes in climate and rises in sea levels; in 1987 came the Brundtland Report from the United Nations's World Commission on Environment and Development, dealing with pov-erty as a major source of environmental degradation, and introducing the concept of 'sustainable development'; and the British Antarctic Survey's discovery in 1988 of a hole in the ozone layer above the Antarctic continent gave dramatic new impetus to the already emerging consensus for limits on the use of chlorofluorocarbons. Secondly, there was the Chernobyl disaster in 1986. Thirdly, the environmentalists began to take their concerns to the ballot box. Green parties sprang into action in a number of countries, some of them winning enough seats to directly influence policy outcomes, but all of them putting pressure on established governments and bureaucracies to act.

Australia has been immune to none of these developments. An immense public, and political, consciousness is now alert not only to the local but also to the international dimensions of environmental issues. It is very widely understood that there is no more clear-cut example of global inter-dependence than the global environment. We cannot erect national fences to insulate us from the threats of environmental degradation which are global in scope. We cannot legislate to keep out of our national territories gases that destroy the ozone layer or upset the finely tuned rhythms of nature.

But for Australia, the imperative to help resolve global and regional environmental problems goes well beyond their implications for our own national environment. Environmental problems, if unchecked, could threaten our security. They could weaken our economic infrastructure and trade prospects. Climate change, for example, has potential implications for our energy exports, especially coal, and for our agricultural productivity. The increased costs incurred by some industries through environmental taxes and regulations may result in pressure on governments to protect these industries through trade restrictions, with flow-on effects for Australia's multilateral trading interests. These are all potential costs which need to be kept under close review. On the other side of the ledger, greater international sensitivity to the causes of climate change could open up new trade opportunities for Australia in such areas as organically grown foodstuffs, alternative power sources and anti-pollution technologies. More importantly, the potential economic, social and security costs of not acting to avert environmental threats are massive.

Even if it were possible for the Australian continent itself to be insulated from environmental degradation, we would still face grave consequences from environmental threats in our region and beyond. A rise in sea levels, to take just one example, would have a devastating effect on the small island countries of the South Pacific. It would destabilise a region of primary strategic interest to Australia. It would create in its wake scores of thousands of 'environmental refugees' who would look mainly to Australia for resettlement. It would place heavy additional demands on our aid program. In short, quite apart from the cost in human misery and dislocation to the island communities, which of course are ample reasons in themselves for our concern, it would jeopardise vital Australian national interests. All these considerations lay behind the decision in 1989 to appoint an extremely distinguished Australian, the former Governor-General Sir Ninian Stephen, to the newly created position of Ambassador for the Environment, to act as the focal point for our international environmental activity.

This chain of enlightened self-interest constitutes a compelling case for international co-operation. But it is not, in itself, a sufficient basis for effective action. Common interests only get us to the starting gate. If we are to finish the course we also need to address the many complex issues of equity, responsibility and development that lie at the heart of the issue. These are, in a sense, the conceptual hurdles which need to be overcome if common interests are to be translated into common action on specific environmental problems.

A fundamental issue is the relationship between growth, development and environmental protection. The Brundtland Report dealt with this linkage within the framework of 'sustainable development', which has since become the guiding principle of the economics of environmental protection. Sustainable development rejects the false dichotomy between economic growth and the protection of the environment. It is elegantly defined in the Brundtland Report as 'meeting the needs of the present without compromising the ability of future generations to meet their own needs'[2] 'Economy' and 'ecology', as has often been observed, both come from the same Greek word—'*oikos*'—meaning household management. They are two sides of the same coin. For sustainable development to become a reality, however, it must not only meet the test of balance but also, in the international context, of equity. There are going to be costs, quite possibly heavy costs, in meeting the new environmental responsibilities that will be forced upon us. Developing countries, trying as they are to cope with major and long-standing existing social deprivation, cannot be expected to share this burden unaided. The adjustment will have to be equitably shared, and in a way that recognises the inter-connection of this problem with other problems—of population growth, international trade, debt and development.

Communities living on the margin of survival are concerned not to endanger their fragile productive base. Individuals and nations in dire straits will seek to survive now at the expense of later survival: deforestation, for example, is widespread in developing countries partly because poor people need firewood and forage for their animals. Even when they well understand the long-term damage that their fuelwood and forage-gathering activities cause, their short-term needs are so urgent that they are prepared to risk the long-term consequences. Nobody understands the harsh trade-offs between short-term and long-term conservation better than poor people in developing countries. Yet these are precisely the sort of desperate trade-offs which it is in everyone's interest to avoid. If the developed nations wish, for self-interest as much as anything else, to encourage developing countries to pursue sustainable development and to thereby refrain from economic policies which contribute to environmental problems on a global scale, they must be prepared to assist them to meet the short-term costs of such an approach. Without an equitable transfer of resources and technology from the North to the South, a new environmental order has as much chance of success as the wasted campaign of the 1970s for a new international economic order.

Climate Change   There are many urgent issues on the agenda of the global environment in which Australia is taking a close interest. Depletion of the world's stock of natural resources; the loss of biological diversity, through such practices as clearing tropical rainforests; land degradation; desertification; the disposal of radioactive and other hazardous wastes; marine pollution; protection of freshwater resources—these are all international environmental problems to which Australia can make a constructive contribution. Important as these problems are, however, they are necessarily of a different order of magnitude to the prospect of irreparable damage to our atmosphere—the canopy over our common home. The threat to our atmosphere, from what has been called the 'exhaling breath of industrialised civilisation', is the biggest ecological problem faced in this or any other age.

From all the scientific evidence accumulated to date, it is evident that something is happening to upset the fragile and delicate atmospheric balance on which life depends. We know that it has the potential to make an impact on sea levels, agriculture, energy use, and indeed on the whole network of international economic and political relations. We do not know at this stage precisely what is happening and how far-reaching the impact will be. In a number of respects—on the timing, magnitude and regional pattern of climate change—the scientific jury is still out. But the problem is that by the time the jury finally returns its verdict, the damage to our planet may be irreversible. So the time to recognise the enormity of the problem, and to make a global response to it, is not one or two decades hence, when the scientific evidence may be complete and irrefutable: the time to act is now.

A good start has been made in the 1987 Montreal Protocol on Substances that Deplete the Ozone Layer; in the 1989 Declaration of The Hague on the preservation of the atmosphere; in the work of the Intergovernmental Panel on Climate Change; and in work being done by the OECD. But we need to promote universal adherence to those conventions already negotiated, and to develop new instruments to deal with climate change. We need more research, including contributions from the private sector, which also has a great deal at stake. We need to extend more practical assistance to countries to implement environment protection programs, and we need to strengthen the institutional authority of the United Nations to deal with environmental issues. It is important that the United Nations system rises to the challenge posed by the environmental threat. It is not enough for it to be a forum for statements of concern about the environment. It must also be able to demonstrate that it can do something; that it has the means of co-ordinating international efforts and of crafting agreements which directly address environmental problems.

Australia needs to continue to inject a regional perspective into the discussions. The South Pacific, with its vast expanses of ocean, low-lying atolls, and dependence on agricultural exports and tourism, has a particular and obvious concern about climate change and rising sea levels. Environmental issues more generally have in fact been an element in the forging of regional co-operation in the South Pacific. Nuclear-waste dumping has been a long-standing regional concern; the destruction of chemical weapons by the United States at Johnston Atoll a more recent one. Opposition to nuclear testing in the South Pacific has been driven largely by worries on the part of island countries that testing would contaminate their ocean environment. More recently, the region has been at the forefront of international efforts to ban driftnet fishing—so aptly described as the 'wall of death' because of its indiscriminate pillaging of marine living resources. Australian policy has been responsive to all these concerns through commitment to exchanging information and undertaking research and monitoring of climate changes; through our support for regional conventions like the South Pacific Regional Environment Protection Convention (SPREP); and through working to ensure that South Pacific interests are addressed in broader international forums and by the major powers.

Antarctica   It is perhaps inevitable that most of the international effort on environmental issues is threat driven, aimed at overcoming or containing problems which are already upon us or just around the corner. Yet, as in health care, prevention is equally if not more important than cure. This is why Prime Minister Bob Hawke and his French counterpart Michel Rocard took the lead in 1989—against the opposition of many important countries —to prevent once and for all any future mining and oil drilling in Antarctica, and to turn this magnificent and fragile wilderness continent into an internationally protected wilderness park.

Prior to the Australia–France initiative, the general consensus among parties to the Antarctic Treaty was that it was possible to reconcile mining and oil drilling in Antarctica with environmental protection. It was argued that it was unrealistic to exclude such activity in Antarctica forever, and that it was better to have mining and drilling take place under strict controls than under no controls at all. Australia was originally part of the consensus to this effect, which was embodied in the 1988 Convention on the Regulation of Antarctic Mineral Resource Activity (CRAMRA), still awaiting ratification. But whatever appeal arguments of this kind may have had in the past, the very clear judgment is now held by Australia, on a bipartisan basis with strong public support, that they should not be our guide for the present or the future.

It is simply not possible to have mining or oil drilling in a unique, fragile and irreplaceable environment such as the Antarctic without the risk of extensive environmental damage, of the kind which occurred with the Exxon Valdez spill off the coast of Alaska in 1989. We do not believe that the international community ought to accept that risk, however distant actual mining in Antarctica may be. A further important consideration is that mining and oil drilling, should they ever come to Antarctica, are most likely to take place in that 2 per cent or so of the continent near the coast, and in off-shore areas—the very areas where wildlife is congregated and where human interference could be disastrous.

So on May 1989 the Government announced that it was opposed to mining taking place in Antarctica and would not sign CRAMRA. Instead, it would seek to persuade its Antarctic Treaty partners to set aside CRAMRA and to negotiate a new instrument which would provide for a comprehensive protection of Antarctica as a 'Nature Reserve—Land of Science'. The Government committed itself to an intense campaign of diplomatic activity by ministers and officials which was itself directed towards persuading treaty parties at the then next Antarctic Treaty Consultative Meeting (ATCM XV), scheduled for Paris in October 1989, to convene a Special Consultative Meeting on comprehensive environmental protection. This was one of the most difficult Antarctic Treaty meetings ever held. Some nineteen Treaty parties had signed CRAMRA, and many were not convinced that it should be set aside or that a new environmental protection instrument was required. However, in a significant diplomatic achievement in the circumstances, the meeting did finally decide to convene a Special Consultative Meeting in 1990 to explore and discuss all proposals relating to the comprehensive protection of the Antarctic environment.

The following twelve months was a period of intense diplomatic and, importantly, public activity by Australia and France in support of their initiative. In March and again in October 1990 they circulated to other Treaty parties further detailed proposals. It had become apparent by the middle of that year that the initiative had taken on considerable momentum and, although many still did not fully accept our ideas on mining, a consensus had begun to emerge on the need for a more comprehensive protection regime. The weight of public opinion, stimulated by the international political campaigning in which non-government organisations had taken an increasingly prominent part, was at last beginning to overwhelm entrenched bureaucratic opposition. National governments, long accustomed to regarding Antarctic Treaty matters as wholly arcane and best left to the technicians, simply had to start giving directions. When the Special Consultative Meeting convened in October 1990, in Vina del Mar in Chile, the negotiating climate was very much better than at the Paris meeting, and agreement was quickly reached to negotiate a legal instrument. An outline draft was accepted as a basis for that negotiation. It contained draft proposals for environmental conduct including prior impact assessment of activity, institutional machinery, compliance and dispute settlement provisions. And it also contained a draft prohibition on Antarctic mineral resource activity.

Expectations were accordingly high by the time the Antarctic Treaty parties met again, in Madrid in April 1991, for the next round of detailed negotiations. But the outcome exceeded even the most optimistic prediction. After long and difficult discussion, consensus was reached to recommend to governments the text of an Environment Protection Protocol which prohibited mining absolutely for fifty years—and continued that prohibition indefinitely so long as any one of the existing consultative parties (i.e. including Australia or France) vetoed a relaxation of the mining ban. All that remained was for governments to formally endorse the Protocol, and a further meeting was convened in Madrid in June 1991 for this purpose.

The euphoria of the conservationists—not to mention the Australian Government—proved, however, to be a little premature. The United States Government refused to endorse the 'Madrid I' consensus, and sent its negotiators back to the table with a much tougher position: although accepting a fifty-year moratorium on mining, they demanded that any country dissatisfied with a continuing prohibition after that time have the right to withdraw from the no-mining clause in the Protocol. But international opinion had by now moved so far in favour of a mining ban that this degree of backsliding was simply unacceptable to the other Treaty parties. After more very difficult negotiations, a compromise was hammered out: the fifty-year prohibition would stay, and relaxation of it thereafter could be blocked by just a quarter of the present consultative parties (i.e. seven countries); moreover, if any country wanted to pursue mining in the face of such a blocking exercise, it would have to walk away not just from the anti-mining clause but from the entire Environment Protection Protocol, and bear the political pain accordingly. 'Madrid II' broke up with the United States still reserving its position, but within a few days —under strong pressure from the rest of the international Antarctic community, led again by Australia and France—President Bush had announced that his country would in fact join the consensus there reached.

For thirty years the Antarctic Treaty has protected the Antarctic environment, kept Antarctica free of political conflict, and preserved it as an area of scientific inquiry from which nuclear weapons and military activities are prohibited. Australia's Antarctic initiative sought to build on this unique achievement, within the framework of the Antarctic Treaty system. In the diplomatic marketplace, where realism is the currency of trade, it is unusual to seek to expand the definition of what is possible. But that is precisely what was required, and it is what our Antarctic initiative set out to achieve. Consensus, as always in Antarctic matters, proved enormously difficult to achieve. But the final outcome provides infinitely greater protection for the Antarctic than could have been anticipated at the outset of the campaign. Australia—with France—has the satisfaction of knowing that we have fundamentally changed the terms of the environmental debate about the future of a whole continent.

PART III

RELATIONSHIPS

11

The South Pacific

THE SOUTH PACIFIC—encompassing New Zealand, Papua New Guinea and the arc of island states and territories stretching across 10 000 kilometres of ocean from Guam to Pitcairn—is for Australia, in all sorts of ways, the part of the world closest to home. It is where we have some of our most long-standing and comfortable diplomatic relationships. It is where we have an intricate maze of economic, political, development, defence, and personal connections. And it is where a good deal of our history has been made.

The South Pacific is also the part of the world where we are thought to exercise most influence—because of our history as a colonial power, our geographic proximity, our very comprehensive diplomatic network, our significance as an aid donor, and simply our combination of massive relative size, wealth and market power. And therein lies a foreign policy problem for Australia. If we do choose to exercise such influence as we possess, and are successful, then we expose ourselves to criticism on the grounds of insensitivity, neo-colonialism or, given our professed commitment to internationalist principles, hypocrisy. If we choose not to seek to impose any particular outcome upon a situation, we expose ourselves to allegations of neglect or policy drift. And if we do seek to exert influence in any overt way, and do not succeed, then we expose ourselves at best to embarrassment and at worst to a much-reduced capacity to exert any influence in the future.

The notion of a country like Australia trying, but failing, to impose its will in a region like the South Pacific is not far-fetched. It is not just a matter of the dangers of backlash, both in the country concerned and in the region at large, in any crude assertion of military or economic power. It means appreciating that in a region of fragile micro-states, where every institution is highly personalised, there is less susceptibility than might be thought to the logic of relative size and power. And it is a matter of recognising that, however small or impecunious a micro-state might be, it wants in every case to be and remain genuinely independent.

CONSTRUCTIVE COMMITMENT

What kind of policy stance should, then, Australia adopt towards its region? The first possible policy option is benign neglect: doing nothing at all to move events, other than reacting *ad hoc* when Australian interests appear to be directly threatened. But this is manifestly not an option at all, given the range and extent of Australian interests in the region, and the expectations that exist about our participation in it. The South Pacific is an area of primary strategic interest for us, in which we have a clear interest in promoting peace and stability, including keeping the region free from destabilising activity by any external power or group. It is an area of commercial importance for us. Not only is New Zealand our third largest export market overall, and Papua New Guinea our fourth largest for elaborately transformed manufactured goods, but the Pacific island states generally buy a range of Australian products, some $1.2 billion worth in 1988/89; the region, moreover, accounts for nearly 20 per cent of Australia's investment overseas. And, not least, the South Pacific area is important to us—as we are to it—simply for good international citizenship reasons, as reflected for example in our very extensive development co-operation programs, and our engagement in crucial regional environmental issues, like driftnet fishing and climate-change induced sea-level rises.

A second option is for us to seek an activist role as the guardian of Western alliance interests, with a mission to deny access to the Soviets or anyone else potentially hostile to those interests. But this founders on a number of rocks. For a start, it rather assumes that Australia has no interests in the region separate and distinct from those of the Western alliance, and that is manifestly not the case. Secondly, there is a conceptual problem in applying the notions of 'gatekeeper', 'policeman' or 'Western lake',[1] all signifying denial of access to some identifiable adversary, when one is dealing with a totally accessible region with diffuse assets not in much demand. Thirdly, the horses seem largely to have bolted anyway, with the Soviet Union concluding fishing arrangements with Kiribati in 1985 and Vanuatu in 1987, and establishing a diplomatic presence in Papua New Guinea in 1990, quite apart from the less-than-effusive contribution made to the Western alliance itself by New Zealand's ship-visits policy since 1985.

Fourthly, there is not much evidence that any horses that have not already bolted would be very interested nowadays in leaving the stable anyway: the Soviet Union has other preoccupations (and has not in fact sought to renew either the Kiribati or Vanuatu agreements), and not much has been heard of the Libyans—let alone anyone else—since 1987.

A third option is for Australia to seek to become a regional hegemonist in its own right, unilaterally mobilising all the influence we can command across the whole range of our own interests. Certainly Australian nationalists of the late nineteenth century believed that in time their country would inherit the dominant position of the European colonial powers. It was thought inconceivable that the Pacific countries themselves could sustain an independent existence. The way of the world was for the strong to dominate, or at best to protect, the weak, and Australia would rise irresistibly to become 'mistress of the South Seas'. This echoed in a minor key the sentiment of the Monroe Doctrine, by which the United States (albeit with the implicit support of the British) declared its intention to keep foreign powers out of Central and South America. But the Monroe Doctrine was proclaimed in 1823, and by the time the colonial powers—the French apart—were prepared to take their leave of the South Pacific a century-and-a-half later, the assumptions underlying the notions of 'hegemony' and 'spheres of influence' were no longer so obvious.

Quite apart from questions of principle, the problem with any country attempting to throw its weight around in a region like the South Pacific is that it is more likely than not to fail. The United States has learned often enough in Latin America that military intervention, while it can bring quick results that seem to unequivocally advantage the interventionist at the time, as often as not merely postpone the resolution of more abiding political problems. And the same applies to the exercise of raw economic power. If the dominance of the United States in its own hemisphere has been a mixed blessing, the dominance of the Soviet Union in East Europe was an unmixed liability, and Japan's attempt to dominate its region in the fashion of the European powers was a disaster. Dominance, by anyone, is not the answer in the South Pacific.

That leaves as the only viable policy option, in our judgment, what the Foreign Minister called 'constructive commitment' when first enunciating it in 1988.[2] This entails maintaining and developing a partnership with Pacific Island countries which promotes regional stability through economic development and the encouragement of shared perceptions of strategic and security interest.

This general approach has a number of specific dimensions to it: promotion of close, confident and broadly based bilateral relations with all Pacific island countries; promotion of effective regional co-operation, especially through the South Pacific Forum and other regional organisations like the South Pacific Commission; recognition that, for Pacific island countries, security hinges on economic and social development, and offering assistance to achieve both; respect for the full sovereignty of all Pacific island states, in relation to their internal affairs and their right to establish diplomatic and commercial links with countries from outside the region; and promotion, at the same time, of shared perceptions of the region's strategic and security interests, laying the basis for a regional approach to situations, internal or external, which put regional stability at risk.

Partnership and mutual respect are the central elements. Constructive commitment simply cannot involve any vestige of old colonialism or new hegemony. Australia is in a position to be a helpful neighbour. We do have assets we can bring to bear including our direct aid support, our connections with the international financial institutions and other multilateral agencies, our defence co-operation programs, and our diplomatic willingness to raise regional concerns bilaterally and in multilateral forums. We may wish to warn, counsel and advise, and there will certainly be many occasions when we will wish to persuade. Partnership implies give and take, and there is no need to be falsely modest, or shrink from being firm in the defence of Australian interests and values. But we should never seek to exercise control. Overall, constructive commitment requires consistency and patience, backed by demonstrable interest, adequate levels of resources, flexibility in the formulation of policy and sensitivity in its implementation.

The concept of constructive commitment was originally formulated with the Pacific island countries other than New Zealand in mind, and some of its elements—in particular economic and social development assistance—clearly are not intended to apply to New Zealand. But its basic elements *are* necessarily applicable to all our South Pacific neighbours, without exception. It would be utterly at odds with the notions of respect for sovereignty and partnership to treat countries with different degrees of respect simply because of their different sizes. In many respects the content of Australia's bilateral relationships does differ as between New Zealand and Papua New Guinea and the smaller island countries—just as it differs between the smaller island countries themselves. But on the fundamental questions at the heart of our relationships with all the countries of the South Pacific region, there can be no differences of approach at all.

NEW ZEALAND

Australia and New Zealand are as close as two countries that almost became one could be. At the National Australasian Convention in Sydney in 1891, at which the trans-Tasman colony was represented along with its six Australian mainland counterparts, Alfred Deakin likened New Zealand to 'a coy maiden, not unwilling, and indeed expecting to be courted, and whose consent would be granted by and by as a favour'.[3] In the event, of course, that consent was not forthcoming. That it was not, perhaps owed something to the spirit personified at the Australasian Federal Conference in Melbourne a year earlier, when Captain William Russell said that he did not think there would be a marriage of affection between New Zealand and the Australian colonies—and if there were to be a *marriage de convenance*, then New Zealand would have to seek refuge in the Married Women's Property Act![4]

A marriage there may not have been in the 1890s, and a marriage there may never be—although that debate has regained a little life in recent years. But a sense of family has, nonetheless, been an omnipresent theme in the relationship ever since. The ANZAC tradition created in 1915 in Gallipoli did more than anything else to bond it, and the language of siblingship—following different career paths, but remaining close—is a better way than most to describe it. People-to-people links across the Tasman are enormously close—with over 200 000 New Zealand citizens living in Australia, and a two-way flow of over a million-and-a-half crossing the Tasman each year—and there is a strong sense of common cultural identity.

The official and institutional ties are endless. The most important of these is unquestionably now the Australian and New Zealand Closer Economic Relationship Trade Agreement (ANZCERTA, or CER for short) which has kept steadily ahead of the timetable proposed when it was established in 1983. All barriers to trans-Tasman trade in goods—creating in this respect a single market—were removed by July 1990, instead of 1995 as originally anticipated. Subsequent decisions by the Australian Government have eased the way for participation in the aviation and telecommunications areas, and remaining outstanding issues, involving some other services and some formal impediments to investment, are being steadily worked through. Systematic attention is also being paid to the harmonisation of business law, customs and quarantine procedures, and everything else that might expand or inhibit, as the case may be, the economic relationship.

Both countries have unquestionably benefited economically from the CER achievement to date. Since 1983 total bilateral trade has grown from A\$1.99 billion (NZ\$2.5 billion) to A\$4.5 billion (NZ\$5.6 billion). This is an average annual growth rate of about 15 per cent, and faster than the growth in either country's trade with the rest of the world. Today New Zealand is Australia's fourth-largest trading partner and Australia is New Zealand's largest. Both countries are significant markets for each other's manufactured goods, and we have become major markets for each other's services. The balance of trade is roughly equal. Even in the absence yet of any special facilitation for investment (inhibited by Australia's commitments under its Treaty of Nara with Japan which prohibits discriminatory favours elsewhere), total trans-Tasman investment has grown from approximately A\$1.5 billion when the CER Agreement came into force, to over A\$10 billion in 1989.

Bilateral issues aside, Australia and New Zealand co-operate closely on international economic issues through, in particular, our joint membership of the Cairns Group and APEC. There is invariably a close working relationship in the whole range of other multilateral bodies—not least in the South Pacific—to which we both belong. The process of co-operation is very much assisted by the fact that New Zealand and Australian ministers and officials see a good deal of each other. In the case of foreign ministers, this has been formalised into full-scale *tour d'horizon* consultations every six months to supplement the numerous other specific meetings which occur on an *ad hoc* basis. But the pattern is similar across the whole portfolio range: New Zealand ministers or senior officials now attend, on a regular formalised basis, fully twenty-two separate Commonwealth–State forums.

Defence ties are no exception to any of this. Apart from the ANZAC Pact of 1944, which was established mainly to assert the rights of the two countries to be principals in the negotiations over Pacific territories following World War II, the main formal expression of the link is the Australia–New Zealand leg of the ANZUS Treaty of 1951. This remains firmly in place even if the New Zealand–United States leg does not, following the decision of the Labour Government in 1985—so far confirmed by its successor—to deny the entry to New Zealand ports of ships which may be nuclear armed. In addition there is our joint membership of the Five Power Defence Arrangements with Malaysia, Singapore and the United Kingdom. Specific co-operative activities between the two countries include regular high-level consultations, combined exercises, training and personnel exchanges, logistic co-operation and joint activity in the region involving, especially, co-ordinated air and naval surveillance with South Pacific countries and the Forum Fisheries Agency. And New Zealand's decision to purchase two ANZAC frigates ensured, apart from anything else, a continued capability to operate effectively with the Australian Navy.

The commonality of approach and outlook that is so much a part of the Australia–New Zealand relationship can sometimes manifest itself in striking ways. An example is the Foreign Minister's 1989 Statement on *Australia's Regional Security*[5] which was criticised in some quarters for not dealing in any detail with the trans-Tasman relationship. The omission, however, was explained by Senator Evans when tabling the Statement in the Senate. It was a function, he said, of the relationship between Australia and New Zealand being *so* close—as an ally, CER partner and otherwise—that it did not call for attention in the context of an outward-looking statement exploring possible risks to security in our regional environment.[6]

All that said, there are differences between the two countries which do manifest themselves from time to time, not just in intense sporting and social rivalry but policy approach. Certainly the social development of the two countries has been different. New Zealand remains closer to its British origins, not having experienced an influx of non-British European and

Asian migration to the extent Australia has. And it does have closer social links with the South Pacific. New Zealand's indigenous Maori community (more than 10 per cent of the population) is of Polynesian origin and, having been in residence for several centuries before Abel Tasman landed in 1642, claims proprietorial rights. Under the Treaty of Waitangi in 1840 the Maoris ceded sovereignty to the British, but recent New Zealand governments have renewed a commitment to honour the terms of the treaty in respect of claims to Crown land, employment and training opportunities. The Maoris, with more recent immigrants from the Cook Islands, Niue and Samoa in particular, provide New Zealand with a concentration of Polynesian population which causes some stresses but also gives the country a store of credit in its dealings with its immediate region, and occasionally a different perspective from Australia in its approach to regional issues.

New Zealand also retains a more traditional economic base than Australia. Like Australia, it has passed through a hectic period of budgetary constraint, financial deregulation and economic restructuring, seeking to become more competitive on a broader base of economic activity. It remains, however, even more dependent than Australia on rural exports. While our views on multilateral trade policy issues are very similar, there are differences in perspective, based not only on the size of the two markets (17 million as compared with 3.4 million), which makes for bilateral sensitivities in various areas from time to time. For instance, the New Zealand Dairy Board's monopoly over the marketing of all dairy products has been perceived as unfair by the less regulated Australian industry, especially where the Board has directly supported New Zealand investment into the Australian market. Equally, the New Zealand car assembly and component industries have deemed Australian levels of government support for its manufacturers in these areas as unfairly impinging upon their ability to compete in their home market, let alone in Australia. Waterfront and shipping reform has also been a recent point of contention as the varying pace of reform on the sides of the Tasman has direct effect on the costs associated with trans-Tasman trade.

There are other differences between the two countries arising naturally from their size and location. New Zealand does not share Australia's interest in the Indian Ocean. It has not had as testing a responsibility as has Australia in divesting itself of the colony of Papua New Guinea nor of forging a relationship with a neighbour as large as Indonesia. It does not have an Asian frontier. And in recent years some quite important differences have opened up around the primacy we have been respectively prepared to give to our membership of the Western alliance.

Australia's views on New Zealand's continuing ship-visit policy, and its implications for ANZUS, remain quite straightforward. First, the 'NCND' (neither confirm nor deny) policy adopted by the United States in respect of its nuclear-capable vessels is a logically consistent and defensible one. It has to be recognised that difficulties would be caused for the United States in a number of other countries if the policy were to be selectively breached or modified, with serious implications for its capacity to play its present global role. And there is a credible operational need to protect information, not only about which ships are, but just as importantly those ships which are *not*, carrying nuclear weapons. Secondly, it is a necessary incident of an alliance relationship that the parties to it be prepared, among other things, to facilitate port access for each other's vessels. Thirdly, it is an inevitable consequence of the incompatible positions adopted by the United States and New Zealand that the United States–New Zealand leg of ANZUS should be suspended so long as that incompatibility remains. Fourthly, given the tripartite character of ANZUS, there is no reason why either the Australia–United States or Australia–New Zealand legs of the relationship should be affected—as indeed they have not been. And fifthly, while it is difficult to see much room for improvement in defence and security matters between New Zealand and the United States so long as the present impasse continues, there is no reason whatever for any other areas of the New Zealand–United States relationship to suffer as a result of it. While Australia has taken the view that the whole controversy is essentially one for the United States and New Zealand to resolve bilaterally, we have sought to make our position on this last aspect of the matter particularly clearly understood in Washington.

The issue will not be an easy one to resolve. The United States seems unlikely to change its policy in any relevant way in the foreseeable future, and looking for a linguistic solution to the problem is like hunting the snark. While one understands any country wanting to be able to engage in such policy luxury as its geography allows it, and while there are many countries who would like to be able to give equally robust expression to their anti-nuclear credentials, hard choices on occasions have to be confronted. The hard choice here goes to participation in the Western alliance: whether one wants to be a contributing partner—as Australia has decided to be for all the reasons spelt out in earlier chapters—or whether one prefers to opt out.

The present New Zealand Government has shown in a number of ways, not only by its military involvement in the Gulf crisis, that it does see it as being in New Zealand's longer term interest to play a larger role in global and regional security matters. But it is finding it very difficult to take the necessary next steps. Until that happens, presumably on the basis of a gradual shift in public opinion, there seems destined to be a continuation of this one major policy difference—and it really is the only one—between Australia and New Zealand.

PAPUA NEW GUINEA

If 'family' metaphors are part of the general charm of the Australia–New Zealand relationship, Papua New Guineans must sometimes feel a little oppressed by their application to Australia's relationship with its closest northern neighbour. This is because the metaphor in this case is invariably parental—inevitably so given the circumstances of Papua New Guinea's birth as an independent nation in 1975. Parents and their offspring can of course be just as close as siblings—and indeed are often more so—but the difficulty is to draw a line that will be universally understood between the parental relationship and a paternal one.

There are those in Australia who will never understand that Papua New Guinea is a child no longer, but a fully grown, independent young nation making its own way in the world and its own decisions about its priorities and its future. Australia's role, given the history of our relationship and the abundant affection we retain for the country, is to be as helpful as we possibly can be with advice, assistance and encouragement. But we are neither entitled nor able to impose our will, in security matters or anything else, in a way that would once—in *Taim Bilong Masta*[7]—have been routine. We do have a responsibility of course to protect and advance our own national interests, economically, strategically and otherwise, which means that from time to time we may well have lively policy disagreements with Papua New Guinea, as with any other country important to us. But just as we can be generous without being patronising, so too can we warn, advise, counsel and cajole, in what we perceive to be both our own interests and Papua New Guinea's, without being paternalistic. Crucial to the conduct of our relationship with Papua New Guinea—as indeed with all our Pacific island neighbours—is that both affection and respect go hand in hand.

There can be no question of Papua New Guinea's importance to Australia. Its geographic proximity and consequent strategic significance alone guarantee that. But it is also, as one would expect with the nature of its resources and the size of its population, a major Australian investment destination, with a stock now of well over $2 billion. It is also a significant trading partner, with total trade in 1990 at $1.12 billion and a trade balance running at over two-to-one in Australia's favour. Over twelve thousand Australians live there, reflecting not only the complex legacy of our colonial past, but the vibrant commitment of the present day. Port Moresby is one of Australia's biggest missions, about the size of our embassy in Beijing and only slightly smaller than the Tokyo and Jakarta missions. The large amount of time spent on relations with Papua New Guinea, not only by the foreign minister and his department, but by the prime minister and his, is further evidence of the importance we attach to the country. It may sometimes be difficult for the Australian public to appreciate the need for this attention except as crisis management, but it is better seen as an investment in a mature relationship in the twenty-first century. Papua New Guinea has such potential, and Australia's interests are so substantial, that getting the relationship right at this still early stage in its evolution must be one of our highest priorities.

A good deal of attention has been paid in recent years to giving some formal shape and direction to the relationship. The Joint Declaration of Principles which Australia signed with Papua New Guinea in 1987 sets out a framework for dealing with each other in a mature and co-operative fashion, with full regard for each other's sovereign interests. The most difficult element to get right in the Declaration proved to be the security clause. Security relations had until then been governed by a 1977 joint statement:

> The two Prime Ministers . . . declared that it was their Governments' intention to consult, at the request of either, about matters affecting their common security interests and about other aspects of their defence relationship.[8]

At the time of this Declaration there had been five hundred members of the Australian defence forces serving with the Papua New Guinea Defence Force: ten years later there were just thirty-eight (albeit, however, with a defence co-operation program running at an annual expenditure of some $40 million). Papua New Guinea proposed that Australia make a more specific security commitment, suggesting language that was a little stronger than either the ANZUS Treaty[9] or the Five Power Defence Arrangements (FPDA).[10] In the result, the agreed formula became:

> The two Governments will consult, at the request of either, about matters affecting their common security interests. In the event of external armed attack threatening the national sovereignty of either country, such consultation would be conducted for the purpose of each Government deciding what measures should be taken, jointly or separately, in relation to that attack.

This language carefully balanced at least three considerations. One was that it reassured Papua New Guinea, but without being an unequivocal or automatic commitment to defend Papua New Guinea territory: Australia could, for example, decide on diplomatic, not military, measures. It thus encouraged Papua New Guinea to strengthen its own armed forces and become militarily self-reliant. Secondly, it restricted consideration to 'external armed attack threatening the national security', so it could not be interpreted to include internal security, or a common threat somewhere else in the region. It thus avoided conveying to others in the region that Australia and Papua New Guinea considered themselves joint gatekeepers or peacekeepers. Thirdly, of all the options it was the closest to the security commitment contained in the Five Power Defence Arrangements. It would have been anomalous to give Papua New Guinea a lesser security commitment than that which Australia joins in with Malaysia and Singapore, but not necessary—or desirable in terms of Australia's other regional relationships—to give it a significantly greater commitment.

Papua New Guinea was no doubt influenced to some extent in originally seeking a more explicit defence relationship with Australia by the then running sore of its border relations with Indonesia. Papuan dissidents, reacting to Indonesia's transmigration program for settling other ethnic groups in West Irian, had been crossing the border in such numbers that about 10 000 were on Papua New Guinea territory. But in early 1987 Papua New Guinea and Indonesia signed a Treaty of Mutual Respect, Friendship and Co-operation, and subsequently a number of practical arrangements—including more substantial, direct and frequent contact between Papua New Guinean and Indonesian ministers and officials—have evolved for handling bilateral issues. Although border incidents will still occur, and a major problem could again flare, a good deal of the heat has gone out of this issue in recent years. With Australia's own relations with Indonesia significantly improving over the same period, a generally more comfortable trilateral relationship between the three countries has evolved, with nothing appearing likely to threaten it in the foreseeable future.

But as Papua New Guinea's external security environment has become more settled, its internal situation has become much more difficult. By far the biggest problem has been the secessionist conflict in Bougainville, which came to a head with the forced closure by Bougainville Revolutionary Army (BRA) militants of the huge Panguna copper mine in May 1989, the subsequent escalation of violent conflict between the militants and the government's defence and police forces, and eventually the withdrawal of all central government personnel from the Province in March 1990. The government, remaining wholly committed to resisting the break-away, then applied a blockade to the main island, established—with local support—a bridgehead on the small neighbouring island of Buka, and has sought to resolve the situation by a course of peaceful negotiation. But well into 1991 the situation remains unresolved, and this continues to place strains not only on the whole Papua New Guinea economy, but on the political and security situation elsewhere in the country. Law and order had for long been a matter of serious concern by nationals and expatriates alike, especially in the larger towns as the familiar developing country problem of urban drift grew steadily larger. But that concern became acute in 1990–91, and the issue became a matter of the highest political, economic and social priority.

Against this background, the Australian and Papua New Guinea governments have embarked on a joint reassessment of the whole pattern of defence and security co-operation between the two countries, with a view to gradually shifting the balance of support from an external to an internal focus, with Papua New Guinea itself embarking on a parallel process of institutional reshaping. That process has not yet worked itself out, but the signs are that a balance of resource allocation better attuned to the real current needs of the country will emerge.

Again, Australia has had a delicate balancing act to perform—being helpful, but not over-intrusive. The use of Australian materiel on Bougainville, including helicopters—supplied in accordance with the defence co-operation arrangements between the two countries—inevitably generated a hostile reaction from some Bougainvillians and their supporters. But our attempts to set restraints on the military use of some of that equipment, and our reluctance to become involved in any more direct way, was equally the subject of some criticism from other quarters. There is simply no other guide to dealing with these situations than first principles: to fully respect our neighbour's sovereignty and independence; to be as helpful as we possibly can be; but to act always in a way that is consistent with the protection and advancement of our own national interests.

Quite apart from the defence relationship, efforts have also been made in recent times to give some general shape and direction to Australia's development assistance to Papua New Guinea. Since independence the pattern had been for Australian aid, very large by any international standards—absolute or relative—to be given in the form of lump-sum budgetary support, with only marginal amounts channelled into specifically identified projects and programs. While from one point of view a measure of respect for Papua New Guinea's independence—in that how the money was spent was essentially a matter for the country itself to decide—from another point of view this approach served only to perpetuate a degree of unhealthy reliance on external support for the day-to-day management of the country's affairs. Following the controversial decision of the Australian Government in its 1986 Budget, as part of a drastic expenditure reduction across the board, to unilaterally cut $10 million from the previously agreed support figure (a decision indelibly etched on the present Foreign Minister's psyche, because he—in his then capacity as Minister Assisting the Foreign Minister—had to go to Port Moresby to explain it), a major effort was made to put Australian assistance on a more satisfactory footing for both sides.

Under the Treaty on Development Co-operation signed by Prime Ministers Hawke and Namaliu on 24 May 1989, Australia committed itself to supplying a further $1.5 billion in development assistance over the five years to 1993/94, but with the balance between budget and project support gradually altering in favour of the latter, and with the overall amount declining in real terms over the period. It was expected that budget support would be able to be phased out entirely by around 2005, if not earlier. Already its contribution to general budget revenue will, on current estimates, have fallen from nearly 30 per cent in the early 1980s to around 10 per cent by the mid 1990s. Much depends on how quickly major revenue-producing resource projects come on-stream (and how the Bougainville conflict is finally resolved), but Papua New Guinea is generally assessed by both governments, and indeed by the whole international community, to have a sound economic future, and one that will not need to rely to the same extent over the long term on the kind of assistance the country has received to date.

Papua New Guinea's historical relationship with Australia, its size and population, its linguistic and cultural diversity, its natural resources base and economic potential, all set it apart from the other Pacific island nations, and give it a unique place in regional affairs from an Australian perspective.

But it does share with other Pacific island nations several common developmental features: an economy dependent on a narrow range of commodity exports, a disproportionately large public sector, strong population growth, rising urbanisation and social dislocation, and an extensive but relatively undeveloped agricultural sector.

THE SMALLER ISLAND COUNTRIES

While life in the South Pacific is often depicted as closer to paradise than anywhere else on earth, many of the smaller island states are struggling to survive. Most of them have a narrow economic base and depend heavily on external financial assistance. Because of this, their most valuable resource is usually their maritime Exclusive Economic Zone (EEZ). Some of these zones are huge by any standards: the fifteen Cook Islands, for example, have a land area of only 240 square kilometres but are spread over 1 800 000 square kilometres of ocean. And Kiribati is made up of thirty-three islands in three groups, with a land area of 690 square kilometres but a sea area of 3 600 000 square kilometres.

Economic growth rates are low, and in some instances coincide with high population growth rates. The drift from outer island village to main island town creates urban problems, such as unemployment and lawlessness. Few countries have a realistic prospect of building self-sustaining economies. Tourism is an important, but for most an insufficient, revenue source; traditional commodities like copra have not been strong enough support bases; fisheries, even with the vast new economic zones recognised in recent years, have not produced the revenue flows, or certainly the employment generation, that had been hoped; sea-bed mining still seems generations away.[11] Foreign aid, coupled with remittances from nationals living abroad, constitutes for all too many island countries their most reliable sources of foreign exchange.

But if there are some recurring similarities among the smaller island countries, so too is there diversity. Fiji has long been an exception to most economic generalisations about the region because of its larger population base; well-developed sugar industry; well-established tourist industry and role as a transport and distribution hub for most of the region; rapid movement into manufacturing, especially clothing, through the establishment of tax-free zones; and attempts to cultivate a variety of economic links with Asian countries of the western Pacific rim. That said, the 1987 coups and their aftermath did produce a dramatic short-term reversal of economic fortunes, and even four years later significant problems persist[12]. But Fiji's longer term economic prospects still look considerably brighter than is the case for most of its smaller neighbours.

Economics apart, there continues to be enormous social, cultural and political diversity in the region. Not only do the sub-regions of Melanesia, Micronesia and Polynesia vary immensely from each other, but so too do

The Pacific Island States and Territories

State or Territory	Constitutional Status	International Org. Membership	Land Area (sq. km)	Sea Area (sq. km)	Population	Per Capita GDP A
Melanesia						
States						
Fiji	Independent (1970) Republic (1987)	UN, SPF, SPC	18 272	1.3m	725 500	2 087
Papua New Guinea	Independent (1975) Monarchy	UN, CW, SPF, SPC	462 243	3.1m	3 463 300	1 272
Solomon Islands	Independent (1978) Monarchy	UN, CW, SPF, SPC	27 556	1.3m	292 000	718
Vanuatu	Independent (1980) Republic (formerly New Hebrides)	UN, CW, SPF, SPC	11 880	0.7m	145 000	1 225
Territory						
New Caledonia	French Overseas Territory (TOM)	SPC	19 103	1.7m	153 500	7 759
Micronesia						
States						
Federated States of Micronesia	Free Assoc. with US (1986) (formerly Caroline Islands)	SPF, SPC	701	3.0m	97 700	1 372
Kiribati	Independent (1979) Republic (formerly Gilbert Islands)	CW, SPF, SPC	690	3.6m	67 700	545
Nauru	Independent (1968) Republic	CW*, SPF, SPC	21	0.3m	8 800	9 179
Republic of the Marshall Islands	*Free Assoc. with US (1986)	SPF, SPC	181	2.1m	37 800	1 514
Territories						
Guam	US Unincorporated Territory	SPC	541	0.2m	119 800	12 913
Northern Marianas	C'wealth of the US (1986)	SPC	471	0.8m	20 600	17 888
Palau	UN Trust Territory/ US Administration	SPC	494	0.6m	14 000	3 342

State or Territory	Constitutional Status	International Org. Membership	Land Area (sq. km)	Sea Area (sq. km)	Population	Per Capita GDP A$
Polynesia						
States						
Cook Islands	Free Assoc. with NZ (1965)	SPF, SPC	240	1.8m	17 100	2 919
Niue	Free Assoc. with NZ (1974)	SPF, SPC	259	0.4m	2 500	1 553
Tonga	Independent (1970) Monarchy (Indigenous)	CW, SPF, SPC	699	0.7m	94 800	865
Tuvalu	Independent (1978) Monarchy (formerly Ellice Islands)	CW, SPF, SPC	26	0.9m	8 500	614
Western Samoa	Independent (1962)	UN, CW, SPF, SPC	2 935	0.1m	162 000	912
Territories						
American Samoa	US Territory	SPC	197	0.4m	36 700	7 336
French Polynesia	French Overseas Territory (TOM)	SPC	3 265	–	176 800	17 168
Pitcairn	British Territory	SPC	5	0.8m	100	–
Tokelau	NZ Territory	SPC	10	0.3m	1 600	–
Wallis and Futuna	French Overseas Territory (TOM)	SPC	255	0.3m	14 700	–
Totals	States 13 Territories 9	UN 5 CW 8 SPF 13 SPC 22	550 044	24.4m	5 660 500	4 799 (av)

Notes

Sources   *Pacific Islands Year Book*, 16th edition, 1989; *South Pacific Economics Statistical Summary*, 11th edition, SPC, Noumea

Dates   Population estimates as at 30 June 1987; GDP figures variable (1983–87)

Abbreviations   UN: United Nations   CW: Commonwealth   SPF: South Pacific Forum SPC: South Pacific Commission

* No right to attend Heads of Government meetings

individual states and indeed islands within states. Some of that flavour should be evident in the accompanying Table, which identifies, quite apart from anything else, a bewildering variety of constitutional arrangements among the twenty-two states and territories listed.

As compared with Melanesia, with its twelve hundred or so languages in five states and territories (including Papua New Guinea), Polynesia, the most recently settled area, looks positively homogenous: it has only thirty separate languages spread over ten states and territories! But there are very real differences even between such near Polynesian neighbours as Tonga and Western Samoa. And a country like Fiji, classified as Melanesian because of its original inhabitants, now has—quite apart from the Fiji-Indians who make up just on half of its population—distinct Polynesian characteristics as a result of strong Tongan influence dating back to the eighteenth century (reflected among other ways in the hereditary chiefdom system—now embedded, if anything, even more strongly following the events of 1987). Governments like Australia, trying to make and implement policy for the region as a whole, have to be sensitive to all these differences and distinctions, and the political currents that flow with them.

A corollary of the individuality of each island state is the increasingly wide-ranging and varied agenda which each relationship with Australia entails. The fabric of relations is becoming more complex year by year, in a way which expands both the opportunities for co-operation and the scope for disagreements on both sides. Our relations are becoming richer, more interesting and challenging—and less predictable. A quite dynamic process of political and economic change is at work in most countries of the region. We are well into the post-colonial age of the Pacific, and generational change is producing new leaders for whom the movement towards independence and away from former colonial relationships is not the starting point in their political thinking. Some quiet evidence of that kind of change is the amendment to the franchise system recently achieved in Western Samoa—away from a chiefly to a genuinely universal suffrage—and the debate that is now occurring about more democratic processes in that most hierarchically structured of all Polynesian societies, Tonga.

Some political generational changes of a more turbulent kind have been occurring in the Melanesian states of Vanuatu and the Solomon Islands, as well as Papua New Guinea, but in each case within the existing constitutional framework. Among the independent states, the only exception so far to this reliance on constitutional process—and it was a spectacular one —has been the successive coups in Fiji in 1987. Launched by the military under the leadership of Lieutenant-Colonel (now Major-General) Sitiveni Rabuka, the coups were a reaction to the election victory that year of the multi-racial coalition led by the Labour Party's Dr Timoci Bavadra. More fundamentally, they were an assertion of ethnic-Fijian pride, a reaction to the perceived humiliation of being reduced to what they saw as minority status in their own country. Either way, the coups were an alarming demonstration that things were no longer as the world had assumed they always would be in the Pacific.

The offence to democratic principle involved in the coups was, and remains, great; and there are similarly profound difficulties with the terms of the new post-coup Constitution, which effectively entrenches a minority role in government for non-Fijians. But in the environment of the South Pacific, and in the policy context of constructive commitment that we have described, there is little that we or any other country can do about it except continue to make clear our views of the issues of principle involved, and hope that attitudes will gradually change. Australia can neither be the region's policeman nor its arbiter of political legitimacy.

Nor, realistically, can Australia be more than a supportive spectator in the remaining decolonisation processes that have yet to work themselves out in the South Pacific. A number of dependencies—e.g. Guam and American Samoa in the case of the United States, the Wallis and Futuna Islands in the case of France, Tokelau in the case of New Zealand—have never really sought to change that status and seem unlikely to do so in the foreseeable future. In others like French Polynesia there is a body of independentist opinion, but conspicuously lacking majority support. In others again like the United States administered United Nations Trust Territory of Palau there is clear majority support for a 'compact of free association' with the United States (of the kind now enjoyed by the effectively independent Federated States of Micronesia and Republic of the Marshall Islands). But Palau's cross-cutting divisions of local opinion, and the complication of an inconsistent nuclear-free clause in the Palau Constitution which requires not just a majority but a 75 per cent vote to override, have produced a prolonged stalemate in bringing this about.

The most sensitive remaining issue of this kind is the future of the French Overseas Territory of New Caledonia, where the overwhelming majority of indigenous Kanaks—constituting around 45 per cent of the population —have long sought independence, but this has been resisted by most European settlers and not supported with any enthusiasm to date by the mixed ethnic groups of Wallisians, Polynesians, Vietnamese and others who make up the balance of the voters. After an extended period of confrontation punctuated by violence, agreement was reached in the 1988 Matignon Accords between the new Socialist French Government under Prime Minister Michel Rocard and representatives of both the Melanesian and European communities, to put the future of the Territory to referendum in 1998. Under the Accords the emphasis until 1998 is to be on political institution-building and regional economic development. The Accords have been wholly successful to date in achieving a process of constructive reconciliation and have been warmly supported by Australia, including in the United Nations and the South Pacific Forum, where it politically counts. We have also taken the opportunity of the more relaxed atmosphere that now generally prevails in Australia–France relations as a result of these developments, and of our joint Antarctic initiative, to start building a substantial bilateral relationship with New Caledonia itself, in the form of trade, investment and training and related assistance. No doubt new tensions may emerge closer to the referendum date, which may create difficult policy choices for Australia, but for the moment the direction of our policy is both clear and uncontroversial.

The one area—quarantined though it may be—where Australia–France relations have manifestly *not* improved concerns the continued nuclear-testing program by the French on Mururoa Atoll in French Polynesia. They remain undeterred by our regular protests, and by the negative reaction of almost the whole South Pacific community, as given formal expression in the Treaty of Rarotonga. But that remains at the moment the only example of an overweening external presence in the region, whether benign, hostile or something in between. The United States military presence is slight and unobtrusive. The presence of the American tuna-boat fleet, which for a long time was neither of these things, has since 1987 been controlled by the Multilateral Fisheries Access Treaty, the United States signature of which did much to restore the country's standing in the region. The United States chemical weapons destruction program on Johnston Atoll caused a stir in 1990, but it now seems generally accepted—as Australia had argued from the outset—that the program here is a limited one, morally defensible in a way that nuclear testing or waste dumping in the region could not be, and as environmentally safe as any technical process could be.

So far as other countries are concerned, the Soviet Union appears to have lost, for the foreseeable future, whatever interest it may have had in the region. Libya came for a time, surreptitiously but disconcertingly, but has now for all practical purposes disappeared, presumably discouraged by the sharp regional reaction and attracted by more fertile revolutionary pastures elsewhere. Japan is becoming a higher-profile presence, as a result of its substantial and growing aid program, a good deal of which continues, incidentally, to be developed and administered in consultation with Aus-tralia. But its commercial presence has not been seen as oppressive, and its driftnet fishing practices—which were seen as wholly unacceptable on environmental as well as economic grounds—have now been suspended as a result of regional pressure, in which Australia again played a leading role.

Regional co-operation to force the driftnet fishing issue to a successful conclusion has been just one of a number of instances in recent years of regional institutional processes maturing and producing results. There is an ever-expanding agenda, in the South Pacific Forum, the South Pacific Commission, the Forum Fisheries Agency and elsewhere of economic, environmental, development and political co-operation issues. Regional economic co-operation has produced privileged access for Pacific island products to Australia and New Zealand under the South Pacific Regional

Trade and Economic Co-operation Agreement (SPARTECA) and to the European Community under the Lome Convention. Whether it will ever be possible for the region, given its fragmented political and geographic environment and all its inherent economic difficulties, to break away from these kinds of lifelines, and its larger aid dependency, is one of the central questions to be addressed in the years ahead.

Region-wide—and bilateral—co-operation on security issues is one of the more important strands in Australia's constructive commitment policy approach. This involves the promotion, as we said, of shared perceptions of the region's strategic and security interests, laying the basis for a regional approach to situations, internal or external, which put regional stability at risk. We do not see much of a security problem looming for the region in the form of major-power competition for influence, military or otherwise. The pressures on the Pacific island countries are of a different kind: illegal fishing, customs evasion, drug-running, commercial violations, financial speculation, and potentially some gun-running and terrorism. To combat these, governments need both internal resilience and external support, the latter both on a bilateral basis from countries like Australia and through regional co-operation arrangements.

In this context Australia has developed, for example, its Pacific Patrol boat project, the largest defence co-operation project Australia has in fact yet undertaken. It is intended to provide the Pacific island countries with a multi-purpose vessel, capable of undertaking surveillance and enforcement, search, rescue and police roles, as well as providing inter-island transport. By mid-1991, the first fourteen boats had been handed over to Papua New Guinea (four), Tonga (three), Federated States of Micronesia (two), Vanuatu, Western Samoa, Cook Islands, Solomon Islands and Marshall Islands (one each). Australia provides Royal Australian Navy advisers to support the vessel and assist with the construction of wharf and shore facilities. The patrol boats are obviously an important beginning for nations with such major maritime areas to police. In 1990/91, the project accounted for $14.1 million out of a total of $23.5 million Australian defence co-operation expenditure in the South Pacific. However, Australia itself also undertakes activities intended to support the Pacific countries' own efforts. Particularly important in this respect are the series of airforce patrol flights and naval ship deployments which are co-ordinated with the patrol boats whenever possible, reporting on fishing infringements, vessels sighted in the EEZs and maritime surveillances generally. This is a program developed and implemented on a co-operative basis with New Zealand and the Forum Fisheries Agency.

Australia's policy of constructive commitment is one that is pitched regionally, pursued so far as possible through regional institutions, but for the most part has to be practised bilaterally. It also has to be practised *personally*. Given the scale of the states and territories involved, the cultural value usually attached to direct personal contact, and the generally highly

personalised, non-ideological character of the political structures concerned, there is simply no substitute for devoting the necessary time and
attention to such contact. The very first overseas visit Gareth Evans made, a
week after his appointment as Minister for Foreign Affairs and Trade in
September 1988, was to nine South Pacific states and territories, and he
remains the only foreign minister ever to have visited all fifteen Forum
countries. If Australia is to effectively honour the commitment it has made
to its closest regional friends and neighbours, then this is a pattern which
simply has to be maintained in the future.

12

South-East Asia

AUSTRALIA HAS HAD DIFFICULTY in becoming part of the South-East Asia neighbourhood, both because of our perception of it and its perception of us. We were British in origin and did not fight for our national independence. Our European racial base and our Western cultural traditions and style of life set us apart in both experience and outlook. While some of our neighbours valued their links with outside powers, our security connections with both Britain and the United States were emotionally, not just strategically, important to us and this detached us from the region in a number of ways. Religion, too, drew attention to our 'otherness'. Indonesia, Malaysia and Brunei are predominantly Muslim. Thailand and Burma are Buddhist. The Philippines, while Catholic, has a Muslim minority movement, as does Thailand.

The six-member Association of South East Asian Nations (ASEAN), formed in 1967, is the institutional expression of a South-East Asian community. Australia is not a member. We were the first country to establish with it, in 1974, a formalised dialogue relationship. But, useful as this is, it involves no closer status than that now enjoyed by other outsiders like Japan, the United States and the European Community.

South-East Asia has tested Australian foreign policy. We have tended to accept it as the touchstone of our success or failure in adapting to our region. It has thus borne the brunt of our own uncertainty, for not all Australians have been convinced that adapting to our regional environment is desirable, even if achievable. Some have believed that security demanded we keep our distance. Others have simply found it difficult to identify with the Third World conditions of parts of South-East Asia. Others again have felt that the cultural changes required are so substantial that, even by trying to adapt, Australians would lose their identity.

But an important shift in perception has occurred in both South-East Asia and in Australia as economic considerations have become dominant in the Asia Pacific region. The obsessive security concerns that culminated in our involvement in the war in Vietnam have retreated, no longer driving either foreign policy or domestic politics. At the same time Australians have come rapidly to appreciate that the economic energy of the Asia Pacific region, generated initially in North-East Asia but now well and truly evident in South-East Asia as well, is not a threat but rather a promise of enormous opportunity. The perception is now almost universal in both South-East Asia and Australia that, to compete successfully in the emerging global economy, our own economies need to be more open to the secular dynamics of commerce. Cultural or racial identity has no status in the markets of the world.

COMPREHENSIVE ENGAGEMENT

From these shifts in perception and appreciation arose the Australian policy of 'comprehensive engagement' with South-East Asia.[1] This seeks to resolve, at least for some time, the dilemma of identity that for so long has underlain the debate about Australia's relationship with South-East Asia—whether we are 'in' it, 'of' it, 'part of' it, or something else. It expresses the idea not of 'belonging', which is an unrealistic aspiration for the foreseeable future, but of 'engagement', which is eminently feasible. 'Engagement' itself implies, importantly, a mutual commitment between countries which are in every sense equals. It has more resonance in this respect than a word like 'commitment', which can appropriately describe an inherently unequal relationship. (Thus the difference between South-East Asia and the South Pacific: 'constructive commitment', as an Australian policy framework for the latter, acknowledges that in the South Pacific context, unlike elsewhere, we are inevitably cast in the role of a major power, although it also makes clear our determination to use that relative power not oppressively but constructively, in a spirit of partnership and mutual respect.)

Engagement can be limited or comprehensive in its scope: Australia's interests clearly demand that our relationship with South-East Asia be as broad-based as possible. In his 1989 Statement on *Australia's Regional Security*, the Foreign Minister has described the essential ingredients of 'comprehensive engagement' with South-East Asia in these terms:

- building a more diverse and substantive array of linkages with the countries of South-East Asia, so that they have an important national interest in the maintenance of a positive relationship with Australia;

- continuing to support the major existing regional association, ASEAN, and working with the countries of the region to shape additional regional organisations or arrangements, such as APEC, which can contribute to the social and economic evolution of the region;

- participating actively in the gradual development of a regional security community based on a sense of shared security interests;

- working for the involvement of Vietnam, Cambodia, Laos and Myanmar in the cooperative framework of regional affairs; and

- recognising that Australia, in vigorously pursuing its national interests in the region, should do so as a confident and natural partner in a common neighbourhood of remarkable diversity, rather than as a cultural misfit trapped by geography.[2]

ASEAN operates in a manner that fits comfortably with Australia's approach. It has not developed into a wholly exclusive grouping, but has remained loosely co-operative and consultative in character, its members equally pursuing bilateral links with each other and with the outside world. It thus reflects that concept of mutual commitment within a network of linkages that is at the heart of Australia's own approach to the region. Australia's formal dialogue with ASEAN is concentrated on three levels. There is the foreign minister's annual participation at the ASEAN Post Ministerial Conference (PMC), attended by the foreign ministers of the six ASEAN countries and of ASEAN's seven dialogue partners (Australia, New Zealand, United States, Canada, Japan, Republic of Korea and the European Community); the annual meetings of the senior officials' level ASEAN–Australia Forum; and the ASEAN–Australia Consultative Meetings (AACM), comprising Australian officials and the Canberra-based ASEAN heads of mission.

The subject matter of that dialogue ranges—as is the case with ASEAN's other partners—over the whole multilateral agenda, political and economic, although naturally varying in breadth and depth with the currency of particular issues. Cambodia—and Indo-China generally, including the refugee question—has been a central preoccupation of ASEAN and its dialogue process for most of the organisation's history; economic co-operation has been a similarly recurring theme, traditionally focusing on market access questions, but more recently on wider sectoral issues; development assistance issues loomed large at the outset, when ASEAN countries were in much more of a recipient—donor relationship with their dialogue partners, but has become noticeably less prominent; other 'third agenda' issues, including the environment, have by contrast been growing in prominence in recent years.

Until very recently security issues have not been (other than in very specific contexts, like Cambodia) part of ASEAN's dialogue process, either internal or external. This is notwithstanding that one stimulus for ASEAN's formation in the mid-1960s—and explanation for its cohesion thereafter—

was the status of its six members as anti-communist states in a region long perceived to be threatened, within and without, by communist forces. Its members had different attitudes towards external alliances, the involvement of great powers in the region and indeed the whole philosophy of power balance. There was, moreover, a history of mutual sensitivity on security issues between many of its members (e.g. as between Indonesia and Malaysia over Confrontation, or the Philippines and Malaysia over Sabah). ASEAN thus chose from the outset to stress its economic, social and cultural objectives, and not to pursue with any vigour the question of ensuring 'stability and security from external interference'.[3] The dramatic and tumultuous world events of 1989–90, and their implications for the Asia Pacific region as elsewhere, have stimulated a much less cautious approach to dialogue on strategic and security issues. Beginning with the ASEAN Post Ministerial Conference in Jakarta in July 1990, a very lively debate has in fact now commenced. That said, there is certainly still no sign of any mood to transform ASEAN itself into any kind of defence organisation.

While ASEAN's interest in multilateral economic issues, like Australia's, has been growing rapidly (with four of its six members—all the agricultural producers—being members of the Cairns Group, and all being members of APEC), the organisation's record in internal economic co-operation, an objective to which its members have from the outset been committed without reservation, has been less substantial than many of them might have hoped. Not only has a common market been rejected, but various more selective efforts to stimulate intra-ASEAN trade, through tariff preferences and the like, have by and large been lost in the rush to do business with outside countries.[4]

Australia has certainly been participating in that rush, conscious of the market potential of a combined population of 315 million, albeit at the moment with a total GDP more or less equal to Australia's alone. Two-way trade between ASEAN and Australia stood at $8.8 billion in 1990, an increase of nearly 50 per cent since 1988. In that same period, exports increased by 70 per cent to $5.8 billion (making ASEAN rank behind only Japan and the European Community, and ahead of the United States, as an Australian export market). All this trade has of course been not with ASEAN itself, but with its individual member countries. And important as the formal ASEAN consultative process is, it is with those separate bilateral relationships that, in practice, most of the texture of comprehensive engagement has to be developed.

INDONESIA

No two neighbours anywhere in the world are as comprehensively unlike as Australia and Indonesia. We differ in language, culture, religion, history, ethnicity, population size and in political, legal and social systems. Usually neighbours share at least some characteristics brought about by proximity over time, but the Indonesian archipelago and the continental land mass of Australia might well have been half a world apart.

Indonesia is the fifth most populous country in the world and, as about 90 per cent of its 180 million people are Muslim, it is also the largest Islamic country in the world. After a period of parliamentary democracy in the 1950s, it followed a form of personal presidential rule under Sukarno. After an abortive coup d'état on 30 September 1965, the armed forces assumed effective power under the leadership of General Suharto, who became President in 1968. They have ever since exercised the dual functions ('*dwifungsi*') not only of standing ready to defend the country, but of governing it and maintaining its internal security. Elections are held for both the presidency and the representative assembly, but the Indonesian political system remains tightly controlled.

Indonesia is also an old civilisation with deeply rooted traditions. It is the site of discovery of one of the earliest of human remains (Java Man). All the major religions have washed up on its shores at some time and have been incorporated with older traditional beliefs. Several kingdoms flourished in the archipelago before the arrival of Islam, such as Srivijaya (seventh–fourteenth centuries) in southern Sumatra and Majapahit (thirteenth–fifteenth centuries) in east Java. The domination of the Dutch, first as the Dutch East India Company and then as the Netherlands government, was eventually the catalyst for Indonesian nationalism, but it was only the most recent episode in a history of absorbing foreign influences.

Indonesian nationalism has sought its own ideology in the form of Pancasila, or five principles: Belief in One God, Humanitarianism, Unity, Democracy, and Social Justice. This is flexible enough to accommodate most beliefs and practices, but it has been interpreted in the light of Indonesia's perceived national security weaknesses, deriving from its archipelagic character (coupled with its ethnic diversity), to exclude, as well as communism, both Islamic fundamentalism and Western-style liberalism. They are believed to represent foreign ideologies which pose a threat to internal security. At times this inward-looking form of Indonesian nationalism has seemed to work against more open foreign and economic policies. But in recent years, with Indonesia engaged both in highly activist external relations and in the deregulation and reshaping of its economy, there has been little or no sign of this.

The Indonesian economy was traditionally dependent on agriculture— much of it small-scale and carried out at subsistence level—and, in its more recent history, on oil and gas. The latter dependence—amounting to around 70 per cent of exports a decade ago—was, however, thought to be excessive, and over the last five years Indonesia has in fact been transformed from a commodity-driven economy to one substantially geared to industrial expansion and manufactured exports. Always well regarded for its macro-economic management, but less so for its business regulation, Indonesia has, again since the mid-1980s, set in train a major reform program which has fundamentally transformed the commercial landscape. That program has included trade reforms (easing of tariff and non-tariff barriers), the introduction of a more attractive regime for foreign investors (simplified investment procedures, incentives for export-oriented joint ventures) and significant financial sector reform to ensure that business has access to the financial services necessary to support an increasingly diversified and sophisticated economy. Real growth has been averaging over 5 per cent during this period and, although per capita income is still the lowest in ASEAN, it is clear that by the turn of the century Indonesia will be both a massive and wealthy market.

Australia's relations with the Republic of Indonesia were off to a flying start at the birth of the nation in 1945. Most Australians opposed Dutch colonialism and sympathised with Indonesia's struggle for independence. This was especially true of many of the Australian soldiers who served in Indonesia at the end of the World War II. Australian workers rallied to the aid of the Republic, embargoing cargoes of Dutch supplies, munitions and troops. The Indonesian cause also attracted Australian government assistance. Many hundreds of Indonesians, evacuated to Australia after the Dutch surrender to Japan in 1942, were later voluntarily repatriated by the Australian government to Republican territory. In 1947 Australia represented Indonesia's interests on the United Nations Good Offices Committee, arguing in favour of international recognition for an independent Indonesia. Australia co-sponsored Indonesia's admission to the United Nations in 1950, the same year in which the first Australian Ambassador to Indonesia was appointed.

But after these good beginnings, things seemed to drift apart. Indonesia turned towards others for its more important relationships. Under Sukarno it was an active founder-member of the Non-Aligned Movement and, in an attempt to balance the influence of the British and the Americans in South-East Asia (also reflecting the balance of political forces within Indonesia, which then included a powerful communist party), sought the attention of the Soviet Union and later the People's Republic of China. Under President Suharto, Indonesia attached prime importance to ASEAN and to good relations with the United States, and has been active in consolidating relationships with Arab countries.

Australia, for its part, has always acknowledged the importance of Indonesia, but developed more substantial links in South-East Asia with Singapore and Malaysia. Economically, the focus was overwhelmingly on Japan. After 1972, Australia's enthusiasm was directed towards establishing a substantial political and economic relationship with the People's Republic of China (which re-established diplomatic relations with Indonesia only in 1990, after a breach of many years). The relations that we went out of our way to cultivate in Asia always seemed to be with other countries.

The relationship with Indonesia not only did not develop the substance that might originally have been expected, but over the years became quite brittle. The general wariness of Australians about security threats from the north did not exclude our nearest neighbour. And there was particular concern that incidents on the border between Papua New Guinea and Irian Jaya might escalate into major conflict. But the strongest negative Australian reaction was to the Indonesian takeover of East Timor in 1975, when the military moved with less than decent haste to take the place of the hastily departed Portuguese colonialists, with five Australian journalists being killed in the process. There was little or nothing any Australian government could have done at the time to limit or reverse the annexation, and successive Australian governments since, conscious of international realities, have accepted its irreversibility, with *de jure* recognition being given in February 1979. They have concentrated efforts, rather, on pressuring the Indonesian government to improve the situation of the East Timorese people, pressing for economic development and proper attention to human rights. But that has not stopped the issue of East Timor—and the activities of expatriate East Timorese in Australia—being a recurring irritant.

Indonesian irritation with all things Australian became acute with the publication in April 1986 of a front page *Sydney Morning Herald* article by David Jenkins, focusing on the financial dealings of the President and his family, and comparing them with the Marcoses in the Philippines. The Indonesian Government lodged an official protest, cancelled ministerial visits, refused entry to Australian journalists to Bali to cover a visit by President Reagan and temporarily hindered visa-free entry for Australian tourists. The immediate tension ended shortly thereafter, but a general disquiet about the relationship remained. Differences between the two countries, natural and inevitable as many of them were, kept being magnified and identified as obstacles to be overcome. The 'relationship' itself, rather than its content, was becoming a preoccupation.

In 1988, with the appointment of new Foreign Ministers in both Jakarta and Canberra—Ali Alatas and Gareth Evans, who quickly established a warm personal relationship—the opportunity arose to explore a more practical approach. It was based on a mutual desire to build up the relationship, layer by layer, across a wide range of activities, including defence, culture and commerce. The Australian Foreign Minister, in a speech in Bali shortly after his appointment, urged that we no longer talk of 'the relationship' as though it were a patient in precarious health: what mattered more than taking its temperature was getting on with the task of building it.[5]

It was decided to reinstitute annual talks between senior officials and to hold regular ministerial discussions. The Australia–Indonesia Institute was established, on the model of the Australia–Japan Foundation and the Australia–China Council, to increase people-to-people contact alongside the official relationship. But more important than a new framework was an acknowledgement that the political will was present, on both sides, to make the relationship more fruitful. This arose in part from a recognition by both countries that they were facing critical challenges in a rapidly changing region and a rapidly changing world, and that each had an interest in seeing that the other met these challenges successfully. The tension between Indonesia and Australia as putative rivals, which led the two countries to focus on differences and bilateral irritations, was largely replaced by a desire for practical outcomes.

The most substantial achievement in this respect was the Timor Gap Zone of Cooperation Treaty, signed by the two Ministers for Foreign Affairs in an aircraft ceremony above the Timor Sea in December 1989, and which entered into force in February 1991. Differences over where to draw the sea boundary line for the exploration and exploitation of potentially rich resources of oil and gas under the Timor Sea had delayed the completion of an agreement for almost a decade. When the political will was applied, an imaginative solution was found. Instead of trying to draw a line through the area in dispute (due to differing interpretations by Australia and Indonesia of sovereign rights over the continental shelf), a 'box' of some 40,000 square kilometres was drawn around the immediately disputed area and agreement reached to establish co-operative arrangements for the mutual exploration of the enclosed resources.

The Timor Gap Treaty deals not only with petroleum exploration and exploitation, but also matters as diverse as labour relations, environmental protection, criminal law and security, and customs, quarantine and immigration requirements. Unlike other joint development arrangements, it does not simply divide the area into two separate zones in which each country's regime operates. It reflects a synthesis of approaches, practices and legal principles of both countries. The Treaty is the most substantial bilateral agreement ever reached between our two countries and illustrates eloquently how differences between the two systems can be overcome for our mutual benefit.

An equally eloquent indication of the relationship's new vigour has been the number of ministerial-level visits. From August 1988 to June 1991 there were thirty such visits, fifteen from each side, with several ministers visiting more than once. The broad range of sectoral interests represented during these visits, including education and culture, environment and forestry, transport, resources, immigration and defence indicates the breadth of our common interests. These and other visits have begun new initiatives which are adding further ballast and substance to the overall relationship. Senior Officials Talks have resumed; a High Level group on Energy and Mineral Resources has been established; discussions on environmental co-operation are to begin; discussions on fisheries—including the recurring encroachment by non-traditional fisherman into Australian waters—are well advanced; an agreement on nuclear science co-operation is being negotiated: and arrangements for co-operation in defence, search and rescue, and quarantine continue to develop. The development assistance program to Indonesia, our second largest after that to Papua New Guinea, continues to itself make a significant contribution to bilateral relations, with disbursements to Indonesia running at close to $100 million per annum in the five years to 1991/92. This reflects Indonesia's development needs, its close proximity to Australia, and the importance Australia places on the bilateral relationship. Its geographic focus is on the less developed eastern provinces of Indonesia

In addition to all these bilateral developments, both countries have begun to realise more fully the degree to which they share similar interests in important global and regional issues. Both have worked closely at both ministerial and official level in the Cairns Group to achieve the opening up of agricultural trade in the Uruguay Round of trade negotiations. Both have perceived the threat to regional security of continued strife in Cambodia and have worked together extremely closely in continuing efforts to resolve the problem. And both are working to make the Asia Pacific Economic Co-Operation (APEC) initiative a process that will foster greater economic interdependence in the region, take better advantage of Asia Pacific economic dynamism, and make a major contribution to both global and regional trade liberalisation.

Commercial links between Australia and Indonesia are also at last showing signs of coming of age. For a long time they were inhibited by the limited complementarity between the two economies, the ignorance in each country of conditions and opportunities in the other and, where there was knowledge, a genuine concern about the regulatory environment. But the liberal, market-oriented policies now being followed by both countries offer real prospects for enhancing trade and investment, and business has been responding. During the five years to 1990, Australian exports to Indonesia more than doubled, reaching some $1330 million, and Indonesia became our eighth largest export market. In the same period, Indonesian exports to Australia have risen by 83 per cent to $522 million, a large portion of this increase being non-petroleum exports. Australian investment in Indonesia has increased rapidly, particularly in coal and gold mining and more recently in banking. Indonesian companies are showing greater interest in investing in Australia, at least in the property development and pastoral industries. A double tax agreement will facilitate economic links. So too will the expansion of civil aviation capacity between Indonesia and Australia, set to increase by 43 per cent in two stages beginning in April 1991. The Indonesian national carrier, Garuda, was due to commence new services between Bali and Brisbane and Adelaide and Cairns in mid-1991.

Trade in services has grown substantially. Over 170 000 Australian tourists visited Indonesia in 1989. Around 6500 Indonesians were studying in Australia in 1990, making Australia the second most popular study destination for Indonesian students after the United States. The rapid growth of investment by Australian mining companies in Indonesia is being followed by an increase in activity by mining support industries such as goods suppliers, engineering, consulting, finance, legal and accounting firms. There is also a growing awareness in Indonesia of the quality of Australia's medical services, leading more Indonesians to seek specialist treatment in Australia rather than, as traditionally, in Singapore, the United States or Western Europe. As the Indonesian economy booms, the growing affluence of many Indonesians and their capacity to pay for top quality foreign education and medical treatment means that Indonesia should continue to develop as a destination for export of these services.

The transformation of Indonesia from a producer of agricultural commodities, minerals and fuels to a country with a huge manufacturing sector has already begun to create opportunities for Australia. During the five years to 1990, Indonesian imports of cotton from Australia increased by 400 per cent, making Indonesia the second largest market for Australian cotton. At the same time, there has been a large increase in Australian exports of manufactured inputs into the textile and clothing industry, such as dyes, pigments and paints. Over the same period Australian imports of a range of Indonesian textile products rose by nearly 300 per cent. In general, Australian exports to Indonesia are increasingly oriented towards providing inputs into Indonesia's rapidly growing export industries.

The days when the bilateral relationship was characterised, at best, by non-specific good-will and expressions of 'good neighbourly relations' are now over. The last three years have been a period of rapid expansion as both Australia and Indonesia came to realise that they share an ever-expanding range of fundamental interests. Both sides have a stake in maintaining this relationship. It is inevitable from time to time that issues will emerge or events take place which will cause friction. To suggest otherwise is to court disappointment. Certainly Australian media reporting here, as elsewhere in South-East Asia, always has squall potential. The value of the ballast that has been laid down in recent times is that it should prevent any single problem in the relationship from assuming too much importance, as has occurred in the past. Traditionally, when a dispute arose, there was little to prevent that particular issue from dominating the relationship, and assuming an unwarranted prominence and seriousness. The situation today is very different. The relationship is so much more substantial that it is reasonable to assume that only a very large storm would seriously disturb it.

MALAYSIA, SINGAPORE AND BRUNEI

In one sense, Australia is less close to these countries than it was a few decades ago, when our South-East Asia policies were considerably less developed. The seeming paradox is not hard to explain. Australia established its first contact with them as part of the British connection, the flow-on of consequences from World War II, and as something of a regional patron. The British played a major role—with Australia in a lesser support role—in the 1950s and 1960s in combating the communist-led Malayan Emergency (1948–60) and in resisting Indonesia's 'Konfrontasi' against Malaysia in 1965. The world then was a simpler place. In the robust anti-communist atmosphere of the mainstream Cold War years, Australia found a niche as a sympathetic and helpful neighbour, as well as a substantial supplier of development assistance through the Colombo Plan and related programs.

The difference now is that Malaysia, independent since 1957 (as Malaya, and since 1963 as Malaysia), has both embarked on a rapid economic development drive and developed a more deliberately Islamic character as well as an association with the Non-Aligned Movement. Brunei, independent since 1984, describes itself as a 'Malay Islamic Monarchy'. And Singapore, independent since 1965, has become one of the major economic success stories of the Asia Pacific region, and disinclined to look to Australia for advice. Today, Australia's relations with Malaysia, Singapore and Brunei are based on mutual respect and shared interests, but without the intimacy of the earlier period: that has given way to a rather more complex set of relationships as the international and regional agendas have changed.

Malaysia shares membership with us of the Five Power Defence Arrangements (FDPA), the Cairns Group, Asia Pacific Economic Co-operation (APEC) and the Commonwealth. Australia maintained for thirty years, until 1988, a fighter squadron at Butterworth Air Base and now deploys a squadron on a rotating basis; a rifle company continues to be based there. Trade has increased recently and in 1990 totalled $1.6 billion (the balance slightly in Australia's favour), ranking Malaysia seventeenth among our trading partners. Total investment is now around $1.5 billion, with slightly more Malaysian investment in Australia than the other way round.

Malaysia's population is about the same as Australia's—nearly 18 million in 1990—and, given the pace at which the Malaysian economy has been expanding in recent years, trade and investment figures could be higher. Malaysia's main export markets are Japan, Singapore, West Germany, Britain, United States, other European countries, ASEAN countries other than Singapore, China and Taiwan; the list of its major importers is in almost exactly the same order. Trade has been an issue in Australia's relations with Malaysia in recent years, reflecting a Malaysian view that our tariff and industry policies restrict access to the Australian market and that Australia's free trade arrangement with New Zealand (ANZCERTA) diverts trade away from the ASEAN countries. Australia has had to explain the long-term effects of its policies to make Australian industry more competitive, including the phased reduction of tariffs on most goods, and the removal of quotas and tariff reduction on import of textiles, clothing and footwear: the task has been much easier since the Australian Industry Policy Statement of March 1991. Our response on ANZCERTA has been that while it may cause some trade diversion in the short term, it will create a stronger Australia–New Zealand economy in the longer term and therefore a large market for ASEAN goods.

The most evident of Australia's links with Malaysia is educational. Many thousands of Malaysians have completed secondary and tertiary studies in Australia and, largely for this reason, Australia is well known. In 1988 (prior to changes to the Australian government funded scholarship scheme), 90 per cent of the value of Australia's development assistance in Malaysia was in subsidies for 10 000 students studying in Australia—more students than from all other countries combined.

Malaysia has been sensitive at times about Australia's role and attitudes. Like Indonesia, it is watchful of our liberal democratic values, perhaps even more so because Islam is institutionalised through the monarchy in Malaysia and is the national religion. Racial issues tend also to be a little more sharply etched, because of the large Chinese (32 per cent) and Indian (nearly 9 per cent) minorities. Malaysia's strongest reaction to Australia in recent times followed the screening in Australia late in 1990 of the ABC television serial *Embassy*. Although dealing with a wholly fictional country, 'Ragaan', incorporating characteristics of perhaps twenty real-life ones, and with plot-lines drawn from incidents and issues arising all over the world, the producers had—in a map appearing in the first episode— located 'Ragaan' not only in South-East Asia, but in a bulge half-way up the Malay peninsula. They had also, apparently inadvertently, included one or two other matters in various scripts which seemed to have Malaysian origins. Evidently for these reasons, the program was perceived by Prime Minister Mahathir and others in Kuala Lumpur to refer, adversely, to Malaysia, and offence was taken. Malaysia's reaction—which involved a freeze on official contact, with some spill-over occurring in the commercial relationship as well—was the stronger because it tended to reinforce lingering resentment against Australia for the public stance taken by Australian parliamentarians and others over the years on such questions as the logging of tropical timber, the future of the Penan people in Sarawak, arrests under the Internal Security Act in 1987, and the execution in 1986 of two convicted Australian drug traffickers.

It is clear that Australia's relationship with Malaysia, and the kind of close association that existed between many of our political leaders in the past, can no longer be taken for granted. While its pro-Western disposition remains, it is obviously not as clear or as strong as it was when the threat to Malaysia was Chinese communism. The country has become more fiercely conscious of its Asian identity, and that needs to be acknowledged and respected.

The elements of comprehensive engagement are already present in our relations with Malaysia, spanning the full range of activities including defence, immigration, aid, trade, investment and political co-operation. But that engagement needs to be updated and refreshed. We have to learn that the influence which our assistance earned us in the early period of post-independence must be won anew as the region and the world changes, and Malaysia's interests change with them.

Singapore is now Australia's third largest market in Asia (after Japan and the Republic of Korea) and fifth largest overall. Its remarkable economic achievement since independence in 1965 has made it the most prosperous country in Asia after Japan and oil-rich Brunei. As one of the most trade dependent countries in the world, and with a population of 2.7 million living in a tiny island state, Singapore's economy is always vulnerable to events beyond its control. However, its success in weathering several downturns in the world economy in the 1970s and 1980s has given investors confidence. Singapore is the largest recipient of Australian direct investment among the ASEAN countries, with over three hundred companies and four major banks represented. Australia is also a major recipient of investment funds from Singapore: the actual scale of funds originating from Singapore is, however, difficult to assess as Singapore acts as financial intermediary for other sources.

Australia ranks (outside ASEAN) second only to Japan as a source of tourists for Singapore, accounting for 10 per cent of arrivals in 1988/89. In 1988/89, nearly 2000 Singaporeans were studying in Australia, most paying their own fees. Australia is also increasingly attractive to migrants from Singapore: in 1988/89, 2659 permanent residence visas were issued, 17 per cent of which were for business migrants. This category has been increasing steadily, as have skilled and independent migrants, which prompted former Prime Minister Lee Kuan Yew, to draw attention in his final state of the nation address in 1990 to the 'brain drain' from Singapore, despite its economic achievements and rewards for talent.

Singapore is a member, with Australia, of the Five Power Defence Arrangements, Asia Pacific Economic Co-operation (APEC) and the Commonwealth. Under Lee Kuan Yew's brilliant, adversarial leadership, Singapore's views on international affairs always commanded respect, even if their sharpness did not always win universal support. Singapore's attitude to the world, and foreign policy priorities, can be described as ultra-pragmatic. Its attitude to external powers, including its two best customers, the United States and Japan, can be prickly. However, Singapore's relations with Malaysia, for long a source of some regional tension, have improved recently, subsumed by and large within their wider regional responsibilities as members of ASEAN. And each has improved its relations with Indonesia. Both are members of APEC, and each has been involved in the long negotiations for a peace settlement in Cambodia.

One of the continuing differences of Singapore with Australia has been over human rights, including press freedom. For Australia, as for the United States, one such issue arose when the Singapore Government refused to allow two major economic journals, the *Far Eastern Economic Review* and the *Asian Wall Street Journal* to be represented at the second APEC meeting, held in Singapore in July 1990. But overall, the general state of Australia's relations with Singapore seems to be soundly based on a mixture of historical ties, shared strategic outlook, economic opportunities and a large dose of common-sense.

Brunei Darussalam, a small (240 000 people) and very rich (per capita GNP over US$14 000) nation on the northern coast of Borneo is the third largest oil producer in South-East Asia after Indonesia and Malaysia. It is ruled by a Sultan—the twenty-ninth in one of the oldest continuous lines of monarchy in the world. The population is predominantly of Malay stock, and the national religion Islam. Brunei is a member of ASEAN, APEC and the Commonwealth. It conducts its foreign policy cautiously, conservatively and squarely within the ASEAN mainstream.

Australia's relations with Brunei follow the pattern of our earlier relations with Malaysia and Singapore in the wake of Britain's withdrawal. Training for civil servants, military personnel and students has had a high priority, especially useful in the defence area. The Royal Brunei Armed Forces are comprised of two infantry battalions as well as a naval flotilla and an air wing. A force of retired Gurkhas is employed to guard buildings and utilities, and a battalion of British Gurkhas, home-based in Hong Kong, is stationed there. The entire RBAF infantry has undergone training in Australia and some officers have completed courses at the Joint Services Staff College and other military establishments in Australia.

Trade and investment between the two countries is modest—total trade was $56 million in 1990—although increasing. As it has with Indonesia, the Northern Territory has formed a niche in trade with Brunei, especially for food and horticultural products, and in a joint venture in the hardware and housing sectors: there is a direct airlink between Darwin and Brunei's capital, Bandar Seri Begawan.

THAILAND, BURMA AND THE PHILIPPINES

Thailand has a long history of independence. It is the only country in South-East Asia not to become a European colony, which it achieved by making territorial and commercial concessions to the French in Indo-China and to the British in Burma and Malaya. The northern tip of Thailand is separated from China by Laos and Burma, a small geographical fact which may account for its relatively comfortable relationship with China. The Chinese population in Thailand is also extensively integrated, and does not represent a distinct and somewhat mistrusted minority, as so often elsewhere in South-East Asia. Thailand has long shared the anti-communist preoccupations of its fellow ASEAN members, and has been particularly resistant to Vietnamese aspirations. It was an active ally of the United States through the Vietnam War period, not least as a base for B52 bombing operations. When Vietnam invaded Cambodia in 1978–79, it sought closer links with China and actively assisted the resistance forces—both communist and non-communist—in Cambodia.

The country has historically tended to be open to Western educational and political influence and Indian cultural—including religious—influence: 95 per cent of the population profess Theravada Buddhism. Notwithstanding the country's long tradition of military governments, the political culture is more free-wheeling than repressive. The country's major economic links are with Japan, now its largest trading partner and foreign investor.

Australia's relations with Thailand have been growing steadily in complexity and importance. One of our largest embassies anywhere is in Bangkok: with 33 Australia-based Foreign Affairs and Trade staff, it is bigger than Beijing and only a shade smaller than Jakarta. There has been a significant focus over the years on defence links, due to our common involvement as allies of the United States—although the unfortunate return to military government in February 1991, when civilian democracy had seemed at last to be getting established, required that defence relationship to be downgraded. There has also been close co-operation on police matters in the suppression of the trafficking of narcotic drugs. And political dialogue has been strong, particularly in the context of the Cambodian problem, where Thailand has played an active mediating role, especially as host to key meetings of the four Cambodian parties. But it is in trade and investment that the relationship holds most potential for growth.

Thailand's economy has been growing in recent years, for three reasons. It has natural resources—fertile farmlands; minerals, including tin; natural gas and oil; a large population (55 million); and a productive workforce. The society is stable, based on a widely accepted religious and monarchical system which has remained relatively undisturbed by recurring military coups (usually bloodless) and political upheavals. And the private sector has always been the main engine of growth, allowed by government a fairly free hand. All these factors came together in the 1980s to produce growth rates in Thailand—over 10 per cent in 1988—that were comparable with the fabled achievements of North-East Asia.

Recognition that the country's growth will continue to depend crucially on growth in world trade has forged a good working relationship between Thailand and Australia on multilateral trade issues. Although Thailand has diversified its economy, with manufacturing now contributing more than agriculture to Gross Domestic Product and even more to exports, Thailand has been an active member of the Cairns Group, and more recently also of APEC. But there is some distance to go on bilateral economic matters.

Two-way trade between the two countries remains relatively small—just over $1 billion in 1990, making Thailand our nineteenth largest trading partner—and investment flows are minor. Australians sometimes have found Thailand a difficult country in which to do business, particularly with major public sector infrastructure projects, but it is crucial that the effort continue to be made.

Thailand occupies a key position in the mosaic of South-East Asia. Part of ASEAN, it is a strong economic performer, with well developed instincts about the economic potential of the whole region, particularly when Indo-China finally gets its political and military conflicts behind it. Locking into Thailand's links with both the mainland and the archipelago will add scope and strength to the network of connections that is central in Australia's strategy of comprehensive engagement.

Burma—or Myanmar, as its present government prefers[6]—is a telling example of the liabilities of isolation. Independent in 1948, a country now of some 40 million people and well endowed with natural resources, it could undoubtedly play a more active and constructive role in the region's affairs. But the country experienced under the leadership or influence of General Ne Win nearly three decades of the 'Burmese way to Socialism', which effectively meant military rule, economic hardship and political isolation. In 1988 student protests against Ne Win were crushed, with widespread loss of life. Another military regime under General Saw Maung was installed, but prospects were held out of a return to democratic civilian rule. National elections for a constituent assembly in May 1990 saw the opposition National League of Democracy win 392 of the 485 seats. But then the military junta, styling itself the State Law and Order Restoration Council (SLORC), refused to allow the assembly to even convene, let alone transfer power to it, and continued to crack down on NLD political activists.

The SLORC did promise a move towards a more market-oriented 'open door' economic system. Fishing and forestry production increased with the granting of concessions to foreign (mostly Thai) operators. Singapore and South Korea investors showed interest, while nine foreign oil companies, seven of them Western, signed off-shore exploration agreements with the SLORC. Yet the performance of the economy remained sluggish, at low 1980s levels, with continued large budget deficits and high inflation. Burma remains one of the poorest countries, not only in the region but the world.

Australia's economic interests in Burma are not substantial. Before the suspension of aid in response to the events of 1988, Australia was third largest donor, with $12 million annually. Two-way trade was under $40 million in 1990, with Burma ranking sixty-ninth among our trading partners. BHP, however, is one of the nine foreign companies granted off-shore oil concessions, and there is unquestionably major trade and investment potential in the country. Australia's basic policy approach has been to encourage Burma to increase its economic links with the outside world, while at the same time continuing to support the restoration of democracy and to draw attention to human rights abuses. Thus it was decided late in 1990, despite deep misgivings about SLORC's treatment of the democratic movement, not to withdraw Burma's status as a developing country under the Australian System of Tariff Preference (ASTP).

But Burma continues to test Australian foreign policy. By early 1991 any hope that the SLORC regime may simply have been dragging its feet, in not yet recognising the result of the May 1990 election, had well and truly evaporated. Perhaps relying on the Gulf for distraction, the months of late 1990 and early 1991 were spent banning minor opposition parties; imprisoning hundreds more political opponents—including most of the remaining leadership of the NLD; flushing out dissident monks from the Buddhist monasteries; and ensuring that dissident students did not return to the universities. It became difficult to resist the conclusion that the 1990 election may have been from the outset no more than a fraud, designed to flush out the next generation of democratic leaders.

Close attention has been paid to ways of increasing external pressure on the SLORC regime to heed the voice of its own people. The Government has canvassed the possibility of trade and economic sanctions (supported by the United States Congress); political pressure through the United Nations General Assembly (proposed in 1990 by Sweden); and an arms embargo.[7] International concern with the situation was building—being expressed, for example, quite strenuously by the European Community in its annual consultations with ASEAN in June 1991. But by mid-1991 it was apparent that a number of difficulties clearly confronted any major international campaign.

One difficulty was that there was little or no support for such an exercise within Burma's own region. A number of countries were concerned at SLORC's failure to honour its undertakings, and at the implications of a major blow-up in Burma for regional security generally, but none were willing to apply public political pressure, let alone sanctions. Among its immediate neighbours, China remained a willing arms supplier and Thailand a willing trader. India was unhappy with Burma, but cautious about any question of interference. ASEAN retained its usual resistance to censuring internal human rights matters—and its interest in Burma's future membership of the organisation. Outside the region, countries were not so much reluctant to act, as unpersuaded of the utility of doing so. They have pointed to the reality that Burma's indifference to international opinion has been legendary; that its trade with the West has been so small that its disruption would barely be noticed; and that Burma's aid support has been so reduced that its complete cessation would scarcely be noticed either.

Options for assisting the process of change by externally applied pressure will need to continue to be actively considered by countries like Australia. But it seems that there is little alternative but to rely on a gradualist approach: to ease Burma, step by step, out of its isolation and into the international community. As elsewhere in Asia, differences have to be acknowledged and an effort made to quietly accommodate them. Indirect approaches can sometimes be more productive, if less satisfying to domestic audiences, than direct ones. In the context of Burma, this would involve Australia encouraging those with greater direct influence—the ASEAN countries and China—to apply that influence in a way that will enhance the longer-term peace and stability of the region.

The Philippines, from the moment of its independence in 1946 (from the Americans, after three centuries of Spanish rule), has been troubled by populist insurgencies and political instability. The war-time 'People's Army against Japan' (Hukbalahap, or Huks) became a communist-led insurgency which seriously threatened the central government until the mid-1950s. The boisterous style of political democracy that the Philippines inherited from the United States seemed to be working until 1972, when President Marcos—first elected in 1965—declared martial law, dissolved Congress and ruled by decree, ostensibly to deal with an insurgency led by the New People's Army and with a Muslim rebellion in the south. The assassination of the Opposition leader Senator Benigno Aquino in 1983 brought about a series of anti-government demonstrations, as well as a flight of capital from an already weak economy. Then in a special election for president and vice-president, called unexpectedly by Marcos in 1986, the declared result in favour of Marcos was rejected by the Opposition leader, Mrs Corazon Aquino, widow of the assassinated Senator, and denounced by the Catholic Bishops Conference of the Philippines as having been gained by means of electoral fraud and violence. The 'Four Day Revolution' of February 1986 saw hundreds of thousands of civilians in the streets of Manila as a demonstration of 'people power', and culminated in the installation of Mrs Aquino as President.

The restoration of democracy in such dramatic form meant that Mrs Aquino took office with a high degree of local and international credibility. After an initial period of goodwill, however, her government was subjected to pressure from the insurgency, a disaffected military and an increasingly impatient populace. A number of unsuccessful military coup attempts were made, economic reform was sporadic and business confidence declined in the wake of political uncertainty. But in mid-1991, rather against the odds, the government and the country were still holding together.

With its largely English-speaking population of more than 60 million, Christian heritage and long exposure to Western culture, the Philippines is a country with which Australia might expect to have a close association, and that is largely the case. The Philippines is Australia's sixth largest source of immigrants, about half of whom are brides and fiancés. Tourism levels to the Philippines are high (a perhaps not un-related phenomenon). Development assistance is a major Australian activity, and Australia also has a defence co-operation program with the country. Bilateral trade and investment are improving, but there is little doubt that the full potential of the relationship here remains to be realised. Total trade (significantly in Australia's favour) was $612 million in 1990, making the country our twenty-sixth largest trading partner, and Australia is the seventh largest investor in the Philippines.

Probably the most important single contribution that the Philippines makes to its region—and to Australian national interests—is its hosting of the major United States military facilities at Subic Bay Naval Base and Clark Field Air Base. The two bases have not only given the United States an 'over-the-horizon' presence throughout South-East Asia and Indo-China, but have linked the Seventh Fleet operations in the Pacific with the Indian Ocean and Persian Gulf, and in the process provided an assurance to Japan—among others—that the sealanes between the two oceans are protected.

The twenty-five year bilateral agreement covering the bases was due to expire in September 1991. The outcome of the negotiations between the United States and the Philippines about the future of the bases has been the subject of close attention by the whole region for several years. Minds have been particularly concentrated by their conduct in an atmosphere where nationalist anti-base sentiment is strong, and where budgetary and other pressures have made it less easy for the United States to offer a very generous compensation package for continued occupancy. Then, on the verge of a deal being closed, Mount Pinatubo erupted in June 1991 with disastrous consequences not only for the people and agricultural economy of central Luzon, but also for the infrastructure of both bases. At the time of writing, it seemed likely that the cost of rehabilitating Clark Field would be too great to sustain, and that any continued major United States military presence—and even then probably only for a limited further period—would be confined to Subic Bay.

The bases issue apart, Philippine foreign and trade policy has generally been conducted squarely within an ASEAN–APEC–Cairns Group framework, in a way that has meshed well with Australia's interests and concerns. It is appropriate that we continue to stress, in our own dealings with the Philippines, the security benefits of a continued substantial United States presence in the region; the importance of the democratic process; the need for social reform to ensure the delivery of basic services to the people; and the expansion of trade and commercial ties with Australia.

13

Indo-China

THE STORY OF Australia's relations with Indo-China since the end of World War II is also, in many important ways, the story of Australian foreign policy. It is concerned with threats to the Australian continent, the place of Asia in our national consciousness, and our continuing efforts to reconcile history and tradition with geography and security. We can see in the evolution of our Indo-China policy—from our taking sides in the Vietnam War to our attempts to bring warring sides together in Cambodia—nearly all the themes, mistakes, aspirations and shifts which characterise the broader narrative of Australia's still-evolving sense of our place in the international scheme of things.

Of all the South-East Asian nations that came to independence after World War II, the three countries of Indo-China—Vietnam, Cambodia and Laos—have been the least understood by Australia. With the other South-East Asian nations, Australia at least had links of some sort, whether born of proximity, shared security concerns, commerce or an Imperial connection. Malaysia, Singapore and Burma shared a British background with Australia. In the case of the first two, Australia continued to have defence links, and we had a security link with two other South-East Asian nations —the Philippines and Thailand—through SEATO. And in the case of Indonesia, Australia was closely involved both with its birth as a nation and in a recurring series of policy issues thereafter.

Our understanding of Indo-China, by contrast, was very limited. This was partly because the region had been colonised by the French, which created a cultural and institutional gap as well as political distance. And its location outside our area of primary security interest did not in itself compel attention. Nor was there any particular commercial opportunity perceived. In any event North Vietnam was a communist state, and therefore automatically viewed with suspicion. This was the only country in larger South-East Asia in which power had been effectively handed over, however tempestuously, by the departing colonial authorities to a communist government after a military defeat. In all other cases, power was handed over to the non-communist nationalists (Sukarno, Lee Kuan Yew, Tunku Abdul Rahman), and the communists had to try and seize power from them.

By the mid-1950s, the plummeting temperature of the Cold War had brought Indo-China closer to the centre of Australian security thinking, even if its history and culture remained on the periphery of our thoughts. Australia was not a direct participant in the Geneva Conference of 1954 which divided Vietnam at the seventeenth parallel but, equally, we did not question it. This division was intended to be temporary, but quickly became entrenched with the refusal of Ngo Dinh Diem in the South, supported by the United States, to participate in elections. According to the politics of anti-colonial nationalism, Vietnam was one nation. According to history, it was three not two: Vietnam under French administration was divided into Annam, Tonkin and Cochin-China, this trilateral division corresponding with slight linguistic differences and political regionalisms which had emerged as Vietnamese settlement gradually moved southward over several centuries. The carving of the nation into two was a strategic expedient which defied both history and nationalism, and the consequences were all too inevitable.

THE VIETNAM WAR AND ITS LESSONS

From the early 1950s onwards, Australia's view of Vietnam gradually changed from one of neglect to a belief that it lay between Australia and the 'downward thrust' of an expansionist communist China. The reasons depended not so much on what was happening on the ground in Vietnam as on the politics of the Cold War, Australia's changing views of regional security, and our long search for reassurance that a great and powerful friend could be relied on to protect Australia should it ever face invasion. To this list could be added another factor: the demands and dynamics of Australian domestic politics of the period, when the politics of anti-communism were also those of electoral victory.

By the 1950s, Australian defence planners were already regarding Indo-China as important to Australian security. The 1952 Strategic Basis paper noted that Indo-China was the 'key to the defence of South-East Asia'. 'While Indo-China is held', the paper argued, 'defence in depth is provided for the Australia-New Zealand main support area'.[1] It is easy enough to see in this analysis the basis of the forward defence policy on which Australian involvement in the Vietnam War was later to be justified. But it is also worth noting that, notwithstanding the views of defence planners in the early 1950s, there was little enthusiasm on the part of the Australian Government of the day for Western intervention in Vietnam. In 1954, at a time when the United States administration was considering what needed to be done to contain communism in South-East Asia, Foreign Minister Casey advised the Australian Cabinet that Australia should use its influence to restrain the United States from embarking upon active military intervention in Indo-China without adequate consideration of its military and political aims.

By the 1960s, however, that caution had given way to the crusading view that Vietnam was the place where the West, and most particularly the United States, should take a stand against expansionist Chinese communism. President Eisenhower coined the image of Vietnam as the first of a series of precariously poised dominoes. It was an image, and an analysis, which the Australian Government enthusiastically embraced. As Prime Minister Menzies put it in April 1965 when announcing to Parliament the sending of Australian troops to Vietnam:

> The takeover of South Vietnam would be a direct military threat to Australia and all the countries of South and South East Asia. It must be seen as part of a thrust by communist China between the Indian and Pacific Oceans.[2]

The war to which Australian troops were thus committed had been gradually building up since 1959, when the political struggle being directed by North Vietnam (the Democratic Republic of Vietnam, or DRV) against South Vietnam (the Republic of Vietnam, or RVN) first took a significant guerrilla warfare form. United States advisers had been involved in relatively small numbers supporting the South since 1961, but massive American intervention—with forces exceeding 540 000 at their height—began only in 1965. Five other nations joined in: Australia, New Zealand, the Republic of Korea, the Philippines and Thailand. Australia's contribution was in one sense small: our peak strength of 8300 represented about a quarter of the US commitment in population terms. But nearly 47 000 Australian military personnel (including over 17 000 National Servicemen) served in Vietnam between 1965 and 1972, by far our largest commitment overseas outside the two World Wars. And 496 of them were killed.

The war was never one that, in retrospect, even looked like being won by the South and its allies. The Tet Offensive of March 1968 was the psychological turning point. The bombing of the North halted shortly thereafter, peace negotiations began in Paris in May, and phased allied troop withdrawals began in mid-1969. Australia's participation—which had been fiercely controversial domestically for the duration of the war, particularly the sending of conscripts—ended so far as combat troops were concerned in 1971, with the very last forces being withdrawn by direction of the incoming Whitlam Government in December 1972. The Paris Peace Agreement was signed in January 1973, but after the United States withdrawal in March that year, hostilities continued between the North and South until the latter's defeat in 1975. The tragically delayed unification of Vietnam took place formally in July 1976.[3]

It is sometimes said that Australia's involvement in the Vietnam War flowed not from any considered assessment of Australian national interests but from a mindless following of the United States. But the failure of Australian policy on the Vietnam War was not, primarily, a failure to consider Australia's interests. They were considered, but on the basis of assumptions which were inherently flawed. It was in the end not a failure of national self-assertion, but a failure of analysis.

There were three essential justifications for Australia's involvement, not all of them stated with equal frankness at the time. First, as Menzies had told Parliament, it was to stop the advance of expansionist Chinese communism before it reached Australia. In its essentials this justification was a combination of the domino theory and the strategy of forward defence. If South Vietnam, the first domino, fell, it would only be a matter of time before the other dominoes in South-East Asia collapsed, thereby precipitating the fall of the ultimate domino—Australia. Australia could not afford to wait until it was directly threatened. Against the background of the Korean War, Chinese support for various insurgency groups in South-East Asia, the experience of Indonesian '*Konfrontasi*' and the challenge of the insurgency in Malaya, concern about the intentions of China had a certain surface plausibility when measured against the fears of the time. This was a period when many feared that communism was on the march in South-East Asia, and that Thailand, in particular, faced a critical domestic challenge from communist insurgents. It should be recalled that United States and Australian involvement in Vietnam had the support—in some instances active, in others tacit—of most of the South-East Asian governments of the day. These governments saw the war as a means of keeping communism in North Vietnam in check, thereby creating a breathing space during which they could tackle their own problems of underdevelopment and internal communist insurgencies.

The second essential reason for Australian involvement in the war was the calculation that if Australia showed beyond reasonable doubt that it was willing to share the United States burden in South-East Asia, especially at a time when other US allies were reluctant to contribute, then such good deeds would not be forgotten by the United States in the event that Australia faced a threat. As the Australian Embassy in Washington at the time put it in a cable to Canberra:

> Our objective should be to achieve such an habitual closeness of relations with the US and sense of mutual alliance that in our time of need, after we have shown all reasonable restraint and good sense, the US would have little option but to respond as we would want.[4]

The third justification was closely linked to the first two. It was to help keep the United States actively engaged in the security of South-East Asia. By lending support to the US effort in Vietnam, Australia was helping to ensure the presence of US forces in the region, thereby reinforcing the region's defences against communism. Battalions on the ground were considered much more reassuring than untested commitments, however sincere.

None of these assessments of national interest, either separately or together, stand up to scrutiny. Forward defence was a flawed policy which was both tested and defeated by the Vietnam War. It was directed at the defence of Australia, but its burden could not be borne by Australia. It depended ultimately on the presence of United States forces on the ground to act as a shield for Australian forces. But the idea that Australia could somehow buy a US security guarantee for itself by providing modest military support for the US effort in Vietnam was naive. One does not need the realism of a Metternich to see that it was folly actually to believe that Australia could manoeuvre the United States into a position where it would have no alternative but to respond 'as we would want'. The Australian desire to see the United States actively engaged in the security of South-East Asia was more understandable. Here the problem lay not in the objective but in a failure to appreciate that the US strategy in Vietnam would not succeed. Australia failed to see what even Anthony Eden perceived as far back as the early 1950s: that Vietnam was 'the wrong war against the wrong man in the wrong place'.[5]

The most important lesson of the Vietnam War for Australian foreign policy was the need for rigorous analysis in the definition of national interests and in the formulation of strategies to advance those interests. Such analysis had not only to be based on judgments independently arrived at, but also reflect a proper understanding of the various influences at work. When Australia moved to the assessment that Indo-China was of direct strategic concern—which in fact occurred some time before Australian combat troops were despatched to Vietnam in 1965—it was an assessment made without an adequate understanding of Vietnamese history, and indeed defied Vietnamese history. The assumption that North Vietnam was a puppet of China and serving Chinese interests ignored the long history of Vietnam's resentment of Chinese political hegemony. It ignored the fact that Chinese domination of Vietnam had been a vital ingredient in the complex amalgam of forces which nourished Vietnamese nationalism.

The combination of imperfect knowledge and the great simplifications so much a feature of the Cold War was a recipe for bad policy decisions. It meant that we knew little about the degree of real popular support for the successive ineffective governments of South Vietnam. And it meant that we underestimated the nationalist impulses behind Ho Chi Minh's policy and political philosophy. A better understanding of Vietnam and its history would have led us to the view that Ho, while undoubtedly a man deeply committed to the cause of international communism, was not a Chinese puppet playing out some scripted drama for the extension of Chinese communism through all of South-East Asia and beyond. Had we known more of Vietnam we might have seen more grey and less red.[6]

The second big lesson of Vietnam was the need to comprehensively rethink our whole approach to the larger South-East Asia region. Australian involvement in the Vietnam War bore witness to that pungent observation of MacMahon Ball that, historically, fear has been the tap-root of Australia's interest in Asia.[7] It was an expression of that psychology of exile, that sense of vulnerability of a European outpost isolated from its cultural roots, inhabiting a rich but sparsely populated continent on the edge of a pressing Asian land mass. Subsequent Australian governments learnt from the war that Australia simply had no alternative but to come to grips with its neighbouring region, and to try and define a positive relationship with it. It had to be a relationship based on an acceptance of the region not as a buffer zone between us and invasion but as an area of opportunity where Australia must be comprehensively engaged. An area of continuing security significance to Australia it most certainly was, but one in which Australia had to develop many-faceted relationships—political, cultural, commercial, social and individual.

The Vietnam War also taught us about the relationship between foreign policy and defence policy and the way in which we define national security. It highlighted the crucial link between economic security and strategic security: a link of which Australian governments after World War II seemed to be aware (as shown in the initiation of the Colombo Plan and Australian development assistance programs in South-East Asia), but one which was not given sufficient weight in our assessments of whether to become involved in the Vietnam War. Our engagement in Vietnam represented a subordination of foreign policy to defence. Not only was foreign policy driven by a presumed sense of defence vulnerability which was perhaps mistaken in a strategic sense; it was also pursued without due regard for the type of long-term relationships we wished to build up with the nations of the region. It was a case of over-valuing the role that great and powerful friends, no matter how valuable and powerful, could play in protecting and promoting Australian interests. It was a case, too, of seeking purely military solutions—and quick ones—to problems which required long-term political management.

There are, to be sure, moments of real threat when defence considerations properly loom large. But short of this—and since World War II we have always been short of it, and look like remaining so—there are dangers in adopting a narrow view of national security and in having foreign policy determined by defence requirements. The war in Vietnam taught us that an effective national policy required both a credible defence policy and a constructive foreign policy. It taught us that a sound external policy is one based on an integrated, multi-dimensional approach to security: an approach which recognises the value of diplomacy in helping to advance national security, which involves a prudent mix of defence preparedness and diplomatic reassurance, and which also understands that economic security is the bedrock of national stability.

Finally, the experience of Vietnam taught Australia a lesson about the value of bipartisanship in foreign policy. The end of the Vietnam War saw a convergence of views about Australian foreign policy—which, despite some ups and downs, still survives. Unreality is a great spur to partisanship; realism tends to encourage bipartisanship. We can take some comfort in the fact that since Vietnam there has been broad agreement in Australia on many fundamentals. In particular, the reality of our place in the region, and our need to attach priority to our relations with it, has become a commonplace.

THE TRAGEDY OF CAMBODIA

The horror of Cambodia's experience in the killing fields of the Khmer Rouge has captured the attention, and emotions, of the world more than almost any other contemporary tragedy. Australia's efforts to help achieve a durable peace for Cambodia have occupied more time and attention in our diplomacy than any other single issue in recent years. These efforts, moreover, have probably done more than anything else to establish and define the essential character of Australian foreign policy as it is now practised. For all these reasons, the story of Australia's involvement in the Cambodian problem—unfinished though it still is—is worth telling in some detail.

The complex modern tragedy of Cambodia effectively began with the deposition in 1970 of Prince Sihanouk—head of state, head of government, quicksilver personality and for years the sole effective guarantor of his country's independence.[8] This culturally rich and gentle land of seven million people, which had managed hitherto to avoid being caught up in the region's bloodier conflicts, was plunged into a civil war variously involving North and South Vietnamese, United States forces and republican and anti-republican Khmer troops, which culminated in the capture of Phnom Penh by the communist Khmer Rouge in 1975.

There was then instituted, under the Democratic Kampuchea (DK) government of the Khmer Rouge, and its leader Pol Pot, a genocidal reign of terror exceeded probably only by the Nazis. The country was cut off from the world, all foreigners expelled, the cities and towns forcibly evacuated, the whole population set to work in the fields, and the systematic extermination ordered of professionals, intellectuals, senior bureaucrats, 'Khmer bodies with Vietnamese minds',[9] and anyone else who might conceivably challenge Khmer Rouge authority. News of the scale of the horror was slow to filter out, but by 1979 it was becoming clear that at least one million people—perhaps double that number: the truth will never finally be known—had died.

The virulent anti-Vietnamese attitudes of the Khmer Rouge led to border clashes with Vietnam and eventually to invasion by Vietnam on 22 December 1978. Phnom Penh was captured on 7 January 1979, the DK Government ousted, and the People's Republic of Kampuchea (PRK) proclaimed on 11 January under the leadership of Heng Samrin; Hun Sen became in 1985 Prime Minister of the PRK, which subsequently was renamed the State of Cambodia (SOC). In June 1982 the Coalition Government of Democratic Kampuchea (CGDK) was established in Kuala Lumpur, bringing the non-communist Sihanoukists and Son Sann's Khmer Peoples National Liberation Front (KPLNF) together with the communist Khmer Rouge. Nothing could have united these two non-communist resistance groups with the Khmer Rouge other than their common opposition to the Vietnamese invasion, and to what they regarded as the Vietnamese puppet SOC government. The CGDK government-in-exile—always a fragile coalition—was renamed the National Government of Cambodia (NGC) in February 1990.

The end result of all this was simply to replace one kind of killing by another, albeit on a less horrific scale. The Khmer Rouge's reign of terror came to an end, but an endlessly protracted civil war recommenced. Recurring bloody military engagements, guerrilla assaults and ambushes, the displacement of large numbers of civilians, and the inability of life generally to return to any kind of pre-1970 normality all took their further toll of a people who have already suffered more than most in the twentieth century. This civil war has proved immensely difficult to bring to an end, not least because it has involved three distinct sets of players, all with agendas of their own. First, there have been the four internal parties, all—whatever their degree of political alliance—immensely distrustful of each other; secondly, there have been the major-power patrons—in particular, China supporting the Khmer Rouge and Prince Sihanouk, the Soviet Union supporting the SOC, and the United States supporting the two non-communist resistance groups; and thirdly, there have been the involved regional countries, most importantly Vietnam on the SOC side and the ASEAN nations on the other. In this kind of environment, even a situation like Lebanon begins to look almost straightforward by comparison.

Australia first became involved with the Cambodia issue in reaction to the Vietnam invasion in 1978. When that invasion occurred—ostensibly to save the Cambodian people from the genocidal regime of Pol Pot, but in manifest breach of the most fundamental of all international relations principles, that of non-intervention—it became politically impossible for any Australian government to pursue a normal, let alone an expanding, relationship with Vietnam. In January 1979, with the support of the then Labor

Opposition, the Fraser Government cancelled Australia's modest aid program to Vietnam and bilateral relations—which had been quietly normalising—were put on ice.

Australia's position on the political and strategic issues raised by Vietnam's aggression was essentially to be supportive of ASEAN policy. The one significant exception occurred in February 1981 when, after two years of growing domestic pressure, the Fraser Government broke ranks with ASEAN and 'de-recognised' the ousted Khmer Rouge, or DK, Government, whose cause ASEAN had been sponsoring in the United Nations. This decision, while it generated quite a strong negative reaction from ASEAN at the time (especially from Singapore), did not reflect any assessment by Australia that on this issue our national interests differed from those of the ASEAN states. Rather it reflected the very strong domestic opinion in the Australian community that it was immoral for Australia formally to recognise any claimant to government associated with the odious Pol Pot regime.[10]

Early Settlement Efforts   The Hawke Government came to power in 1983 with a commitment—born of the very strong views in the Labor Party on Australia's role in the Vietnam War—to play a both more independent and more active role in a Cambodian settlement, and to re-establish bilateral relations with Vietnam. However, the Labor Party's platform on the resumption of aid to Vietnam ran up against the firm opposition of both the United States and ASEAN, who saw this as running counter to their strategy of continuing to isolate Vietnam over its invasion of Cambodia. It was clear to the new Government that, if aid to Vietnam were to be resumed, it would have to be within the context of, and not in advance of, a comprehensive Cambodian settlement.

The Hawke Government's Indo-China policy thus focused from the outset on exploring various options for a Cambodian settlement. Activities included visits by Foreign Minister Hayden to Vietnam and Laos in 1983 and 1985, and to Australia by Vietnamese Foreign Minister Thach in 1984 and Prince Sihanouk in 1985. Specific Australian initiatives designed to help break the stalemate included the proposal for an international war crimes tribunal to try Pol Pot and his senior associates, and the series of seminars organised by Griffith University and supported financially by the Australian Government. The policy was driven generally by a desire to more strongly assert Australia's regional interests and to present and pursue our own distinctive policies there and elsewhere. Another important assumption driving the activity was that a military solution to the Cambodia problem was neither possible nor desirable, and that failure to resolve the problem held the potential for increasing regional instability, particularly in the context of superpower confrontation, regional polarisation and even a regional arms race.

The ASEAN reaction to a more independent Australian approach on

Indo-China was at first highly critical. The first significant manifestation of the new approach was the Australian decision in 1983 to withdraw from co-sponsorship, in favour merely of support, of the annual ASEAN Cambodia resolution in the United Nations General Assembly. That decision was taken on the basis that, among other things, the resolution was too one-sidedly critical of Vietnam, and did not sufficiently acknowledge the enormity of the human rights desecration that had occurred in Cambodia under Pol Pot. ASEAN feared that Australia's actions, coming as they did on top of the earlier decision not to recognise the CGDK's entitlement to the Cambodian United Nations seat, would disrupt the fairly solid phalanx of Western support for ASEAN and lead to an unacceptable erosion of such support. In some ASEAN circles, there was probably also a feeling that Australia was being used by Vietnam in ways which could work to ASEAN's long-term disadvantage. Certainly the war crimes tribunal call by Bill Hayden in 1986 (which continues to be fondly remembered in Vietnam and Laos, and by the SOC) was not greeted with any enthusiasm by ASEAN. It was some time—probably not until Australia resumed its co-sponsorship of the ASEAN resolution in 1988—before ASEAN accepted that Australia did not seek to erode the ASEAN position on Cambodia, that our involvement was legitimate and that we were acting on assessments independently arrived at.

The achievement of the Hayden years, notwithstanding the problems with ASEAN, was to have Australia accepted by the international community, including ASEAN, as a responsible and knowledgeable voice on the issue of a Cambodian settlement. Our views at this time were not necessarily welcomed by all the parties, but they were given weight and taken into account, and Australia's activities did impart a sense of urgency, previously absent, to the effort to find a solution. Something of a consensus was emerging at least on broad principles—that there needed to be withdrawal of all Vietnamese forces from Cambodia, matched by an effective arrangement to prevent Pol Pot and his Khmer Rouge forces from returning to power in Cambodia; free and fair elections for Cambodia; the creation of conditions for the peaceful return of displaced Cambodians; and guarantees that a post-settlement Cambodia would be neutral, independent and non-aligned.

Following these efforts other regional countries, and in particular Indonesia, sought to play a more active diplomatic role in pursuit of a solution to the Cambodia problem, which resulted in the two Jakarta Informal Meetings (JIMs) in July 1988 and February 1989. These meetings were inconclusive: although they did result in some clearer definitions of the issues involved, there was no significant lessening of the differences among the four Khmer factions. But hopes for a major move forward had arisen with the announcement by Vietnam in January 1989 that it was prepared to withdraw all its troops from Cambodia by September that year. Seeking to force a breakthrough, France—the former colonial power and still a significant influence in the region—judged in mid-1989 that the time was ripe for a full international conference on Cambodia. The Paris International Conference on Cambodia (PICC) was accordingly convened, with joint Indonesian chairmanship, in Paris in July–August 1989. This brought together all four Cambodian factions, the six ASEAN countries, the Permanent Five Members of the UN Security Council, Vietnam, Laos, Australia, Canada and India as well as Zimbabwe (representing the Non-Aligned Movement) and a representative of the UN Secretary-General.

In the event the Paris Conference failed, but not without coming close to succeeding. A comprehensive settlement strategy was mapped out involving, in broad terms, the monitored withdrawal of all Vietnamese forces; a ceasefire; the cessation of external support; the creation of a transitional administration; and the holding of free elections—all under the supervision of an international control mechanism. It also involved measures to guarantee the neutrality of Cambodia and non-interference in its internal affairs; to deal with the repatriation of refugees and displaced persons; and to ensure the reconstruction of the country. That settlement strategy foundered for a number of stated reasons, but only one of them was really crucial. One side to the conflict, the combined resistance forces of Prince Sihanouk, Son Sann and the Khmer Rouge, together with their international backers, demanded a place for each of the four internal parties, including the Khmer Rouge, in the transitional administration. To this demand, the SOC Government of Hun Sen, and its international backers, were simply not prepared to concede.

Vietnam proceeded to withdraw its formed military units more or less on schedule in September 1989, but this was accompanied not by a renewed momentum for peace—despite various efforts by the Paris Co-Chairmen, the Thai Prime Minister and the US Secretary of State—but rather a resurgence of fighting, continued external supplies of arms and materiel, and a general hardening of diplomatic positions. Although international opinion remained overwhelmingly in favour of a comprehensive settlement— as the UN General Assembly vote on the ASEAN resolution again proved —the stumbling block remained the composition of the proposed transitional administration, and in particular the role proposed in it for the Khmer Rouge. This was so even given that the Khmer Rouge would have but a minor role in a quadripartite administration, and that it would be shorn of its former leadership.

Australia's United Nations Peace Plan
It was to break this impasse that the Australian peace proposal, announced in outline by Gareth Evans in the Senate on 24 November 1989, was put forward. The central concept of the Australian proposal to reinvigorate the peace process was very simple. So as to sidestep the power-sharing issue which had bedevilled the Paris Conference, and constrain the role of the Khmer Rouge in the transitional arrangements, it was proposed that the United Nations be directly

involved in the civil administration of Cambodia during the transitional period. Along with a UN military presence to monitor the ceasefire and cessation of external military assistance, and a UN role in organising and conducting elections, UN involvement in the transitional administrative arrangements would ensure a neutral political environment conducive to free and fair general elections. The proposal recognised that a logical consequence of such a role for the United Nations would mean having the Cambodian seat at the United Nations either declared vacant or transferred to a neutral representative Cambodian body for the duration of the transitional period. In other important regards, it preserved the objectives of a comprehensive political settlement as defined at the Paris Conference.

The idea of United Nations involvement in a transitional authority was not in itself new, although the degree of detail with which the concept was subsequently developed certainly was. Prince Sihanouk had in March 1981, and occasionally subsequently, raised the idea of some form of United Nations trusteeship. And during 1989, US Congressman Stephen Solarz had developed the specific idea of a neutral United Nations interim administration: discussions Gareth Evans had with Solarz in New York in October 1989 and subsequently were crucial in shaping Australia's thinking.

In advocating a very substantially enhanced UN role in the settlement, the Australian Government recognised that it was being ambitious. Though well experienced in peace-keeping operations and monitoring elections, the United Nations had not to date had a role in the civil administration of one of its member states, nor primary responsibility for organising and conducting elections as distinct from monitoring them. In addition, conditions within Cambodia—including the potentially fragile character of any ceasefire, the difficulty of monitoring guerrilla forces, and the lack of developed transport and communications infrastructure— would mean that the overall UN operation would be much more difficult than had been experienced in most other situations.

While recognising from the outset the inherent difficulty and complexity of what we were proposing, Australia was encouraged by the new vitality and credibility the United Nations had been able to demonstrate through its success in facilitating an end to the Iran–Iraq war and the Soviet withdrawal from Afghanistan, and its role in implementing the Namibian settlement. The transformation of East–West relations under way in 1989 was also relevant to our calculations in two ways. First, close collaboration between the United States and the Soviet Union in a number of international disputes had strengthened markedly the collective authority and influence of the Five Permanent Members of the UN Security Council. Secondly, as the effects of historic changes in the Soviet Union and Europe worked their way through to the Asia Pacific region, it was becoming clear that the Soviet Union, Vietnam and probably China were more interested than before in achieving a Cambodian settlement if their minimum objectives could be obtained. Despite these positive pointers, however, it was appreciated that a long, gruelling effort would be required to translate the Australian proposal into reality.

In preparing its plan, Australia had to take account of the prospect that the Khmer Rouge would be able to exploit the process politically, militarily, or both—particularly in the proposed transitional period under United Nations administration—and would not in any event accept any final outcome which did not leave them in control of the country. Why not simply take the position that their past record of atrocities entitled them to no consideration at all, and that the best option in these circumstances was to establish relations with the Phnom Penh government and encourage it to hold free elections—in which at least the non-communist resistance would be able to participate—as soon as possible? After Vietnam had withdrawn virtually all its troops from Cambodia and was no longer sustaining by occupation the government it had installed, was it not now possible to accept, at least pending elections, the SOC as the legitimate government of Cambodia?

If it were simply a matter of adopting a strategy that would effectively isolate and marginalise the Khmer Rouge, not very many voices would be heard in strenuous opposition. But the critical point was that the Khmer Rouge could not be effectively isolated and marginalised, and its military influence nullified, so long as it continued to be supplied, especially by China, with arms, money and diplomatic support. China (determined as always to neutralise Vietnam's influence over Cambodia, actual or perceived) has consistently maintained that it will give a commitment to cease military support to the Khmer Rouge, and support a ceasefire, *only* in the context of a comprehensive settlement agreed by all four Cambodian parties and which guarantees the future independence and neutrality of the country. Unless and until China was prepared to withdraw from the picture —and only the UN peace plan seemed capable of delivering that—then whatever Australia and other countries might choose to do, the continuation of bloody civil war was inevitable.

It was also possible that the protracted process involved in the plan's negotiation and implementation would be exploited by the Khmer Rouge to make major military gains and extend their political influence. The media carried exaggerated and sometimes unfounded accounts of Khmer Rouge advances, but the situation reflected in intelligence assessments available to the Australian government was less dramatic. These assessments indicated that the Khmer Rouge was making steady long-term progress with the same sort of guerrilla strategy which brought it to power in 1975 (combined with a softer 'hearts and minds' political strategy), but that there was no prospect of an early takeover. The only exception made, and it was an important one, was in the event of a total collapse in the military, political and social morale of the Hun Sen administration, but that was not assessed as likely in the medium term.

Another possibility was that the Khmer Rouge would be able to exploit the transitional arrangements to facilitate their return to power. This was given close attention in the Australian plan and in the international deliberations that followed. An important threshold consideration here, however, was that the proposed Supreme National Council (SNC), while comprising representatives from the four parties and fully embodying the sovereignty of the Cambodian nation, was not expected to itself exercise the full range of executive authority that one would associate with an ordinary government. (Certainly the Phnom Penh government was prepared from the outset to accept that the presence of just two Khmer Rouge nominees within the body of twelve constituting the SNC was not in itself a ground for concern: it regarded the SNC quite differently from the quadripartite transitional administration proposal which had been opposed in Paris.) Nor was it anticipated that the SOC regime would resist the idea of letting the Khmer Rouge contest UN-supervised elections, provided Pol Pot and his most notorious associates were not candidates. Although it appeared they were not in fact proposing to stand, a further safeguard was that the United Nations and most relevant national governments, including Australia, would no doubt have refused to co-operate with a process which was belittled by the presence of candidates of such notoriety.

A further important election safeguard proposed by Australia was that the elections should take place with secret balloting for a single national constituency with proportional representation. This would minimise the risk of intimidation of voters in areas controlled by the Khmer Rouge, for example. As to likely election outcomes, it was difficult to believe that the Khmer Rouge would win more than a minor share of the vote in any genuinely free and fair election, although it was unwise to underestimate the degree of support they had been winning—with their fiercely anti-Vietnamese nationalism and freedom from accusations of corruption—especially among some segments of the rural population who had not suffered directly their earlier brutality.

Certainly in these circumstances, given no evidence that the Khmer Rouge's stated abandonment of their previous ideology and methods was anything more than tactical, there could be no guarantee that they would not resume fighting after the transitional period with weapons which had been hidden from the UN monitoring teams. But, while acknowledging there could be no absolute guarantee that renewed fighting would not occur, it was thought that two crucial new factors would have a positive bearing on the outcome. First, China would have given an international legal undertaking to cease arms supply to the Khmer Rouge, would be under close international scrutiny to uphold that undertaking, and could be reasonably expected to honour it. While the Khmer Rouge may well have access to two or three years supplies of arms in caches, and would be able to make a major nuisance of themselves during that time, thereafter—

without continued external support—the danger they pose would be dramatically reduced.

A second consideration was that the new Cambodian administration would be accepted by the whole international community as the government of the country and was very likely to receive substantial economic, social and technical assistance during the rehabilitation and reconstruction process envisaged under the comprehensive settlement. Taken together, these factors would mean that the newly elected Cambodian government would be in a much better position than the present SOC regime to withstand any renewed challenge from what would be in any event a considerably constrained Khmer Rouge.

The Diplomatic Marathon   The initial international response to the Australian proposal was nothing less than remarkable. It very quickly became clear that the idea was one whose time had come. Within a matter of weeks, most of the participants in the Paris Conference had picked up the proposal for an enhanced United Nations role as a viable way around the power-sharing impasse and the problem of the Khmer Rouge, and given it varying degrees of public as well as private endorsement. This process was considerably assisted by an extraordinary feat of diplomatically effective endurance by Department of Foreign Affairs and Trade Deputy Secretary, Michael Costello. He had been tasked by the Foreign Minister early in December 1989 to pay a quick visit to Hanoi—in between talks scheduled on other matters in Hawaii and Tokyo—to take preliminary soundings. The response was so encouraging, and developed with each successive meeting such a snowball effect, that this initial detour turned into a series of thirty major meetings with key players in thirteen countries over twenty-one days straddling the December 1989–January 1990 period. During the course of this odyssey— in which all the pros and cons of the proposal were exhaustively discussed—the Australian 'idea' became a fully fledged Australian 'initiative' or 'plan', as the Foreign Minister and the officials working with him constantly refined and developed the detailed elements of the proposal and responded to suggestions or criticisms from our various interlocutors.

Particularly encouraging was the positive reaction of the United States Administration, which had the foresight to propose to the Soviet Union in late 1989 that they join the other three Permanent Members of the Security Council in a series of consultations on Cambodia. Representatives of the Permanent Five met in Paris on 15–16 January and agreed by consensus on a set of sixteen principles which would form the basis of their future discussions. Those principles included strong endorsement of the concept of an enhanced United Nations role in the transitional period. The January meeting of the Permanent Five was significant in another sense. It marked the start of a two-track international approach to the Cambodia problem the Permanent Five process and the Paris Conference process—between which a productive interaction has subsequently been maintained.

By late January 1990, Indonesian Foreign Minister Ali Alatas, who, as Co-Chairman of the Paris Conference, had been exploring the possibility of an informal regional meeting on Cambodia, felt sufficiently encouraged to convene a meeting in Jakarta on 26–28 February involving the four Cambodian parties, Vietnam and Laos and the ASEAN countries. In recognition of the contribution we were making to the peace process, Australia was invited to attend as a resource delegation.

In preparation for the Jakarta Informal Meeting on Cambodia (IMC), as it became known, an Australian technical mission visited Cambodia, Bangkok and the Thai–Cambodia border area from 2–16 February to gather information on the administrative structures of the State of Cambodia and of the National Government of Cambodia, with a view to filling in gaps in data necessary for the development of a United Nations role in Cambodia leading to free and fair elections. With a Departmental task force now numbering over a dozen senior officers working directly to the Foreign Minister, there was produced in time for distribution at the Jakarta Meeting a 155-page series of Working Papers, incorporating the technical mission's findings and covering in some detail all the necessary elements of a comprehensive settlement.

The Papers were subsequently published as *Cambodia: an Australian Peace Proposal*—the so-called (from the colour of its binding) 'Red Book'.[11] They examined in particular detail roles for the United Nations in civil administration, organising and conducting elections, and maintaining a secure environment in which Cambodians might exercise their electoral choice free from fear, intimidation and violence. The Papers also explored a range of costings. Conventional wisdom had it that such an exercise would be beyond the resources of the United Nations. Australian indicative calculations showed that such a proposal (estimated, for the preferred 'mid-range' scenario, to cost US$1.3 billion for 18 months) was both practicable and affordable.

The Jakarta IMC came very close to reaching agreement on a statement of principles providing for an enhanced role for the United Nations in a comprehensive settlement, but in the end it just failed to do so, consensus breaking down on the question of whether the agreed record should make specific reference to 'the prevention of recurrence of genocidal policies and practices'. While the outcome was disappointing in that regard, the meeting did begin a process of consensus-building. It also confirmed that if there was to be a way forward, it must be through an enhanced role for the United Nations.

Steady diplomatic progress was made throughout the rest of 1990 in the refinement and development of the Australian plan, with the Permanent Five and the Paris Conference Co-Chairmen in close consultation with the

UN Secretariat now playing the central role. The Permanent Five held six major consultative meetings on the subject between January and August, reaching agreement in New York on 27–28 August on a 'framework' document setting out the key elements of a comprehensive political settlement, based on an enhanced UN role, in a skilful and judicious balance of the various interests involved.

Then, at a meeting in Jakarta on 9–10 September, hosted by Indonesia and France as Paris Conference Co-Chairmen, the four Cambodian parties accepted this Permanent Five framework in its entirety as a basis for settling the Cambodian conflict, and agreed to establish a Supreme National Council (SNC)—part of the original Australian proposal, and called for in the framework—which would, among other things occupy the Cambodian seat in the United Nations. At Indonesia's invitation, Australian representatives attended this meeting and helped behind the scenes to achieve a successful outcome.

The next step was for the United Nations itself to endorse the basic elements of the peace plan. It did so, urging the parties to elaborate the Permanent Five framework into a concluded comprehensive political settlement, in UN Security Council Resolution 668 of 20 September and UN General Assembly Resolution 45/3 of 15 October 1990. These resolutions also welcomed the agreement of the Cambodian parties to form an SNC 'as the unique legitimate body and source of authority in which, throughout the transitional period, the independence, national unity and sovereignty of Cambodia is embodied', noting that the SNC would 'designate its representatives to occupy the seat of Cambodia at the United Nations'.

The last of the settlement building blocks to be put in place was the preparation of a detailed negotiating text. Agreement was reached on the form and structure of such a text at a Working Group Meeting in Jakarta on 9–10 November, hosted by the Paris Conference Co-Chairmen (Indonesia and France), and attended by the Co-Chairmen of the Conference's three Working Committees (Canada and India, Malaysia and Laos, Japan and Australia), the other four Permanent Members of the Security Council and a representative of the UN Secretary-General. Australia had prepared and circulated a full draft negotiating test as an input to the Working Group meeting, and this work was substantially drawn upon during the discussions. The meeting gave a mandate to its Co-Chairmen to complete the draft: their representatives, and the Secretary-General's, met with Permanent Five officials on 23–26 November and reached consensus on a full draft comprehensive agreement.

By the end of 1990, then, all the necessary foundations had been laid. All that remained to complete the settlement process were three steps: first, for the SNC to meet, resolve outstanding questions about its composition and chairmanship, and indicate its willingness to join in a resumed Paris Conference; secondly, for the PICC Co-ordination Committee, involving all

Paris Conference participants, including the SNC representing Cambodia, to meet to settle the text of the comprehensive settlement agreement; and thirdly, for a ministerial session of the Paris Conference to convene to endorse and sign that agreement. It would be then for the UN Security Council to pass a resolution instructing the Secretary-General to take the necessary action to implement the settlement.

As 1991 dawned, there seemed likely to be a relatively swift and painless run home to the tape. But despite all the momentum and expectations generated over the long months since the Australian plan was first put on the table in November 1989, the process faltered and seemed—five months into the year—in danger of stalling completely. Phnom Penh—supported by Hanoi—expressed a series of reservations about the Permanent Five negotiating text. Some of them—in particular the issue of army demobilization, and the relative vulnerability of each side following it—raised serious questions requiring further thought and negotiation; others —like the question of the implications of a UN role for Cambodian sovereignty—seemed to be trying to prise open agreements in principle long since reached; others were essentially minor quibbles, but capable of endlessly protracting the settlement process. Many meetings were held between various combinations of players—a number of them with Australian diplomats working quietly in the wings—but while no major backward steps were taken, nor was there any real movement forward.

Despair, however, was as premature as exultation would have been in 1990. A rush of events in June 1991 injected immense new life into the settlement process. Prince Sihanouk emerged from months of self-imposed isolation; formed an improbable liaison with Hun Sen (which, with the apparent approval of China, pushed the Khmer Rouge into something of a corner); convened a meeting of the SNC in Pattaya, Thailand on 24–26 June (the first since its notional formation the previous September); and at that meeting brokered a series of agreements between the four Cambodian parties which engendered a great deal of international confidence that a final settlement might, after all, be quite quickly attainable.

The key agreements were an immediate and unconditional ceasefire of unlimited duration; acceptance that all Cambodian parties would stop receiving external military assistance forthwith; and—in relation to the SNC itself—that future meetings would be chaired by Prince Sihanouk; that it would set up headquarters in Phnom Penh in a matter of months; and that countries participating in the peace process would be invited to accredit missions to it. Australia, a few days later, was the first country to announce that it would seek such accreditation to the SNC: in the first place on a non-resident basis through its Ambassador to Thailand, and subsequently by the establishment of a resident mission in Phnom Penh as the SNC was itself there established.

Crucially, all the Cambodian parties at Pattaya reiterated their support for the Permanent Five framework, and for a comprehensive settlement in which the United Nations would have a central role. There remained many issues of detail—not least the question of interim enforcement of the ceasefire and arms cessation agreements, and resolution of the demobilisation question which was continuing to worry the SOC. But there was general agreement on a course of future meetings to address these issue— involving, again, the Paris Conference Co-Chairmen, the Permanent Five, and ultimately the reconvened Paris Conference. At the time of writing it did seem, at last, that the comprehensive settlement process had moved to its decisive end-phase.

Whatever the final outcome proves to be—and there have been many false dawns before in the Cambodian tragedy—Australia's contribution to the settlement process has been major, and acknowledged as such by the international community. Our United Nations peace initiative was not taken at anyone's behest. It was not the kind of 'good offices' role that Australia had undertaken in the past (when, say, it represented Indonesia in its independence struggle against the Dutch), nor the kind of 'representation' role that Menzies had assumed for Australia in heading the delegation of Suez Canal users to Nasser in 1956. It was neither front- nor back-seat driving, but the more demanding, although less visible, role of mapmaker. It was, in short, an intellectual, rather than a political or military role. It represented not only a sharp new turn in the implementation of Australia's Indo-China policy but a major development in Australian diplomacy.

FROM BATTLEFIELD TO MARKETPLACE

One of Thailand Prime Minister Chatichai's enduring legacies will undoubtedly be his stated determination, expressed to reporters at his inauguration on 4 August 1988, 'to turn Indo-China into markets for products instead of a battleground'. Entering the literature thereafter as 'from battlefield to marketplace', or 'from war zone to trade zone',[12] this aspiration seemed to catch the mood of the time not only throughout ASEAN, but in Indo-China itself.

The Indo-China region—particularly Vietnam, with its 65 million people and substantial natural resource base—lags far behind in its development as a result of the conflict in which it has been immersed for so long. A reformed, expanding Vietnamese economy would be good for everyone else's business, not least Australia's. But despite the tentative internal liberalisation that had begun to occur, major rehabilitation, reconstruction and growth will not be possible without large-scale external trade, aid and investment. And in practice—largely because of pressures maintained by the United States and its allies—this will not happen until the Cambodian question has been resolved. So Prime Minister Chatichai's call—though it was capable of, and given, various intrepretations—became a rallying cry of its own, and quite a helpful one at that, for all those trying to move the peace process forward. More generally it also reflected a growing feeling—certainly shared in Australia—that the countries of Indo-China should be embraced within, and more comprehensively engaged within, the policy framework of regional co-operation. This should be the case not only in economic issues, but on political and strategic issues and on the new 'third agenda' ones as well, in particular in relation to the problem of drugs and refugees.

Australia's economic and trade interests in Indo-China are at present insignificant, but the potential for growth—particularly in Vietnam—is immense, and we are particularly well poised, because of our diplomatic engagement, to take advantage of this opportunity. Two-way trade with Vietnam grew steadily from under $5 million in 1984 to nearly $40 million in 1990, with a significant component of this—reflecting intense infra-structure activity by OTC and Telecom on the ground—being telecommunications equipment. Trade with Cambodia and Laos, by contrast, was negligible—less than $2 million in each case, essentially exports associated with Australia's aid program. Laos, the smallest of the Indo-China countries, with a population of under 4 million essentially dependent on agriculture, and ruled by the communist Pathet Lao since the end of its own twenty-year civil war in 1973, is the only country in Indo-China which in recent times has received direct bilateral aid from Australia. Vietnam and Cambodia have, however, received Australian support indirectly through multilateral and non-government organisation aid programs.

One of the endemic problems of the region that should be capable of resolution with the transition from war zone to trade zone, and the peace and prosperity going with it, is the outflow of refugees. Since the fall of Saigon in 1975, Australia has accepted over 130 000 Indo-Chinese refugees—on a per capita basis the highest ratio of all resettlement countries. Australia has also accepted nearly 30 000 other persons direct from Vietnam under our bilateral Vietnam Migration Program. It is estimated that the cost to the Australian community over the years from 1975 to mid-1991 has been some $720 million (measured in present-day terms) for initial transport and settlement expenses alone, quite apart from the additional food and cash aid contributions we had made to Indo-Chinese refugee programs.

The 'boat people' brought to the forefront two seemingly different Australian national interests. One is the value of Australia subscribing to an international system which ensures that refugees are given asylum. This interest arises partly from the axiom that everyone benefits from rules that apply to everyone, but more particularly from the belief that Australia benefits by practising what, as a liberal, democratic society, it professes—such as the right of the individual to a private life, protection of the weak against the strong, and equality before the law. Refugees, who by definition are victims of persecution, obviously offer a test of these principles.

The other Australian interest lies in restricting, not encouraging, the flow of refugees. It is always likely that Australia will be the target of refugee movements, as a relatively prosperous society with a small population occupying a large land mass. Our distance from the main centres of refugee activity protected Australia in the past from the involuntary flow of large numbers of refugees, who normally move over the nearest border. It had been easier for Australia to maintain the first kind of national interest when we decided to bring large numbers of refugees from war-stricken Europe, where they were carefully selected by trained immigration officers thousands of miles from Australian shores. The 'boat people' arrived without any such preparation. Although controversy broke out over the question of their status—whether they were actually refugees, in fear of persecution, or merely seekers of good, or better, fortune—many of them were indisputably refugees. That they had undertaken a hazardous voyage, through seas subject to storms and piracy, to some extent supported their claim. Whereas the European refugees were brought to Australia as part of deliberate immigration strategy, the Vietnamese were, from the standpoint of Australian policy, less wanted. This applies also to more recent 'boat people' from Cambodia.

The resolution of these two national interests is achieved in principle by establishing that every country has the right to determine who enters its territory. Through experience of grappling with the Indo-China refugee issue at first hand, Australia remains committed to its humanitarian principles, but has realised that it must be more active in managing the refugee problem. It has done this by establishing an 'orderly departure program' with Vietnam; persisting in a dialogue with other governments in South-East Asia about restraining the flow of refugees southward to Australia; impressing countries outside the region with the need to resettle refugees at present held in camps of first asylum; and, above all, by making an end to the conflict in Cambodia—and the isolation of Vietnam—one of the top priorities of Australian foreign policy. In that sense Australia owed it not only to innocent victims of war and conflict but also to ourselves to find a lasting solution to the last remaining source of serious conflict in Indo-China.

14

North-East Asia

AUSTRALIA'S RELATIONS with North-East Asia—Japan, the People's Republic of China, the Republic of Korea (ROK), Taiwan and Hong Kong in particular—have developed more rapidly over recent decades than our relations with any other part of the world. This is partly because of policy priorities decided deliberately by Australia, but also because North-East Asia is one of the world's power points, both as an economic force and as a strategic nerve centre. Almost every economy in the region is characterised by unusual industry and achievement: the growth rates achieved by the region as a whole have been breathtaking, without historical precedent. And with the strategic interests of four of the world's major powers—Japan, China, the Soviet Union and the United States—intersecting in various ways in North-East Asia, it has been unquestionably the most sensitive, as well as the most dynamic, area in the Asia Pacific region.

It is not difficult to see, country-by-country, why North-East Asia demands, and gets, so much of the world's attention. Japan's economic capacity is a global by-word, and remains at the core both of North-East Asia's economic achievement, and of its potential. Japan is also a country of major strategic importance: both because of its alliance with the United States, and the contribution its substantial armed forces make in their own right—albeit constitutionally limited to self-defence—to the military balance in North-East Asia. Its continuing dispute with the Soviet Union over the occupation of the four northern islands remains a major regional pressure point. China is a permanent member of the United Nations Security

Council, the world's most populous nation, a civilisation of remarkable endurance and a nuclear-armed communist state. It not only has huge weight in regional affairs but is a world power. How China chooses to handle its relations with other countries in the region is always a profound force for stability, or instability, as the case may be.

The two Koreas, both strong and ambitious—but with the ROK in the south by far the higher economic achiever—divide the Korean peninsula, itself separating China and Japan, uneasily between them. While some tortuously slow moves toward rapprochement have occurred, the Korean peninsula remains the region's most dangerous potential flashpoint. Taiwan and Hong Kong are both immense economic achievers, but their political status—linked to China past and future—remains unresolved. Whether Hong Kong's transition to Chinese rule in 1997 can be peacefully and smoothly accomplished, and whether a *modus vivendi* can be found to suit both the People's Republic of China and Taiwan, are issues of more than merely regional significance.

The countries mentioned so far are not the only ones making up North-East Asia, but they are the ones around which Australia's relationships with the region are built. The Soviet Union is of course an Asian as well as a European power, and the Soviet Far East—with its seven million people and vast mineral and energy resources—is bound in due course to become an influential regional economic player. But the Soviet Union's significance for the moment is as a global superpower with a major military presence in the region, rather than as a regional country in any other sense. Mongolia, which is unequivocally a regional country, has had a fascinating history, not least since it rebalanced its relations with China and the Soviet Union in 1989, and abandoned communism in favour of multi-party democratic elections in 1990. But its tiny population of two million people and its land-locked Third World economy mean that it will be a long time yet before it assumes significance in either regional or bilateral terms.

In recent decades the dominant dimension in Australia's relations with the major North-East Asian countries has been, unquestionably, economics. Japan has been for twenty-five years by far our largest market anywhere; the Republic of Korea is our third largest export destination. In 1990 Taiwan, Hong Kong and China ranked seventh, ninth and tenth respectively as Australian export markets. The region as a whole accounts for over one-third of our total trade (as compared with less than one-fifth each for Europe and North America). And from the perspective of the region itself, the economic relationship with Australia has been a crucial one: for instance, Japan relies upon Australia for 70 per cent of its steaming coal and 45 per cent of its iron ore and coking coal.

Reflecting all this, our relationships in the region over the last thirty years have been dominated by bilateral trade issues. (China has perhaps been the exception, with our relationship from the time the diplomatic ice was broken in 1972 being characterised by an interplay between political and economic themes. The breach which followed June 1989 was all the more jarring for that reason.) But more recently, those relationships have become much less one-dimensional in character. With Japan we have been exploring for some time the scope for co-operation on a wide range of political, strategic and economic issues of regional and global significance. As Japan feels its way, still rather uncertainly, into a political role more commensurate with its economic status, it is looking for the kind of support that countries like Australia—diplomatically active and with no particular competitive axes to grind—can give. Similarly with the ROK, ministerial and official exchanges have steadily become more wide-ranging and productive, reaching into subject areas—for example, Asia Pacific security and economic co-operation—which were simply not on the table for serious dialogue until very recently.

ECONOMIC ASCENDANCY

North-East Asia has, with dramatic speed, become one of the three main centres of world production, trade and savings. Its sustained pace of economic growth has been both unprecedented and stunning: economic output has more than doubled over each of the last four decades in Japan, Hong Kong, the Republic of Korea, Taiwan and China, with growth throughout the period averaging nearly 8 per cent per annum. North-East Asia's share of production has grown over the period from one-third of North America's to a quarter of the world's.[1] Since the end of World War II, Japan has become the second largest global economy, the largest international creditor and the world leader in fields as diverse as automobiles, consumer electronics, industrial robotics, semi-conductors and banking. The ROK and Taiwan have grown from underdeveloped economies, heavily dependent on United States aid, to upper-middle income economies and major world traders. China, over the same period, emerged from chaos and civil war to the point where it is now the world's major exporter of labour-intensive goods.

Explanations have been offered for these transformations. It has been argued by some that Confucian values and the relationship between government and business in some of the economies have played a part. But the main explanation can also be couched in orthodox economic terms. The successful economies of North-East Asia have saved and invested a high proportion of output. Their rapid growth has been associated with effective economic management, and particularly with outward looking policies which have drawn strength from a comparative advantage in supplying manufactured products to the world market. They have proved willing to absorb and adapt technology from abroad, and—more importantly—to undertake structural adjustments. And they have benefited from labour forces that are diligent, skilled and productive in relation to labour costs.

Rapid growth in North-East Asia has also depended critically on the relatively open post-War international economic order. This order has been weakened over the years by significant difficulties and restrictions in areas such as agriculture and textiles, and by a proliferation of voluntary export restraints and other protective measures, often directed at the North-East Asian economies. Nevertheless, a relatively liberal trading system has been an essential foundation for the strategies of export-oriented industrialis-ation which economies in North-East Asia have pursued.

China is, as in many other respects, something of a special case. Here, the momentum of development has, on more than one occasion, been inter-rupted by significant policy reversals and instability. Rapid growth since the end of the Cultural Revolution in 1976 has been associated with market-oriented reform, and an increasingly outward orientation for its centrally planned economy. Growth over the next decade will equally depend on a continuing commitment to reform and to the political changes required to make economic reform effective.

North-East Asia's extraordinary economic performance has provided an immense opportunity for Australia, and will go on doing so. Australia has, until now, responded well to that challenge. Japan had become our biggest export market—displacing the United Kingdom—by 1966, and overall our biggest trading partner by 1970. By 1967 North-East Asia as a whole had replaced West Europe as our major export region: it now takes over two-fifths of our exports (providing five of our ten top export markets), provides just under one-third of our imports, and is a major source of foreign invest-ment and tourism. None of this is especially surprising, given the inherent complementarity of our respective economies. As Ross Garnaut points out in his 1989 Report on *Australia and the Northeast Asian Ascendancy*:

> The Northeast Asian economies are more closely complementary to Australia in their resource endowments and in the commodity composition of their trade than any other economies on earth. This close complementarity survives the changes of economic structure that accompany economic growth: from the natu-ral fibres required for the textiles industries which dominate the early stages of Northeast Asian industrialisation, through the mineral raw materials used so intensively in later heavy industrialisation to the high-value foodstuffs and visits to less densely populated places that mark the high consumption of advanced economic development in Northeast Asia.[2]

Japan has led the way with each successive new layer of trade—from fibres and foodstuffs, to minerals, to processed raw materials, to high quality goods and services—with Taiwan and the Republic of Korea following a decade or so behind, and China a good deal further back again.

The real challenge for Australia in the years ahead will be to maintain and build upon this momentum. There is no doubt that North-East Asia will continue to be a major world engine of growth for the foreseeable future, and it is crucial to *our* future that we stay with that pace. The scale of the task is amply and effectively documented in the Garnaut Report. This combines a thorough analysis of the scale of the economic growth and restructuring achieved in the region with a wide-ranging checklist of the opportunities thus created for Australia and a prescription of the strategies —in both domestic and foreign policy—needed to effectively grasp those opportunities.

The prescriptive themes of the Garnaut Report echo, in a specifically North-East Asian context, those which in fact recur throughout this book. Australia's primary diplomatic weapon, as a middle-power, is persuasion, and to be effective in this respect we have to be clever and disciplined in identifying and pursuing shared interests. Our economic diplomacy should be directed at securing open, non-discriminatory trade; we must develop professional excellence in the management of our international relations, both in diplomacy and commerce; and we must accelerate progress in domestic economic reform, to build a flexible, internationally oriented economy capable of grasping opportunities in the decades ahead.[3] Garnaut also gives special emphasis to the need for effective public diplomacy to ensure that Australians and North-East Asians get more attention 'in each other's minds'[4] He advocates, in a way we entirely endorse, persistent efforts to build people-to-people links; to overcome some of the more damaging stereotypes held about us (especially that we are a better place in which to relax than to do business); and generally to project Australia as a constructive and outward-looking partner with something to offer the region.

THE SECURITY ENVIRONMENT

Economic success cannot be achieved without strategic stability, and Australia has almost as big a stake as do the North-East Asian countries themselves in ensuring that the region remains peaceful. That will not be an easy task: of all the sub-regions of the Asia Pacific, the North-East is in security terms the most complex and least stable. Economic dynamism and growing interdependence coincide with an increasingly fluid strategic landscape. The complexity of that landscape flows primarily from the simple fact that the interests of four major powers—the United States, the Soviet Union, China and Japan—intersect there. Additional elements of uncertainty include the evolving political situation in China, the future of Hong Kong and Taiwan, territorial disputes in the South China Sea, possible changes in the United States–Japan security relationship, the direction in which Japan–Soviet relations might develop, and—above all—the situation on the Korean peninsula.

There has been some recent relaxation of traditional tensions as ripple effects flow into the region from the profound and dramatic changes that have occurred in Europe. Sino-Soviet relations have been normalised. The Soviet Union and the ROK have established diplomatic relations, and the Democratic People's Republic of Korea (DPRK) has proposed a normalisation of relations with Japan. The DPRK has announced its intention to seek, in parallel rather than in competition with the ROK, a seat in the United Nations. Mongolia has embraced parliamentary democracy. China–Taiwan relations are thawing, with Taiwan declaring the communist rebellion over, and direct personal and commercial contacts rapidly growing. The Soviet Union has revived its vision of a resource-rich Soviet Far East which will attract investors from capital-rich north Asia, especially Japan, and has indicated to Japan that it no longer regards the United States–Japan alliance as an impediment to the Soviet Union concluding a peace treaty with Japan. It has also acknowledged that the future of the four northern islands occupied by the Soviet Union since the end of World War II—Etorofu, Kunashiri, Shikotan and Habomai—is a question that needs to be resolved (although it is evident that a combination of domestic political and military anxieties in the Soviet Union will make that resolution extremely difficult).

What continues to distinguish North-East Asia from Europe is that the driving force of change in East Europe—the rejection of communist ideology and political structures—still has a great distance to go: China and the DPRK show no signs of following Mongolia's democratic example. Cold War tensions remain most evident of all on the Korean peninsula, which for forty years has been the eastern fulcrum of global East–West conflict. The gap between the two Koreas, although beginning to close, remains wide. A particularly disturbing element in the DPRK's approach is the indication that it may not only be keeping open the option of acquiring nuclear weapons, but actively developing them. This concern has not been entirely dispelled by the DPRK's announcement in June 1991—under intense diplomatic pressure, and after years of foot-dragging—that it would move to conclude a safeguards agreement with the International Atomic Energy Agency pursuant to its signature in 1985 of the Nuclear Non-Proliferation Treaty.

The Korean peninsula is a specific challenge to the capacity of the United States and the Soviet Union to co-operate in the 1990s. We have seen with the sudden political reunification of Germany and the protracted military reunification of Vietnam that nationalism remains potent in a divided country, and we should not expect Korea to be any different. There are some parallels with the situation in Europe, as two large land armies face each other across a demilitarised zone with support from allies armed with nuclear weapons. The United States's reluctance to engage the Soviet Union in discussions aimed at a balance of naval forces in the Asia Pacific region is not therefore a factor. The Soviet Union has powerful economic imperatives to ease Korean tensions, reduce its military patronage of the DPRK and attract interest from the ROK in infrastructure development and construction in the Soviet Far East. It is reluctant, however, to act too quickly, as China might be prepared to move into the gap left by the Soviet Union. The well-based concern about DPRK development of nuclear weapons adds a note of dangerous urgency to this uncertain situation. The United States has accepted that the Korean peninsula is one neuralgic point in Asia which could respond to the kind of confidence-building measures, including arms reductions, that have been successful in Europe. An obstacle in the path has been the absence of any substantive dialogue between the two Koreas, but a series of meetings, starting in September 1990, of delegations headed by Prime Ministers—the highest level contact between the two Koreas since 1945—has given some small hope that progress could be made on a non-aggression pact, and ultimately on reunification.

Australia has an obvious interest in making what contribution it can to the security of North-East Asia. There are fewer opportunities than in the South Pacific and South-East Asia, but our influence is not negligible. Our main role must continue to be as a persistent, consistent voice urging a frank and open dialogue between all the countries on security issues. The decade of the 1990s presents the world with a major opportunity for systematic confidence building: the development of arrangements—military, diplomatic and otherwise—designed to build, over time, assurance of mind and belief in the trustworthiness of other states and their actions. This will be harder to achieve in North-East Asia than in most other regions of the globe, but the need for it is commensurately greater.

JAPAN

Japan is, and has been since 1970, Australia's major trading partner. There is every reason to believe that its importance to us will continue well into the next century, and the first pillar of our policy in relation to the country must be to maintain and enhance—in both breadth and depth—that economic relationship. This will involve, here as elsewhere, not just relying on our established laurels as an efficient commodity supplier. We have to make clear the extent of the structural changes that have been taking place in the Australian economy, and the opportunities this creates for Japan in Australia. While we expect that mineral resources, energy products and agricultural commodities will continue to underpin the bilateral trading relationship, we are looking to encourage a much broader, more diversified economic interchange.

This process is, in fact, well under way, with Japan already the largest market for Australian manufactures (albeit largely of the 'simply transformed', or processed mineral, variety), and Japanese investment in Australia accounting for about one-third of the total annual investment inflow. The Multi-Function Polis Project (MFP), initiated by Japan at the Australia–Japan Ministerial Committee (AJMC) in 1987, has become an important barometer of our success in diversifying and upgrading the sophistication of our economic relationship. Following four years of bilateral co-operation to define and test the MFP concept (essentially designed to unite new thinking about high technology industry and leisure in the context of a newly created working-living environment), a physical site in Adelaide has been earmarked, a new International Advisory Board established, and wide-ranging international business participation in the development of the project actively sought.

An important new characteristic of Australia's relationship with Japan is the way in which growing diversification of our economic relationship is now being matched by the adding of new dimensions to the relationship as a whole—and the way in which this is being pushed at least as much by the Japanese as by ourselves. At the tenth meeting of the two-yearly AJMC in January 1989, Japan proposed that the bilateral relationship be designated henceforth as one of 'constructive partnership', in which we jointly co-operated on regional and global security, economic and environmental issues. As refined at that meeting, and at the next one in Canberra in May 1991—attended by an unprecedentedly large group of six Japanese Cabinet Ministers and two Parliamentary Vice Ministers—the concept is now agreed to embrace four key components. They are, in the first place, security—in particular co-operation in securing peace and prosperity in our own Asia-Pacific region; secondly, international trade—co-operation in maintaining and strengthening a free and open world economic system; thirdly, the resolution of international problems requiring co-operation for their solution—in particular protection of the environment; and fourthly, bilateral relations—co-operation in the further development and diversification of the Japan–Australia relationship.

Underlying the 'constructive partnership' is a recognition that, for all the disparities of size and wealth between the two countries, we do bring together important assets. In security and strategic terms, Australia and Japan *are* properly described as the northern and southern anchors of the Western alliance, with both countries sharing the view that a continuing significant United States presence in the region is wholly desirable. In economic terms, we are the two major advanced market economies of the region, and still (with New Zealand) the only eyes and ears of the OECD in the Asian hemisphere. Japan's ranking at the head of the regional wealth table is clear, but Australia ranks third (after China) with a GNP equal to India's, or all six ASEAN countries combined.

Australia, moreover, has a long-standing record of active involvement in international diplomacy—especially in multilateral forums—which makes us a useful dialogue partner for a country still searching for its role in this area. Japan in many ways is now at a watershed in its history, having to make domestically very difficult decisions about how to respond to expectations from abroad that it accept the kind of responsibilities of international political and economic leadership that are appropriate to its status as the world's second largest economy. It has been the view of successive Australian governments that Japan should play a wider role in world affairs, but it is only quite recently—in the context of Japan's very public agonising as to the role it should play in the Gulf conflict—that the issue has come fully into the open.

During his visit to Japan in September 1990, Prime Minister Hawke publicly supported Japan's permanent membership of the United Nations Security Council, and said that Japanese armed forces as a contribution to a UN peacekeeping role in Cambodia or the Gulf would be acceptable to Australia. He argued for a generally enhanced Japanese role in these terms:

> Indeed, it is true to say that no framework for the conduct of international affairs could be regarded as adequate or complete if it lacked Japanese commitment and involvement. The days are gone when Japan's international political influence can or should lag behind its economic strength and economic interests.[5]

Memories of Japan's attempt to subdue the Pacific in World War II, in alliance with Nazi Germany and Fascist Italy, remain powerful in Australia, as they do throughout South-East Asia and the South Pacific, and the Prime Minister's comments did cause a degree of public reaction in Australia. However, it is a fact of international life, acknowledged by the great majority of Australians, that substantial national interests are now very much involved in Australia's relations with Japan and that, nearly half a century after World War II, it is time to treat the Japanese as full participants in public affairs—not as paymasters who are called in only to handle the bill.

Australia cannot be prescriptive about a Japanese role in world affairs. How the Japanese people and government intend to meet their national responsibilities is a matter to be determined by Japan itself. In the past, Japanese nationalism has been associated with militarism, and this is what concerns foreign observers today when nationalism again asserts itself. However, the form in which Japan chose as a nation to assert itself at the end of the nineteenth century was copied from the aggressive nationalism of the European nation-state. Whatever we may think about the way it went about realising its ambitions, Japan was attempting in its part of the world something not very different from what the European powers had been doing for centuries.

Mainstream Japanese nationalism today is associated not with military aggression so much as with resistance to military alliances and strict support for the pacifist constitution—forced on the Japanese after World War II but later somewhat compromised by the development of armed forces which, Self-Defence Forces though they may be, are now supported by the third largest military budget in the world. Popular and political resistance by Japanese to the suggestion that their country should again be a military power remains formidable. In these circumstances, Japan needs to be encouraged to develop politically and militarily according to the new concepts of security that are likely to determine the shape of the twenty-first century, rather than to those that shaped this century or the last.

The issue of Japan's role in world strategic and security affairs is therefore contained within a bigger issue—whether a real international community is emerging and, if so, what kind of enforcement it can provide of accepted international behaviour in the interests of peace and stability. Japan, the most nationalist of nations, has also shown itself to be increasingly internationalist in outlook and sensitive to universalist tendencies in world politics as they have developed with the decline of the Cold War. If these tendencies are strengthened, as is to be hoped will be the case, Japan will be able to play a role in the world's security affairs not in any way at odds with the spirit of its constitution.

It is being edged in this direction by the nature of the Asia Pacific region, especially as the two superpowers move away from policies of strategic denial to accommodation and even co-operation. The Asia Pacific region—potentially volatile though it may be in some corners, especially North-East Asia—is open and dispersed. Only rarely do the major powers impinge upon, or threaten, each other. It is for this reason that the Asia Pacific is not readily susceptible to nineteenth century 'balance of power' theory, and is amenable to co-operative ideas of powersharing and accommodation.

Japan's role in international economic policy-making is a much less sensitive issue internationally than its involvement in strategic and security issues, but here the country's policy-makers have again—for domestic political reasons—trodden extremely cautiously. Given the vital interests that both Australia and Japan have in strengthening the multilateral trading system, and securing the further liberalisation of trade in both goods and services, Australia has consistently urged that Japan play a leadership, rather than merely subsidiary, role in exercises such as the Uruguay Round of multilateral trade negotiations—not least by being prepared to make some significant further gestures in the liberalisation of access to its own markets, particularly rice.

So far as regional economic co-operation is concerned, Japan has been—while not taking a leadership role—strongly supportive of the development of the APEC process. In particular, it has supported APEC's development *not* as a closed Asian-region, yen-dominated bloc established to do battle with the giants of North America and Europe, but rather as an open-textured vehicle for both global and non-discriminatory regional trade liberalisation. In all of this, Japan's policy co-operation with Australia has been very close. It is crucially important, not just for the health of the region but the global economy, that this perspective continue.

In the area of international problem-solving generally—those matters of international concern, like the environment, that increasingly worry governments of all political persuasions in countries big and small—Japan is increasingly playing a much more active role, and being universally encouraged to do so. Two significant initiatives in 1991 were to host a major United Nations Disarmament Conference in Kyoto—addressing the whole range of post-Gulf War multilateral disarmament and arms control options

—and a major meeting on drug abuse issues for the Asia Pacific region. Japan has also substantially upgraded its involvement in international environment issues, and has started to explore the scope for collaborative research work with Australia in this field, drawing on our success in developing a number of world competitive technologies. Japan's contribution, again, to aid and humanitarian programs has long been substantial in quantitative terms. In this area, as in others, the change has been in its willingness to engage with ourselves and other countries in co-operative policy and program development, as for example in the South Pacific.

Thus the basic course of Australia's future relationship with Japan has, then, been set: it simply has to be assiduously pursued. Here as elsewhere there are plenty of competitors for our partner's attention, and Australia will have to work hard to consolidate and develop such influence as we have. And here as elsewhere this will require as much attention to broad-ranging perceptions of each country by the other as it will to high-level policy-making: public diplomacy again. Japanese and Australians *are* gradually getting to know each other better—through massive increases in tourism, and through cultural and educational exchanges and the like. There are, moreover, proportionately more youngsters studying the Japanese language here than in any other country in the world. But, in a bilateral relationship as important to Australia as this one, this is no time to be resting on our oars.

CHINA, TAIWAN AND HONG KONG

Relations with the People's Republic of China have been a priority of Australian foreign policy since we established diplomatic relations in 1972—after having refused for twenty-three years to acknowledge the country's existence. The ascent of the relationship was dramatic, and it has not been without turbulence since, not least following the tragic events in Beijing of 4 June 1989 which led to a nearly two-year severance of economic and technical assistance and high-level political visits.

The rise of China in Australia's foreign policy priorities was due partly to the simple fact that it had been suppressed for so long. The sudden surfacing of such a major fact of international life could not help but dominate policy thinking in Canberra. Australia had trade with the People's Republic of China from its beginning, and from the 1960s it became an important, if irregular, market for our wheat and, later, wool. It was believed that, without diplomatic recognition, the Chinese market would never be fully open to Australia. So there was substantial business interest in opening relations with China as well as a political and strategic fascination with the awakened giant of Asia. What catapulted China into such an important place in Australian foreign policy, so that it was even later suggested that we had a special relationship, was the unexpected bipartisan enthusiasm it generated in Australia. Recognition of communist China was one of Gough Whitlam's magnificent obsessions, which he handled with courage and flair, demolishing his political opponents while making history. Essentially, however, the Whitlam Government expressed in its China policy, as in its Vietnam policy, the pent-up resistance of the left of Australian politics to the Cold War. By the time the Fraser Government took office, playing the China card had become the prerogative of the political right. With the United States withdrawn and angry after its defeat in Vietnam, China was viewed as a bulwark against the Soviet Union and a check on Hanoi. This was a theme that Malcolm Fraser employed successfully on his early visit to China in 1976, and it became a chorus after Vietnam invaded Cambodia in 1978.

The Hawke Government concentrated on the economic potential for Australia. Ministerial visits were frequent. An umbrella mechanism—the Joint Ministerial Economic Commission (JMEC)—was established to co-ordinate economic relations. Institutional arrangements for economic co-operation were made in iron and steel, wool, agriculture, coal, non-ferrous metals, education, transport and communications, machinery and electronics, energy, science and technology, and space. The Australian business community responded enthusiastically. But even before the check to relations that occurred with the Beijing massacre in June 1989, some fatigue was beginning to show in business and government circles in Australia. Despite the warmth of high-level political contact—expressed in two visits to China by Mr Hawke and visits to Australia by Hu Yaobang, then General Secretary of the Communist party of China, and Li Peng, China's Premier—the economic relationship did not develop as quickly as had been hoped. Some major achievements, such as the Mount Channar iron ore mine in Western Australia and a 10 per cent investment in the Portland Aluminium Smelter in Victoria (China's two largest overseas investments), coupled with a diminishing trading surplus in Australia's favour, kept hopes alive, but two-way trade did not increase markedly in value. The far-reaching economic reforms in China from 1984 to 1988 made the economy more dynamic, but did create problems—including rapid over-heating in certain sectors and a stop-go approach to macro-economic management.

It is notable that despite all the evident warmth and appreciation in bilateral relations, the media attention given to high level visits, the fulsome official rhetoric, the preferred location in Canberra for a large Chinese embassy, and all the rest, Australia's two-way trade with the renegade Chinese outpost of Taiwan—with its 20 million people as compared with the mainland's 1.1 billion, and with whom there were no official dealings at all—was as substantial as that with mainland China. And with the small and truncated Republic of Korea, trade was significantly greater. Moreover, Australia's exports to Taiwan and the Republic of Korea were strongest in the preferred category of manufactures and value-added goods, while our exports to China remained heavily in commodities (see Chart 6).

After June 1989—with the crushing of the democracy movement and the loss of position or influence for many politicians, intellectuals and officials who had been at the forefront of reform in China—enthusiasm for the relationship rapidly subsided in Australia. Critics emerged—such as the former Australian Ambassador to China, Dr Stephen FitzGerald, and, inevitably, the Opposition—arguing that Australia had overplayed its hand in the past. It is true that Australians had taken up the relationship with an unusual display of enthusiasm and indeed emotion; that the material benefits had not been as great as expected; and that, in the future, Australia's political relations with China are unlikely, in the absence of really fundamental change in that country, to reach again the height they did. However, the importance of this early period should not be lost in a dazzle of hindsight. There were at least three benefits to Australia.

First, the political struggle in Australia over recognition of the communist regime in China, although long and costly as an exercise in foreign policy decision-making, was eventually won. Probably the most dramatic example since World War II of an Australian initiative in Asia maintained in the face of United States disapproval, this was a landmark in Australia's development as a nation-state in our region. Hitherto we had been immensely reluctant to venture into Asia in defiance of our more powerful kith and kin, and the recognition of the People's Republic of China entered the history books as a win, if overly delayed, for Australian national confidence.

Secondly, the attempt to create a substantial relationship with China was a major test for Australian foreign policy resourcefulness. China was—and still is—a huge, self-absorbed country, one of the world's great civilisations, and one committed to a system of government and economic management totally different from Australia's. Japan, India and Indonesia in their different ways all presented problems for Australia in seeking a relationship of substance, but nothing quite comparable with the task in China. The management of such an asymmetrical and cumbersome relationship was a challenge for Australian foreign policy which for the most part was met with some accomplishment.

Thirdly, Australian and Chinese cultural exchanges were significant in opening up an awareness of the other country that had not been there before. China made a point of sending to Australia major exhibitions (such as the 'Entombed Warriors') which would not normally have gone to a nation off the beaten track of international cultural exchanges. The Melbourne *Age* helped establish an English-language newspaper, *China Daily*. Acrobatic training provided by Chinese experts to the Flying Fruit Fly children's circus in Albury–Wodonga was a major, sustained exercise. Teacher and student exchanges with Australia were substantial. For its part, Australia sent more cultural delegations to China than almost anyone else. Arts companies excitedly queued up to tour, and even such an idiosyncratically Australian offering as playwright Jack Hibberd's *A Stretch of the Imagination* was given an airing. Considering how preoccupied the Australian arts community tends to be with the standing of our arts in the United States and Europe, this excursion into the unknown cultural marketplace of Asia was an important innovation, in which new seeds of Australia's uniquely developing culture may have been sown.

As to the future, the Australian Government must remain committed to a long-term co-operative relationship with China, where Australia has enduring strategic and economic interests. It is manifestly not in the interests of our country, nor indeed of the region or the broader international community, to have an isolated and inward-looking China. Regional stability will be influenced by China's key role in issues such as Cambodia, and by the results of its economic modernisation program. The extent of China's openness to outside economic forces will have crucial influence on the future of Asia Pacific regional economic growth and integration, with obvious implications for Australia. China is also an important player on issues of global importance, such as disarmament and the environment.

It will be difficult to the point of impossibility to restore the warmth of the previous bilateral relationship while the generation of leaders responsible for the violent suppression of the pro-democracy movement in June 1989 remains in place. But it is important that as many lines of access, communication and dialogue as possible be kept open, not least to the legion of institutions and individuals within China who remain as appalled by those events as anyone in the West. Given the monolithic and inherently repressive nature of the Chinese political system since 1949, and the ingrained hostility of that system to the democratic and libertarian values of the United Nations Charter and Universal Declaration of Human Rights, the circumstance that was, in a way, even more remarkable than the awful massacre of Beijing was the rapid growth and strength of feeling underlying the democratic movement that preceded it. From all that we know about the continued force of that feeling, and the nature of the next generation of potential political leaders now waiting in the wings, it is difficult to believe that the eventual changing of the present leadership guard will not herald a reaffirmation of that humanitarian and democratic impulse.

Economic reform and modernisation does continue in China, and it has its own momentum. There are those who will cling for some time yet to the notion that a measure of economic liberalism can be conceded without having any implications for political democracy or the respect for human rights that goes with it. But this is as misconceived as President Gorbachev's disastrous reverse conclusion in 1990 that a measure of political democratisation did not need to be accompanied by any concession to economic rationality. The point is simply—as good Marxists should be prepared to concede—that economic and political change is inseparable.

Australia's political relations with Taiwan have been governed by our relations with mainland China: inevitably connected, because each claimed to be hosting the true government of all the peoples of China, but also separated because at times each had made an association with Australia dependent on not having an association with the other. Until 1972 we recognised the government in Taipei, and refused to recognise that in Beijing. There was always some ambivalence about the Australian position. Successive governments long remained reluctant to establish a formal diplomatic post in Taiwan. Political and strategic support did not extend to backing the Chinese Nationalists to the point of going to war with the People's Republic, for example in the context of the mid-1950s tension over the Taiwanese fortification of the off-shore islands of Quemoy and Matsu. And, despite United States pressure for an embargo, Australia developed through the 1950s and 1960s a significant trade with mainland China, especially in wool and wheat.

In December 1972 the Whitlam Government recognised the government of the People's Republic of China as the 'sole legal Government of China' and acknowledged 'the position of the Chinese Government that Taiwan is a province of the People's Republic of China'[6]. That commitment to a 'one China' policy has been firmly maintained since on a bipartisan basis—as it has been since around that time by most other Western countries. Taiwan, while making unremitting efforts to recapture diplomatic ground, in these circumstances has had to be content—in its dealings with Australia as with others—with relationships almost wholly economic in character. While some hesitant steps have been taken in recent times towards establishing a working relationship between Taiwan and the mainland, there is a very long way to travel—and with a great deal of ideological baggage needing to be jettisoned along the way—before the prospect of reunification could be seriously contemplated.

Taiwan's political setbacks have done nothing to inhibit its economic stocks. The island's economy was mainly agricultural when the Kuomintang (KMT) Government of the Republic of China fled there from the mainland in 1949: Taiwan had been ceded to Japan by China after its defeat in 1895, but the Japanese maintained it as a prosperous rural outpost of their economy. The KMT set about land reform and establishing industry for export, and succeeded with a vengeance. From 1961 to 1970 the real value of exports grew by an annual rate of 22 per cent and real GNP by an average rate of about 10 per cent. Although given considerable aid by the United States, investment was supported by one of the highest savings ratios in the world—rising as a proportion of the GNP from around 10 per cent in the 1950s to nearly 40 per cent in the late 1980s. By then Taiwan was the world's thirteenth largest trader. On current growth rates it is set to be one of the world's ten largest trading entities by the end of the century.

Taiwan's economic drive was achieved under tight government direction, in the form both of a series of four-year plans, beginning in 1953, and of martial law, which was not lifted until 1987. Recently restrictions have been eased, leading to a reduction in tariffs and some opening of banking and finance to outside competition but, like a number of other aggressive traders in the region, its instincts remain protectionist. Indirect trade between Taiwan and China, mainly through Hong Kong, has rapidly expanded, passing the US$1 billion mark in the late 1980s. Taiwan has a substantial trade surplus with the United States, and is under the same kind of pressure as Japan and the Republic of Korea to open up its domestic markets to foreign goods.

Australia has shared in the growth boom, with trade trebling since 1983 to be worth $3.6 billion in 1990. Taiwan is now our seventh largest export market, ranking ahead of Hong Kong and China itself. Our major exports have been coal, aluminium, wool, beef, iron ore, dairy products and cotton; imports have focused on automatic data processing equipment, toys and sporting goods, textiles, clothing and footwear, motorcycles, furniture and travel goods. Bilateral trade is presently close to balance. It would likely be less so if Australia had easier access for our exports of beef, wheat and fresh fruit: recurring efforts have been made to break down discriminatory restrictions in these areas, but the combination of protectionist sentiment and favourable arrangements for the United States has so far proved a difficult one to beat.

The one-China policy necessarily limits Australian relations with Taiwan to commercial and unofficial dealings, but within these constraints the relationship is strong, and growing. Australian commercial interests—including visa facilitation—are looked after in Taiwan by the Australian Commerce and Industry Office (ACIO), run under the auspices of the Australian Chamber of Commerce, but with a number of employees with extensive public sector, including diplomatic, experience. Taiwan maintains a reciprocal network of Taipei Economic and Cultural Offices in Australia.

Australia has actively sought investment from Taiwan—including by legislating to provide investment security for companies registered there—and the business links are extensive at all levels. A long-standing issue of difficulty has been direct aviation links between Australia and Taiwan, but after a protracted course of intensive negotiations—requiring Australia to engage in a delicate balancing act with the People's Republic of China, which for many years resisted such links—a commercial aviation understanding was signed in March 1991, providing the basis for a direct service to proceed. No government-to-government negotiation or agreement was involved, and it is an important element of the arrangement that neither Australia's flag carrier (Qantas) nor Taiwan's (China Airlines) will fly the route.

The Territory of Hong Kong, including Kowloon and the New Territories—a thriving, vibrant community of six million, possibly the most dedicated capitalists in the world—will be given back by the British to China when its ninety-nine year lease expires in 1997. Under the terms of the Sino–British Joint Declaration of 1984, Hong Kong is to be established thereafter as a Special Administrative Region, where the existing social and economic systems, and the present life style, would remain unchanged for another fifty years. The imminence of the transfer colours every aspect of Australian, like everyone else's, policy towards Hong Kong.

Australia has had a long association with Hong Kong as a British colony —as a tourist attraction, a listening post on China for foreign correspondents and intelligence analysts, a mercantile and financial centre and a trading partner—and the relationship continues to grow and develop. Two-way trade amounted to over $2 billion in 1990—with Hong Kong being Australia's ninth most important export market. Our main exports are gold, coal, seafood and photographic supplies; our main imports are garments, office machinery and electrical appliances. Hong Kong is the fifth most important destination for Australian investment abroad ($2.5 billion), and by mid-1989 had invested some $6.8 billion in Australia. Hong Kong is Australia's third largest source of migrants and largest source of business migrants, with over 14 000 in 1989/90. Hong Kong is an important and growing source of tourists (47 000 in 1989/90) and fee-paying students (5120 in 1989/90). Over 12 500 Australians live in Hong Kong, and some 250 Australian companies operate on Hong Kong soil.

For all these reasons, quite apart from the welfare of the colony's citizens, Australia is intensely interested in the process of transferring Hong Kong to China. Whether it goes smoothly or chaotically will affect our relations with both Hong Kong and China, and to some extent with the United Kingdom. While Australia is in no way a party to the transaction, and can do little to directly influence its terms, our voice is not without its value. We have strongly supported the transitional principles and arrangements agreed to in the 1984 Joint Declaration, and have done our best to help Hong Kong position itself for the transition, in particular by promoting its international autonomy. Australia has played a leading role in supporting Hong Kong's succession to the GATT in 1985 as a separate Contracting Party; its application (accepted in September 1990) to join the Pacific Economic Co-operation Committee (PECC); and its efforts to participate in the APEC process. We have also sought ourselves, wherever appropriate, to conclude separate bilateral treaties and agreements with Hong Kong.

In addition, we have sought to help by taking a robustly narrow view of the appropriate definition of refugee status to be applied to the Indo-Chinese boat people (but at the same time accepting a significant proportion of those screened in as genuine refugees); by making strong direct representations to China, at ministerial level, in support of Hong Kong's need to carry through its massive new airport development project without intrusive interference from Beijing; and, simply, by continuing to actively encourage bilateral trade and investment links, including educational exports, which simultaneously help Australia to improve its trade account and Hong Kong to overcome its skilled labour shortage.

THE KOREAS

There is a dramatic imbalance in Australia's relations between the Republic of Korea (ROK) in the south, and the Democratic People's Republic of Korea (DPRK) in the north, reflecting both political and economic history.

Politically united since the seventh century, Korea's present division at the thirty-eighth parallel originated with the United States–Soviet military occupation in 1945, was consolidated by the outcome of the Korean War (1950–53) and the Cold War years that followed, and seems certain— despite recent moves to re-establish dialogue—to continue for a long time yet. Australia's support for the South in the Korean War (two infantry battalions were sent together with naval and airforce units, and nearly 300 servicemen killed) and in post-war reconstruction has translated into strong continuing bilateral relations with the ROK, notwithstanding recurring concerns on human rights issues during its less democratic periods.

By contrast, diplomatic relations with Kim Il Sung's bleakly and consistently authoritarian DPRK were not established until 1974, and then abruptly suspended the following year when, in response to a perceived slight in the United Nations, the DPRK withdrew its mission from Canberra and expelled ours from Pyongyang. Indeed, so abrupt was the withdrawal, so the story goes, that one flustered North Korean official crashed his car on the way to Canberra airport; rushing into the nearest house for assistance, he found that his would-be good Samaritan was the South Korean Ambassador! Although overtures have been made in recent times for the restoration of full relations, Australia's position has been that this would depend on developments in ROK–DPRK relations, the DPRK's own international behaviour, and our own level of confidence (so far not high) that there is in fact a basis for an improved relationship.

Economic relations are, similarly, buoyant with the ROK and negligible with the DPRK. Although only around half the ROK's population size and with less arable land, the DPRK was considered at the outset to have much greater economic potential, with major mineral resources, hydro-electric power and greater industrialisation under the Japanese. But the rigours of the command economy, combined with the absence of Western aid, led to the DPRK being rapidly outstripped by its southern neighbour. By the late 1980s the ROK's national output was over five times greater, and its per capita income more than treble.

The ROK's trade with Australia has been dramatically expanding, topping $4 billion in 1990. The ROK is now Australia's sixth largest trading partner overall, and our third largest export market, with steel-making and energy-based raw materials, minerals and agricultural products the basis of this trade. The ROK is also actively expanding its own trade with Australia: over the past five years imports from Korea averaged 27 per cent growth each year, double the rate of imports from the world as a whole. Moreover, the growing economic links between the two countries are based, as elsewhere in North-East Asia, on strong complementarities. Australia in recent years has provided many of the inputs which have fuelled Korea's remarkable economic growth and spectacular export performance, and this growth has contributed to the rapid increase in living standards in Korea.

At the moment, this trade and commercial relationship is relatively narrowly based. We export mainly raw materials, and import mainly finished goods. Korean business does not perceive Australia as much more than a raw material supplier, and Australian business does not know a great deal about the ROK. This narrowness reflects the relative newness of the relationship. But the Garnaut Report makes clear that, as our two economics restructure, the complementarities are increasing. Australia is well placed not only to continue to supply the vital ingredients of industrial activity—coal and iron ore for example—but also to supply a wide range of services and manufactures for which the Korean market is rapidly expanding. In particular, good markets exist for tourism, education services, processed foodstuffs and other agricultural products, automotive components, building materials and equipment, and information-based services.

As with Japan, Australia's relationship with the ROK has in recent times been developing new depth and variety. Our traditional trade dialogue is itself becoming more sophisticated and wide ranging, focusing strongly on international and regional issues—with all the complex policy and diplomacy that goes with them—as well as the familiar narrowly defined bilateral ones. The APEC process, conceived in Seoul in January 1989 and born in Canberra ten months later, with the third annual ministerial-level meeting scheduled for Seoul in late 1991, is the clearest example of that co-operation at work. The relationship between Australian and Korean officials has been very close throughout, reflecting not only the genesis of the project but our very similar views about the potential benefits of greater regional economic co-operation, and the pivotal role that an open and non-discriminatory trading system has for our economic future.

Australia has been working hard—it has had to—to correct the very narrow and stereotype perception of Koreans about us and create the human basis for a broader relationship. In education, for example, Australia is now the third most important destination for Korean students. An Australian Education Centre was established in Seoul in 1990 to inform Koreans about the prospects for study in Australia, and a National Korean Studies Centre has been established in Melbourne to build a stronger profile here in Korean studies and language.

Perhaps the most encouraging development in bilateral relations has been the establishment—following highly successful reciprocal visits of

President Roh Tae Woo in 1988 and Prime Minister Hawke in 1989—of a high-level Australia–Korea Forum to consolidate and stimulate ideas about the future of the relationship. Bringing together fifteen eminent people from each country, from diverse backgrounds in industry, academe, media and culture, the Forum has generated a strong flow of useful, awareness-enhancing ideas. At its second meeting in April 1991, for example, the Forum recommended a more intense dialogue, at both the governmental and non-governmental levels, on political and security issues; the establishment of reciprocal Australia–Korea Foundations to promote closer bilateral relations and to broaden and strengthen existing co-operation in the education, media and other cultural fields; the establishment of a Korea–Australia Science and Industry Program to promote and co-ordinate research and development efforts by the two countries; and the establishment of an Australian–Korean Industrial Relations Research Group which could facilitate, through greater understanding of the different systems, joint ventures and other collaborative economic activities.

Taken together with such recent initiatives as an air services agreement and memoranda of understanding on science and technology and two-way investment, these various developments suggest that governments have done about as much as they can to bring the Australia–ROK relationship to the point of take-off. But formal institutional arrangements are by themselves usually not too difficult to put in place, and—as in all Australia's North-East Asian relationships—the business, in a sense, has looked after itself. The hard part is to break through the cultural barriers and establish wide-ranging networks of personal relationships, not only at points of obvious influence but at a more general social level. Without this yeast, it is very difficult to create bilateral relationships of any real diversity or maturity. It is not surprising that this process should have taken some time to develop between Australians and Koreans; the good news is that, on all available evidence, it is now happening.

15

South Asia and the Indian Ocean

THE STRATEGIC FOCUS of Australian policy has always been north and east, rather than west and north-west across the Indian Ocean. It has been the Pacific Ocean and the regions associated with it—South-East Asia, North-East Asia, the South Pacific and the Americas—that have commanded our attention. From one point of view, this is hardly surprising given the economic, political and strategic importance of these regions to Australia—and perhaps also the reality that the east coast is where Australia's population, and its foreign policy establishment, is concentrated. But Australia does have real interests, actual and potential, in the Indian Ocean and South Asia—certainly no less with India than with China—and it is important that they not be neglected.

One should not exaggerate the extent to which this area *has* been neglected. We had extensive early contacts with the South Asian sub-continent through the Imperial link; we were influential, in the early years of post-colonial nationalism, in establishing the Colombo Plan, one of the first and most successful development assistance schemes; we were active as a mediator in the early stages of the Kashmir dispute, when Sir Owen Dixon accepted appointment in 1950 as the United Nations's Representative for India and Pakistan; and we have maintained good personal relations with South Asian leaders—and a number of others elsewhere in the Indian Ocean islands and littoral—through the Commonwealth's dialogue processes. But if trade statistics are any guide to the real intensity of relationships, the facts speak for themselves: in 1990 Australia's trade with all the South Asian countries together constituted just $1.4 billion, or 1.3 per cent of our total trade.

AUSTRALIA IN THE INDIAN OCEAN

Australia is an Indian Ocean nation, and our interests in the region are essentially strategic and commercial. Our main security interest in its eastern reaches is to protect our maritime approaches and ocean resources, and the strategically important Cocos and Christmas Islands. It is for this reason that we now have a two-ocean navy. We have particular concerns about the potentially destabilising effects of nuclear proliferation in the Indian Ocean region, and we wish to see superpower rivalry there contained. The latter is a declining problem with the broader changes in East–West relations, but it has been a persistent feature of the Indian Ocean strategic environment for the last several decades, when the Cold War extended to these waters—and nobody can yet be certain what the future shape and behaviour of the Soviet Union will be.

We also have an interest in maintaining the security of trade and communications routes through the region. Some 30 per cent of our total foreign trade crosses the Indian Ocean, and access to airspace—and to a lesser extent airports—in South Asia and the Gulf region are still important to our civil aviation links with Europe. Overall our goal is to see a stable regional environment which provides maximum scope for economic development and trade, and where difficulties are resolved peacefully.

Part of the comparative neglect may be due to the fact that the Indian Ocean region is so diffuse. The once 'British lake' contains around it now a score or more of new states with little or no natural cohesion. There is room for argument as to where, as a region, it begins and ends, and it contains, moreover, a variety of sub-regions. Its cultural and religious diversity is extraordinary. If one extends the region to the Gulf littoral, it contains the richest as well as the poorest of nations, and states ranging in size from India with over 850 million people to the Seychelles with less than 80 000. The Indian Ocean itself is very different from the Pacific Ocean, notwithstanding the similar development problems faced by island states in both. Whereas the Pacific is a convex environment, with small island populations dotted across a limitless sea, the Indian Ocean, is concave—defined by its littoral with very few people in the middle.

While Australia has obvious strategic interests in the Indian Ocean, they are not pressing and they are not easily given regional cohesion. The protracted negotiations over the Indian Ocean Zone of Peace (IOZOP) proposal, compared with those leading to the South Pacific Nuclear Free Zone, have been partly due to the difficulty in defining the Indian Ocean 'zone' itself, and partly to the absence of any real consensus about basic objectives. The IOZOP proposal dates back to a conference of non-aligned states in Lusaka in 1970, which adopted at the urging of Ceylon (now Sri Lanka) a declaration:

> calling upon all states to consider and respect the Indian Ocean as a zone of peace from which great power rivalries and competition as well as bases conceived in the context of such rivalries and competition, either army, navy or air force bases, are excluded . . . The area should also be free of nuclear weapons.[1]

The Whitlam Government supported the proposal and obtained a place for Australia on the UN Ad Hoc Committee established to consider it. From the outset there was some tension between that support and our hosting of the Naval Communications Station at North West Cape, one function of which has always been communications with United States ballistic missile submarines.[2] In recent years the Ad Hoc Committee, while continuing to meet, has been stalemated by the withdrawal from its deliberations of all Western states (including the nuclear weapons states) except Australia, and by differences of view—often concealed within procedural arguments—about the continued utility of the 'no foreign bases' objective, and even the extent to which the 'nuclear free' objective should be actively pursued.

It may be that the thaw in East–West relations will act to break this logjam and give fresh impetus to the negotiations. It is to be hoped that this proves to be the case, although it must frankly be acknowledged that there are any number of other problems which could cause yet further delays. What is needed is for the littoral countries, and other key players with legitimate interests in the region, to agree on measures which build confidence. These could include military exchanges and visits, the more open publication and communication of military data, co-operative approaches to the protection of sea-lanes and sea lines of communication and to dealing with incidents at sea, and wholly non-military measures like environmental security arrangements for the protection of reefs and coastal waters. Confidence building measures, tailored to local needs and circumstances, lend themselves particularly well to regional arrangements, and the European experience shows they can work.

It is difficult for Australia to bring any of its Indian Ocean relationships within a supportive regional institutional framework as with, say, Indonesia or Japan. India is not, for example, a dialogue partner in the ASEAN Post Ministerial Conference, the Asia Pacific's most important political discussion forum; nor is its membership under consideration in APEC, the Asia Pacific's most important economic discussion forum, although speculation has already begun about APEC ultimately extending its reach to Mexico and the Pacific littoral of South America. By the same token, the one regional consultative body (the Ad Hoc Committee on IOZOP apart) embracing the major South Asian countries—the South Asian Association for Regional Co-operation (SAARC)—does not have dialogue relationships with any other country. Other regional bodies are even more narrowly focused. The Indian Ocean Commission (IOC), formed in 1982 with the general aim of fostering economic development through regional co-operation, has a membership confined to Mauritius, Madagascar, the Seychelles, Comoros and Réunion (represented by France). The Indian Ocean Marine Affairs Co-operation Council (IOMAC) was initiated by Sri Lanka in 1985 to provide a framework for dealing with marine resource and environment issues: seven regional countries are now formal members (Sri Lanka, Pakistan, Mozambique, Kenya, Tanzania, Indonesia and Nepal), but India's resistance to the organisation has been strong, and its achievements to date have been slight.

Australia's insufficient attention to its west and north-west may be remedied naturally by time with the further economic development of Western Australia and, in particular, the dispersal of previously east-concentrated defence forces to the west and north. The process will be slow. Unlike the United States, where the shift of the focus of political power was the effect of incremental shifts of population and industry from the old east coast states through the mid-west to California, the western part of Australia is more isolated from the east and lacks the infrastructure support it will need to become a power centre in its own right. There is no iron law of transcontinental progress which will make Western Australia the economic equal of eastern Australia. Even when Australia's Imperial lifeline meant that Western Australia was first port of call from across the Indian Ocean, the natural advantages of the east held sway. But coupled with the global tendency towards economic interdependence, the loosening up of political alignments due to the dismantling of the Cold War, and the need for Australia to maximise its economic opportunities wherever they may arise, a corrective can be expected to apply steadily to Australian foreign policy priorities in future years. The Pacific focus will not be supplanted, but it should, and will, be modified.

INDIA

India is the predominant power in South Asia and among the littoral states of the Indian Ocean. It is the second most populous country in the world—over 850 million people now, and expected to outstrip China's population by 2010—and is a practising democracy. It has a substantial land mass, a highly developed manufacturing and industrial sector, an advanced nuclear capability and substantial resources of professional, scientific and technological talent. The Indian economy is the twelfth largest in the world (Australia's is eleventh),[3] and is rapidly developing, with a middle class market of perhaps 100 million people. Although India has had limited success to date in improving the lot of its poorest people, the country is able basically to feed itself.

A leader of the Non-Aligned Movement (NAM), India has always been active politically on a wide range of international issues. It is an impressive military power, in manpower terms the fourth largest in the world (after

China, the Soviet Union and the United States). India's location gives it a commanding central position in the Indian Ocean, merging with South-East Asia to the east and with the Middle East and the Horn of Africa to the west. The stated aim of its naval build-up in recent years has been to protect a 7500 kilometres coastline, together with ports, off-shore installations, island territories and Exclusive Economic Zone (EEZ) maritime resources. By its military involvement in Sri Lanka and the Maldives, and its robust response to some pin-pricks from Nepal and Bhutan in recent years, India has given notice that it is prepared to exert authority in its region. India's most long-standing and genuinely felt security concern has been the intentions of its neighbour Pakistan. As a response to this concern—and sensitive to the role of the United States in South Asia—India formed close links in the 1960s with the Soviet Union. But with that Soviet connection losing some value in the post-Cold War era, India has shown a desire to improve relations with China and with the United States. And its defence budget, given massive boosts in the late 1980s, has now levelled off in response to financial constraints.

India has always been conscious of its status in the region and internationally, and keen to demonstrate the legitimacy of its claim to attention as a major power, certainly one in the same class as China. When newly independent, India sought to influence the world's power brokers by itself playing an international role. It did this effectively under the inspiration of Jawaharlal Nehru's leadership, in a period when both the emotional tides of anti-colonialism and the fortunes of the United Nations were rising fast. At the same time, the early conflicts with Pakistan (which had become a member of the pro-Western military pact SEATO) meant that India had to look to its own resources in defence. In the later Nehru years, under the additional pressure of intractable economic difficulties and disillusionment over the border war with China, India turned towards establishing itself as a regional power in order to strengthen its global claim to major power status. That disposition has continued, although economic pressures are now tending to redirect the focus of government inwards more than has been the case for some time.

Australia has good relations with India—of long standing, but of less weight than we would like. The issue for our foreign policy is to create enough substance in the relationship to support our capacity to influence the future course of events in areas of interest to us. Some progress has already been made, but there is scope for plenty more.

Politics Australia's first concern is to assist India, to the extent we appropriately can, to remain a democracy. Insufficient emphasis has perhaps been given by democracies like Australia to this aspect of their relations. Because India was non-aligned during the height of the Cold War and developed close relations with the Soviet Union for its own security reasons, its achievement as a large developing country in sustaining a working political democracy has been, while recognised, given less respect than it deserves. But its existence, quite apart from other values, provides mutual institutional access and understanding of a kind which helps a great deal in the conduct of foreign policy. Democracies do not always produce strong governments that seem to know their own minds. But their sensitivity to domestic currents does seem to make them better international citizens. By and large, the relationships between democracies, throughout history, have been peaceful and productive.[4]

The assassination of Rajiv Gandhi during the national election campaign of May 1991 was a shock to Indian democracy in more ways than one. Not only was there the immediate crisis to weather, but the assassination brought to an end the persistent connection between independent India's democratic tradition and the creation of a modern dynasty of prime ministers through the Nehru family. Almost continuously in office since 1947, Pandit Nehru, his daughter and then his grandson had provided a link with the hereditary leadership style of old India. But Indian democracy was now on its own without the support of an attractive 'royal' family.

The challenges it is facing are severe. The turnout for the postponed 1991 election was the lowest on record, suggesting if not disillusionment with the democratic process at least a fear of violence (although in the event this proved largely unrealised). Congress won the election only narrowly (242 seats out of 506, making it a minority government) despite a presumed sympathy vote. The significant showing—at least in the north—of the Hindu fundamentalist Bharatiya Janata Party (BJP), which won in the former Congress strongholds of Uttar Pradesh and Bihar, and became, with 117 seats, the second largest party, suggests that the issue of communalism will continue to haunt the political process. But Indian democracy has proved its resilience in the past, and should do so again. While it may be a mistake to believe that democracy will itself remove communalism—or caste or poverty—it has shown in India's case a remarkable capacity to incorporate them within the political system and thus, even if tragically at times, to manage them in a way which maintains the integrity of the nation-state.

The interest of Australia, among others, in seeing that India survives and prospers as a democratic entity means that we must be prepared to be as supportive as we can, both materially and politically. India continues to be the most important test-bed for democracy in the social and economic conditions in which most of the world's people live. If democracy works only for rich and stable societies, it does not have much of a future. Part of that support should necessarily be directed to developing more intensive people-to-people contacts, particularly at opinion-influencing levels, between the two countries. In this respect, the establishment of an Australia–India Council—as recommended by the 1990 Senate Committee Report on *Australia–India Relations*[5]—would be desirable, following similar arrangements in the cases of China, Japan and Indonesia. The function of education is crucial, in providing an expert base, as well as a better informed community. The Asian Studies Postgraduate Scheme, the National Asian Languages Scholarship Scheme and the targeted Institutional Links Program have all been aimed at increasing Australian expertise on Asia, including India. The establishment in 1990 of the Indian Ocean Peace Studies Centre, to be jointly managed by the University of Western Australia and Curtin University of Technology, also helps us in moving towards the goal of a better informed Australia.

Economics Australia has an obvious interest in India's economic potential. At its lowest, this is an interest in seeing that India as a nation successfully feeds, clothes and provides minimum welfare for the hundreds of millions of people for whom it has responsibility. The consequences of failure would not only be tragic for India itself: they would spread throughout South Asia and beyond. At its highest, Australia's interest is in an economy which could become a major trader, not just with Australia but globally.

The Congress Government led by Narasimha Rao, elected in June 1991, has been quick to recognise the need for a more competitive Indian private sector. Prime Minister Rao has evoked the memory of Indians as traders for thousands of years, and has described aid as a 'crutch'. The ideas of self-reliance and of state occupancy of the commanding heights of the economy, which had guided Congress governments for four decades (although briefly contested by Rajiv Gandhi), were largely discarded in the new Government's early decisions—devaluing the rupee, deregulating the manufacturing sector and offering incentives for foreign investment. It seemed to be accepted that some radical measures were needed to address a deteriorating economy affected by the Gulf War, the fall of two minority governments in eighteen months, and communal turmoil—not least if large loans from the International Monetary Fund were to be forthcoming.

To the extent that Indian economic management is being set on a new path, this should also be seen as a reflection of a worldwide trend away from the state-directed economy. This model, attractive to so many countries emerging from colonialism, had been followed with enthusiasm by India—creating excessive controls, sustaining an excessively large bureaucracy, inviting corruption and inducing in the business community an expectation of state protection. Like many other countries which had formed economic links—including barter and artificial currency arrangements—with the Soviet Union and East Europe, India also had to adapt to the collapse of these socialist economies and the arrival of a highly competitive trading world.

Even before the impact of these policy shifts, there had been promising developments in the Australia–India relationship, including a more than 200 per cent increase in total two-way trade between 1983 and 1990 in dollar terms; the establishment of a Joint Ministerial Commission, an

Australia–India Joint Business Council, a Joint Trade Committee and a Joint Working Group on Coal; the initiation of a $35 million, three-year development co-operation program and a treaty to facilitate it; and the signing of an umbrella agreement fostering co-operation in science and technology, under which a number of projects are being pursued in fields such as space science and monsoon meteorology. In addition, the relationship has been supported by the development of bilateral defence exchanges; a Mixed Commission which is actively promoting cultural and political exchanges; and a significantly expanded political agenda, which includes regular bilateral disarmament talks. Perhaps reflecting the expanded level of commercial and political contact, migration applications during 1990 rose 74 per cent and migrant visa issues rose 32 per cent.

When Prime Ministers Hawke and Gandhi agreed in 1986 in Canberra to make major efforts to enhance the bilateral relationship, their main focus was commercial. During the Joint Ministerial Commission in 1989, the Indian and Australian negotiators reached an agreement to work towards doubling the two-way trade by 1992. This target is on the way toward being met, with two-way trade now approaching the A$1 billion mark. Australia has also set a specific target, in consultation with the Indian government, whereby 1 per cent of our total imports of engineering products should come from India—subject to quality and price competitiveness. Particular emphasis has been placed, from the Australian side, on the development of several large, long-term projects of significant 'demonstration' status. The Piparwar open-cut mine and the Karwar naval base consultancy are two important successes for Australian companies in this respect, being showcases for Australian expertise and technology. Their achievement has required a dextrous use of diplomatic, marketing and financial resources. Through the Development Import Finance Facility (DIFF), Australia has been able to offer an attractive mixture of aid funds and commercial export finance: the grant aid component of the Piparwar project was A$60 million.

It has acknowledged that India, for all its large size and growth in GDP, actually imports fewer goods than does Australia. There are difficulties faced by Australian companies in establishing a bridge-head for goods in India, although a number of companies which have been prepared to persevere have succeeded in doing good business there. Australia must continue to press for further progress in trade liberalisation in India, but all the signs are that from now on we will be pushing at a much more open door.

Security   Finally, Australia has an interest in creating with others an international security system which can accommodate India's concerns and aspirations, and in which India plays a strong and effective role. At the same time, we would obviously be concerned at any change in Indian military capabilities or objectives which operated to reduce rather than strengthen regional security. In recent times, concern has been expressed at the rapid growth in the size of the Indian Armed Forces and in particular its Navy—with an expenditure on equipment of US$20 billion over six years, and defence expenditure generally constituting nearly 20 per cent of government outlays and more than 3.5 per cent of GDP.[6]

A full analysis of Indian capabilities and objectives was made by the Australian Senate Committee on Foreign Affairs, Defence and Trade in its report on *Australia–India Relations: Trade and Security*, tabled in Parliament in July 1990.[7] The Committee's conclusions, as to capabilities, were that India was probably capable of defending its borders and containing any surprise attack from Pakistan[8] and any incursions involving less than full-scale attack by China; that India had a capability to patrol its Exclusive Economic Zone (EEZ) along the both eastern and western coasts, but not to offer a credible defence against the United States or Soviet navies; that it had the capability to launch small-scale rapid deployment operations in the northern Indian Ocean, as with its action in the Maldives; that it had the ability to deploy substantial numbers of ground troops overseas in collaboration with host governments, as shown in Sri Lanka; that the use of the Andaman or Nicobar Islands as a staging point for the deployment of Indian military power to South-East Asia was at least a theoretical possibility; and that generally India had developed a significant deterrent capability, even in relation to the superpowers, making it unlikely that India itself could be subject to 'coercive naval diplomacy'.

The Committee further concluded that India had not developed new military doctrines to suggest that it was developing capabilities for contingencies other than those that have concerned it in the past—i.e. ones associated with South Asian problems and great power intervention in the region. Overall, it found that India's military build-up was far less threatening for the foreseeable future outside the South Asian region than some views had suggested. Certainly, such prospects as direct military intervention in support of the Indian population of Fiji could be regarded as hypothetical at best. At the same time, India was the predominant military power in South Asia, with an already very powerful capability. Should continued expansion of that capability occur over the next decade, it would probably reduce the security not only of India's South Asian neighbours, but also of India itself as its neighbours responded with build-ups of their own.

In the Australian Government's response to the Report in December 1990, the Foreign Minister broadly endorsed the Committee's findings, making clear that the Government understood the historical facts which had helped to fashion India's perception of its strategic environment.[9] The point was made that in the four decades since Independence, India has fought a number of wars, still has disputed borders, and faces some serious separatist and insurgency problems. India must be able to protect its long coastline, its scattered island territories and its off-shore interests: its strategic circumstances mean that it needs to maintain a certain level of military capacity. The Foreign Minister acknowledged that while India's military build-up has enhanced its power projection capability in the South Asia region, it does not constitute a threat to the security of Australia or South-East Asia. He emphasised, though, the need for openness and dialogue to allay any regional concerns that may arise from time to time, and referred to the range of visits and defence staff exchanges that were occurring with India, together with the re-establishment of the Defence Adviser position in New Delhi. These measures would contribute to a better comprehension of, and means of dialogue about, India's defence preoccupations, and thus to a better understanding of India's strategic concerns and objectives.

The particular problem of nuclear proliferation pressures in South Asia continues to cause concern, as the Senate Committee Report also pointed out and the Government reply acknowledged.[10] Australia has considered it to be in the interests of all nations that both India and Pakistan demonstrate conclusively that they are not pursuing a nuclear option. This could be done by their acceding to the Nuclear Non-Proliferation Treaty (NPT) or, at the very least, placing all their nuclear facilities under fullscope safeguards applied by the International Atomic Energy Agency. In mid-1991 there was still no sign of any shift from India's traditional strong opposition to the NPT—an opposition founded essentially on claims of double-standards by the existing nuclear weapon states.

But at least there was no sign, either, of any imminent move toward the overt acquisition of a nuclear weapons capability. However, the opposition BJP's stated commitment, in its 1991 Election Manifesto, to acquire 'nuclear teeth' for the Indian military (together with its commitment to developing 'the first navy in the Indian Ocean from Aden to Singapore') suggests that there will be continuing overt domestic pressure for such a move. It will be a continuing task for the international community to discourage it. It can only be hoped that the changing world environment, the associated recent changes in attitude toward the NPT of countries like France, China and South Africa—and the avoidance of provocation by Pakistan—will work to encourage revision of India's traditional position.

There are other signs that India may be moderating some of its traditional non-aligned articles of faith. An important example was agreement with the United States during the Gulf Crisis to allow aircraft on the way from the Philippines to the Gulf to refuel in Bombay. The practicalities of India's position appeared to be that, quite apart from the particular circumstances of the Gulf conflict, good relations with the United States were an asset, not least with the declining substance of its relationship with the Soviet Union. It would certainly, from Australia's point of view, be a bonus from the collapse of the Cold War if India were to continue the process of shedding its sometimes artificial anti-Americanism, while maintaining its independent and non-aligned stance in a genuinely detached manner.

In our perception, an important regional, and perhaps global, role awaits an India that is able to adjust its policies to the post-Cold War era. It may be that some Australians, who have liked to think of India as a source of spiritual enlightenment and an example of neutralism in a world gripped by military pactomania, will find the 'new' India a worrying prospect. In terms of Australia's national interests it is not, and we should be encouraging India to think creatively about its future strategic role. At the very least there is a case for India being drawn more systematically into the security dialogue process now developing rapidly in the larger Asia Pacific region.

PAKISTAN, BANGLADESH AND THE HIMALAYAN STATES

Australia's relations with the countries of South Asia other than India are generally friendly and useful, but necessarily reflect the fact that since 1971, when Pakistan lost its eastern provinces and Bangladesh was born, India has been dominant on the sub-continent. Pakistan remains a country of more than 100 million people, with strengthening links in the Islamic countries of the Middle East and North Africa. Its strategic value was evident in its role as a frontline state following the Soviet invasion of Afghanistan in 1979, which won it support from its Islamic neighbours and also from the United States. However, Pakistan has not been able to recapture American backing to the same extent as during the Cold War. The United States placed a ban on economic aid to Pakistan in 1979, and again in 1991 because of its suspicion that Pakistan was developing a nuclear weapons capability.

Australia's relations with Pakistan are still somewhat in the cricket—hockey—squash—Commonwealth mould.[11] Our two-way trade actually declined for a period in the 1980s, and is now running at only around $250 million (two-to-one in our favour, with Australia exporting coal, iron ore, steel, wool and wheat, and importing mainly cotton textiles). As we do not have a dialogue relationship with the South Asian Association for Regional Co-operation (SAARC) of which Pakistan is a founding member, our dealings are conducted mainly on a bilateral basis or within the Commonwealth. Our main concern—not that we have been in a position to do more about it than anyone else—is that Pakistan's historically bad relationship with India has not shown much sign of long-term improvement. There have been three wars already between the two countries: after partition in 1947–48, when the still unresolved issue of control of Kashmir arose; in 1965, again over Kashmir; and in 1971 over East Pakistan, which became Bangladesh. The issues, though no longer subject to Cold War manipulation, still simmer, fanned by increasing Muslim–Hindu tensions and an arms race that remains perilously close to becoming nuclear (with India justifying its nuclear option because China has it, and Pakistan justifying its nuclear option because India has it).

Pakistan's return to democracy after the death of General Zia in August 1988 provided a firm basis for the re-establishment of a substantial relationship between Australia and Pakistan. This was underlined by Prime Minister Hawke's visit in February 1989, in the course of which he announced a three year $15 million aid program with a largely commercial focus. The dismissal of the Bhutto Government in August 1990 was an unhappy interruption, leading the Australian Government to express its strong concern and its support for the rapid restoration of democratic process. With the October 1990 elections, and the lifting of the state of emergency, conditions for a closer relationship were again restored. In this context there is potential for a significant expansion of trade with Pakistan, and a framework was set in July 1990 with the establishment of a Joint Trade Committee.

Bangladesh is one of the most densely populated countries in the world (110 million) and one of the United Nations's 'least developed countries' (US$180 per capita income), with its economic and social problems constantly made worse by the country's appalling vulnerability to flood and cyclone. Australia was one of the first countries to recognise Bangladesh, and goodwill has been sustained by an aid program which is the main element of our relationship. Bangladesh is normally around the fifth largest overall recipient of Australian bilateral aid (about $20 million in 1990/91, 66 per cent in the form of food aid). Disaster relief has, unhappily, been a significant additional component of our aid in recent years. Australia is also contributing around $10 million over four years to a population and family-health project of the International Development Association. Total two-way trade is small—$85 million in 1990—and substantially in Australia's favour.

Our interest in Bangladesh lies not just in its enormous humanitarian problems, but in its occupancy of a key position in a volatile region of continuing concern to Australia. Unfortunately for Bangladesh's post-Independence development, its history has been marked by a series of coups, military governments, martial law periods and states of emergency. But since April 1991 the country has again experienced the pleasures of a democratically elected parliament and government, and there is reason to hope that the Bangladeshis—a people of extraordinary resilience—will have a significantly more stable political future.

Sandwiched between India and China, the mountainous, landlocked kingdom of Nepal has been forced to play a delicate balancing act between its two powerful neighbours. Until free multi-party elections in May 1991,

Nepal had been governed under the constitution of 1962 which enshrined Royal authority through the system of panchayat ('council') government without political parties. However, while parties were officially banned they did exist, and functioned to a limited degree though often subject to severe repression leading to increasing complaints about human rights violations. In November 1990 King Birenda proclaimed a new constitution guaranteeing fundamental human rights and multi-party democracy. The process initiated under this constitution culminated in the May 1991 election which, while it had some irregularities, was generally considered to have been free and fair. In response to a Nepalese request, two Australia parliamentarians joined an international observer commission for the election. Our participation in this exercise not only underpinned Australia's interests in Nepal's development, but also enhanced our image in the region as a friendly and reliable democratic state with a commitment to democratic values and fundamental human rights.

Apart from our interest in encouraging the democratic process and respect for human rights, aid and tourism are the main elements in our bilateral relationship, and consular matters the mainstay of Australia's small mission in Khatmandu. Nepal—with a population about the size of Australia's—is one of the world's lowest income countries. Australia has been involved through its aid program in the development of hydro-electricity, forestry regeneration, civil aviation and grain management. Bilateral trade is very small—less than $5 million—but there is potential for the development of commercial links through involvement of Australian companies in development project work, and Nepal has participated on a regular basis in trade displays run by the Market Advisory Service (MAS) of the Department of Foreign Affairs and Trade.

Australia's relations with Nepal's Himalayan neighbour, the kingdom of Bhutan, are necessarily limited. Its population is under 1.5 million, and—although a UN member since 1971—its external relations continue to be 'guided' by India (as they were previously by Britain) under a treaty of 1949. Australia was one of the earliest providers of development assistance to the country, with funding in recent years running at close to $1 million per year, principally to update Bhutan's sheep industry. Another Australian rural connection has been the Leader of the National Party (and keen mountain climber) Tim Fischer, who perhaps has been Bhutan's most regular tourist in recent years, and certainly one of its most fervent boosters abroad.

Beyond the western end of the Himalayan range lies a rather bigger country, which has given the world many more headaches. The future of Afghanistan continues to be uncertain. Despite expectations that Soviet troop withdrawal from the country in early 1989 would lead to the fall of the Najibullah regime installed by the Soviet Union and its replacement by a government of the resistance, the Kabul regime has remained in place. Neither it nor the Mujahaddin have been able to impose their rule throughout Afghanistan: both sides have been riven by internal dissent. Australia, in the United Nations and elsewhere, has consistently affirmed the right of the Afghan people to self-determination, and supported efforts to establish a government acceptable to Afghans, but we have no special interest to give us any more leverage over the situation than any other member of the international community.

Australia has had, nonetheless, a solid record of practical assistance to Afghans, providing $58 million between 1980 and mid-1991 as food aid to refugees in Pakistan, and a further $13.5 million for the rehabilitation of Afghanistan and the return of refugees. Australia has also contributed several teams of mine-clearing instructors from the Engineer Corps of the Army to assist in the training of Afghans in de-mining techniques: it is estimated that Soviet troops laid as many as 15 million mines in Afghanistan, and unless and until they are cleared the reconstruction of the country will be very substantially hampered.

SRI LANKA AND THE ISLAND STATES

Sri Lanka—an island about the size of Tasmania, but with a population as large as Australia's—was once a popular stop for Australians on their way to the United Kingdom and Europe by sea. The major air routes have now directed tourist traffic elsewhere, and communal tensions and violence since 1983 have also dissuaded visitors—unhappily so, for the country remains one of the most beautiful and culturally rich in the world.

Since Ceylon gained its independence from the British in 1948—and became the Democratic Socialist Republic of Sri Lanka in 1978 (the change to 'Sri Lanka' came six years earlier)—the politics of the country have always been lively. But it has been conflict between the Tamil and Sinhalese communities, deteriorating into more-or-less constant civil war since 1983, that has overwhelmingly preoccupied the country in recent years. The conflict, over the issue of a separate state for Tamils in the north of the island, has not attracted the involvement or attention of any major power except India. Concerned at the spillover implications, especially in its own State of Tamil Nadu, the Indian Government secured an invitation from Colombo to intervene directly in the dispute in 1987, with a peace-keeping force that reached 50 000 men going on the offensive against the main militant group, the Liberation Tigers of Tamil Eelam (LTTE). Following a negotiated ceasefire—and agreement by the Sri Lankan Government to establish a merged and largely autonomous North-Eastern Province—the Indian forces eventually withdrew in March 1990. The uneasy peace was, however, broken by the LTTE in June. The cycle of violence has since escalated massively, and in mid-1991 showed no signs of abating.

The tragic situation in Sri Lanka has been a particular concern for Australia as a fellow member of the Commonwealth, and as a country with over 60 000 Tamil and Sinhalese immigrants. Human rights violations on both sides have led the Australian Government to repeatedly express concern. Atrocities on the LTTE side have been legion. On the government side, the focus has been on the high number of extra-judicial killings, allegations of disappearances, torture and detentions without charges, and the operation of 'death squads'—a good many of these in the context of Colombo's suppression not just of the Tamil Tigers in the north but of the Sinhala Buddhist Marxist Youth Group, Janatha Vimukthi Peramuna (JVP), in the south. An encouraging development, however, was the establishment by the Sri Lankan Government in late 1990 of a special task force to examine charges of human rights violations. And through all its difficulties, Sri Lanka has maintained its democratic system intact.

Australia has also made active efforts to encourage a negotiated political settlement. During a visit in August 1990, Foreign Minister Evans discussed with President Premadasa the possibility of the Commonwealth's involvement in this respect, and Prime Minister Hawke subsequently wrote to the President proposing a specific Commonwealth good offices role to facilitate resumption of negotiations between the government and the LTTE[12]. While the President did not, in response, rule out the possibility of Commonwealth involvement in the future, it was made clear that for the moment the Sri Lankan Government believed that there was no basis on which constructive negotiations with the Tamils, under any auspices, could proceed. And clearly neither the Commonwealth nor any external mediator can act without support from the Sri Lankan Government.

Australia's relations with Sri Lanka have historically been close, and remain warm, notwithstanding the vigour with which we have pursued human rights concerns in recent years. Whether they can expand depends very much on Sri Lanka's economic development. In this respect Sri Lanka's troubles have set back the program of economic liberalisation that began in the early 1980s. Defence spending has risen sharply, and an expanding balance of payments deficit and rising inflation are causing concern. There has been a slowing, moreover, in the so-called 'peoplisation', or limited privatisation, of some state-owned enterprises. Two-way trade, although recently increasing (to around $90 million in 1990), is still not worth what it was in the mid-1980s. While Sri Lankan exports to Australia are consistent (tea, spices, textiles and chemicals), Australian exports (cereals, dairy and food products) have been volatile. However, Australian investment has increased substantially, and a lasting peace will undoubtedly generate more.

Mauritius, whose economic performance in the last five years has been one of the success stories of the third world, is a tiny island (just half the size of Kangaroo Island in South Australia) but with a population of just over one million—and already a community in Australia of around 20 000. Our relationship with Mauritius—from Australia's perspective the major country in the south-west Indian Ocean—is significant not just because of the growing Mauritian community in Australia but also because of the Commonwealth connection. The establishment of a mission in Port Louis in 1984 with oversight responsibilities for other Indian Ocean states reflected the Government's Indian Ocean policy guidelines. Australia is a reasonably large bilateral aid donor to Mauritius—$3.4 million in 1990/91 —and the country is in fact our largest market (apart from South Africa) in the sub-Saharan region, though exports amount to under $40 million a year and have remained fairly static.

Our relations with the other island states are very limited, though without any difficulties. The Seychelles and the Maldives have, as members of the Commonwealth, greater relative importance. Both receive Australian aid ($1.1 million and $1.9 million respectively in 1990/91), enough in the case of the Maldives to make Australia the second largest donor after Japan. Madagascar is the physical giant of the Indian Ocean, with a population of over 10 million, but has failed to capitalise on its potential. There are, nonetheless, signs of rethinking in its political and economic orientation which may lead to new economic development and, in time, opportunities for Australian trade. The Indian Ocean Commission (IOC)—with its development co-operation focus—has proved something of a disappointment, but there are signs that it may seek to adopt a more practical approach to development assistance and greater involvement from Australia. All the island states face common problems of land degradation and marine resource conservation, and some of them potentially from sea level rise. They also lack experience in environmental management and there will be clear opportunities for Australia to assist in that field, particularly through training. Relations with the Indian Ocean island states are not likely for the foreseeable future to assume the same importance as those with Australia's Pacific island neighbours, but they should certainly not be neglected.

16

The Middle East and Africa

AUSTRALIA IS CONNECTED with the Middle East and Africa by the Indian Ocean, but not an enormous amount else. In any tough-minded comparative assessment of the nature and extent of Australian foreign policy interests at stake, both regions have to rank at the lower end of the scale, along with East Europe and South America. Even our trade with the Middle East—which it most definitely *is* in Australia's interests to cultivate—in 1990 constituted only 4.1 per cent of our trade with the world.[1] Taking into account how Australian interests are affected, and what we might be able to do about it if they are, the attention devoted to certain Middle East and African issues in the Australian media—not to mention the passion devoted by various ethnic-based and other lobby groups, and by parliamentarians from all sides—does often seem disproportionate.

We do, nonetheless, have a number of specific interests engaged in the Middle East and Africa, and no assessment of Australia's foreign relations in theory or practice can afford to ignore them, even if we are never likely to be as closely engaged as West Europe, the United States or (to a lesser extent these days) the Soviet Union. In the first place, there is the interest we share with the rest of the world in maintaining global security, including the resolution of regional conflicts of potentially global significance. This demands not only that we follow closely the course of events in the Middle East, still the world's most volatile and dangerous region, but that we do what we can to help resolve them—for example by participating, as we did in the Gulf crisis of 1990–91, in UN collective security responses.

257

Secondly, as good international citizens we cannot help but be moved by the great moral and humanitarian issues in these regions—securing the destruction of apartheid in South Africa, achieving the reconciliation of the tragically competing interests and claims of the Jewish and Palestinian peoples, and overcoming the recurring nightmares of food shortage and massive population displacements in Africa. Thirdly, we do have obvious economic interests involved. We are affected, like everyone else, by the impact of Middle East conflict on world oil prices. And we do have to maximise, here as elsewhere, the bilateral trade and investment potential of the Middle East and Africa.

THE MIDDLE EAST AFTER THE GULF

A harsh climate, representing a disastrous ecological decline from the 'fertile crescent' of early civilisation; extremes of poverty and wealth; control of most of the world's oil, the lifeblood of twentieth century industrial society; an alarmingly high level of armaments; smouldering resentment among Arabs at their historical treatment by the Western powers and the planting of Israel in their midst; the Israelis, struggling to find a way of guaranteeing, once and for all, their country's survival; the Palestinians, adrift in search of a homeland; Iraq, decisively defeated in its attempted military dominance of the Gulf, but with a mass of security, political and economic problems unresolved; intense feeling generated by all these issues, for whatever reasons, in domestic political debate—the Middle East is not an easy area for anyone's foreign policy.

The task is not made any less difficult by the region's diversity.[2] There are the wealthy Gulf Arab oil states with relatively small populations—Saudi Arabia, Kuwait, Bahrain, Qatar, the United Arab Emirates and Oman. There are the Arab states with little oil and, for the most part, large populations—Egypt, Syria, Yemen and Jordan. There are Iraq and Iran, which have both oil wealth and large populations, together with broader based economies including agriculture and mining, but which have been burdened with large defence budgets and—now—the costs of post-War reconstruction. And, there are Lebanon and Israel, both small, unique and without oil: the former struggling to re-create its identity after being torn apart by a generation of conflict, and the latter with high military spending, high immigration and a tendency to budget and trade deficits manageable only by major military and economic subventions from the United States. The total population of the region, thus defined, is around 170 million and growing rapidly, with half its people less than twenty years of age. There are fewer economic links between Middle East countries than might be expected, and intra-regional trade and investment is low. And the major regional organisations—the Arab League and the Gulf Co-operation Council—have had, at best, mixed success in forging a sense of common economic and political purpose among their respective members.[3]

At the time of writing, the abiding policy issues of the region—political, security and economic—had not been resolved in the aftermath of the Gulf War, but hopes continued that the new dynamics operating in the region would make major progress possible: Iraq's invasion of Kuwait on 2 August 1990; the concerted reaction of the international community resulting in the United States-led multinational forces ejecting the Iraqis in the six-week war of January–March 1991; the co-operation of hard-line Arab States like Syria in that process; the credit won by Israel for its restraint under SCUD-missile attack; the credit lost by the Palestine Liberation Organisation (PLO), not only in the wider international community but within the region itself, for its support of Iraq; the central role of United Nations institutional processes; and the rapport of the United States and the Soviet Union throughout the crisis. All these events, and reactions, suggest that not only was it imperative to address the outstanding problems of the region, but that this might at last be possible.

Security The most immediate security imperative after the Gulf War was to implement the series of resolutions of the UN Security Council designed to stop Iraq from again attacking its neighbours, or from undermining the hard-won international protection of its Kurdish minority. The key resolution was UNSCR 687 of 3 April 1991, which affirmed all thirteen previous UNSCR resolutions during the Gulf War and set out in detail conditions for the destruction of Iraq's chemical and biological weapons and ballistic missiles with a range of more than 150 kilometres, and the placing under international control of any material which could be used to construct nuclear weapons. It was important for the international coalition which brought about the downfall of Iraq to keep up the pressure after the threat against Kuwait had receded. If the effort of political will, diplomatic skill and military organisation that constituted the coalition's response was not to be lost in the vast store of cynicism accumulated from past efforts in the Middle East, Iraq could not be permitted simply to walk away from the obligations it had accepted in defeat, living to fight another day.

In mid-1991 the international community's main weapon in this respect was the continued rigorous application of the sanctions regime imposed in the lead-up to the War. But provision was also made to enable the United States and some of its allies to retain a discreet presence in the Middle East through naval forces in the Persian Gulf, through some pre-positioned equipment on land in the Gulf, and through a land-based rapid reaction force in Turkey. The presence of these forces, with their potential for swift retaliation, would complement continued United Nations sanctions and other Security Council resolutions in keeping up the pressure on Iraq.

The second security imperative was to establish an effective longer-term disarmament and arms control regime, not just for Iraq but for the region as a whole. The Gulf crisis showed up in stark relief almost every one of the world's fears about proliferation of weapons of mass destruction—nuclear, chemical and biological—the extension of missile technology, and the alarming implications of the build-up of massive amounts of conventional weaponry.

Ideally, this problem would be tackled by pursuing simultaneously some fully international measures together with some region-specific ones.[4] The former would involve, in particular, the speedy conclusion of the proposed Chemical Weapons Convention; improvements to the existing Biological Weapons Convention (especially its verification regime); extension of the Missile Technology Control Regime (MTCR); the establishment of the UN Register of Arms Transfers to improve transparency in relation to conventional weapons; and redoubled efforts to extend the reach and effectiveness of the Nuclear Non-Proliferation Treaty—in all of which areas Australia is, as it should be, an active diplomatic player.

Region-specific measures would involve not only the completion of the work of the UN Special Commission in overseeing the destruction of Iraqi nuclear, biological and chemical weapons capability, but also the negotiation of more broadly focused agreements—involving, hopefully, all categories of weapons and forces—designed to ensure a more stable and equitable regional military balance. Presumably such an exercise would succeed only it were conducted in tandem with the resolution of outstanding political questions, but the immensity of that task should not in itself be deterrent to the attempt. Here as in Europe and elsewhere, it would be helpful if smaller-scale confidence building measures could be put in place along the way to improve the negotiation environment.

Economics   A further imperative, if the Gulf War and its aftermath are to produce a really durable peace in the Middle East, is to achieve a more even pattern of economic development through a better distribution of the region's resources. The economic complementarities of the Middle East are striking. Resource-rich countries of small populations need the skilled labour that the region's larger states possess in such abundance. The population-rich countries are in desperate need of the investment funds that the oil producers can supply. The necessity of developing scarce supplies of water, the sources of which defy political boundaries, puts a clear premium on economic co-operation. Recent Middle East history is littered with the wrecks of grand schemes for regional co-operation and union. One starting point for the future might be a less ambitious proposal modelled on the lines of the Asia Pacific Economic Cooperation (APEC) process, which has succeeded to date by avoiding over-ambitious goals, defining areas of practical co-operation fairly precisely and, above all, recognising that the future of the region lies in preserving and developing its open and dynamic trading character.

The recovery of the Middle East from the Gulf War depends in the short term on re-establishing the flow of oil, at reasonable prices. Kuwait, facing a huge reconstruction program, has the foreign assets to back it. However, it has had to overcome severe environmental hazards with the oil fires started by the fleeing Iraqis expected to take a year or more to extinguish; creating health, agricultural and fishing problems, and delaying the recovery of Kuwait's economy. Saudi Arabia and the United Arab Emirates have substantial financial reserves, although the Saudi treasury has not avoided strain in accommodating the cost of the Gulf War. Countries facing severe post-war financial constraints are Egypt, Jordan, Syria and, most seriously, Iraq itself. It was obvious that the rich Middle East countries would need to help their poorer neighbours with loans; the West responded with aid-supported credits for capital projects and some debt write-off. In the longer term, however, the Middle East is clearly a candidate for a self-help program of regional co-operation and a more rational distribution of its wealth.

Australia's interest in a durable peace for the Middle East lies not least in the opportunity it will provide for the economic development of the region and the growth of Arab markets for Australian goods. Australia's trade with the Middle East has been concentrated in key commodities—the export of wheat, barley, processed food, meat, iron and steel, and the import of oil and refined petroleum. In 1990 exports were $2.4 billion (4.8 per cent of total Australian exports), mainly to Iran ($614 million), Egypt ($413 million), Saudi Arabia ($295 million) and the United Arab Emirates ($271 million) with important markets also in Iraq, Bahrain, Yemen, Oman and Israel. Imports were $1.6 billion (3.2 per cent of total imports), mainly from Saudi Arabia ($720 million) and the United Arab Emirates ($477 million) as well as Israel and Kuwait. Australia's post-Gulf War trade strategy had three objectives: to resume our traditional commodities trade, to diversify and expand our exports into new products and new regional markets, and to contribute to the reconstruction and restocking of Kuwait.

While Australia has had a high profile in the region in specific commodities, we have not had any significant success in manufactures trade (with the exception of simply transformed manufactures like iron and steel ingots). However, Australia has had considerably more success in supplying services to the region, especially in agriculture-related consultancy. An important new development was an $80 million contract between Telecom and Saudi Arabia, won in 1988. Such 'operations and maintenance' contracts in the services sector involving, in particular, joint ventures with regional and international partners, will offer further opportunities as the demand for services grows. However the same stricture applies as elsewhere: Australian firms which are serious about doing business in the

Middle East need to establish a long-term presence in the region, and develop close relationships with local firms and personalities.

ISRAEL AND ITS NEIGHBOURS

The central political problem of the Middle East is much easier to state than to solve: achieving secure and recognised borders for Israel behind which it can live in peace with its Arab neighbours, and at the same time achieving a just future for the Palestinian people. The problem has existed, in its essentials, since the birth of Israel in 1948–49, and has been made no less intractable as a result of the three wars that Israel fought since, in 1956, 1967 and 1973, to protect itself against real or anticipated attack, and its experience under SCUD missile attack in the Gulf War. United Nations Security Council Resolution 242, passed at the end of the 1967 war, neatly illustrates the problem. (Resolution 338, with which it is usually bracketed, followed the 1973 war and essentially called on the parties to implement UNSCR 242). Resolution 242 provides for both the withdrawal of Israel from occupied territories and:

> the termination of all claims or states of belligerence and respect for and acknowledgement of the sovereignty and territorial integrity and political independence of every state in the area and their right to live in peace within secure and recognised boundaries free from threats or acts of force.

Israel's position has been that there could be no withdrawal unless or until secure boundaries were established and its sovereignty within them recognised. Israel would not commence talks unless the Arabs acknowledged Israel's sovereignty and negotiated directly with it; the Arabs, however, would not negotiate with Israel while it occupied their territories. Egypt's President Sadat partially broke this deadlock with his peace initiative in 1977 which, followed by the Camp David Agreement of 1979, led to Israel returning the Sinai. But the deadlock persists with the continued occupation of the West Bank, Gaza Strip and Golan Heights.

A separate but related problem continues with Israel's occupancy of part of southern Lebanon since 1982, which it has been reluctant to relinquish while faced with a continuing active Palestinian presence there, pending the full restoration of Lebanese sovereignty and the re-establishment of stable government. The Taif Agreement, brokered by the Arab League in 1989, offers the best prospect for a very long time that this result may at last be achievable. Indeed, by the middle of 1991 the Lebanese Government had succeeded, to an extent unimaginable during the long years of civil war since 1975, in asserting its authority over the various militias and the remaining Palestinian forces in southern Lebanon. For many, in particular the Maronite community, this success had come at the expense of accepting a Pax Syriana, reflected in the Treaty of Cooperation signed with that country in May 1991. It is too early to assess whether Syrian influence will be as pervasive as might be feared, or whether Syria will be simply satisfied with arrangements which ensure that its perceived basic security needs are accommodated. What is clear, however, is that for the first time in sixteen years the Lebanese have a real opportunity to negotiate their differences, and work towards re-establishing Lebanon's economic prosperity.

In the months after the Gulf War, US Secretary of State James Baker made multiple visits to the Middle East in pursuit of a process designed to change the ground rules for peace talks by breaking the taboos on direct dialogue between the parties. Baker sought consensus on several points: that the objective was a comprehensive settlement, based on UN Security Council Resolutions 242 and 338; that negotiations would proceed along two tracks, between Israel and Arab states, and between Israel and Palestinians; that negotiations between Israel and Palestinians would proceed in stages, with talks on interim self-government preceding negotiation over the permanent status of the occupied territories; and that a conference co-sponsored by the United States and the Soviet Union would be a launching pad for direct negotiations, leading also to multilateral talks on arms control, regional security and the issues of the environment and water supply.

By mid-1991 it appeared that the convening of such an initial conference before the end of the year might be achievable. But very difficult problems remained to be resolved, not least the question of Palestinian representation—one of the most sensitive of all issues for Israel, and the one on which the Labour-Likud coalition government had collapsed in May 1990. A further difficulty confronting the peace process was continued Israeli settlement activity in the occupied territories: almost a textbook example of a confidence-*destroying* measure, this led Baker to remark in Congressional testimony in May 1991 that 'nothing has made my job of trying to find Arab and Palestinian partners for Israel more difficult'. And certainly no-one could be confident that even if an international conference were convened, it would in fact generate substantive negotiations.

Australia's position, on these efforts as with earlier ones, has been to support all reasonable peace efforts aimed at achieving the twin objectives of security for Israel and a just outcome for the Palestinians. We have not, sensibly, seen ourselves as having any more direct role as a mediator, negotiator or conference participant. There has never been any question, and is none now, about the intensity of our commitment to Israel. It originated as a product of World War II and the Holocaust, and was consolidated by the intellectual link between the Jewish community in Australia —many of whom had fled from Nazi persecution—and the Australian Labor Party in office through the 1940s. The Chifley Government and Dr Evatt, then President of the United Nations General Assembly, gave important political support to Israel at the time of its creation at the United Nations; generations of Australian political leaders since have maintained unwavering support (perhaps excessively so in 1956 when Australia—like Israel itself—played a dubious hand in the Suez Crisis and was exposed accordingly); we participated in the Multi-national Force and Observers (MFO) group monitoring the return of the Sinai following Camp David; and we have been among those leading the international campaign to have the United Nations General Assembly overturn its indefensible Resolution 3379 equating Zionism with racism.

Australia has also had—at least since the 1970s—an even-handed appreciation of the merits of the Palestinian side of the argument. Moreover, in successive Government statements since 1983 it has been made clear that there should be acknowledged 'the right of self determination for the Palestinian people, including their right, if they so choose, to independence and the possibility of their own independent state'.[5] How the Palestinian people exercise that right—whether to establish their own independent state or choose something less, like confederation with Jordan—would depend on the realistic options available to them when the opportunity to exercise the right arrived.

Australia has also been prepared to engage in a dialogue with the Palestine Liberation Organisation (PLO), at least by way of responding to overtures in circumstances where this has seemed likely to be productive. We have recognised that, for all its sins of omission and commission over the years—not least during the Gulf crisis in 1990–91—and despite the ground it appears to have lost since 1988 to those controlling the *intifada* within the occupied territories, there is still no more broadly based representative Palestinian organisation in existence. Clearly the PLO significantly improved its credentials with the December 1988 statement of its chairman Yasser Arafat in Geneva. Expressly speaking on behalf of the Organisation, Arafat then renounced terrorism, recognised Israel's right to exist and committed the PLO to the terms of Resolutions 242 and 338. But equally clearly the PLO would further improve its credentials in this respect if it were to formally amend its constitutional charter—or Covenant—to make clear beyond doubt its acceptance of Israel's right to exist.

Australia has been strongly arguing for some time that Israel's manifest unwillingness to embrace any kind of 'land for peace' strategy, or at least to enter into the kind of serious negotiations which might produce this outcome, is short-sighted and very much against the country's own long-term interests. The reasons are straightforward.

First, there is the strategic time-bomb. Ten years ago Israel spent as much on defence as all its potential regional adversaries combined. But in 1990 Iraq and Syria alone—leaving aside Jordan, Saudi Arabia, Libya and Egypt —were spending between them nearly three times as much as Israel. The size of Israel's armed force has changed little over the last decade, whereas Syria's and Libya's have doubled. The number of Iraqi divisions increased in that time from 10 to 55, and the number of its tanks from 1700 to 5500.

That capability was dramatically reduced by the Gulf War, but there is as yet no guarantee that it cannot and will not be rebuilt.

For the time being, Israel can be confident of its superior organisational and technical capability, and of continued disunity among its neighbours making a combined assault highly unlikely. Certainly it is unlikely as long as Egypt, Saudi Arabia and Syria maintain their present alignment, or at least rapprochement, with the United States. But it is unlikely that President Assad, for one, has permanently changed Syrian spots, or that current alliances will prove any more lasting than their predecessors. The one enduring constant in Arab rhetoric (if not always reflected in Arab countries' behaviour) has been commitment to the Palestinian cause against Israel, and it simply cannot be assumed, with the military balance moving as it is, that some combined assault against Israel is out of the question indefinitely. All the more reason to move now, while the balance of Arab forces are, for whatever reason, working constructively with the West, to defuse the Palestinian issue (and the associated problems of relations with Jordan, Syria and Lebanon) as far as possible and as soon as possible.

Secondly, there is the demographic time-bomb. The Palestinian birth rate is much higher than that of the Jewish population of Israel. There are already more than 750 000 Arabs living inside the pre-1967 borders of Israel, and another 1.3 million or more living in the occupied territories. If Israel retains control of those territories, it is only a matter of time before Jews become a minority in their own country. Even the mass arrival of Soviet Jews will, on recent estimates, postpone that date by only ten years, from 2015 to 2025.

Thirdly, there is the fact that Palestinian opposition to the status quo in Israel has become in recent times a much more home-grown phenomenon —less dependent on external PLO and Arab leadership to sustain and nourish it. Until December 1988, when Israel was confronted by Palestinian terrorism or frontal attack, it was a matter of outside organisation, based on the Palestine diaspora and the confrontationist Arab States. Within the occupied territories there was an apparently quiescent, indeed compliant, Palestinian population, notwithstanding its lack of fundamental democratic and human rights. The *intifada* changed all that. While the stone throwing can be suppressed—more or less effectively depending on the relentlessness of the methods employed—the underlying dynamics of the Palestinian cause have permanently changed. Yasser Arafat and the external leadership of the PLO may not matter quite as much in the future as they have in the past, but the new generation of Palestinian leaders inside Israel and the occupied territories will matter a good deal more. And, as time goes on, it may become harder and harder to find moderates among them.

These internal factors point up starkly the nature of the dilemma that has always existed for Israel: what kind of nation does it want to be? As Thomas Friedman has pointed out in his perceptive and stimulating analysis of

Middle East politics, *From Beirut to Jerusalem,*[6] David Ben-Gurion answered that question in the only way possible. He said, in effect, that Israel could be a Jewish state, it could be a democratic state and it could be a state occupying the whole of what was considered to be the historical land of Israel. But it could not be all three. In 1947 Ben-Gurion persuaded his fledgling nation that Israel could at best secure two-and-a-half of these objectives: a Jewish and democratic State occupying part of the historical Israel. In 1967, with the occupation of the West Bank, the choice between those three options became much starker, though this was perhaps not at the time as fully understood as it could have been. The demographic reality has brought home that the nation of Israel could not occupy the historical land of Israel yet at the same time indefinitely continue to be both Jewish and democratic, short of a totally unacceptable solution such as the mass deportation of Palestinians. But since 1967 Israeli leaders have effectively avoided making that hard choice, and the consequences are plainly visible.

Since 1988, and the coming of the *intifada*, the dilemma has become even more stark. If the *intifada* is about nothing else it is about democracy, about people's right to determine their own political destiny, and about the claim of right of the Palestinians to self-determination. It brought home clearly to Israelis and the rest of the world that if Israel continued to turn a blind eye to that Palestinian claim of political right—and even worse if the Israeli military were to continue to physically suppress it—then Israel as a democracy would be fundamentally flawed.

Israelis sometimes claim that they are judged in these matters by harsher and higher standards than their neighbours. And they are. But this is for the very good reason—as Thomas Friedman again points out—that Israelis have always wanted to be so judged, and the very foundation of the State depended on their being so regarded. The Jewish people have become for the world, by virtue of their history and their achievement, the yardstick of morality and the symbol of hope, and if that status is ever lost—if the world ever becomes as cynical about Israel as it is about almost everything else—then something of enormous value will be lost. Friedman quotes Abba Eban, looking back to the United Nations debate in 1947:

> So we based our claim on the exceptionality of Israel, in terms of the affliction suffered by its people and in terms of our historical and spiritual lineage . . . We chose to emphasise at the beginning of our statehood that Israel would represent the ancient Jewish morality. Some Israelis now complain about being judged by a different standard [from other countries in the Middle East]. But the world is only comparing us to the standard we set for ourselves.[7]

If Israel is to go on being an exceptional country, as it should be, then the time is fast approaching when it will have to compromise. The Palestine issue and the Palestinian people will simply not go away. The nature of Israel's history, and the world spotlight that will always be on the biblical land of Israel, means that the Palestinian issue will not just drift off to the far fringes of public consciousness, like the plight of the Kurds or Armenians or other comparable minorities who equally have been victims of history, only momentarily ever able to capture its attention. And the demographic imperative, if nothing else, means that it is not a problem that Israel itself can forever ignore. Compromise has not been easy for Israelis to contemplate. As Friedman again nicely puts it, they have wavered between two poles. When we are weak, how can we compromise? When we are strong, why should we compromise?[8] Israel is strong at the moment, but it cannot forever assume that it will remain so. To find a way through the morass will involve a demonstration of strength, not a confession of weakness. Certainly it will require a good measure of statesmanship.

AFRICA

Australia's relations with Africa have tended to develop on a largely *ad hoc* basis, often as a consequence of policies on other issues, such as human rights, the Commonwealth and, especially, apartheid. While Australia lacks a history of involvement with the continent, and few Australians are well acquainted with African countries or issues, it is also the case that Africa has not made the sort of demands on Australian foreign policy—the issue of apartheid excepted—that were expected in the 1960s and 1970s. Africa simply did not develop its economic potential as hoped in an era dominated by economic issues. Once the struggles for independence were over and its strategic significance declined as the Cold War gradually lost ascendancy in the international agenda, Africa's poor record in economic development told against the kind of links with Australia anticipated when our first diplomatic missions were established in the 1960s. In 1990 Australia's exports to Africa accounted for only $325 million, or half of one per cent of total exports. And imports accounted for only $187 million, again less than half of one per cent of total imports.

However, it would be wrong for Australia to ignore Africa, or to allow our relations to drift without substance. African nations are able to exert considerable influence internationally, especially at international forums and in developing Third World strategies. In the United Nations and its various agencies, and in the Commonwealth, the African group is the largest and the Africans have shown cohesiveness and discipline on issues of importance to them. Australia must take close account of African views if we are to maintain our international standing and achieve our particular objectives in the multilateral sphere. Our position within the Commonwealth, and our uncompromising record against apartheid, has given us a high standing. But as Africa's attention switches to the resolution of its economic and social problems, expectations from those regarded as friends will increase. They will certainly expect Australia to play a positive role in development and humanitarian aid, and African support for Australian concerns will depend increasingly upon how these expectations are met.

Despite the strength of African cohesion in international forums it is, of course, misleading to talk of 'Africa' as if it were a single entity. There are many different 'Africas' and Australia's interests vary accordingly. The Africas with which Australia has been most involved are those—usually focusing on countries to whom we have been bound through the Commonwealth—where we have established missions from time to time, including Nigeria in West Africa, Kenya in East Africa and Harare and Pretoria in Southern Africa. We have done our best to foster commercial relationships, and to direct as much development assistance—humanitarian and otherwise—as we possibly could to the endemic regional problems of food shortage and population displacement (Africa is host to around half of the world's refugee population of over 13 million). We played a constructive role in the Lusaka Commonwealth meeting in 1979 which assisted Zimbabwe (formerly Southern Rhodesia) to independence within the Commonwealth. We contributed to the cease-fire monitoring force and sent a team to observe the elections in 1989 in Namibia: perhaps an appropriate gesture, given Sir Percy Spender's casting vote in the South West Africa Case in the International Court of Justice in 1966, which delayed Namibian independence for the best part of a generation. But the overwhelming focus of our policy has been, since the early 1970s, the struggle against apartheid—initiated in Australia by the Whitlam Labor Government; sustained, not without personal cost, by Malcolm Fraser; and picked up and taken several stages further by the Hawke Government.

Southern Africa   Southern Africa—embracing South Africa, Lesotho, Swaziland and the 'Frontline States'[9] of Angola, Botswana, Mozambique, Namibia, Tanzania, Zambia and Zimbabwe—has been over the years the area of most direct Australian interest, with the issues of decolonisation and apartheid at the forefront, but economic and development assistance matters not far behind.

The economic failures and disappointments experienced in this part of the continent have had much to do with apartheid itself. Not only have the economically irrational restrictions imposed by the apartheid system dramatically limited South Africa's own growth potential—not to mention the international sanctions imposed in response[10]—but from the mid-1970s South Africa pursued, in aggressive defence of its system, a debilitating policy of 'destabilisation' against its Southern African regional opponents, especially Angola, Mozambique and Zimbabwe. As the African nationalist 'wind of change' blew south, South Africa sought first to prolong the existence of European-controlled buffer states on its northern borders and then to weaken their successors. In the case of Angola, which the Portuguese had left in a state of civil war, South Africa became involved in a Cold War imbroglio in which the United States, the Soviet Union and Cuba flooded the country with weapons. With Mozambique, again Portuguese, a fragile economy which had long been dependent on South Africa was the initial principal target after independence; that was followed, when P. W. Botha came to power in Pretoria in 1978, by more direct military intervention. In Zimbabwe, which won its independence from Britain in 1980, South Africa's task was complicated by the policy of reconciliation unexpectedly pursued by the new leader, Robert Mugabe. But its land-locked geography made it vulnerable to economic pressure, and this was later supplemented by the full range of destabilisation techniques, including 'direct military action and sabotage, clandestine support for action by surrogates, assassination and indiscriminate terror bombings, propaganda and disinformation'.[11] One estimate of the cost of South Africa's 'total strategy' against its neighbours during the 1980s is US$45 billion in material and economic damage, and 1.5 million lives lost through direct military action, disruption of the delivery or production of food, and destruction of health facilities and immunisation programs.[12]

Southern Africa has been the principal focus of Australia's development assistance to Africa over the last twenty-five years. The ten member countries of the Southern Africa Development Co-ordination Conference (SADCC)[13] have been the major beneficiaries of AIDAB's Southern Africa program, amounting to $100 million over the three years 1987–90, with a further $110 million program commencing in 1990. This expenditure incorporates—to the extent of $6.9 million in 1990/91—the Special Assistance Program for South Africans (SAPSA) which was established in 1986 in order to directly help those disadvantaged by apartheid, as well as provide a means for increasing Australian awareness and involvement, particularly through the work of Australian non-government aid organisations.[14]

Despite the closure of the Australian Trade Commission office in Johannesburg in 1985, and our strict adherence to other specific trade sanctions agreed by the United Nations and the Commonwealth, South Africa is our largest trading partner in Africa (with the exception of Egypt, which is treated for most purposes as part of the Middle East rather than Africa). Total two-way trade in 1990 was just over $240 million. While the lifting of trade sanctions will create new openings, they should not be regarded as an automatic guarantee of greatly increased bilateral trade. The South African and Australian economies are far more competitive—especially in commodities—than complementary.

One of the most important of our bilateral African relationships, certainly in terms of political dialogue, is with Zimbabwe. The commercial relationship has increased quietly but steadily since Zimbabwe became independent in 1980, and the Qantas link with Harare has operated successfully. Zimbabwe is one of the few African countries which has continued to maintain modest levels of economic growth. It has abundant agricultural and mining resources and an expanding manufacturing industry. Yet so volatile has been the African political scene, and so disheartening the overall economic prospects, that Australian business has hastened slowly in consolidating what could still, ultimately, be a strong Australian connection. Total trade in 1990 was only $31 million, but despite the difficulties, trade has grown by more than 200 per cent since independence in 1980. Zimbabwe, like Mozambique, could well become in the post-apartheid era one of the key pillars in a South Africa-stimulated regional economy.

Despite the strong Commonwealth focus of Australia's relations with Africa, Mozambique has been the largest recipient of Australian bilateral aid in Southern Africa. Almost $45 million was given in assistance during the triennium ending in June 1990—$21.5 million for development purposes and $23 million in emergency assistance—reflecting Mozambique's precipitous economic and social decline in the 1980s, due essentially to destabilisation. But Mozambique has a significant natural resource base and is strategically very important to the region's transport infrastructure (as the natural land, rail and seaport for land-locked Zambia, Zimbabwe, Botswana and Malawi). It has a much brighter long-term future than its present parlous circumstances would suggest.

The Other Africas   East Africa comprises important African members of the Commonwealth—Kenya, Uganda and Malawi (also, geographically, Tanzania, although its political links have been more with Southern Africa), and their support has been important in developing and promoting the broad international acceptance of Australian and Commonwealth policies on Southern Africa. As neighbours in the Indian Ocean, Australia and the countries of East Africa have a common interest in strategic developments in the region, while Kenya's position as the host of the United Nations Environment Programme reflects the close involvement of East African states in the environmental issues which are of growing concern to Australia and the international community. Also of concern, but in a rather less attractive way, has been the human rights situation in this region— particularly the brutality of the Amin and Obote years in Uganda, and the increasing authoritarianism of the Kenyan government during the 1980s: the latter has been the subject of active, if not always easy, representations by the Australian resident mission in Nairobi. Economically, Kenya remains an important potential market for Australia, but present trade is limited. Commercial opportunities exist for Australian agricultural equipment and services, as well as expertise in other areas such as the energy sector, but there is little expectation of major breakthroughs. In Kenya and Uganda in particular, Australia has provided assistance with special emphasis on training in promoting economic and social development.

Central Africa, dominated by Zaire and including Rwanda and Burundi, Congo, Gabon, Equatorial Guinea and the Central African Republic, is an area with which Australia has had very limited relations, reflecting the historical background of these countries, which tend to look to Europe first.

In terms of our priorities in Africa, and the resources which we can devote, it is unlikely that relations will develop beyond their current very modest level.

Developments in the Horn of Africa, by contrast, have created considerable interest in Australia. Ethiopia, Sudan and Somalia have all experienced major civil unrest. In particular, the secession struggles in the Ethiopian provinces of Eritrea and Tigray, and the associated refugee flows, have engaged a good deal of parliamentary and community attention—and sympathy. Concern over the 1974 famine was largely responsible for the initial growth of widespread community interest in Black Africa; regrettably, as drought and war have continued to take their toll, this interest has had to be regenerated over and again. Australian Government relief aid to Ethiopia alone amounted to nearly $60 million between 1985 and 1990.

West Africa is in many respects the most diverse of the 'Africas', dominated by Nigeria but also comprising significant states of francophone Africa like Senegal, the Ivory Coast and Guinea, with whom Australia has little direct contact or, realistically, much in common. Nigeria is the giant of Africa, in size, in potential and in the assertiveness of its national pride. It has abundant natural resources, especially oil, and a population of at least 110 million, with a growth rate of 3.4 per cent per annum, one of the highest in the world. The down-turn in oil prices in the 1980s had severe consequences for Nigeria, creating a familiar pattern of increasing debt, expenditure cuts, and depreciation of the exchange rate. There are again encouraging signs of a strengthening economy, although unemployment and inflation are biting hard, and the health of the economy will be an important element in managing the return of civilian rule, now targeted for 1992. Australia's trade with Nigeria has been low, despite optimistic expectations ever since our mission in Lagos was opened in 1960, tending to fluctuate with specific commodity contracts such as wheat and salt. Nigeria has, nonetheless, continued to express interest in trade and technical cooperation with, and investment from, Australia, especially in agriculture-related areas. In recent years the main focus of our bilateral assistance program has been on in-Australia training but, as with other areas of Africa outside Southern Africa, the proportion of Australian aid to Nigeria has declined in recent years, as attention has had to be directed to higher priority areas.

The Maghreb (literally 'West') stretching from Libya through Tunisia, Algeria and Morocco to Mauritania is an area which, politically at least, we tend to view as an extension of the Arab states of the Middle East rather than Africa. In the 1970s and early 1980s the region was regarded as one of considerable potential for Australian commercial interests, but a combination of economic difficulties (in the case of Algeria) and political dispute with Libya over the regime's sponsoring of destabilising activity in the South Pacific, have limited opportunities for its realisation. However, apart from Libya, relations have been warm. Algeria in particular, with its strong non-aligned credentials, has been a very valuable interlocutor in international forums. Although resource constraints have caused both Australia and Algeria recently to close their respective missions in each other's capitals, Algeria remains both a useful dialogue partner and a potentially significant market in which Australia has an established, and good, reputation. The long-running dispute over the former Spanish Western Sahara between Morocco and the indigenous Polisario has been a continuing problem for the region, but now at last one moving toward resolution through the efforts of the United Nations Secretary-General. Australia's decision in mid-1991 to contribute to the United Nations supervision of a referendum to determine the future of Western Sahara was an important development in the history of our contribution to peace-keeping operations, given that it involved an area and dispute with which Australia had had only limited involvement in the past.

THE STRUGGLE AGAINST APARTHEID

The history of apartheid began effectively with the victory of the South African National Party in the general election of May 1948 on a platform of strict racial segregation. Within a few years the National Party legislated the basics of the system of apartheid—the Population Registration Act, the Group Areas Act, the Separate Amenities Act, the Bantu Education Act, the prohibition of black trade union activity, and the abolition of coloured voting rights. In addition, the government introduced the Suppression of Communism Act, the initial stage in the introduction of broad-ranging, immensely repressive security legislation. Internal opposition grew steadily with organised defiance campaigns and nation-wide protests led by the African National Congress (ANC)—which had been founded as far back as 1912—supported by groups such as the Indian National Congress and the white Congress of Democrats. That opposition culminated in an event which drew the iniquity of the apartheid system to world attention as nothing else had—the horrifying Sharpeville massacre of March 1960. But far from persuading the South African Government of its error, a new round of even more severe repression began, starting with the banning of both the ANC and its offshoot, the Pan Africanist Congress (PAC).

In May 1961 South Africa became a republic and ceased to be a member of the Commonwealth. At the same time the government began its pursuit of separate development through the homelands policy. The original intention was that South Africa be completely divested of its black population. Each of the ten 'homelands' would eventually be granted total 'independence' and cease to be part of 'South Africa'. Black workers in 'South Africa' would be allowed back only as aliens on the basis of temporary work permits. Every African, even though born and brought up in 'white' South Africa was to be regarded as a citizen of a homeland which he or she may never have seen. The political and moral bankruptcy of the homelands policy was amply demonstrated by the fact that, as developed by the late 1980s, the homelands constituted only 13 per cent of all South Africa, were hopelessly fragmented in shape, non-viable economically, and the actual place of residence of only about 40 per cent of South African Blacks.

By the mid-1970s the South African Government faced increasing pressure, both internal and external. Within its immediate region, the collapse of Portuguese administration in Angola and Mozambique made the country much more vulnerable to guerrilla activity by ANC and PAC exiles—a situation exacerbated at the end of the decade by the achievement of Zimbabwe's independence. At home, South Africa faced the most serious social violence since the Union in 1910 when violence erupted in the black townships, beginning with Soweto in June 1976. These pressures led to some reform of the more restrictive 'separate development' and 'petty apartheid' restrictions during the early 1980s. But constitutional reforms designed to provide for power-sharing for the Coloured and Indian communities led to a renewal of urban violence, starting in late 1984 and continuing throughout 1985 and into 1986. The proclamation of a limited state of emergency in July 1985, and then an effectively permanent one from June 1986, brought with it a major new cycle of repression and reaction. More than twenty million Black people—over 70 per cent of the population of South Africa—were in the mid-1980s as far away as they had ever been from acceptance as equal citizens in their own country.

Sanctions against South Africa have had a long history. Initial phases involved India imposing a trade ban as early as 1946, a few countries imposing selective measures during the 1960s (e.g. Japanese ban on direct investment in 1964), and a number of countries imposing oil and arms embargoes, and sports and cultural boycotts, in the 1970s. The Commonwealth—and Australia in particular—played a particularly vital role in launching the sports boycott. Gough Whitlam announced in December 1972 that sporting teams selected on the basis of race would not be allowed to enter Australia. This position was further strengthened by the Fraser Government which in November 1976 supported the United Nations General Assembly Resolution on apartheid in sport, and in June 1977 became a party to the Gleneagles Agreement.[15] In October 1983, Foreign Minister Bill Hayden announced significant further tightening of the restrictions on sporting contacts.[16]

Overall, it would be fair to say that in terms of the breadth and domestic profile of the sporting contacts forbidden, Australia (closely followed by New Zealand) probably sacrificed more by its sports boycott policy than any other country in the world. But in the judgment of successive Australian governments (and a largely supportive Australian populace) that sacrifice has been very much worth it. There can be no doubt about the psychological pain—the sense of isolation and deprivation—that has been caused by the boycott policy to the rugby-mad and cricket-mad and generally sports-mad white South African community. And that impact in turn must have had some effect in forcing appreciation of the painful implications of apartheid itself.

It was not until 1985–86, in reaction to the further cycle of violence and repression then occurring, that really wide-ranging and substantial economic sanctions were put in place by the international community. The Commonwealth, European Community, United States and individual Nordic countries led the way, each drawing successively on precedents set by the others in what has been accurately described as a 'wave' phenomenon.[17] So far as the Commonwealth was concerned, an initial range of measures was agreed at the Nassau Commonwealth Heads of Government Meeting (CHOGM) in October 1985: some consistent with recently introduced Australian measures (e.g. a ban on new government loans), others giving further content to the existing 1977 United Nations Security Council Resolution banning arms sales, and others imposing new restrictions (e.g. on the importation of krugerrands, the export of oil, trade promotion and cultural and scientific links).

Following the failure of the Eminent Persons Group (EPG) mission to make progress in moving the South African Government towards negotiations,[18] Commonwealth Heads of Government met again in London in August 1986, and agreed to recommend the imposition of the 'second tranche' of measures previously agreed in Nassau (including bans on airlinks, the importation of agricultural products, government procurement and contracts, and tourist promotion). For good measure, they added a series of further restrictions to the list (the withdrawal of consular facilities, and bans on all new bank loans and on the importation of uranium, coal, iron and steel). Most of these measures were picked up, and in some cases exceeded, elsewhere. For example, in October 1986 the United States Congress overrode a Presidential Veto to pass the Comprehensive Anti-apartheid Act (CAAA). Drafted on a 'carrot and stick' basis, this Act was in many ways tougher than the Commonwealth package, but the American legislators openly acknowledged their debt to the Commonwealth for laying the groundwork.[19]

Undoubtedly the most effective of all the economic measures introduced in the mid-1980s were the financial sanctions—those involving the denial or limitation of credit to the South African government and companies. Partly these were imposed directly by national governments—as with the action taken by most Commonwealth countries in 1986 to ban (or at least seek the voluntary cessation of) new bank lending, and the Gramm Amendment passed by the United States Congress in 1983 to effectively veto IMF loans to South Africa. Partly they were driven by the decisions of many lower-level governments, particularly states and cities in the United States, to refuse to deal with companies, including banks, that had South African links: the pressure came from both voters and customers. And partly it was simply a matter of boardrooms making assessments of the credit risk of a country that seemed on the verge of violent explosion. The whole process has been self-reinforcing in a way that trade sanctions could never have been. Every new bank that refuses credit, or sets tougher terms, increases the credit risk for other suppliers still in the field. This is, in effect, what happened in the years after the initial decision in 1985 of a number of New York banks not to roll over short-term loans—the decision which first plunged South Africa into real financial crisis.

The pain caused by financial sanctions, both formal and informal, was readily acknowledged from the late 1980s by spokesmen like Finance Minister Barend du Plessis and Reserve Bank Governor Gerhard de Kock. Ways had been found to circumvent trade sanctions, and disinvestment had run its course, but the level of access to new international capital was dramatically and comprehensively strangling the economy. South Africa could fund internally growth of no more than 2 per cent a year, but it needed to grow at 4 per cent or more to create jobs for its expanding population and to maintain existing standards of living. It was conceded in discussions Gareth Evans had with a number of ministers and officials during his visit to South Africa in June 1991—the first by an Australian Foreign Minister to South Africa since 1948—that it was financial sanctions more than any other form of external pressure that had ultimately forced South Africa to the negotiating table.

In this respect, the role played by Australia has not been unimportant, even though our own financial institutions have never been significant bilateral creditors. We strongly supported the initial imposition and subsequent extension of financial sanctions at successive Commonwealth meetings. It was Prime Minister Hawke at the Vancouver CHOGM in 1987 who initiated the ground-breaking expert study on the impact of financial sanctions which became widely influential in international financial circles,[20] and which subsequently influenced a wider public to understand the centrality of these sanctions when it was published (again at Australian initiative) in book form in 1989.[21] And it was Australia which proposed, at the Kuala Lumpur CHOGM in 1989, and largely funded, the establishment at the London School of Economics of the Centre for the Study of the South African Economy and International Finance, designed among other things to assess on a continuing basis the role of international capital flows into and out of South Africa.

The relentless international pressure for change, and the ever-mounting internal tension, had created all the necessary conditions for reform, but there was need still of a white political leadership clear-headed enough to grasp the moment. That came at last with the succession to the Presidency in February 1989 of F. W. de Klerk, replacing the ailing hardliner P. W. Botha, and his election victory in September that year on a platform of political reform. The speech which President de Klerk made to launch the reform process on 2 February 1990 was genuinely historic, announcing as it did the unbanning of the ANC and other opposition political organisations, the release of ANC leader Nelson Mandela after twenty-seven years in prison, and the Government's willingness to enter into serious negotiations on a wholly new democratic and non-racial constitutional dispensation.

De Klerk's speech opened the way for 'talks about talks' throughout 1990 between the ANC and the Government. These were highlighted by the Groote Schuur meeting in early May and the Pretoria meeting on 7 August, which set out the preconditions for formal negotiations on a new consti-tution and the end of the apartheid system, including agreements relating to the release of prisoners and the return of exiles. The process was carried further by de Klerk in a 'first anniversary' speech on 1 February 1991, in which he confirmed the Government's intention to repeal all the legislative pillars of apartheid and clear away the outstanding obstacles inhibiting detailed constitutional negotiations, and also set out a human rights oriented 'Manifesto for a New South Africa'.

All this movement created reverse pressures for the relaxation in sanc-tions in a number of countries, particularly Europe. The European Com-munity acted accordingly by lifting its sanction on new investment in December 1990, and in April 1991 announcing the removal of barriers to importing South African iron, steel and kruggerands. But developments during the first half of 1991 made it appear that this relaxation of pressure may have been premature. While the Government did honour its promise to repeal the 'pillars' legislation (the Group Areas, Population Registration, Separate Amenities and Land Acts), it failed to meet deadlines on the prisoners-release and exiles-return questions. And, even more worryingly, violence in the Black townships broke out again on a major scale, with frequent bloody clashes involving supporters of the ANC and the Zulu-based Inkatha Party of Chief Buthelezi. That violence was accompanied, moreover, by frequent and apparently well-founded allegations of overt security-force (and covert government) support for Inkatha. It seemed to many observers that the Government, confident now of its international backing, felt that it could afford to spend more energy building and con-solidating its political support for the future—including division of the Black community—than seeing the reform process through to fruition.

There was still, in mid-1991, a reasonable level of confidence that the reform momentum was effectively irreversible, and could be expected to result eventually in a wholly new South Africa. The task for the inter-national community was to work out how best to encourage the working out of that process in the fastest and most peaceful way. The Com-monwealth's response has been to adopt a phased and selective approach to the lifting of sanctions. As devised by the Committee of Foreign Min-isters on Southern Africa (CFMSA)—the nine nation body established by the 1987 Vancouver CHOGM, chaired by Canada, which operates in close consultation with the liberation movements and Frontline States, and on which Australia has been actively engaged since its inception—the approach has four elements.

'People-oriented' sanctions—including cultural boycotts, the ban on direct airlinks and visa restrictions—could be lifted once the preliminary obstacles to formal constitutional negotiations had been overcome (namely, repeal of the 'pillars', review of security legislation, and resolution of the prisoners and exiles issues). Trade, investment and financial sanctions would not be lifted until some further major step (e.g. the establishment of an interim government or constituent assembly) had been taken towards constitutional reform. And the arms embargo would not be lifted until a new constitution and government were actually in place. But the sports boycott could be lifted selectively as non-racial administrative integration was achieved and endorsed in a given sport, and a commitment made to the development of Black facilities: thus the new United Cricket Board of South Africa was readmitted to the International Cricket Council, with both Commonwealth and ANC support, on 29 June 1991.

Many disappointments and reverses can be expected as the process of rebuilding South Africa, and welcoming it back into the international community, works itself out. But nobody can doubt the justice or necessity of the cause. Apartheid has involved a tragic waste of human potential and human resources; it has been disastrous for the millions of lives it has blighted or destroyed, and in its impact on the South African economy; and it has run against the tide not only of humanity but of rationality.

We live in a world of many inequalities and many injustices, and it may be questioned why a country like Australia should have committed so much to an issue so little of our making. But the system of apartheid, based as it has been on an assertion that whites are superior to Blacks and that this self-proclaimed superiority entitles one race to rule the other, stands so far beyond the pale that it simply could not be regarded as just another unpalatable regime. If we in Australia had washed our hands of apartheid, on the comfortable but indecent justification that it was too far away or too intractable a problem, we would not only have failed in our humanitarian duty, but have debased the very values which are at the core of our sense of human dignity.

17

Europe

EUROPE'S CONTRIBUTION to the modern world has been so enormous that it has been tempting at various stages of this century to think that it might have ended. The exhaustion of two world wars, fought mainly in Europe; the rise of fascism and communism to contest the liberal-bourgeois values that seemed to typify European civilisation; the end of European colonialism; the arrival of an era of nuclear weapons in which the United States and the Soviet Union were dominant; and, by no means least, the emergence of the Asia Pacific region as a productive centre of a global economy—each seemed to signal imminent completion of the great European contribution to world affairs. Yet Europe continues to change and develop in ways that renew its claim to intense international attention. And since 1989 that renewal has been so dramatic as not merely to absorb but to dominate world attention.

In West Europe, in 1989 and subsequently, there was an extraordinary acceleration towards economic and political union, not least with a united Germany becoming part of the European Community and, inconceivable only a year before, part of NATO as well. In East Europe there was also acceleration, but in the opposite direction towards disintegration and disunity. The formerly Soviet-dominated structure of East Europe collapsed like a house of cards. The Soviet Union itself, a massive combination of republics covering a sixth of the earth's surface, and seemingly invulnerable to the nationalism that had earlier undermined the European empires, found itself facing internal dissension and irredentism that threatened to break the country apart.

Growing cohesion in one half of Europe and fragmentation in the other: it seemed like a recipe for the kind of conflict with which Europe was only too familiar. Equally, however, it could be seen as the first stirrings of a European response to the reshaping of the world that had been going on in fits and starts since the beginning of the nuclear age. Europe was centre stage in confronting the dilemma of nuclear war, with the Warsaw Pact and NATO forces attuned to every nuance in the peculiar stalemate of military power that had developed—one of competing armouries of nuclear weapons that could never rationally be used. It was in Europe that, in response, new concepts of security began to emerge. It was in Europe that the two nuclear superpowers offered each other the reassurances of confidence-building measures and the transparent observation of each other's military preparedness. And it was in Europe that the breakthrough in disarmament came, with the dramatic dismantling of much, though by no means all, of the weaponry laboriously built up from the beginning of the Cold War.

What is now revealed had long been suspected. It was in military power, and little else, that the Soviet Union and its East European associates could claim parity with West Europe and its North American allies, the United States and Canada. When the imperative of military equality was relaxed and economic, political and cultural factors were allowed to determine the priorities of governments, West Europe prospered and East Europe faltered. West Europe went on moving away from local conflict and historic rivalry, while East Europe and the Soviet Union were rediscovering their pasts with a vengeance. They discovered that communism had subdued or suppressed tradition, in particular ethnicity and religion, without replacing it with any new religion, any new national identity or a sufficient abundance of material life to make that loss of tradition desirable or even palatable. Mikhail Gorbachev, determined to change the Soviet Union and prepared to accept its diminished grip on East Europe, believed that the result would be a shake-up, not a break-down. His political skills and his confidence may have commanded respect, but his belief was not universally shared.

By mid-1991 the future shape of Europe was still an open question. The Soviet Union and the East European republics were all in economic distress of varying degrees. All faced political instability and internal disorder as they set about moving from centrally planned and controlled economies to ones primarily responsive to the marketplace. Theory and instinct suggest a clear connection between liberal democracy and market economy, but no-one can adequately predict how things will finally turn out. In the established democracies of West Europe, the marketplace acts as a unifier, providing a common secular language across religious and ethnic divides. However, in the Soviet Union and East Europe, the market is still breaking through the upper reaches of the command economy; without the momentum for integration already established in West Europe, it is not clear what the overall effect will be, or the extent of the likely differences, country by country. Nor is it clear what the relationship will be between the European Community, the Soviet Union and the countries of East Europe.

In these circumstances, Australian foreign policy has to deal with several interrelated realities, developing within different and still uncertain time-frames. One is the European Community, with the Single Market set to be achieved by 1992, and further economic and political union following. Another is the Soviet Union which, in whatever form it emerges from its current crises, will remain at the very least a massive military power, and a great force accordingly in world politics. A third reality is the continuing individuality of many countries in both West and East Europe with whom Australia has relationships of importance, be it for reasons of trade and investment, politics, immigration or culture.

It is difficult to believe that countries with the identity and accumulated national experience of Britain, Germany, France and Italy—not to mention Sweden and Greece and a good many others—will ever submerge their identity and their national freedom of action in something yet to be defined called 'Europe'. But that is just what may be happening. For Australia, it is necessary, accordingly, while maintaining our bilateral links—with all the history, culture, commerce and sentiment that defines their character—to be at the same time responsive to the momentum in Europe as each definable stage in the process of integration is reached.

A NEW EUROPEAN ARCHITECTURE

By mid-1991, some of the more ambitious ideas about the re-ordering of Europe after the democratic revolutions of 1989 were being scaled down. The idea of a 'common European home', with Mikhail Gorbachev promoting the Soviet Union as a tenant, was seen by West Europe as, quite apart from anything else, too expensive: the early euphoria over German reunification had subsided as West Germans counted the cost and, with the Soviet Union in desperate financial need, a close association with it became unpalatable. Then there was the idea of a Europe of concentric circles, with the twelve European Community (EC) countries[1] at the centre, the six European Free Trade Association (EFTA) countries[2] in a second ring, the seven former socialist countries of East Europe[3] on the periphery, and the Soviet Union farther afield, but still very closely associated. Events have somewhat overtaken this model, with the EFTA countries pulled in closer and the Soviet Union—for the time being anyway—pushed rather further away. And Francois Mitterrand seems to have abandoned, at least for the time being, the notion of a grand European 'confederation'.

For Australians, aware of the economic nit-picking and political back-biting of the sovereign Australian states before Federation in 1901—not, for that matter, a phenomenon much diminished thereafter—it is no surprise that the vision of a united Europe is taking some time to implement.

The European Community countries, which will be the core of whatever emerges as the new Europe, have since the Single European Act of 1987 been committed as a first step to the Single Market, an internal barrier-free trading zone of 340 million consumers. This has been a major exercise in itself, involving protracted negotiations over a central stock market, tax standardisation and innumerable other regulatory issues, but it is expected to be in place on schedule by the end of 1992. It is the foundation stone of the new Europe. However, the speed of political change in Europe since 1989 and the Gulf crisis, which showed up differences among the Europeans, set in motion further wide-ranging negotiations not only about economic integration but also about political union including defence and security issues. While the new architecture is mostly still on the designing board, it is possible to give an outline sketch of what is emerging.

On economic matters, the European Community continues to set the pace. Not only is the Single Market well on track for the end of 1992 but, on the question of European Monetary Union (EMU), the EC countries have now agreed, in June 1991, on a detailed negotiating text. The core of the case against monetary union—most vociferously expressed by Britain—had been the loss of national sovereignty and the possible adverse economic consequences of handing over to a European central bank the management of a single currency. There still remain many difficult issues to be resolved—including the precise powers to be transferred to a European central bank, the extent to which there would have to be complete convergence of the weaker and stronger EC economies before EMU was finalised, and the timing of the crucial steps—but it is hard to resist the conclusion that a single currency and fully co-ordinated monetary policy is not many years away.

The pace of the EC's own economic integration has tended to cut across the protracted negotiations for a 'European Economic Area' (EEA)—previously, and rather oddly, known as the 'European Economic Space'—between the EC and the six countries, mainly Nordic, of the European Free Trade Area. A number of EFTA countries have now decided to seek full EC membership, because the laborious negotiations to date had made it clear that they would, without acquiring the full rights and privileges of membership, nonetheless have to accept the copious body of law and regulations governing the EC. This is not to say that the seven years already spent on negotiating an EEA have been a waste of time: in bringing governments and their key agricultural and industrial constituencies to the realisation of the need to go all the way to EC membership, notwithstanding various historical, conceptual and ideological differences, they may well have been an indispensable bridging process.

If EC economic and monetary union was well advanced in mid-1991, political union was some distance behind. Discussion had accelerated, papers and conferences had proliferated, but all the hard decisions about political union had yet to be made. One of the threshold problems was linguistic, with Britain in particular objecting strenuously to the use of the 'f word'—federalism—to describe the target outcome. Foreign Secretary Douglas Hurd said that while, in French, the term 'means something loose with a good deal of power dispersed', for the British it 'means something pretty centralised and integrated': others might be willing to accept the term in the belief that realistically it was something a long way off, but the British were 'brought up differently'.[4] Faced with this robust position, and anxious not to jeopardise progress at the June 1991 EC Summit on the more immediately important issue of EMU, French President Mitterrand and German Chancellor Kohl agreed with Prime Minister Major to shelve substantive consideration of political union until at least the end of 1991.

Three specific political union questions remain particularly controversial. First is the role and power of the European Parliament, and the correction of the so-called 'democratic deficit' whereby the 518 directly elected European parliamentarians—confined to a largely consultative and advisory role—have very little impact on EC decisions as compared to the 'executive' of 17 Commissioners nominated by the member-state governments. Secondly, is extension of the EC's competence into new areas, such as social security, health, education, the environment, immigration, drugs and law enforcement, each a minefield in its own right—not least for a Britain whose vision of political union does not include 'the idea of a centralised Europe with the basic decisions being taken in Brussels'.[5] Thirdly, and most controversial of all, is a common foreign and security policy. While considerable progress has been made in the evolution of common EC positions on 'pure' foreign policy questions, there remain quite fundamental differences on more narrowly defined security and defence issues.

Foreign policy has developed through the European Political Co-operation (EPC) process whereby EC foreign ministers meet regularly with each other—and with other countries and groups including Australia and ASEAN—to consider and formulate joint positions on international issues, for example South African sanctions, the Middle East peace process and relations with the Soviet Union and East Europe. The EC 'troika' (of present, past and future occupants of the six-monthly rotating Presidency of the EC Council of Ministers) has become in recent times almost as visible and significant a participant in international meetings as the major individual European countries themselves. Policy formulation presently occurs on a consensus basis, and one of the political union issues still to be resolved is whether this should be modified to majority rule. Another question requiring further attention as the process further evolves, here as elsewhere in the European system, is the precise working relationship between ministers, the European Commission and the European Parliament. Presently, in foreign policy, effective authority lies squarely with the ministers, and its implementation much more with national governments than with Brussels, but that cannot be assumed indefinitely.

There is much less consensus now, or in prospect, about the handling of defence and security matters, as was evident during the Gulf crisis. At one pole stands the European Commission and its President, Jacques Delors, who envisage an EC defence force to carry out EC policy, and want to absorb the Western European Union (WEU) into the EC. France is sympathetic to this approach, as to a lesser extent are Germany and Italy. Others, led by Britain and the Netherlands, believe that, quite apart from questions of financial feasibility, this would weaken NATO, alienate the United States and alarm the Soviet Union. They would prefer a formula that would leave all European contingencies—including those in East Europe—in NATO's hands, while proposing the WEU as an out-of-area vehicle for European security policy. Overarching all these various structures, and East Europe as well—at least in terms of its comprehensive membership—is the Conference on Security and Co-operation in Europe (CSCE). Presently not much more than a medium for dialogue, the CSCE may nonetheless evolve into a body able to play a much more substantial role in conflict resolution. But in mid-1991 there was no more agreement about this than about any other aspect of the future security architecture of Europe.

The primary raison d'être for the sixteen-nation[6] North Atlantic Treaty Organization (NATO) remains the risks—if no longer the threat—associated with Soviet military power. For all its internal problems, the Soviet Union still has enormous, and at least in some respect ultra-modern, military capabilities, which make it by far Europe's most powerful nation. While much energy has been expended, since the collapse of the Warsaw Pact and the dissipation of the more obvious dimensions of the Soviet menace, in trying to rethink NATO's role, at least two familiar components have been agreed to be still crucial: a continued United States troop presence in Europe, and continued reliance on nuclear deterrence. Thinking in mid-1991 about a new role for NATO was focused on the need for a more mobile, flexible and multinational 'ready reaction force'. How effective this will be in practice will depend on the quality of the resources and quantity of the financial backing allocated to it—both still somewhat uncertain—and larger questions such as whether the NATO Charter limitation on 'out-of-area' operations is dropped, whether France changes its position of non-involvement in NATO's military activities, and whether NATO's present membership is expanded to include some or all of those East European countries making overtures about joining it. There are those who believe that there will be little in practice for NATO to do, that European public and governmental commitment to it will quietly wither away, and that it will eventually become moribund. On the other hand, the United States continues to vigorously insist that NATO should continue to be regarded as the cornerstone of Western security, in its preservation of the strategic balance within Europe.[7] It is certainly too early now to make any confident prediction about the Organization's long-term future.

The Western European Union (WEU) originated in the Brussels Treaty of

1948, a 50-year pact 'for collaboration on economic, social and cultural matters and for collective self-defence', which was signed originally by the United Kingdom, France, the Netherlands, Belgium and Luxemburg, then in 1954 by Germany and Italy, and in 1988 by Spain and Portugal. Long thought to be an empty vessel, it developed a new lease of life in the late 1980s, and especially in the Gulf crisis, when it became a useful vehicle for co-ordinating various national naval deployments. (EC foreign ministers' meetings during the Gulf War—limited in their capacity to discuss military issues by, among other things, the presence of neutral Ireland—were on occasions transmogrified temporarily into 'WEU' meetings for this purpose.) Britain has been advocating the development of a NATO-model 'rapid reaction force' under WEU auspices to give the Europeans the option of intervention—without American involvement—in situations where this might be appropriate. But the organisation has—at least as yet—no unified command, no dedicated troops and a still limited membership coverage. Whether the WEU operates as some kind of bridge between the EC and NATO for the foreseeable future, or whether its role will prove to be slight and merely transient, is again at this stage impossible to predict.

The CSCE—formally established in 1975 with the signing of the Helsinki Final Act, after West Europe and the United States eventually responded favourably to a long-evolving Soviet proposal—embraces the whole of West and East Europe (except Andorra!), and the United States and Canada as well.[8] Its charter has always extended beyond military security to economic co-operation and 'the human dimension': it is now generally acknowledged that the pressures put upon the East bloc countries by their formal adherence to its human rights principles, however sporadic and cynical their real commitment, was an important element in generating the atmosphere for *glasnost* and the revolutions of 1989–90. But for present —and future—purposes, the most important role of the CSCE has been as a forum for security dialogue, with major contributions to its credit in mutual confidence-building, not least the negotiation, under its auspices, of the treaty on Conventional Armed Forces in Europe (CFE) signed at the Paris CSCE Summit in November 1990.

More recent CSCE preoccupations have been with the establishment of a conflict resolution centre (with a focus on prevention rather than resolution), and an emergency mechanism—able to be initiated on a majority rather than consensus basis—to react quickly, at least politically, to regional problems. The first test for the CSCE in this respect came in mid-1991 with the crisis in Yugoslavia. In the event it was the EC which led the effort at political mediation, but with its troika acting also as the appointed representative of CSCE, and maintaining contact throughout with the chairman of the CSCE emergency mechanism (who happened to be at the time its initiator, German Foreign Minister Genscher). It is not expected that, for the foreseeable future, the CSCE will play any enforcement role in situations erupting within its area of coverage—military intervention would be a matter for NATO, the WEU or the UN—but again, at this stage, it is simply impossible to foresee how institutional arrangements will ultimately evolve.

Overall, there is a strong economic logic pushing European unity. If real economic and monetary union is reached by the middle of the 1990s, it can be reasonably assumed that a significant measure of political union will follow, and that even defence and security integration may emerge in time. The habit of contact and consultation has its own momentum, and the natural coincidences of interest are very strong. It can also be assumed that the number of European countries embraced by that unity will, by the end of the 1990s, have significantly increased. Certainly for most of the 1990s European countries will continue to make their own national decisions according to their own perceived interests and with a good deal of continuing individuality. In their forward thinking and planning, however, they will be aware of the increasing importance of Brussels, the new fact of economic life of the Single Market, the effectiveness of a common front on all external policy issues, and the uses that can be made of institutions like the CSCE and the WEU to create a new framework for security in Europe.

It is easy to focus on the areas of difference and hesitancy, but the curve on the graph of European unity continues to rise. It has been remarked that observing EC proceedings can be as deceptive as watching a glacier: there are no sudden movements, but the landscape is being transformed. Unprecedented co-operation exists among EC countries already, and the trend in the whole of Europe is unmistakeable. The rest of the world, including Australia, will be watching carefully the shape and content of European unity as it develops during the 1990s. Traditional bilateral relationships, strong as they may have been, will become of less relative significance, and the new multilateral ones of much greater importance. But bilateral relationships will have their place, and none more so in Europe than Australia's with Britain.

THE UNITED KINGDOM

Britain's influence on Australia has been so extensive that it is difficult to apply the normal tests of foreign policy to our relationship. The ties of history, kinship and culture are so pervasive that the relationship seems to exist independently of governments and their policies. It is in that respect the opposite of the relationship, say, with Indonesia, which is physically close but culturally distant, making contacts between the two peoples more dependent on the actions of governments. While there has been a great deal of effort in both Canberra and Jakarta to improve understanding and create more substance in Australia–Indonesia relations, the Anglo–Australian relationship has been regarded as so uniquely close that such effort has not been really necessary.

This may no longer be a satisfactory assumption. Just as there has been a tendency to believe that a 'special relationship' with the United States was a substitute for the real content of foreign policy, the emotional overhang in relations between Britain and Australia has led to a tendency to be disappointed when real policy issues obtrude, as if their practicality is unseemly. On the contrary, for a healthy relationship it is necessary at this time for both London and Canberra to pay attention to the real substance that already exists, as well as to any potential that can be exploited in the future. In some respects, Britain and Australia may be heading in different directions, but this can be turned to advantage for both by using the opportunity to extend the habits of a comfortable old relationship into new and practical forms of partnership.

It is a fact that there is a consciousness of Australia in Britain that is not found anywhere else in the world, except perhaps in New Zealand. Australian television programs are widely shown, news of Australian sport is popular, advertising of Australian products is common, Australian personalities are well known. Similarly, Britain's profile in Australia remains high. Political, social (especially royal) and economic news about Britain is widely used in the Australian media. If there has been a decline in British influence in Australia since its post-war peak in the 1950s, when the first visit of a reigning monarch was made and the British High Commissioner was sometimes mistaken for the Australian Governor-General who also was British, the intangible assets remain substantial enough to ensure that what happens in Britain, and what Britain does, will be given more prominence and more detailed discussion in Australia than, say, what happens in France or Germany or what the governments of those countries decide. These are assets which can be deployed in both our interests. They are assets of an intense historical experience, coupled with continuing financial links, investment, trade opportunities, and immigration as well as longstanding political and military intelligence connections.

Trade with the United Kingdom—despite its focus on Europe and ours on Asia—was worth nearly $5.3 billion in 1990, making it our third largest country source of imports and sixth largest market for exports (compared with Germany, fourth for imports and eleventh for exports; Italy, seventh for imports and fourteenth for exports; and France, eleventh for imports and seventeenth for exports). While our bilateral trading pattern is old-fashioned—commodity-based on our part, and two-to-one in Britain's favour—on multilateral trade issues we more often than not take similar positions (even on agricultural reform in the Uruguay Round, where Britain has been much less difficult than, say, France or Germany).

The United Kingdom is the largest foreign investor in Australia (with the United States second and Japan third), its stock of $44.5 billion in 1989/90 representing nearly 60 per cent of all West European investment in Australia. Britain is second only to the United States as the destination for Australian investment overseas. The extent of mutual investment reflects partly historical legacy and partly familiarity with political, legal and economic systems, a common language and close links between the two banking systems. But, for the future, it also represents a significant resource linking each with the other's region.

Both political and military co-operation between Australia and Britain—which links both of us and the United States—was particularly close during the Gulf crisis. 'Anglo-Saxon' camaraderie may be declining but there are nevertheless real national security interests which from time to time are mutually strongly supportive and which include, for both the United Kingdom and Australia, a ready acceptance of the continuing leadership role of the United States. Our security links with Britain include long established intelligence-sharing arrangements and common membership of the Five Power Defence Arrangements (FPDA).

Differences with the United Kingdom Government are usually highly specific and do not unbalance the relationship—the tussles over responsibility for cleaning up the Maralinga nuclear test site, and the provision of British welfare services for British residents in Australia are examples. Problems in the relationship are mainly created by false hopes that we can both continue to live in the past. While governments in both London and Canberra have long relinquished such illusions, the close family and other links between the two populations sometimes nourish them.

Australian nationalism has been spiced with anti-British and pro-Irish sentiment, but as Britain is irresistibly drawn into the European context, Australian nationalists will no doubt discover useful qualities in the British connection. This has been the experience of the United States, where the links with Britain have remained especially strong despite such contrary pressures as France's support for America's original revolt against British rule, the cultural appeal of Italy to America, and the central role of Germany in Europe. In Australia's case, the sentimental attachment to Britain will probably continue to be rather stronger than it is in the United States because we have retained, not rejected, many British institutional models still in good working order—especially in our parliamentary system, education and the law. Nor, presumably, should we overlook that mystical influence on national character, cricket.

THE EUROPEAN COMMUNITY AND WEST EUROPE

The European Community is the world's largest trading community, and the EC Single Market will—with some 340 million people —overtake the United States and Japan as the developed world's largest consumer market. Four of the Group of Seven (G7) leading market economies are found in Europe—Germany, France, Italy and the United Kingdom—and Germany is the world's largest exporter. What happens inside the European economy is going to have implications for the trade prospects of most countries, and Australia is no exception. The EC as a whole is our second biggest export market after Japan, and our largest source of imports. It has provided (mainly through the British) more than twice the amount of investment in Australia as has Japan, and is a third as big again an investor as the United States.

The changes currently taking place in Europe pose several questions relevant to Australia's interests. What impact will the creation of a single EC market by the end of 1992 have for Australian exports of goods and services to the EC? Is Europe entering a period of internal preoccupation to the detriment of its capacity to liberalise trade practices and to make a constructive contribution to the crucial Uruguay Round of multilateral trade negotiations? Will the economic problems of East Europe mean that the EC will have less aid and investment for the Asia Pacific? These are just some of the questions which require attention if Australia is to protect and promote its interests in an increasingly fluid European environment.

Clearly the EC is entering a dynamic phase. The Single Market involves the deepening and sharpening of existing commitments, which have been accumulating over many years. Exactly on what terms and in what time-frame the core countries of Single Market Europe will have co-operative economic arrangements with other European countries remains unclear. So too is the time-frame within which other countries who have made overtures to join the EC—including most of the EFTA Group, Malta, Cyprus and Turkey—will in fact be embraced by it. But it is already obvious that the creation of the Single Market means that a 'European' way of doing business—whether it is handling imports, assessing standards, managing investment flows, organising banking, or co-ordinating transport and tele-communications systems—is being established, from which others will stand aside at their economic peril.

Integration of the various already powerful European economies in itself holds no danger for Australian interests, although each dimension of this process will inevitably present particular challenges in specific sectors for Australian business. Indeed, integration offers several advantages. It both simplifies and liberalises opportunities for Australian business. It is likely to result in a more competitive and dynamic European economy with greater economies of scale, a wider choice of base for investment, and a bigger pool of skilled labour. Already some Australian banks and insurance companies have taken advantage of the liberalisation of EC financial markets, and Australian transport companies, including Brambles and TNT, have established extensive EC-wide transport networks and secured significant market share. But if a wider range of Australian businesses are going to meet the standards of intensified competition and business acumen that success in the Single Market will demand, they will need to approach the task with rather greater purpose, imagination and cohesion than has been common in the past. With this in mind, the Australian Government established the Business Advisory Group on Europe (BADGE), a higher level consultative group comprising some of the country's most senior and experienced businessmen, with wide terms of reference covering both West and East Europe and ranging from identifying impediments to better Australian business performance to examining critically the links between Commonwealth and State government efforts to promote trade and investment.

As the work on the nearly three hundred separate measures needed to constitute the European Single Market nears completion, earlier fears by Australia and others that the exercise would prove to be trade-diverting rather than trade-creating (with restrictions achieved through such measures as standards definitions, anti-dumping regimes and lowest common denominator quantitative restrictions) have proved largely unrealised. But while there is little evidence to date to support the 'fortress Europe' spectre, continuing Australian suspicions are understandable given our experience in the past with EC policies in the agricultural and mineral sectors, where the ramparts have long been in place—with the drawbridge up, the portcullis down and all the bolts shot home for good measure. The architects of the Single Market are the same people who gave the world the highly protectionist Common Agricultural Policy. And they are the same people whose intransigence until now—mid-1991—in the Uruguay Round threatens to jeopardize the very international trading circumstances most conducive to the well-being of both the new Europe, and the trading partners on whom it will depend.

Within the EC, Germany is Australia's second largest trading partner after the United Kingdom. In 1990, our exports were $1.2 billion (primarily wool and minerals, some motor vehicle engines, hospital-medical equipment and computer software) and our imports $3.3 billion (motor vehicles, heavy engineering plant and power generation equipment). Germany has the fourth largest stock of foreign investment in Australia ($7.5 billion in 1989). As the world's largest trader, it has an open, highly industrialised economy; the outlook is for continued growth, but at a slower rate, as the weak east German economy is digested. Australia is not expecting major improvements in our exports to Germany, which supports the EC's Common Agricultural Policy and has massively subsidised its coal industry. There could be opportunities in east Germany, with the rapid dismantling of state ownership, but the situation there is clouded by lack of information, social unrest and disputes over property ownership, and it may be assumed that any plums on offer will fall first into the laps of their new fellow countrymen.

Germany is the motor of European integration and Franco–German co-operation its driver. Especially since unification, Germany has made considerable efforts to develop its relationship with the Soviet Union and East Europe generally. Its political and strategic influence in the region, and to some extent the wider world, is becoming ever greater and, even though some national uncertainties about the country's non-economic role were on full display during the Gulf crisis, it can be expected to play an extremely important role in determining the future political and strategic structure of both West and East Europe. Australia's dialogue relations with Germany are sound in both economic and political areas—but given the country's present understandable preoccupation with its own part of the world, there will be a continuing need for us to work all available levers to register and defend our own interests.

Australia's relations with France have been more intense, although a little less economically substantial. Our two-way trade was over $1.9 billion in 1990, making France our twelfth largest trading partner (with exports of $784 million, mainly wool and coal; and imports of nearly $1.2 billion, mainly medicinal, pharmaceutical, electrical plant and beverages). Investment between the countries is lower than it should be, but exchanges of investment missions are currently being actively pursued. Political relations, by contrast, have long been lively. We have co-operated very closely in recent years on important issues as diverse as Cambodia and Antarctica, while remaining at odds over France's nuclear testing in the South Pacific and its unashamed support for subsidies on farm exports. Co-operation on Pacific matters generally—and over New Caledonia in particular—has improved dramatically since the signing of the Matignon Accords by the Rocard Government in 1988. For Australia, France remains a distinctive nation, whatever the progress towards European integration. Although by no means consistently easy to deal with, as the rest of the world has long been aware, it is a country of great flair and style, with whom we seem able from time to time to form unexpected alliances, as over Antarctica. France is a country with wide-ranging interests and capabilities, prepared to act, and one with which the pursuit of Australian 'niche diplomacy' is always an option.

Australia's relationship with Italy has a solid human and historical basis—not least in the well over 600 000 Australians of Italian birth or ancestry—but it has taken on special importance over recent years because of Italy's role as a major member of the EC, its membership of the G7, its direct economic importance to us and its booming economy. Italy is Australia's tenth largest trading partner, with two-way trade worth $2.5 billion in 1999, slightly in Italy's favour. The bilateral trade relationship has traditionally been unsophisticated—raw material (chiefly wool, raw hides and coal) from Australia, for manufactures (particularly machinery, data processing and telecommunications equipment, textiles, clothing and furniture) from Italy—but the proportion of manufactures in Australian exports has recently risen. These have included semi-processed leather and a range of specialised high-technology products, and there is scope for further work in processing (especially in scouring wool). Two-way investment is, as with France, lower than it should and could be, but Italian business interest in Australia and in the general Asia Pacific area is increasing.

Despite frequent changes in government, Italy maintains a consistent foreign policy, pro-Atlanticist yet firmly 'Europeanist' in its attitude to the EC and European union. It's economic interests, including the need for oil, have kept it active in the Middle East, where it is on good terms with all parties, and it also has historical ties which have kept it engaged in the Horn of Africa. With Spain, Italy launched an initiative in 1990 for a 'Conference on Security and Co-operation in the Mediterranean' ('CSCM'), modelled on the CSCE, bringing together Middle East and Mediterranean countries. Italy is also the instigator of the *Pentagonale*, again launched in 1990, designed to strengthen its economic, cultural and political ties with Austria, Yugoslavia, Hungary and Czechoslovakia, and which has already begun projects for joint monitoring of toxic wastes, new rail and road links and shared energy resources. Although much tends to depend on changes of ministerial personality—not all foreign ministers are quite like Gianni de Michelis, who along with his considerable intellectual accomplishments acknowledges authorship of a guide to Italy's one-hundred best discotheques—Italy has been in recent times a lively and helpful political dialogue partner for Australia, on both bilateral and multilateral issues.

Although Australia's most substantial relations in West Europe are undoubtedly with Britain, Germany, France and Italy, that by no means exhausts the list of significant bilateral relations. We have, for example, strong and growing trade links and an excellent political dialogue relationship, on both bilateral and a wide range of multilateral issues, with the major Nordics—Sweden, Denmark and Norway. The instinctive 'like-mindedness' has been particularly evident in the context of such Australian policy interests as Antarctic environmental protection, chemical and biological weapons control, Indo-China and South Africa. Much the same can be said of our relations with the Benelux Group—Belgium, the Netherlands (now our sixteenth largest trading partner) and Luxembourg. Our relations with Spain and Portugal have been slower to develop (with the East Timor issue continuing to be an irritant in the case of the latter), but both are significant dialogue partners in an EC context and there is increasing attention being devoted in Australia, as indeed world-wide, to Spain's enormous economic potential as it continues to rapidly modernise. With a number of other countries—especially Greece, Cyprus, Malta and Ireland —there is a strong human dimension to the bilateral relationship based on very high rates of migration to Australia. The same is true for Turkey— hardly a West European country by geography or culture, despite its NATO membership, but not quite anything else—and certainly a keen aspirant for EC membership. There is an additional emotional link between Australia and Turkey born of our common nation-forging experience at Gallipoli— as was movingly demonstrated at the seventy-fifth anniversary commemoration in 1990—but so far, despite some high expectations, the relationship has not lived up to its economic potential.

While there is no basis for any return to the Euro-centric days of Australian foreign policy, Europe continues to be important to Australia, as it does to the rest of the world, from both a strategic and economic perspective. It is not just intellectual curiosity and sentiment which invite our interest in what is happening there. We bring to the diplomatic task of maintaining and developing our relationship with Europe several assets: historical and cultural links, a close military relationship with the United States and the United Kingdom, close links with other NATO countries, a high profile in multilateral diplomacy generally, and an increasing engagement in Asia Pacific affairs which makes us an important interlocutor in the eyes of many Europeans. But we will have to continue to adapt our diplomacy to the changing face of Europe. In particular, we will need increasingly to think of Europe as a single political and economic entity, and this will call over time for some rationalising and reshaping of our presently very widely scattered diplomatic resources.

THE SOVIET UNION

Mikhail Gorbachev came to power as General Secretary of the Communist Party of the Soviet Union in March 1985 with what seemed in retrospect to have been a significant, but still modest, reform agenda. He knew that the almost total domination of the Soviet budget by the military under Brezhnev could not continue. The failed intervention in Afghanistan —the Soviet Union's Vietnam—had cast doubt on the value of its force projection in the Third World. No political breakthroughs had been won by massive continuing military deployments against West Europe. Soviet research and development was in any event falling behind the advanced-technology weapons being produced in the West (as was later dramatically confirmed in action in the Gulf War). Above all, the Soviet economy itself was in rapid decline, not least because of huge military spending and the unproductive influence of the military bureaucracy. So there had to be some restructuring of institutional priorities at home—with some more open discussion and debate to help that process along—and some serious attempts made abroad to systematically reduce tensions, and resolve the outstanding problems, so as to enable pressing domestic problems to be attended to without major distraction or diversion of resources.

The first steps down these various paths were sure-footed, refreshing and won applause both at home and abroad. But six years later the Soviet economy was in deep crisis, Soviet political life was in turmoil, the national territory of the Union was in dispute, and every fundamental of the Soviet system was either dead or subject to head-on challenge. Gorbachev himself still survived, elected President in 1990 by a Congress of People's Deputies itself elected for the first time in seventy years—and was still dazzling the crowds (if not the economists) abroad. But at home in the Soviet Union, if he had not exhausted his store of political virtuosity, or luck, or both, he certainly seemed by mid-1991 to have completely exhausted his popular support. How much longer he would be able to weave a zig-zag course between reliance on progressives and traditionalists was a matter of open conjecture. It all seemed ample confirmation of de Tocqueville's observation that 'the most dangerous time for a bad government is when it starts to reform itself'.[9]

Gorbachev's difficulties really all stemmed from the reality that his task in the mid-1980s, whether realised at the time or not, was not simply to trim sail on a different tack, but to deal with a storm brewing about the fundamental issues of the Soviet Union's status as a superpower, its security and the relationship between the army, the party and the state. It may be that the logical contradictions of the Soviet system were such that these issues could not be addressed short of a complete dismantling of the whole system. But before Gorbachev could address them, he was faced with developments in East Europe that took not only the Soviet Union, but the world, by surprise, bringing about the collapse of political establishments taken for granted since the 'Prague Spring' had been blown away in 1968. Gorbachev had announced in 1988 the withdrawal of some Soviet forces from East Europe, but in the latter half of 1989 the internal revolutions against communist regimes, especially in East Germany, undermined overnight the costly military structure that Moscow had been building as a buffer between its borders and West Europe since the end of World War II. Gorbachev made the crucial—and in Soviet terms very courageous—decision not to intervene in support of the old guard. The Brezhnev Doctrine—whereby the Soviet Union reserved the right to use force to control its East European satellites—was dead, and the Soviet military leadership to that extent humiliated.

In such a cauldron of nationalist politics, ideology and bureaucratic survival, Gorbachev's rational instruments of reform—*glasnost*, or openness, and *perestroika*, or restructuring—became lightning rods of discontent. Glasnost left no taboo untouched: not only Stalin, but Lenin and Gorbachev himself, have been subject to often vitriolic criticism; previously banned literary works have been published; dissent on a variety of issues broke out in street demonstrations and strikes; imprisonment for political reasons was drastically curtailed; tens of thousands of Soviet citizens were allowed to emigrate; the Communist Party's authority moved into terminal decline; and the genies of long-repressed nationalist sentiment, and centuries-old ethnic rivalries, sprang from their bottles.

The two huge problems confronting the Soviet Union in mid-1991 were the state of the economy and its survival as a political entity. They were closely interconnected: without political stability—the emergence of workable new political institutions, both at and between central and republican levels—effective economic reform could not proceed; but without economic reform political stability simply could not be maintained.

President Gorbachev's economic endeavours to date have been aimed at weakening the overwhelming powers of the centralised planning structure by decentralising responsibility and incentives for economic decision-making, and by attracting foreign commercial participation through joint ventures and favourable investment climate, including the establishment of special economic zones and foreign-owned subsidiaries. In practical terms, however, the reforms have remained a chimera, partly because of resistance by a bureaucracy mindful of losing its power; partly through inherent contradictions in the limited reforms introduced so far (e.g. punitive taxes on private co-operatives); and partly because the key elements of the change—price reforms, the associated abolition of state subsidies, and freeing up of the wholesale trade—have been postponed or at best half-heartedly implemented. Despite the absolute clarity with which the prescription has been spelt out for him, not least in the West, Gorbachev does not seem to have appreciated that, when it comes to embracing market economics, there are stark choices to be made. He failed to understand that he could not go on being both Luther and the Pope.

Many of the measures implemented to date have been actually dislocating the Soviet economy, in that old structures have been destroyed or undermined but not replaced by new and better models. A tug-of-war has continued between central, republican and local authorities over economic decision-making—taxation, banking, monetary policy and the like. The supply of food and other key consumer goods has diminished rapidly while wage increases, stimulated by the devolution of authority to enterprises, outstripped labour productivity and fuelled inflation. Overall output in 1990 fell by about 5 per cent, and the economic slide was approaching catastrophic proportions in mid-1991. Production in the first quarter had fallen some 12 per cent from the same period a year earlier, and observers were predicting an overall decline in 1991 of anywhere between 10 and 30 per cent.[10]

Political reform brought hope to Soviet nationalities, spilling over into civil disorder in the Baltic States, the Transcaucasus and Central Asia. The Union of Soviet Socialist Republics is made up of fifteen separate republics; all of them in varying degrees asserted their sovereignty. The most clear-cut dispute was between Moscow and the Baltic States—Estonia, Latvia and Lithuania—whose declarations of independence in 1990 were declared invalid. Pressure on the Baltic States was applied by the intimidation of Soviet Army and Interior Ministry troops, culminating in the killing of some eighteen Lithuanians and Latvians when troops stormed buildings in Vilnius and Riga in January 1991. Soviet troop actions since then have included interference in peaceful demonstrations; searches for unwilling Baltic conscripts; actions against Baltic customs checkpoints and, in June 1991, the encirclement of the Lithuanian Parliament building. Whether such activity was approved by Moscow—and in which case by whom—or ordered by local commanders, has been unclear. Australia has joined the strong international condemnation of these actions, repeating our refusal to accept in international law the incorporation of the Baltic States in 1940, and our willingness to recognise their statehood as soon as the formal criteria—in particular the effective control of their own territory—are satisfied.

However, the political heavyweight was the Russian Soviet Federative Socialist Republic (RSFSR, or Russia). Russia stretches from Leningrad on the Baltic Sea to Vladivostok on the Pacific coast, and is by far the largest of the Soviet republics, with around half the Soviet Union's population (147 million of a total of 287 million) and economic production, and three-quarters of its territory. In the Russian elections of March 1990, featuring multi-party candidates for the first time, the reformist Democratic Russia grouping won a significant number of seats to the new Supreme Soviet. Boris Yeltsin, the former head of the Moscow City Communist Party organisation, was elected Chairman of the Supreme Soviet, and a republican government was formed largely from reformist and non-communist groupings. Yeltsin was subsequently then elected first President of the RSFSR, gaining some 64 per cent of votes cast in a field of six candidates—the first time in Russia's history that its highest state post had been filled by direct popular election. The central contemporary dynamic in Soviet politics is the tempestuous personal relationship between Yeltsin and Gorbachev. If the rapprochement binding them in mid-1991 has any durability then there is some prospect of both a reformist momentum being maintained in the central government structure and some reasonable resolution being achieved on the Union Treaty issue. But there is little prospect otherwise.

Russia is among the nine (out of fifteen) Soviet republics which have indicated, with varying degrees of consistency and enthusiasm, their intention to sign a new Union Treaty. The others are Azerbaijan, Byelorussia, Kazakhstan, Kirghizia, Tadzhikistan, Turkmenistan, the Ukraine and Uzbekistan; those who have refused are the Baltic Republics, Georgia, Moldavia and Armenia. The so-called 'Nine-plus-One' agreement concluded with President Gorbachev in April 1991 called for a radical enhancement of the role of the republics in policy formulation, joint crisis measures for the economy, and drafting of a new constitution. That agreement, by setting out at least a broad framework for co-operation between Gorbachev and Yeltsin, has given impetus to the reform process in the Soviet Union, and remains the best hope that at least the whole country will not fragment. Whether President Gorbachev is able, however, to realise his stated ambition of achieving a 'strong centre and strong republics' remains to be seen. With the crucial criterion of political allegiance now tending to be one's attitude to the division of power, this may be another case of Luther and the Pope.

In all the domestic tumult that has been raging, the most encouraging element from an international perspective is the way in which the 'new thinking' in Soviet foreign policy has stayed resolutely on track. Fears of a traditionalist backlash—particularly from a military leadership humiliated by the forced withdrawal from East Europe, or anxious for its future employment—while realistic, remain unfulfilled. The most significant departures from the doctrine prevailing in the pre-Gorbachev era are rejection of the concept of irreconcilable competition between capitalism and communism; disavowal of the necessity for revolution in the Third World; stress on interdependence in the contemporary world; and acceptance that security can be achieved by political means and 'reasonable defence sufficiency' rather than being dependent on military superiority. The fruits of this new attitude have been seen particularly in the new era of co-operative relations in the Security Council, not least during the Gulf crisis; in the attempted resolution of the Israel–Palestinian–Arab problem; and in arms control and disarmament negotiations. In our own Asia Pacific region the signals have been somewhat more mixed—with only a marginally more conciliatory line being evident on such issues as the four-islands dispute with Japan, and the United States naval presence in the region, but equally there has been a strongly positive approach apparent on such matters as Cambodia and the Korean Peninsula. While it is reasonable to assume that, other things being equal, a generally responsible and co-operative approach will emerge—along with a somewhat diminished physical presence—it is too early to make any concluded judgment to that effect.

Australia's bilateral relations with the Soviet Union in the light of all these recent developments have recently been the subject of extensive report—to which the Government has fully responded—by the Senate Standing Committee on Foreign Affairs, Defence and Trade.[11] Among the agreed implications for Australian action, so far as political relations are concerned, are that we should continue to encourage reform within the limits of our capacity to do so, including through technical assistance; make clear that any recourse to violence, as has occurred with the Baltic republics, cannot help but affect Australian co-operation, and that of the West generally; encourage a peaceful and democratic resolution of the problems of centre–republic relations; and continue to strengthen the web of dialogue, exchanges and formal arrangements, paying special attention to fostering ties with the Soviet republics.

There is a strong basis on which to build in all these respects. The year 1992 marks the fiftieth anniversary of the establishment of diplomatic relations between Australia and the Soviet Union. During the period to 1983, the quality of the relationship essentially reflected the ups and downs in East–West relations, ranging from undisguised adversarial attitudes to a constrained thaw during détente in the mid-1970s, with serious disruptions in the aftermath of the Petrov affair and the Soviet invasion of Afghanistan. In May 1983 the Australian Government announced its decision to pursue relations with the Soviet Union on a more pragmatic basis, including a clear national priority for resuming commercial links. Those relations have since been fully normalised and given a broad-based substance. A dialogue on international issues has been established, allowing Australia to explore Soviet thinking and register its own views at a high level. Ministerial visits in both directions have taken place at regular intervals. In particular, those by Prime Minister Hawke to the Soviet Union in 1987 and by Premier Ryzhkov to Australia in 1990—in which the path-breaking Human Contacts Agreement was, respectively, initiated and signed—significantly broadened the framework of the bilateral relationship.

So far as bilateral economic relations are concerned, there is again a solid base of formal arrangements in place, with an Australia–USSR Mixed Commission meeting biennially to review trade performance and to promote new opportunities; with new agreements recently signed on co-operation in agriculture, fisheries, trade in commodities, medical services and space research, and with a major effort being made—including a large Australian Trade Exhibition in Vladivostok in 1990—to generate commercial opportunities in the resource-rich Soviet Far East.

But while the Soviet Union has long been an important and stable trading partner for Australia, the recent upheavals have put that status at significant risk, as has indeed been the case with everyone else. Australian exports, for example, fell from just under $1 billion in 1989 to $421 million in 1990, largely reflecting the hard currency crunch the Soviet Union was facing. Government efforts have been aimed at protecting, so far as possible, existing levels of trade: the decision in November 1990 to extend credit facilities of $525 million was designed to encourage a resumption of wool buying and other commodity trade, including in wheat and manganese. Imports from the Soviet Union, based on refined petroleum, tractors and goods vehicles, have always been low: growth has been inhibited by design, quality and supply problems endemic to the Soviet economy. Obviously the opportunities for expanding and diversifying Australian trade with the Soviet Union will depend primarily on the scope and pace, and ultimate success, of Soviet economic reform, and on the political cohesion the country maintains. But we should not be neglecting, in the meantime, opportunities that present themselves with some of the more reform-minded and efficient republics—e.g. the second largest, Kazakhstan, which is entrepreneurially minded, outward-looking, resource-rich and in population terms about Australia's size.

THE NEW EAST EUROPE

It is difficult to overstate the sense of sheer exhilaration that coursed through East Europe in 1989. It was a year that saw the Solidarity movement, having campaigned relentlessly and courageously for nearly a decade, claw its way at last into government in Poland. It saw Vaclav Havel, the dissident playwright outcast, rise as President of Czechoslovakia to declare that government had at last been returned to the people. It was the year that the Hungarian Communist Party turned itself inside out, disavowed the 'crimes and mistakes' of the past, committed itself to a mixed economy, and contritely submitted its management to the scrutiny of the IMF. (The then Foreign Minister Gyula Horn, fresh from one such encounter, told Gareth Evans in Budapest that his remaining wish in life was 'to chair a crisis management conference at which the IMF itself was the supplicant'!) It was a year that saw a demonstration in Bucharest, arranged to show support for Ceausescu, spontaneously turning against the Romanian tyrant. And it was the year that saw the most graphic and exuberant image of all—the breaking down of the Berlin Wall.

By mid-1991 the atmosphere was rather more subdued. The road back to economic prosperity was clearly going to be longer and rockier than many had anticipated. But while there are similarities in the problems facing other countries of East Europe with those of the Soviet Union—in that governments in each case have to face up to the consequences of fouled economic systems, and manage the transition from badly planned economies to market economies—there are also important differences, and not just in scale. The crucial difference is that most of the East European countries have had no doubts or hesitations about throwing overboard their ideological baggage. The communist model was thrust upon them by the Soviet Union, not least as a means of maintaining control over the western flank of the Soviet imperium. East Europeans were Hungarians, Czechs or Poles first, and communists only an unavoidable second. When given the opportunity to avoid the latter, they quickly made it clear that Soviet-style communism held little attraction for them. Nationalism was a very strong force at work in the defeat of the old communist order in East Europe, but so too was in many places a memory and preference for a free-market economic system. When public opinion was released, so too were both these currents.

The pace and manner in which the countries of East Europe manage the transition from communism to democracy and a market economy will vary according to national circumstances. But in no case can the political and economic aspects of transition be viewed in isolation: the future of democracy is at least partly linked to the capacity of these countries to deliver the economic goods. The simple urge towards democracy and away from command economies becomes less simple when, in each country, precise choices have to be made based on history, culture and economic circumstances. In a number of countries of the region, the habits of dictatorship have a rather more substantial history than the habits of democracy. Poland, Czechoslovakia and Hungary were the most likely of the East Europeans to adopt both democracy and a market economy, but even among these three leaders there were substantial differences, with Poland having to struggle the hardest to hold together popular support. As Polish Prime Minister Bielecki put it in April 1991:

> And don't forget the fragility of the democratic spirit in the newly freed countries of Central and Eastern Europe. Huge rallies were organised this year in Germany

by the born-again communist party. People raised in the dullness of communism are afraid of the future. The market brings risk and risk brings fear.[12]

In geo-political terms, Europe's disintegration and transformation has from the beginning offered three possibilities. A new bipolar structure could emerge if the East Europeans were absorbed into a West Europe which retained its ties with the United States, leaving an isolated Soviet Union. Secondly, the fragmentation of East Europe and the Soviet Union, alongside a united Germany, could bring about one of those historic revivals which analysts of the 'German question' and the 'Russian enigma' have been fond of predicting—a contest between a weakened Soviet Union (essentially Russia) and a strong Germany for control of East Europe. Some congenital pessimists suggest that in this respect the future stability of Europe depends on Germany remaining central to NATO—and being contained by it. Others, not least within the Soviet Union itself, are watching anxiously the course of events in Yugoslavia, with concern that a successful assertion of independent statehood by its constituent republics—or minority nationalities within them—might create major new pressures for fragmentation elsewhere. The third possibility is for a pan-European system of economic co-operation and security to develop, with both the United States and the Soviet Union actively participating. This is the CSCE model, which in many ways is the most attractive, but which has to surmount a number of practical problems if it is to be more than merely a dialogue forum—not to mention the attitude of those who think that neither the United States nor the Soviet Union should dilute the 'real' Europe.

The changes in East Europe, and some at least of their pan-European consequences, have implications for Australian interests. There are some potentially negative consequences. A Europe pre-occupied with pan-European issues may conceivably be less constructive—although that is difficult to imagine—on multilateral trade reform. There may be less funds available for investment in our part of the world—although that again seems unlikely, given the disposition of potential investors to be guided by return rather than sentiment. But it is the case that the needs of the East European countries for development assistance funds could reduce the amount of aid funds that the EC countries and the international financial institutions are able or prepared to give to developing nations, including those in the Asia Pacific, with consequent implications for Australia's own stretched aid budget.

The positive implications are more obvious. On the face of it, potentially significant commercial opportunities have been opened up for Australian companies to engage in projects of benefit to both sides, at a time when East Europe is looking westwards for trade and investment, technology and training. Australian companies should be looking closely at what the East European market has to offer in areas like telecommunications, transport, agricultural processing and environment protection, as well as in the more traditional areas of agriculture, raw materials and manufactures. This is not, however, at this stage a market for the inexperienced or impatient.

The dislocation in East Europe means that it will inevitably take time for trade efforts fully to bear fruit. In the short term, moreover, these fruits are most likely to fall the way only of reasonably large companies, given the limited managerial, analytic and risk assessment skills on the ground in East Europe. For Australian companies to be effective in this area of transition, they will probably need to take these skills and resources with them from the start. Australia is not, however, without some advantages in dealing with this new situation. We have hundreds of thousands of Australians who have roots in these countries—some 140 000 Poles, 50 000 Hungarians and 25 000 Czechs and Slovaks for a start, not to mention over 250 000 from the various Yugoslav republics—a great many of whom have retained their language skills and contacts with the 'old country'.[13]

The Australian Government has done its best to position us to take advantage of such opportunities as do flow from a revitalised East Europe. Already represented in Moscow, Belgrade, Warsaw and Budapest, we opened an embassy in Prague in 1990. Australia is particularly well established, and placed to do business, with Hungary; with Czechoslovakia we have targeted a country close to Australia's size in population terms, with a strong entrepreneurial spirit, a like-minded approach to most international issues, and an apparent instinct for bilateral dialogue and co-operation with us. Other steps taken have included the speedy negotiation—beginning with Hungary and Poland—of bilateral investment protection and double taxation agreements, a contribution to the stabilisation fund for Poland, a grant to the Soviet and East European studies program at the Australian National University, the establishment of a $5 million Australian program of training for Eastern Europe—focusing on the development of business management skills in the countries involved—and, probably most importantly, our membership stake in the new European Bank of Reconstruction and Development (EBRD). The diplomatic returns from all this may be self-evident. But when it comes to economic returns, it is only the business sector which—here as elsewhere—can translate opportunities into deals.

18

The Americas

THE AMERICAN HEMISPHERE stretches from the Arctic to the Antarctic, with a total population of around 700 million. It is not a bloc, but a conglomerate of thirty-five sovereign states, with market economies and, by world standards, high to middle incomes, but in many countries with big gaps still between rich and poor.[1] The United States of America has dominated the hemisphere since the early nineteenth century. The Monroe Doctrine of 1823 gave foreign powers warning that the new nation which had thrown off its British colonial masters did not propose to allow Britain's European rivals to sneak in its back door, through Central and South America. Towards Canada, which remained a British territory until 1867, the young American nation adopted a generally benign attitude, assisted by the fact that during the nineteenth century British sea power had unchallenged command of the approaches to the Americas and the government of the United States relied on British co-operation to enforce its exclusion of the European powers.

The stability of the American hemisphere has enabled the United States to feel relatively assured in its relations with the rest of the world. The contrast with the Soviet Union is dramatic. While the United States has neighbours like Canada and Mexico, who may have shown irritation at times with the giant next door but not animosity, the Soviet Union has had China and Japan on one flank and Europe—bolstered by the United States and Canada—on the other. While the US role in Latin America has had its critics, it has not been so heavy-handed as to require massive military power to sustain it. Attempts by the Germans to exploit tensions between

Latin America and the United States during World Wars I and II came to nothing.

The stability of the hemisphere, and North America's distance from the rest of the world, has also tended to reinforce the isolationist strain in US thinking. That strain was most evident in the country's agonised hesitation about intervening in the two World Wars this century, but had its roots in the creation of the republic itself. In President Washington's famous encapsulation:

> Europe has a set of primary interests, which to us have none, or a very remote relation. Hence she must be engaged in frequent controversies, the causes of which are essentially foreign to our concerns.[2]

The advent of nuclear weapons and the Cold War seemed to bring to an end once and for all any lingering American notion that it could be detached from Europe, or indeed from anywhere else in the world. But the reverse in Vietnam led to a mood of at least partial retrenchment, embodied in Richard Nixon's 'Guam Doctrine'—enunciated first in the Pacific in July 1969 and then to Congress in February 1970—which, while ambiguously phrased, emphasised that America's allies and partners must accept primary responsibility for their own defence. And the collapse of the Cold War in 1989, reinforced by the burgeoning economic difficulties of the 1980s, generated a debate once more on the timeless dilemma:

> Some see the Cold War as having been a special, aberrant case in the American experience and maintain that now it is over it is time for America to 'come home' and return to an earlier pattern of behaviour based on a much more restricted view of the country's interests and commitments. At the other end of the spectrum it is argued that, having just won a great victory and become the world's only genuine superpower, the United States should exploit its primacy, accept its historic mission and 'wage democracy' throughout the world.[3]

The Gulf crisis of 1990–91, and the world's reliance once more on the diplomatic and military leadership of the United States to right an alarming wrong—albeit carefully exercised through the processes of the United Nations—stilled that debate for the time being. But no doubt it will be only a matter of time before the old familiar question—about whether it really is the United States's business to be looking after anyone else's interests but its own—is asked again, as it has been now for two centuries.

THE UNITED STATES

Contemporary Australians are so familiar with the United States as a global power—seemingly involved in everything, with its political culture, media and entertainment so pervasive—that it is useful, in the context of exploring our bilateral relationship with it, to see the country in its geographical and historical setting. Impressive though its achievements and authority are, the United States is not so much an all-powerful force as a nation like any other, with interests like any other, and domestic pressures upon it to act (or react, or not to act) like any other. This perspective is not, of course, the only basis on which Australia does, or should, approach its relationship with the United States. We are very conscious of the role for good the United States has played as a global superpower, and the great importance, both globally and regionally, of maintaining our alliance relationship with it. But that relationship will be much the healthier if we do not approach it overwhelmed by awe and reverence. Although of particular importance, the Australia–United States relationship is not something different in essence from other international relationships, etherealised in some way above the atmosphere of ordinary life. It has to be assessed like any other relationship. It has to be managed. And, from time to time, it will be tested.

It has been both a strength and a weakness of Australian attitudes to the United States that we see ourselves as so similar: both democracies; both beneficiaries of the English language; both inheritors of the rule of law, a free press and a strong private sector; both a part of what used to be called the New World. Yet just as George Bernard Shaw described Britain and the United States as separated by the same language, the broad similarities between Australians and Americans mask striking institutional and cultural differences. The strong role of government in Australia followed necessarily from our beginnings as a penal settlement. In America the early settlers were disparate, self-reliant communities more likely to be governed, if at all, by commercial enterprise or religious conviction. While we still have an hereditary British monarch as our head of state, the Americans broke with their British colonial masters in a revolutionary war. We evolved slowly as a nation state; some might say too slowly, through self-government, dominion status and finally independence.

The major difference, however, is simply that the United States is an established society which for most of this century has been the world's greatest power, whereas Australia is, by comparison, a middle-ranking nation with an evolving sense of its place in the world. We are a nation for which the American model of the way to wealth and power may not so readily apply. The important question is not why or how these differences exist but how can they be successfully managed. Each country needs to make the effort to understand the other and not just assume that we are natural allies. The nature of the effort required of each side differs in important ways. For Australians, it means at the very least penetrating the global avalanche of simplistic popular images of American culture to come to grips with the real flesh and blood—the human complexities and competitive pressures which make the American polity such a vigorous and fertile one. For Americans, nurtured on a profound belief in the intrinsic and unique virtues of American society and in America's democracy—a belief for which history has in this century given them plenty of reinforcement—it calls for an often difficult leap of imagination to understand, simply, what it is to be a non-American, and to accept wholeheartedly the legitimacy of non-American interests and the value of friends who are true to themselves.

The alliance has experienced the highs and lows of diplomacy. Perhaps the lowest was, instructively, the misconstrued effect of a high—the late Harold Holt's well-intentioned yet exultant cry in 1966, 'All the way with LBJ', which suggested to Australians grappling with the trauma of the military commitment in Vietnam that the Australian Prime Minister had lost sight of *their* way. Highs in alliance diplomacy, as distinct from war-time camaraderie, have included the creation of sensible understandings with the United States during the period of Indonesia's *'Konfrontasi'* with Malaysia, when major regional conflict seemed imminent, and, more recently, Australia's role in maintaining links with both New Zealand and the United States since the former's policy barring visits by nuclear-capable ships led to the suspension of the US–NZ leg of ANZUS in 1986. In each case Australia was clear sighted about its interests and subtle in pursuit of them.

The experience of both sides of Australian politics in managing the alliance, after the politicising of ANZUS during the 1950s and 1960s, has brought in recent times a maturing of our relations with the United States. We have made clear for some time now that we no longer seek, with the United States or with any other country, what is often called in the rhetoric of international relations a 'special relationship'. Special relationships suggest free rides, and free rides, like free lunches, do not exist. Special relationships have a cost, tending to involve as they do an unhealthy dependence of one partner on another. Special relationships can be an excuse for not having a foreign policy, an invitation to laziness and—at the worst—to lack of integrity in foreign policy, with hard-headed assessments of national interest giving way to indolent fellow-travelling. Far more important than a 'special' relationship is a relationship embodying genuinely mutual interests, one with some real breadth and depth and complexity to it, and one which fully recognizes that alliance membership and sovereign independence, whatever the relative size and clout of the alliance partners, are not incompatible statuses.

Australia now has with the United States not just a military alliance, but a relationship of substance, embracing ties of history, commerce and culture, and a profound mutual interest in maintaining a strong American presence globally and within our region. That the alliance does give expression to mutual interests needs to be clearly understood, because that mutuality lies at the heart of its durability. These interests extend across security issues, economic issues and multilateral or global issues, and there is a ledger of benefits in each from which both sides gain.

First, security. For Australia, our alliance does not absolve us of the responsibility of defending ourselves, of pulling our own weight in our own protection, or of seeking to make our own contribution to multilateral efforts to resolve particular regional security concerns—such as we have done with our Cambodia initiative and with our contribution to the resolution of the Gulf crisis. Australia's defence policy of self-reliance enables us to defend ourselves from within our own resources, and also provides us with the capacity to contribute directly to the maintenance of regional security. But it is self-reliance within an alliance framework. That framework is important to our security, not only because of the deterrent value of the ANZUS alliance—in its guarantee that each country will, in the event of armed attack, 'act to meet the common danger'—but because without the exchange of intelligence, and the technology, resupply and training support that it involves, Australia would find it difficult to sustain a basic defence posture quite as self-reliant as we would like it to be.

The United States contribution to Australia's security of course goes beyond bilateral defence co-operation. It also has a global and a regional dimension. While we have not always agreed with every aspect of US policy in the region—not least in relation to Vietnam—its leadership has been, certainly since World War II, a crucial ingredient in the economic growth and relative strategic stability of the Asia Pacific region. It was the source of the political and economic renaissance of Japan and it supported the economic development and stability of other countries in the region as they came to grips with independence, in some cases with spectacular results. The US–Japan and US–South Korea security pacts, the US naval presence, and its land-based facilities in the Philippines and elsewhere have all been vital stabilising factors ensuring that the regional environment has remained relatively benign from an Australian perspective.

On the other side of the security ledger, important United States interests are served by the alliance. Our location makes us a strategically significant ally. We are currently the only formal US ally in the South West Pacific. And we are in the unique position of straddling both the Indian and Pacific oceans, where the United States and, more generally, the Western alliance have vital interests—although former US National Security Adviser Brzezinski was perhaps engaging in a little rhetorical licence when, in a speech in Melbourne in 1988, he described Australia as the 'Oceanic Geo-Strategic Control Centre'! We offer the United States access to our ports in both oceans, important in sustaining its global role. Again, our contributions to regional security through our Defence Co-operation Program in South-East Asia and the South Pacific, our participation in the Five Power Defence Arrangements, and our capability in analysing regional developments, all serve important alliance as well as specifically Australian interests.

In the larger global context, we make a distinctive contribution to the US defence posture, and through that to global stability, by operating with the United States a number of joint facilities in Australia, most importantly those at Pine Gap and Nurrungar.[4] The ground station at Nurrungar is used for controlling satellites in the United States Defense Support Program, which would give the earliest warning of a ballistic missile attack on the United States or its allies. It thus plays a key role in helping to deter a nuclear attack and to prevent a nuclear exchange starting from an accidental launch. The Pine Gap facility collects intelligence data which supports the national security of both Australia and the United States. In particular, it provides data vital to the verification of arms control and disarmament. The value of this compliance verification role has become increasingly evident as disarmament has moved from being an aspiration to an emerging reality with the INF and START Treaties. Without this verification capacity further major arms control agreements could simply not be concluded; and without Australia's contribution, the risk of nuclear war would be directly and significantly increased.

In economic terms, the relationship with the United States is, has long been, and will for the foreseeable future continue to be a very important one for Australia. In the first half of the nineteenth century, before the Panama canal was built and the railroads joined the east and west coasts of the United States, it was easier to ship goods to California from Sydney than from New York. The trading ties of last century have grown into a substantial commercial relationship. The United States is Australia's second largest trading partner, after Japan, supplying over 23.8 per cent of our imports and taking over 11.3 per cent of our exports, with total trade running at $17.6 billion in 1990. The total stock of US investment in Australia is second only to the United Kingdom. And what happens in the US economy of course directly affects the health of the Australian economy, as it does that of a great many other countries around the world.

Obviously the bilateral commercial relationship looms larger for Australia than it does for the United States. But this is not to say that the Australian market is not important to the United States. Australia is its eleventh largest export market. The United States has a two-to-one trade balance in its favour with Australia, something not to be sneezed at, given its overall trade deficit problems. We have consistently been among the top four cash customers for US defence equipment in recent years, spending in the last three years alone over $3.3 billion on defence purchases. Australian investment in the United States is significant by any standards, and it is increasing: at the end of 1988/89, it stood at $32.5 billion.

Beyond immediate security and economic matters, the United States is important to Australia because of the crucial influence it is able to exert across a range of multilateral issues vital to Australia's long-term security and prosperity. Whether it is the Uruguay Round of multilateral trade negotiations, the establishment of the Asia Pacific Economic Co-operation (APEC) process, the effective operation of the United Nations and its specialised agencies, multilateral negotiations on a Chemical Weapons

Convention and a Comprehensive Test Ban Treaty, or a host of other issues in which Australia has a stake, it matters very much to Australia what position the United States takes.

Appeals for support on multilateral issues work both ways. Australia does not carry the same clout in multilateral forums as a superpower, but we are nevertheless a significant player. And on many multilateral issues, the United States is keen to secure Australian support because of our reputation as active, independent and influential. Examples of issues on which the United States has sought Australian support include human rights resolutions, United Nations consideration of the future of Micronesia, the question of Palestinian representation on bodies like the World Health Organisation, international efforts to strengthen the Nuclear Non-Proliferation Treaty, and the negotiations on a Chemical Weapons Convention and other matters in the Conference on Disarmament (in which context Australia hosted, at the request of the US Secretary of State, the path-breaking 1989 Government–Industry Conference Against Chemical Weapons).

The alliance relationship does not, of course, of itself guarantee United States support for Australian objectives in multilateral negotiations. But the alliance does give us access that we would not otherwise enjoy. Without the alliance it would be that much harder for a geographically remote, medium-sized country to secure and keep the attention of a superpower. It has been a constant complaint of other nations that US policy has been driven too much by either East–West perspectives or domestic imperatives. The alliance relationship has given us the opportunity to inject a different perspective; one that might otherwise be lost in the big picture of United States foreign policy.

The important point in all of this is not the precise balance of benefits, but the fact that each side does reap advantage from the alliance across a whole range of subject areas. Simplistic assumptions that the alliance is only about hypothetical security guarantees patently ignore the range of actual Australian interests which the Australia–United States relationship already serves. Those who would argue that Australia should abandon the alliance —or who urge the government to make threats (for example, to close the joint facilities in order to secure better wheat deals) which could lead to the destruction of the alliance—need to explain how and why Australia should bear the considerable cost to Australian national interests thus involved.

It must equally be stressed, however, that the Australia–United States alliance does not mean—and does not demand—obeisance. While the two countries hold similar views on a great many international political and security issues, in recent years we have also had differences of view on many significant issues. They include the Strategic Defense Initiative, sanctions against South Africa, ratification of the Geneva Protocol on the rules of war, aspects of the South Pacific Nuclear Free Zone Treaty, the urgency of a Comprehensive Test Ban Treaty, the repatriation of Indo-Chinese departees, and the banning of mining and oil drilling in the Antarctic.

The most important of the policy differences have been economic: decisions made in Washington on matters such as export subsidies for wheat, restrictions on agricultural imports of sugar and beef, and so-called Voluntary Restraint Arrangements on steel, and difficulties from time to time with uranium, have all caused a good deal of hurt on our side of the Pacific. While Australia, as chair of the Cairns Group, has been making common cause with the United States in the fight against the European Community's export subsidies and other protectionist agricultural policies, Australia's primary producers, among the most efficient in the world, have found themselves squeezed out of markets by the United States's own subsidies under the Export Enhancement Program (EEP). It is little consolation, when caught in the crossfire of a destructive trans-Atlantic subsidies war of this kind, to be told that the European Community and not Australia is the intended target—or even to be given assurances that 'all possible care will be taken to avoid disruption of traditional markets where Australia, as a non-subsidising exporter, has significant interests'.[5] The importance of meeting these kinds of problems head-on—at the very least by full consultation so that any inevitable harm can be minimised, and better explained to domestic publics—was emphasised by Prime Minister Hawke in his speech on 23 June 1988 to a Joint Session of the United States Congress:

> Australians must not be given reason to believe that while we are first class allies, we are, in trade, second class friends. Trade issues must not be allowed to fester, or to erode our wider friendship or alliance.

It is not the case that the measure of independence in an alliance relationship is the number of disagreements. The point is rather that, whether or not we come out in agreement or in disagreement with the United States on any particular issue, we do so on the basis of an independent Australian judgment. A healthy alliance not only accommodates independence of this kind, but demands it. Our alliance is as relevant as it ever was, as the world changes around us. It is ever more multi-dimensional in character; it is frank and robust when it needs to be; and it is totally mutually supportive when it needs to be. In this sense, ours is not only an alliance of democracies, but also a thoroughly democratic alliance.

In the final analysis the strength of the Australia–United States relationship, its durability and its capacity to adapt to changing circumstances, relies on shared interests. But it is also true that a nation's interests, and the direction of its foreign and defence policies in pursuit of those interests, depend significantly on the instincts, outlook and values of its people—what they believe in. Ultimately, it is because Australians and Americans believe in the same things—democracy, freedom and human rights—that our alliance relationship will endure, will adapt and will go on contributing to the building of a safer and fairer world.

CANADA AND THE CARIBBEAN

If Australia and New Zealand are siblings who have chosen different careers, Australian and Canada have sometimes seemed like siblings who are competing for the same job. There has always been a good-humoured rivalry between us, each reared in the atmosphere of high policy and great events as practised by Britain and the United States. But each, as we matured, has had to come to terms with the world as it is, and the realities each of us has had to face have been markedly different.

It is instructive to contrast our two strategic situations with those that have existed—at least hitherto—for South Africa, the black (or white) sheep of the British Imperial family. South Africa's relations with the rest of Africa were reduced to, at best, a stand-off, and its relations with the rest of the world became so cool that the South Africans had to rely almost wholly on their own defence capacity. They have had, in effect, no strategic neighbourhood. Australia does have a strategic neighbourhood and our defence and foreign policies have lately given a high priority to its cultivation. We are not wholly of the neighbourhood, because of our character as a migrant community, and we retain in our alliance with the United States a crucial connection with the world beyond our region, but we keep coming back to the proposition that we live here and that it is in our particular part of the world that our major opportunities and responsibilities lie.

Canada also has a neighbourhood, but it is so dominated by the United States that the opportunity for Canada to develop regional defence and foreign policies, as Australia has done, has not arisen. Rather Canada, although a middle power like Australia, has undertaken an extensive range of commitments to Western security—in Europe, the north Atlantic, the north Pacific and North America itself—in none of which does it have a major influence. Its contribution to international, especially United Nations, peace-keeping has also been striking. In 1975 Canada agreed to provided as part of a defence review 2000 personnel from the regular forces for peace-keeping duties, and it has had a battalion on standby for UN operations since the mid-1960s. Between 1947 and 1988 approximately 80 000 members of the Canadian armed forces served in twenty-three peace-keeping operations.[6]

Neither the hard realities of defence self-reliance (and it needs to be remembered that Canada is, physically, the second largest country in the world, with a mainland coastline of 59 000 kilometres bordering three oceans, and an exceptionally severe climate) nor a regional security policy have concerned Canadians in the way they have Australians. Canada has sought, rather, to have an influence in international affairs at large. Its voice is moderate and its objective has been to build bridges between different groups or points of view. To balance the overwhelming influence of the United States, Canada has tended to seek its own relationships with the European Community and Japan, and has engaged in successful niche diplomacy, e.g. in Francophone and Southern Africa, the Caribbean and Latin America.

Australia's relations with Canada work productively on several levels. As federations with a comparable pattern of population distribution, and comparable Westminster-derived institutions, our domestic policy arrangements are a source of endless fascination to each other—as testified by the stream of ministers, officials and academics in non-foreign affairs areas who contrive to exchange visits. We share views on many international issues and work closely together in a variety of multilateral forums, for example within the Commonwealth on Southern Africa, within the region on APEC, and within the Cairns Group on the Uruguay Round (although strong domestic protectionist sentiments in some sectors have created pressures on Ottawa threatening on occasions to undermine the Group's solidarity). And our formal bilateral relationship is substantial, certainly on paper, with agreements on trade (CANATA), nuclear cooperation, double taxation, social security reciprocity, air services and the like.

Two-way trade is reasonably substantial, amounting to $1.9 billion in 1990, with Canada our thirteenth largest partner: we export mainly sugar, meat, alumina and canned fruit, and import mainly wood products and a range of manufactures. But both trade and investment are thinner than they might be (even taking into account the significantly competitive rather than complementary character of the two economies), given Canada's status as the seventh largest Western economy, not to mention partnership (with the United States) in the biggest bilateral trading relationship in the world. That trade relationship with the United States—now formalised in the Free Trade Agreement in effect from January 1989 (and now in the process of extension to Mexico)—is in fact a likely source of problems for Australia to the extent that it is allowed by the Canadians to undermine the access concessions enjoyed by us under CANATA. Problems in this respect have already arisen with canned fruit. The lesson for Australia, as in so many of our other markets, is that ultimately our products and services will just have to win access on their own internationally competitive merits. Opportunities for expansion of Australia's trade with Canada seem to exist in this respect for, among other things, high value-added products and services, and food and beverages, including wine.

The Caribbean countries are far better known to Australians for their pirates and fast bowlers than for their politics and economics. They represent nonetheless a modern problem—small economies, usually dependent on one or two products for significant proportions of their export earnings, politically not always totally stable, and in many cases with a legacy of social and racial tensions from the sugar plantation slave economies of the past. If one includes the continental Caribbean countries, whose culture is predominantly West Indian—Belize, Guyana, Suriname, and the territory of French Guiana—the Caribbean area is physically extensive, being only slightly smaller than Australia. Attempts to create a common political identity—by a West Indies Federation or the like—in order to exercise influence in regional affairs have not been very successful, but the Caribbean community (CARICOM), now with thirteen members,[7] has been gradually evolving since 1973 as a significant vehicle for economic and other domestic policy co-operation and for foreign policy co-ordination. Not the least of the problem of a common identity is that so many islands are still under the control of foreign powers.[8] Politically, an intense local focus is characteristic, especially in the island states.

Economically, there is little complementarity, as each country is export-oriented, relying on a few commodities such as sugar, bananas or industrial raw materials like refined petroleum and bauxite. Many Caribbean states have turned to services designed for individuals and companies from the developed world, especially tourism and off-shore finance. But at the same time, the Caribbean countries have been for many years in the forefront of those developing nations seeking through the United Nations—albeit with less than conspicuous success—a new international economic order.

The Caribbean necessarily has a low priority in Australian foreign policy. Given that its Commonwealth countries comprise just on a quarter of the Commonwealth's total membership, we have tended to concentrate our attention on these,[9] with specifically focused consultations periodically occurring on such issues as sports sanctions against South Africa. Our high commissioner in Jamaica—accredited to more countries, and with reporting responsibilities for more countries, than any other Australian representative abroad—is nonetheless responsible for the conduct of Australia's relations (Cuba apart) with Caribbean countries generally. Trade is very light, the most important relationship—US territories apart—being with Trinidad and Tobago, to whom we exported some $7 million worth of meat, cheese and other edible products in 1990, in a total trade of $12 million. Australia has a common interest with Jamaica, Guyana and Suriname in the marketing of bauxite, but the role of the International Bauxite Association (IBA) has, along with that of most comparable international commodity marketing arrangements, nowadays become negligible.

While the Caribbean does not affect Australia's national interests either substantially or directly, it does have the capacity to throw up issues to which Australia has to respond on occasion in the United Nations or elsewhere. One of these is human rights. The social and economic conditions of the Caribbean, coupled with political instability and autocratic rule, have made abuses of human rights almost endemic in some countries, most notably Haiti and Suriname. External intervention in response to internal upheavals is another sensitive issue. In 1983 the United States and contingents from Jamaica, Barbados and four other island states intervened militarily in Grenada to restore order after Maurice Bishop, leader of the leftist New Jewel Movement and prime minister of a Peoples' Revolutionary government, was killed in the course of internal faction fighting: an issue still causing international ripples in 1991 with the death penalty imposed on the main perpetrators.

Cuba after 1959, when Fidel Castro and the Revolutionary 25 July Movement seized power, was throughout the Cold War the most celebrated case of defiance of American power. Upon the nationalisation of foreign business interests in Cuba in 1960, the United States imposed a trade embargo (which it still maintains), sought to overthrow Castro in the Bay of Pigs invasion in 1961 with Cuban exiles based in the United States, and in 1962 forced a showdown with the Soviet Union, which placed, and then withdrew, offensive missiles on Cuban territory. Cuba then extended its assistance to insurgent movements around the world, notably in Central America, Ethiopia and Angola. But the end of the Cold War, the resolution of most of the regional conflicts in which Cuba has been involved, and the economic pressures flowing from the declining Soviet aid to the country, have now given rise to hopes that Cuba may in the future play a more constructive role in regional and world affairs. Australia maintains relations with Cuba through our Embassy in Mexico City, but the main contact tends to be in multilateral organisations or arrangements in which we are both significant players, e.g. the Antarctic Treaty Parties, the Board of Governors of the International Atomic Energy Agency, and the International Sugar Agreement (where Australia, Brazil, Cuba and the EC are the major exporters involved).

MEXICO AND LATIN AMERICA

Mexico has a distinctive role in Latin American affairs, being physically part of the North American land mass but—traditionally anyway—economically, socially and politically focused on Central and South America. The recent changes that have swept Latin America generally are more starkly etched in Mexico than anywhere else, and it is with Mexico that Australia's bilateral relations have recently shown the strongest prospects for new development, after a cordial but insubstantial relationship since embassies were established in 1966 in Mexico City and in 1967 in Canberra.

When President Reagan urged the formation of a North America common market in the early 1980s, Mexico was among the first to reject it. There was a major change of attitude, however, after President Salinas came to power in 1988. In 1990 he formally requested a free-trade agreement with the United States, raising the prospect of an integrated exercise involving all three of the United States, Canada and Mexico. Serious negotiations for a North American Free Trade Agreement (NAFTA) are underway. This change of attitude has been part of a dramatic change of economic policy at almost all levels: an attack on inflation and the national

debt, privatisation (of the telephone system, banking and steel manufacturing) and encouragement to foreign investors, especially in the form of
maquiladoras—bonded assembly plants set up by foreign firms relying on
imported raw material and local labour. Within a remarkably short period,
Mexico has largely stabilised its macro-economic situation (including resolving a hair-raisingly large external debt problem), diversified its export
base away from oil, and moved steadily to tackle a large micro-reform
agenda. At the social level, President Salinas's initiatives have been an
attempt to come to terms with changes that are threatening the traditional
political stability of Mexico. Its population will have grown from 20 million
in 1940 to over 100 million by the end of the century, with dispossessed
rural families searching for a future in the cities and flooding, mostly
illegally, into the United States—an estimated 15 million Mexican emi-
grants now provide a floating labour supply in the southern and western
United States.

What particularly interests Australia is that Mexico's new direction
includes a significant tilt to the Asia Pacific region. It is one of the curiosities
of history that Latin American countries have had little or no role in, or
focus on, the South Pacific. There have been gestures from time to time
towards the Asia Pacific generally, as in the early 1970s when the Andean
Pact countries (then Bolivia, Chile, Colombia, Ecuador, Peru and Venezuela) sought to make economic contacts across the Pacific, but the links are
still tenuous. Mexico has opened embassies in Thailand and Singapore;
and when President Salinas visited Australia in 1990 he raised trade
and investment possibilities, expressed strong interest in joining APEC
and was accompanied by a large business delegation. Already Mexico,
along with Chile and Peru, is a member of the Pacific Basin Economic
Council (PBEC), the private sector's regional business association, and of
the Pacific Economic Co-operation Conference (PECC), the unofficial
organisation of officials, business representatives and academics which
continues to provide, among other things, important inputs into the
APEC process.

Trade between Australia and Mexico, although modest, has been increasing substantially. In 1990 Mexico was Australia's second largest
export market in Latin America (behind Argentina), ranking thirty-ninth of
all Australia's trade partners. In 1990 the total value of bilateral trade was
$217 million, up 57 per cent over 1989. Major Australian exports to Mexico
include skim milk, cream, wool, ores and base metal products, vegetable
oils and, more recently, gold and other legal tender coins. Imports from
Mexico are spread across a large range of products and include automatic
data processing machinery, medical and pharmaceutical products, and al-
coholic beverages. Bilateral investment flows are minimal. With the restructuring of the Mexican economy, and Mexico's heightened interest in
the Asia Pacific region as an area with potential for growth in bilateral and
multilateral political and economic relationships, there is substantial scope

for expansion of Australia–Mexico trade, and great interest in the Australian business community about both trade and investment opportunities. Trade Minister Neal Blewett led the first major Australian business delegation to Mexico in May 1991, reciprocating the Salinas delegation's visit the previous year. Most Australian attention is focusing on the energy sector (where a major power-generation expansion is being planned), transport and communications (including telecommunications and ports), agricultural products, mining and tourism.

The picture elsewhere in Latin America is encouraging, if not quite as fast-moving. For reasons of distance, language and culture Australia has not developed substantial links with the region. Australians have not, by and large, travelled there, done business there or seriously studied the region, despite some intriguing parallels in our national experience, especially with Argentina.[10] A steady, if light, pattern of diplomatic representation has been maintained (in Brasilia, Buenos Aires, Caracas and Santiago) but political interest on both sides has been cursory. Yet the nature of the modern world does not tolerate isolation and in the last decade or so bilateral contacts have increased, due to more trade, investment and immigration, and Australian concern over human rights, reinforced by media and immigrant community interest in particular countries.

Two recent developments have carried this emerging Australian interest in Latin America a stage further. One is rapid political and economic change, almost as dramatic as that sweeping Europe. In 1981 ten of the seventeen Latin American countries were under military rule. Today none is, and almost all have recently held elections for new governments. The economic changes have been no less important. The economies of Latin America almost without exception had been based on a centralised form of state capitalism, with tariff protection of import substitution, large external debts and hyper-inflation. Reforms under way in most countries show over the region as a whole an emphatic drive towards market-based economies, privatisation and trade liberalisation. It would be foolish to assume that the habits of centuries will be swept aside in an avalanche of political and economic reforms that will transform Latin America overnight. The build-up of strategic pressure that helped burst the banks dividing Europe does not exist in Latin America and no doubt, if the economic reforms are not quickly successful, there could be a reversion in some countries to old political habits.

However, the second development may delay, even frustrate, such a reaction. This is the emergence of economic integration within Latin America, and to some extent with North America—along with an inclination, of particular interest to Australia, to be more outward-looking toward the Asia Pacific region. Regionalism is not new in Latin America. It has been popular since World War II, but has not been successful as a form of economic revival because of the tension between economic nationalism—

associated with political centralism, protectionism and solidarity with the adverse fortunes of the Third World—and, on the other hand, structural reform and trade liberalisation. It seems, at least for a moment in Latin American history, that the latter philosophy has won. It is certainly in the ascendant and has been the momentum behind a plethora of recent economic integration initiatives.[11] If these initiatives become established, it will be much more difficult for individual countries to back-track to the comfortable nationalism of the past. The mechanism of integration will itself to a degree be binding but, more importantly, integration will become established on the basis of economic successes which will, it is hoped, improve the living standards of Latin Americans generally and support the democratic process associated with economic reform.

Country by country, Australia's relationships in Latin America have not been significant, if each component is judged by traditional standards and compared with our more substantial relationships. We have no defence arrangement and no cultural agreement with any Latin American country. Our development assistance priorities are elsewhere. Trade and investment, while increasing, remains modest. Yet increasingly, in response to recent developments in Latin America and to the changing agenda of global issues, Australian diplomacy is discovering windows of opportunity, in the context of our joint participation in a whole variety of multilateral endeavours with countries with whom we have not worked closely before.

The Cairns Group includes five Latin Americans—Argentina, Brazil, Chile, Colombia and Uruguay. Sixteen of the Latin American countries are members of the GATT. Although there were differences with Australia (for example, on trade-related intellectual property rights) during the Uruguay Round of multilateral trade negotiations, Australia found that in informal groups on particular issues, Argentina, Brazil, Colombia, Mexico, Peru and Uruguay were actively concerned with increasing access to markets and improving GATT rules and discipline. Australia and Argentina are both major wheat producers and two of the big five exporters—with United States, Canada and the European Community—in the International Wheat Agreement (IWA): Australia and Argentina often share in this context a common position critical of the United States and the EC. Brazil and Australia are two of the four major exporters—with the EC—in the International Sugar Agreement (ISA): again Australia has found common cause in criticism of European and American sugar policies.

Most Latin American nations are involved in the United Nations Conference on Environment and Development (UNCED) which will take place in Brazil in June 1992, and in the negotiations for framework conventions on climate change and biodiversity. Australia is active in both initiatives. We participate with seven Latin American countries in the operation of the Antarctic Treaty system—Argentina, Chile, Brazil, Peru, Ecuador and Uruguay and (as a non-consultative party) Colombia. The Australian and

Argentine Antarctic agencies are developing an agreement for the exchange of information and for staff and research co-operation, and we are working with Argentina on preparations for an international seminar on environmental protection issues to be held in Argentina in 1992. Another issue not unrelated to either the environment or development, and where Australia's interests intersect those of Latin American countries, is our joint support for the 1982 UN Law of the Sea Convention: we share interests with coastal states and, as producers of nickel, copper, manganese and cobalt, in the future of deep seabed mining of these metals.

Five Latin American countries—Argentina, Brazil, Chile, Venezuela and Uruguay—are currently serving with Australia on the Board of Governors of the International Atomic Energy Agency (IAEA). Most Latin Americans are members of the Nuclear Non-Proliferation Treaty (NPT), and although Argentina, Brazil and Chile are presently exceptions, general support for an international nuclear non-proliferation regime is strengthening. Peru and Uruguay were among twenty-eight countries which co-sponsored an Australian proposal at the NPT review conference in 1990 to endorse fullscope safeguards as a condition of new nuclear supply. We share with Latin American countries the desire for a Comprehensive Test Ban Treaty. We find common ground with many of them in opposing French nuclear testing in the South Pacific. There are close similarities between the Treaty of Tlatelolco, which is designed to keep Latin America free of nuclear weapons, and the South Pacific Nuclear Free Zone (SPNFZ) Treaty. Disarmament and arms control co-operation is not confined to the nuclear area. Argentina, Brazil, Mexico, Peru and Venezuela are members with Australia of the Conference on Disarmament (CD). Argentina, like Australia, has begun to prepare nationally to implement a Chemical Weapons Convention (CWC). Venezuela, taking note of Australia's experience, has promoted a regional approach to the implementation of the Convention.

One area of particular sensitivity in both bilateral and multilateral relations with Latin America is human rights. Civilian governments have had varying success in establishing their authority over military forces and security agencies. Extra-judicial executions and 'disappearances' at the hands of government agents have been a brutal feature of Latin American politics, especially in Chile under the Pinochet regime and in Argentina, and at the time of writing are still occurring in Colombia and Peru, both of which have democratic electoral processes. Internal armed conflicts still cause severe loss of life, in particular in Colombia, El Salvador, Guatemala and Peru. The trend towards democracy has, however, begun to affect the Latin American group's approach to the work of the United Nations Commission on Human Rights. Previously sensitive to international criticism and inclined to vote as a bloc, the Latin countries are now taking a more individual approach. This suits Australian policy. While our attitude to human rights is universal, our approach is to raise—non-confrontationally and for the most part quietly—particular cases, and to pursue specific policy issues.

Australia's trade relations with the countries of South and Central America have been modest, even with the big four of Argentina, Brazil, Chile and Venezuela. Its total in 1990 constituted just 0.8 per cent of our exports and 1.3 per cent of our imports. But as between Latin America and East Europe, with whom the trade figures are presently comparable, there is little doubt that the former offers considerably more potential for growth in the short to medium term. Australian business has begun to appreciate this, particularly so far as Chile is concerned. Although trade remains low—just $88 million in 1990—the stock of Australian investment in Chile, particularly in copper and gold mining, is very large. Indeed for a time—before the sale in 1991 of Bond company and other assets—Australia ranked as the second-largest foreign investor in Chile after the United States. The high profile attention that this activity has been getting has its own utility in sensitising Australian business generally to what for most is a wholly new area of external activity.

Fresh Australian interest in Latin America, while it should not be overstated, reflects not only significant political and economic changes globally and in Latin America itself, but also to some extent the maturing of Australian diplomacy. The experience of the tough Uruguay Round negotiations—and especially Australia's leadership of the heterogeneous Cairns Group—brought home to Australians some simple truths about international politics, one of which is that a nation's interests are not necessarily satisfied by clubbing with 'like-minded' or 'comparable' countries. Australia has competitors in Latin America (including Brazil in the resources trade with Japan, and Argentina in the export of meat and grains) but we have found common cause on many multilateral issues. The opening of Latin American markets will make the Latin Americans themselves more competitive, but will also offer opportunities to a range of Australian exports. So our relationships with Latin America will increasingly reflect the more complex, detailed and sophisticated assessment of national interests that Australian foreign policy now demands.

PART IV

CHALLENGES

19

Australia's Role in the World of the 1990s

THE WORLD OF THE 1990s will be fluid, dynamic and uncertain. There will be many new opportunities to tackle old problems, but many accompanying risks as new power relationships work themselves out around the globe. The release of Cold War military tensions; the continuation nonetheless of trade and other economic tensions; the effects of the world-wide ideological mood-shift toward liberal democracy; the escalating need to find co-operative solutions to common problems like global climate warming—these and other developments will leave no country untouched.

The challenge for Australian foreign policy will be, as always, to pursue our own political and economic interests with maximum effectiveness, but in a way that makes as positive a contribution as possible to a more peaceful and prosperous world. In doing so we cannot assume—any more than we ever could—that the protection and advancement of our own interests will be a matter of high priority, or even great concern, for any other country. But there are two very considerable potential assets which Australia can bring to that task. The first is our status as a middle power, with the capacity that implies for effective action and influence. The other is our location alongside South-East Asia in the Asia Pacific region, the most economically dynamic in the world. How substantial and effective a role Australia plays in the world and the region in the years ahead will depend essentially on how well we take advantage of these two attributes.

The late 1980s and early 1990s are watershed years for Australia. We are, whether fully recognising it or not, engaged in nothing less than the reshaping of our national identity. A central element in any country's identity is how it perceives and relates to the external world, and how in turn others respond to it. In this respect Australia's foreign policy is presently acting as an important catalyst in building a new Australian identity—one which is much more internationalist, and regionally focused, than before. A process is at work—by no means fully yet resolved—whereby some new directions in the conduct of Australian foreign policy are generating international responses of a kind which, in turn, are feeding back into and reinforcing domestic perceptions of how we should present ourselves internationally. In this way, our responses to new global and regional challenges have been helping to reveal the kind of country we are, and can become.

BEING AN EFFECTIVE MIDDLE POWER

Australia is a middle power. We are manifestly not a great or even major power; nor, however, are we small or insignificant. The company of nations which tend to be so described is relatively limited—a dozen to twenty at most. There are no agreed criteria: it is a matter of balancing out GDP and population size, and perhaps military capacity and physical size as well, then having regard to the perceptions of others.[1] 'Middle power diplomacy' is an expression less often used than it was in the 1970s, but gradually regaining some currency as the most useful way of describing the kind of role that some nations like Australia have been playing in recent times, or to which they might reasonably aspire.[2] The term 'middle power' (often in conjunction with the adjective 'robust') was used actively by the Whitlam Government to signify both Australia's potential for a creative form of diplomacy in world affairs, and also some room to manoeuvre in our relationship with the United States. One specific way in which Australia was deemed to have the potential for a middle power role was in what was then called 'resources diplomacy': Australia being abundantly endowed with minerals and energy, we were thought to have some cards to play in a world perceived to be short of both.

While middle power diplomacy is ultimately no less self-interested than any other kind, its characteristic methods are these days more often applied to a range of problems which involve the interests of not just a few, but many, nations. Important examples abound in such areas as arms control and disarmament, trade liberalisation, regional conflict resolution and environment protection. Australia, like most other countries, has a self-interested preference for the peaceful resolution of conflict, acceptance of international law, protection of the weak against the strong, and the free exchange of ideas, people and goods. In a world that is increasingly interdependent, the pursuit of a great many of these interests depends on co-operation with others for their fullest satisfaction. The argument is that, in these circumstances, middle powers are as well equipped as anyone else, and in some respects better equipped, to generate acceptable solutions.

The characteristic method of middle power diplomacy is coalition building with 'like-minded' countries. It also usually involves 'niche' diplomacy,
which means concentrating resources in specific areas best able to generate
returns worth having, rather than trying to cover the field. By definition,
middle powers are not powerful enough in most circumstances to impose
their will, but they may be persuasive enough to have like-minded others
see their point of view, and to act accordingly. The countries whom we
have traditionally regarded as 'comparable'—sharing the abiding values of
Western liberal democracy, and the living standards of advanced industrial
societies—have been Britain, the United States, Canada, New Zealand,
and occasionally the Scandinavians and some other West Europeans.[3]
But the term 'like-minded' these days more often describes those who,
whatever their prevailing value systems, share specific interests and are
prepared to join together to do something about pursuing them.

There have been a number of important such like-minded coalitions
formed in recent times. There is the Cairns Group: Argentina, Australia,
Brazil, Canada, Chile, Colombia, Fiji, Hungary, Indonesia, Malaysia, New
Zealand, Philippines, Thailand and Uruguay. There is APEC: at present
Australia, Brunei, Canada, Indonesia, Japan, Republic of Korea, Malaysia,
New Zealand, Philippines, Singapore, Thailand and the United States.
There has been the initiative to ban mining and oil drilling in the Antarctic,
the development of which involved, first, France, then later Belgium and
Italy. There has been the chemical weapons issue, where in organising
the international Government–Industry Conference Against Chemical
Weapons in Canberra in 1989, Australia developed a close working re-
lationship with Brazil, Egypt, Germany, India, Japan, the Netherlands,
Norway, Sweden, the Soviet Union and the United States. By contrast, a
narrower constituency was tapped in our work on chemical weapons in the
'Australia Group': namely, the major chemical-exporting members of the
OECD.

In the case of Cambodia, our coalition building meant working from the
outset with Indonesia, all five permanent members of the Security Council,
Vietnam and the four Cambodian factions themselves. In the ongoing Law
of the Sea negotiations—particularly in the early 1980s—it meant developing, along with Canada and New Zealand, a coalition partnership with the
smaller European democracies of Austria, Denmark, Finland, Iceland,
Ireland, the Netherlands, Norway, Sweden and Switzerland—the 'Group
of Twelve'. In responding to the evil of apartheid, Australia's coalition has
been the Commonwealth itself, and in particular the closely knit group of
nine countries which have since 1987 constituted the Committee of Foreign
Ministers on Southern Africa (CFMSA): Australia, Canada, Guyana, India,
Malaysia, Nigeria, Tanzania, Zambia and Zimbabwe.

It will be evident from these examples that coalitions which Australia has
built in recent years, or in which we have been particularly active, are by
no means confined in their membership to 'middle power' countries. They

often include great or major powers, and those with very much less influence as well. Moreover, the memberships keep changing. Although, for example, trade liberalisation objectives are common to both APEC and the Cairns Group, the countries with whom we made common cause in the former are not all the same as those with whom we have worked in the latter. The point of middle power diplomacy is not who is embraced by it, but how the process of change is initiated and carried through. Coalition building is inherently eclectic: we seek to build in each case the kind of alliance most suited to the particular issue on our international agenda. But the goal is constant: maximising the influence that can be brought to bear by Australia and those countries which share interests with us.

For middle power diplomacy to be effective, a number of conditions have to be met. First, there has to be careful identification of where the opportunities lie for potentially effective action by a middle power. There is no prestige, or likely result, in enthusiastically pursuing ideas which are premature, over-ambitious, or for some other reason unlikely to generate any significant body of support. A good example is regional military security, where we have taken the view that for the foreseeable future the most productive role for a country like Australia is to promote increasing dialogue and the gradual development of confidence building measures, rather than to seek to initiate new structures. On the other hand, APEC, the Cairns Group, the UN peace plan for Cambodia and the Antarctic environment initiative were all examples of ideas whose time had clearly come.

Secondly, there has to be sufficient physical capacity to follow the issue through. This implies a certain minimum of physical resources, including a sufficiently wide network of diplomatic posts, which it may be difficult for any country smaller than a middle power to match. It also means that, for a middle power, there will be a limit to the number of major issues that can be simultaneously pursued: selective 'niche' diplomacy, while often good tactics, is also compelled by realistic necessity. Resources simply have to be concentrated where they are likely to have the most useful impact. Priority setting—involving careful balancing of the importance of the national interests in question against the practical likelihood of their being advanced —becomes extremely important. Thus, for example, in the vast area embraced by what we have described as the 'new internationalist agenda', Australia has tended to focus its major efforts on three specific areas—human rights, the environment and development co-operation. The capacity to follow an issue through also involves energy and stamina. Many good ideas, well capable of implementation, fall by the wayside in international affairs simply because institutions, or the individuals who constitute them, tire. One widely acknowledged reason for the impact made, for example, by Australia's UN peace plan for Cambodia was the sheer persistence with which, over a long period, the proposal was followed through at both official and ministerial level.

Thirdly, there has to be in most cases a degree of intellectual imagination and creativity applied to the issue—an ability to see a way through impasses and to lead, if not by force of authority, then at least by force of ideas. The application of physical resources to a problem without accompanying ideas is unlikely to result in anything more than the appearance of activity. Of course, creativity and imagination are not the prerogative of middle powers; nor should they be assumed to exist in the case of any particular middle power. The point is simply that what middle powers may lack in economic, political or military clout, they can often make up with quick and thoughtful diplomatic footwork. And resolution of just about any significant problem in international affairs—be it bilateral or multilateral in character—needs just that.

Finally, effective middle power diplomacy involves credibility on the part of the country in question. The mix of ingredients here will vary from case to case. Perceived independence from the influence of larger powers will often be one such ingredient. The maintenance of traditional alliance relationships (such as Australia's with the United States) is not in issue here —rather simply the need for any country aspiring to play an active diplomatic role of its own to be able to make clear that it is not acting as a mere cipher or stalking horse for some protector, and that its policy choices and priorities are entirely its own. The maintenance of credibility is also crucially dependent on avoiding any charge of hypocrisy: any country which preaches abroad what it fails to practise at home cannot expect to be taken very seriously for very long. Thus Australia's domestic commitment to internationalising the economy is crucial to our credibility in the Uruguay Round and APEC; similarly, a poor recent race relations performance here would make it very difficult for us to be heard internationally on apartheid. Nor can double standards be applied abroad: we made it clear, for example, in our discussion of Australia's human rights diplomacy that this depended very much for its credibility on both universality in the application of principles, and consistency of approach as between different countries.

Middle powers, simply because they are of less than great or major power status, can occasionally do what great and major powers cannot. It is generally acknowledged that APEC would have had much more difficulty in getting off the ground if the United States or Japan had been its instigator: each side may have feared the worst of the other, and the smaller powers may well have felt that their own interests were at risk. Similarly, Australia's ability to talk comfortably to every country involved in the Cambodian dispute owed much to the fact that we were not carrying any great or major power baggage. We had no axes to grind, and no immediate interests to protect, other than a genuine desire to see a terrible, protracted conflict ended and regional stability improved accordingly.

The approaches we have described as characteristic of effective middle power diplomacy are also, it should be acknowledged, increasingly being embraced by the great powers themselves. The Gulf War, while it demonstrated beyond doubt the effectiveness of US military power, also demonstrated the necessity and utility of acting in concert with others. The global politics of power may not completely have had their day, but there is a real sense in which entrepreneurial diplomacy—exploiting networks of support and influence rather than hierarchical gradations of power—will become an increasingly attractive, and favoured, option. Leadership exercised with one's supporters, rather than over them, is always more durable.

BEING AN ASIA PACIFIC NATION

The great turn-around in contemporary Australian history is that the region from which we sought in the past to protect ourselves—whether by esoteric dictation tests for would-be immigrants, or tariffs, or alliances with the distant great and powerful—is now the region which offers Australia the most. Our future lies, inevitably, in the Asia Pacific region. This is where we live, must survive strategically and economically, and find a place and role if we are to develop our full potential as a nation.

The problem for Australia in fully realising this role does not lie in the 'Pacific' so much as in the 'Asia' component. We have thoroughly well-established working relationships with the United States, Canada and the Pacific Island countries, and are as well placed as any to develop such links with any of the Pacific rim Latin American nations who may in the future choose to reach out into the Asia Pacific region. Of course difficulties will arise from time to time in all these relationships. In dealing with our Pacific Island neighbours there is a particular need for Australians to be conscious that, if we are insufficiently attuned to cultural differences and the cultural sensitivities of the less powerful, we will be perceived as uncomprehending, domineering or patronising. But it is with the Asian countries in our region that the risks of misunderstanding and non-acceptance are very much higher.

It is not surprising that this should be so, given that for most of the two hundred years since European settlement, Australia has fought against the reality of its own geography. We thought of ourselves, and were thought of by just about everyone else, as an Anglophonic and Anglophilic outpost—tied by history, language, culture, economics and emotion to Europe and North America. On the other hand, that perception has been under assault for some time. A long series of developments, stretching back now for several decades, has been gradually changing the picture—including the Colombo Plan and all the development assistance programs that followed; the steady growth of substantial diplomatic relations in both old and newly emerging Asian nations; the rapid rise of Japan to become our major trading partner; the overdue demise of the White Australia policy; the unhappy lessons of our entanglement with Vietnam; the attention paid to building a new political and economic relationship with China, and rebuilding our relationship with Indonesia; and, most recently, the obvious visibility and perceived success to date of our initiatives in Cambodia and with APEC. These and other developments have all contributed to what has now become accepted almost as conventional wisdom: that it is simply no longer an option for Australia to see itself first and foremost as a transplanted European nation.

All that said, there is still a tendency in Australia to view Asia through the distorting lens of old prejudices and fears, seeing a vaguely threatening encirclement and underestimating its adaptability and economic dynamism. The old Asian stereotypes which live on in muted form—of intellectual conformity, political backwardness and economic poverty—were always patronising, and masked the enormous diversity of the region. To the extent that they have any continuing life, they are now dangerously misleading in not equipping us to deal with the reality of modern Asia. It is one thing to recognise that our future lies in this region. It is another to know how to manage that future so as best to protect and promote Australia's own national interests, in a regional environment that is not only culturally and economically diverse, but economically dynamic, clever and competitive, and politically and strategically fluid.

In approaching the management of our Asian future we should not overstate the task. The diversity of the Asian region is part of its challenge, but it also makes it potentially more accessible to any outsider prepared to make the appropriate effort. In the whole sweep of countries from Japan to Afghanistan there was, before the Europeans, no word for 'Asia', and no 'Asian' consciousness—perhaps not surprisingly given the presence of six or more important and distinct cultural traditions, dozens of significant cultures of lesser influence, and a multitude of living languages.[4] That diversity means that, while we in Australia are manifestly not an Asian people, we are nonetheless culturally and demographically more or less equidistant from all its elements. As such, we are well equipped to deal bilaterally with them all, as well as to engage in some region-wide bridge building. Moreover, as the region itself becomes more economically focused—as the battlefields of yesterday turn into the marketplaces of today and tomorrow—questions of cultural and social identity become less dominant. And as the region itself changes, Australia's distinctiveness is less striking. So we no longer need be the odd man out in Asia—even if we are destined to be the oddest man in.

There is no doubt that in the conduct of its relations with the region, Australia still carries some baggage from the past. Stereotyped images die hard. This is true whether they are negative (an immigration policy tainted with racism; a one-dimensional economy; a lazy workforce; an ignorant and patronising approach to non-Europeans), or merely vacuous (open spaces; exotic animals; tennis and surf). But there are plenty of positives on which to build. For a start Australia has, to put it objectively, a more open and tolerant society than any in Asia. That is clearly reflected in immigration policy, where the White Australia policy has been dead for more than two decades; where between a third and a half of our annual migrant intake (amounting to 40 000–50 000 people each year) has since the late 1970s been Asian; and where our per capita absorption of Indo-Chinese refugees, in particular, has been higher than that of any other country in the world. There are presently well over 600 000 people of Asian descent living in Australia; this represents about 3.5 per cent of the population now, but the figure is expected to rise to 7 per cent by the year 2010.

Furthermore, while older generations of Australians were less knowledgeable about Asia and Asians than they might have been, and some wartime prejudices have been slow to evaporate, a major effort is being made to systematically educate current and future generations of young Australians about the region in which they live—not least with the plan now in place, unmatched anywhere else in the region, to have primary and secondary school students routinely taught at least one of six Asian languages. Like our immigration practice, this has just not been fully appreciated in most parts of Asia.[5]

Immigration and education policy are just two of the ways in which Australia has been establishing a new set of credentials for itself as a constructive participant in Asia region affairs. There are other factors at work as well. An indirect, but important, one has been the reshaping of our domestic economy to break down potential barriers and open it up to both the discipline and opportunity of greater trade and two-way investment. Another factor has been the fundamental reshaping of our defence posture around the concept of defence self-reliance—developing the capability to handle all but the most extreme contingencies with our own resources, without resort to others—and with an evolving focus on regional defence co-operation. Most directly of all, there has been the series of regional foreign policy initiatives amply described in earlier chapters.

One of the lessons we have begun to learn is that if Australia is to fully realise the opportunities created by our geography to become a more influential player, politically and economically, in the region—and to reap the rewards in terms of enhanced security, trade and investment flows—then we have to approach Asia in a more deliberately multi-dimensional way than we have in the past. We have to recognise that diplomatic initiatives, defence policy, economic strategies, development assistance, immigration policy, cultural relations, information activities and human contacts generally, all inter-react with each other. And if we want to ensure that Australia's overall interests are advanced, we have to work hard to have them inter-react in a mutually reinforcing way—rather than rub against each other. This was the central theme of the Foreign Minister's 1989 Parliamentary Statement on *Australia's Regional Security*, and it is the underlying practical rationale for recent efforts to co-ordinate and integrate our public diplomacy, in particular through the establishment of the Australia Abroad Council.

Such engagement with Asia—or enmeshment, to use another term periodically in currency—does not imply any sacrifice or subordination of our own distinctively Australian national characteristics. To approach the region with confidence that we can operate successfully within it does not mean we have to thwart our national values and culture, or deny our history. It may well make sense in Asia to moderate some of the directness—or brashness—that we might routinely deploy in encounters within Australia, or with North Americans or Europeans. But that is simply a matter of learning the business of normal neighbourhood civility. It does not mean moderating our commitment to values which are at the core of our sense of national identity and worth—in particular those of democracy and individual liberty.

Australia's disposition, based on our history and culture, has been to emphasise those rights and values enshrined in the International Covenant on Civil and Political Rights. By contrast our neighbours, with their different historical and cultural experience, have been more inclined to give primacy to the rights identified in the International Covenant on Economic, Social and Cultural Rights. Like many developing countries, they have tended to argue that an escape from poverty through economic development is a necessary prerequisite for the application of those political and civil rights which so preoccupy democratic developed countries. They point to the economic and social causes of human rights violations, such as international indebtedness, deteriorating terms of trade, threats to the environment and the like.

But to give continuing attention, as we do, to political and civil rights is not to be engaged in the neo-colonialist imposition of inappropriate values. When frank and serious discussion does take place, away from the spotlight of public attention, one rarely experiences in our wider region any denial of the fundamental, universal nature of the rights set out in *both* International Covenants. Moreover, the great democratic experiment in India, one of the world's poorest and most densely populated countries, continues to work and a whole series of Asian countries have in recent years strengthened their democracies against the odds. Despite recent setbacks the urge to go down this path remains palpable in China. Human dignity is inalienable, and the same human rights exist in every kind of society. The urge to democracy is no more than a reflection of these realities.

The notion of a 'humanitarian right to interfere'[6] has obvious attractions in principle. But foreign policy practice also has to accommodate an acceptance of the integrity of the nation state, on which the United Nations is founded and international law is based. There is no great mystery about this accommodation, articulated as it often is in rhetorical defence of the inviolability of national territory and the sovereignty of states. Equally, there is no mystery about the process of accommodation an individual has to undergo, while holding to his or her inalienable rights, in order to be part of a society. It depends on circumstances and cases. The need, for example, to establish 'humanitarian air corridors' through sovereign territory to deliver food aid in Africa, and the international intervention in Iraq to provide enclaves of safe haven for the Kurdish people, make the point. In pressing its neighbours for recognition of basic human rights, Australia is not raising doubts about their integrity as sovereign states. Of course we recognise the claims of sovereignty, but we ask that the universal rights of human beings be also acknowledged and respected.

Properly handled, there is no reason why these issues should put at risk Australia's regional relationships. While there is no point in provoking arguments needlessly or counterproductively, and while we should always understand and respect the real sensitivities of countries with different cultural traditions, we should not be afraid to tackle issues which cry out for attention. Nor should we be trapped into embracing crude cultural relativism. Australia should make no apology for raising human rights issues— political and civil, as well as economic and social—and for expecting others to acknowledge the integrity of our own values, including respect for freedom in the media. To make our views known, quietly and courteously, about values we regard as universal and hold dear, does not entail condescension or interference in internal affairs. The question in all these circumstances—as so often in Asia—is not whether to act, but how to act.[7]

So Australia can be an Asia Pacific nation in every sense, without modifying any of our commitment to values or principles which are crucial to our own sense of self. Australia will not lose its identity by becoming ever more absorbed and involved in Asia Pacific regional affairs. On the contrary that identity will go on developing, losing attitudes of exclusiveness and superiority which may have been part of it in the past, and gaining in the process a new flexibility, a new capacity to learn and adapt, and a new maturity.

FROM NATIONALISM TO INTERNATIONALISM

We have said often enough in this book that Australia is dealing with a changing world and a changing region. We have perhaps not said enough that we are also dealing with a changing Australia. Attitudes change more slowly than government policies, but the changes in Australia in the last quarter century—and even more so within the last decade— have been remarkable. Some of that change has been generated by the necessity of becoming involved in the region. Even more of it has been generated by the necessity, economically, to join the rest of the world. But today Australians are responding to challenges across the full spectrum of national activity in our region, and to the emerging shape of a twenty-first century world as well.

The search for an Australian identity has been an insistent theme in commentaries about how Australia sees itself and is seen by other countries. After Gallipoli, the 'digger' remained popular, transformed into the 'battler' during the Depression and revived during World War II. However, the notion of the underdog steeled in adversity did not survive the long period of post-War prosperity and the arrival of the Cold War, in which Australia was associated with the 'haves' of the world, providing assistance to those less fortunate and standing firm against the revolutionary egalitarianism of communism. For quite a time we played with the idea of being the 'lucky country', replacing the irony of its author's intention with the sentiment judged proper for official rhetoric. But we learned soon enough that luck, in the form of bountiful natural resources, was not enough to sustain, let alone develop, an economy. More refined ideas were momentarily interesting, such as 'tyranny of distance', which fell victim to the realisation that opportunities abounded near at hand in our own region, and 'loyalty to the protector', which lost its potency when Australia was forced by the experience in Vietnam to look to its own defence. In the 1980s immigrants and entrepreneurs captured attention, with the salad bowl replacing the melting pot as a metaphor for the kind of multicultural society Australia was becoming, and some high-fliers in the business world seeming intent on reincarnating the robber barons of nineteenth century America. We recently faced, and quickly took steps to avoid, the prospect of becoming a 'banana republic'. And we are now offering ourselves as a 'clever' country—perhaps not implausibly, given what we at last seem to have learned from our experience and now understand to be the needs of our future.[8]

It may be that past introspection about our identity was simply a sign that we did not have enough to do. If that were the case it is not so now. Australia can no longer get by looking wholly inward. Channelling what might otherwise have been externally competitive energies into the building and maintenance of high protectionist walls, when the rest of the region and the world have become so competitive, guarantees nothing more than a sustained decline in standard of living. Maintaining a nervous, defensive approach to the world in external policy generally—doing nothing for ourselves in defence policy or diplomacy that we could not rely upon someone else to do for us—makes no positive long-term contribution to either the country's prosperity or its security, particularly in a region and a world where power relationships are rapidly changing, and where protectors who are more focused on our interests than their own are in short supply. Australians can no longer define themselves simply as nationalists who have come to terms with their own history, their own culture, and their own landscape: we now have to come to terms with a region and a world.

In looking to the future in this way, Australians face something of an historical paradox. For long we were dependent upon the traditions we inherited as an Anglo-Saxon settlement in the antipodes. Because of this history, the assertion of our independence was associated with a resurgence of Australian nationalism. At this very point in world affairs, however, we are confronted with a challenge to nationalism that is deep and complex—the tendency, almost amounting to a rush in recent times, towards regional and global interdependence. Simple nationalism, in the world of the 1990s, is an unlikely winner for Australia. We need a more sophisticated kind of nationalism—one, in fact, which has a strongly internationalist flavour running through it.

A new national self-perception of this kind does seem to be emerging, and it is difficult to overstate the impact of the tumultuous events of the last few years in producing it. We have as a nation come to appreciate much more than we ever did that no country or group of countries can any longer sensibly stand outside the mainstream flow; that no country's, or group of countries', interests can usefully be pursued in isolation from everybody else's; that a great many problems on the international agenda can only sensibly be addressed by co-operative action; and that different kinds of problems—economic, security, environmental and the like—can no longer be quite as readily quarantined from each other as might have been the case in the past. We have come to appreciate, moreover, that when a country is of a size and weight of less than major power proportions, then it is very much better for the world to be governed (with a major role in this respect for institutions like the United Nations) by principles of justice, equality and achievement, rather than status and power.

The kind of foreign policy Australia has been crafting and implementing in recent years—which might be broadly characterised as middle power diplomacy with an Asia Pacific orientation—has been designed to respond to this new internationalist understanding manifestly growing in the Australian community. Where that diplomacy has been successful, it has helped in turn to reinforce perceptions in Australia of the kind of nation we need to be in the 1990s. National and international perceptions of Australia's role in the region and the world are in this sense inter-related, and there is no reason why they should significantly differ.

Australia's national interests do not conflict with those of our neighbours. We do not threaten anyone. We want to be a modern, co-operative and inventive society. We are large enough to have influence, small enough to be flexible and innovative, and new enough not to be rigid. At a pivotal period in world history—when opportunities are present for fundamental new approaches to the conduct of international affairs—Australia's pursuit of its national interests is consistent with those tendencies in international affairs working towards a peaceful and prosperous region and a more humane and interdependent world.

From the vantage point of mid-1991, we believe we can be reasonably confident that this message has been heard and understood. We do seem to be generally regarded as a concerned, constructive and innovative member of the world community. Regionally, we do seem to be viewed nowadays as a participant, aware of the complex interplay of different roles in the various issues on the regional agenda, and able to make a valuable and original contribution. But if we have responded reasonably astutely to the great changes of the last two years or so, it must also be said that that change has not yet run its course. We will not be able to linger on past achievements; nor will we have the luxury of stepping back from the flow of events. We need now to build on our achievements, develop the capabilities we have established, and have the stamina to pursue favourable outcomes to the many courses of action already initiated, and the many new activities which the future holds. And we need to do this in a way which is sensitive to the particular currents and nuances of our own region.

All this will require both nous and energy. As we said at the outset, in international affairs, as in the domestic economy, Australia cannot afford the mentality of the plodder or the recluse. Responding effectively to change means keeping our wits about us—in anticipating the currents of change, in reacting to events as they occur, and above all else in being constantly alert to new opportunities for influence in the protection and advancement of Australia's national interests.

Charts

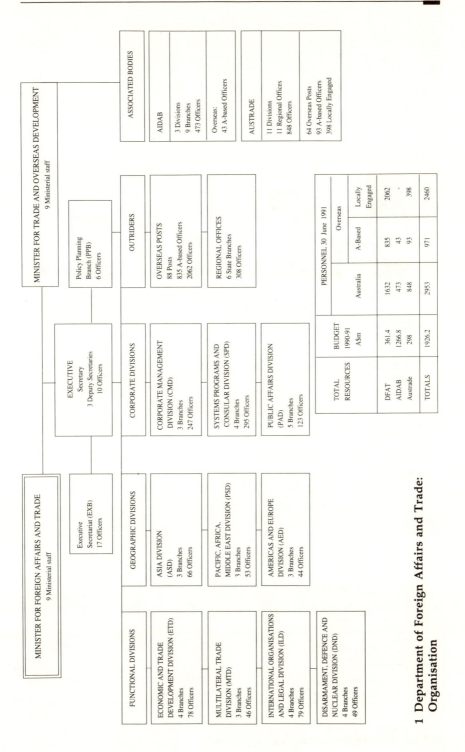

1 Department of Foreign Affairs and Trade: Organisation

MINISTER FOR FOREIGN AFFAIRS AND TRADE
9 Ministerial staff

MINISTER FOR TRADE AND OVERSEAS DEVELOPMENT
9 Ministerial staff

Executive Secretariat (EXB)
17 Officers

EXECUTIVE
Secretary
3 Deputy Secretaries
10 Officers

Policy Planning Branch (PPB)
6 Officers

ASSOCIATED BODIES

AIDAB
3 Divisions
9 Branches
473 Officers
Overseas:
43 A-based Officers

AUSTRADE
11 Divisions
11 Regional Offices
848 Officers
64 Overseas Posts
93 A-based Officers
398 Locally Engaged

OUTRIDERS

OVERSEAS POSTS
88 Posts
835 A-based Officers
2062 Officers

REGIONAL OFFICES
6 State Branches
308 Officers

CORPORATE DIVISIONS

CORPORATE MANAGEMENT DIVISION (CMD)
3 Branches
247 Officers

SYSTEMS PROGRAMS AND CONSULAR DIVISION (SPD)
4 Branches
295 Officers

PUBLIC AFFAIRS DIVISION (PAD)
5 Branches
123 Officers

GEOGRAPHIC DIVISIONS

ASIA DIVISION (ASD)
3 Branches
66 Officers

PACIFIC, AFRICA, MIDDLE EAST DIVISION (PSD)
3 Branches
53 Officers

AMERICAS AND EUROPE DIVISION (AED)
3 Branches
44 Officers

FUNCTIONAL DIVISIONS

ECONOMIC AND TRADE DEVELOPMENT DIVISION (ETD)
4 Branches
78 Officers

MULTILATERAL TRADE DIVISION (MTD)
3 Branches
46 Officers

INTERNATIONAL ORGANISATIONS AND LEGAL DIVISION (ILD)
4 Branches
79 Officers

DISARMAMENT, DEFENCE AND NUCLEAR DIVISION (DND)
4 Branches
49 Officers

TOTAL RESOURCES	BUDGET 1990-91 A$m	Australia	Overseas A-Based	Overseas Locally Engaged
DFAT	361.4	1632	835	2062
AIDAB	1266.8	473	43	-
Austrade	298	848	93	398
TOTALS	1926.2	2953	971	2460

PERSONNEL 30 June 1991

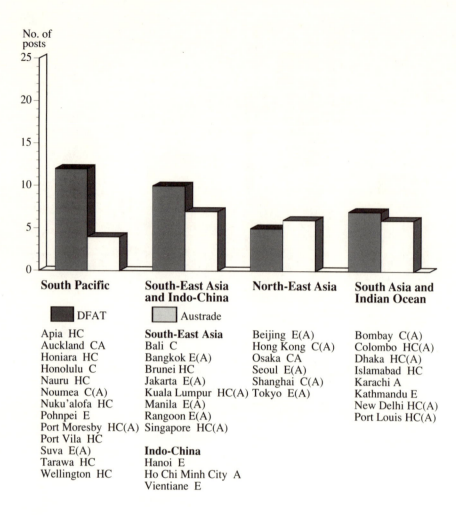

No. of posts

Type	Symbol	Number
Department of Foreign Affairs & Trade (DFAT)		
Embassy	E	51
High Commission (Commonwealth countries)	HC	24
Consulate (DFAT Managed)	C	13
		88
Austrade		
Consulate (Austrade Managed)	CA	4
Office managed by Austrade	A	9
		13
Austrade presence: Post managed by DFAT	(A)	(51)

2 Australia's Overseas Missions

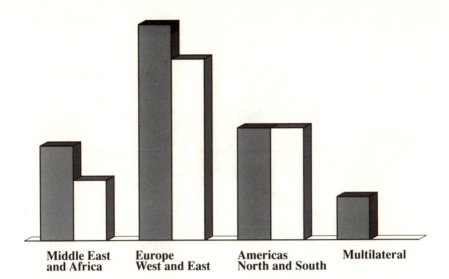

**Middle East
and Africa** **Europe
West and East** **Americas
North and South** **Multilateral**

World Population (1989: 5.2 billion)

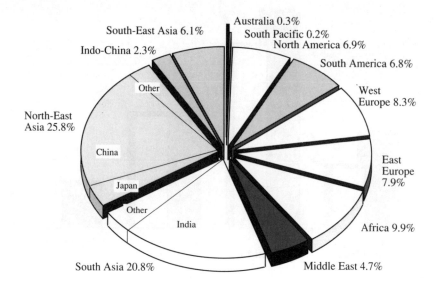

World GDP (1989: US$20 194 billion)

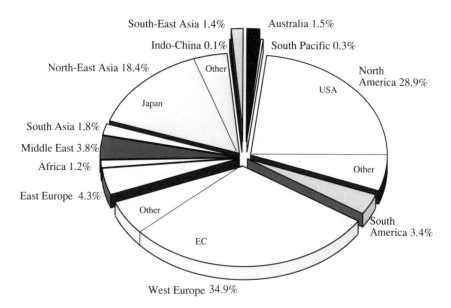

3 Australia in the World: Population and Gross Domestic Product

Regional Population (1989: 2.9 billion)

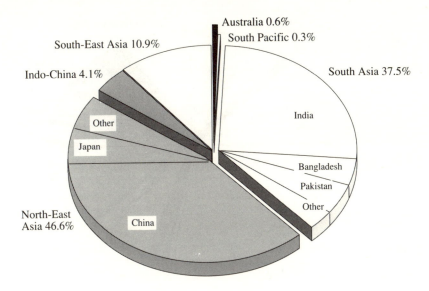

Regional GDP (1989: US$4722 billion)

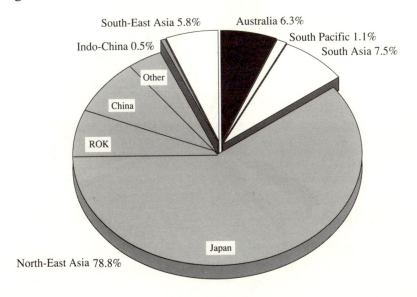

4 **Australia in the Region: Population and Gross Domestic Product**

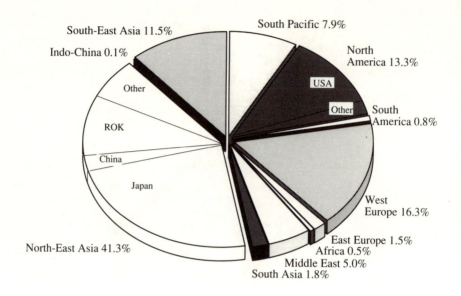

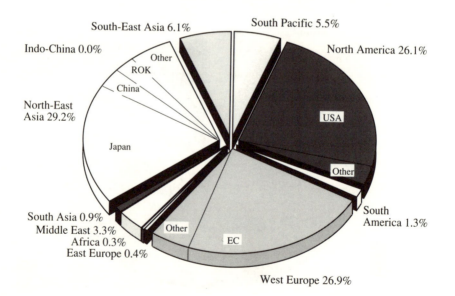

5 Australia's Trade with the World

A$m.

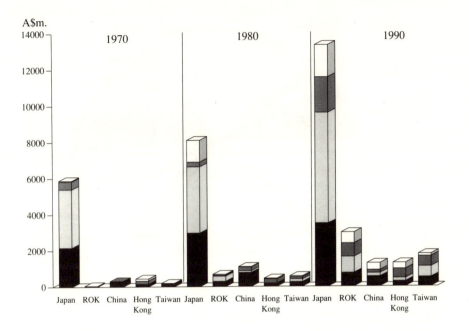

A$m.

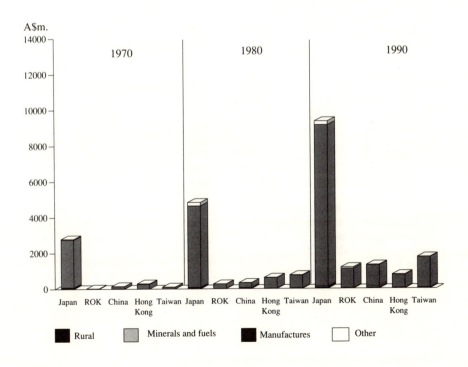

| ■ Rural | ▨ Minerals and fuels | ■ Manufactures | ☐ Other |

Distribution (1990/91)

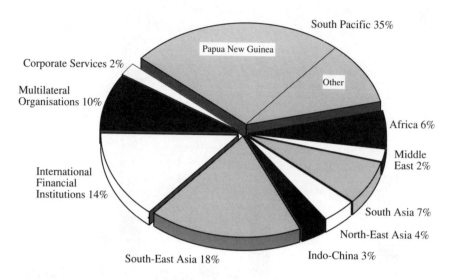

Distribution (1986/87 to 1990/91)

Recipient	1986/87	1987/88	1988/89	1989/90	1990/91
			(A$m.)		
Papua New Guinea	334.4	306.0	315.1	337.8	333.1
Other South Pacific	85.6	86.6	106.8	108.0	109.7
Total South Pacific	420.9	392.6	421.9	445.8	442.8
Africa	46.3	59.3	77.7	95.6	72.2
Middle East	14.0	24.1	21.6	22.9	22.7
South Asia	36.0	36.6	77.8	98.3	90.5
North-East Asia	30.6	43.3	39.2	48.9	45.3
Indo-China	32.6	50.6	49.1	40.0	40.5
South-East Asia	189.5	200.0	206.3	222.2	229.4
Other Countries	4.4	1.3	4.3	5.8	5.3
International Financial Institutions	88.9	84.8	180.3	65.2	181.0
Other Multilateral Organisations	93.0	104.6	92.5	97.9	112.3
Corporate Services	19.5	22.4	23.9	31.2	31.5
Total	975.6	1019.6	1194.6	1173.8	1273.5

7 **Australia's Overseas Development Assistance**

NOTES TO THE CHARTS

Definition of Regions

South Pacific: New Zealand, Papua New Guinea, Pacific Island countries
South-East Asia: Brunei, Indonesia, Malaysia, Philippines, Singapore, Thailand (ASEAN)
Indo-China: Burma, Cambodia, Laos, Vietnam
North-East Asia: People's Republic of China, Hong Kong, Japan, Democratic People's Republic of Korea, Republic of Korea, Macao, Mongolia, Taiwan
South Asia: Afghanistan, Bangladesh, Bhutan, India, Maldives, Nepal, Pakistan, Sri Lanka
Middle East: includes Algeria, Egypt, Libya, Morocco, Tunisia
Africa: all countries in continental Africa except those included in Middle East
West Europe: EC 12 (including German Democratic Republic), EFTA 6, Malta, Cyprus, Turkey
East Europe: Albania, Bulgaria, Czechoslovakia, Hungary, Poland, Romania, USSR, Yugoslavia
North America: Canada, USA, Mexico
South America: Central and South America, Caribbean

Charts 1 and 2

- As is now standard within the Australian Public Service, DFAT and AIDAB staff levels are based on the Average Staffing Levels (ASL) formula budgeted for 1990/91: i.e., one unit equals 26 fortnightly pays per annum. Within this framework *actual* staff numbers may vary from time to time.
- Austrade, as a statutory corporation, is not required to adhere to the ASL formula. Staff numbers for Austrade are therefore based on actual staff employed as of 30 June 1991.
- At the time of writing, the Board of Austrade was considering a report it had commissioned from McKinsey and Company into the Commission's organisational structure, *Organising to Deliver Export Impact* (20 December 1990). *Inter alia*, the report recommended a shift in resources from domestic to offshore operations, the implementation of which is expected to commence early in 1992. The Federal Government also announced on 12 March 1991 that, in tandem with the move of Austrade to the DFAT portfolio, the Export Finance Insurance Corporation (EFIC), which had operated as part of Austrade, would be established as a separate entity operating within the Industry, Technology and Commerce portfolio. These moves will see a significant shift in the allocation of Austrade personnel in 1991/92.
- Austrade employs local representatives in six locations not illustrated who perform on a part-time basis as required. Designated as either Trade Advisers or Trade Correspondents, they represent Austrade in Papeete, Kuching, Hokkaido, Khartoum, Bucharest and Lima.
- Australia is also represented in seven locations by Honorary Consuls not illustrated in the charts: they are Barcelona, Bogota, Boston, Kuching, Lae, Managua and Sao Paulo. At the time of writing, negotiations were under way to add another ten locations to this list.

Charts 3 and 4

- *Sources of data: International Financial Statistics*, International Monetary Fund, Washington, February 1991; *The World Bank Atlas*, The World Bank, Washington

Notes

1 THE CHANGING INTERNATIONAL ENVIRONMENT

1 Francis Fukuyama, 'The End of History?', *National Interest*, No. 16, 1989, pp. 3–18.
2 Paul Kennedy, *The Rise and Fall of the Great Powers: Economic Change and Military Conflict from 1500 to 2000*, Random House, New York, 1987, pp. 514ff.
3 United Nations World Commission for the Environment and Development, *Our Common Future*, New York, 1987.
4 Dr Kenichi Ohmae, Head of Japan Branch of McKinseys, reported in the *Age*, Melbourne, 3 March 1990.

Annotated Bibliography A good summary of the world as it appeared in early 1991 (although better on Europe, the Middle East and Africa than the Asia Pacific region) is contained in the annual survey of the International Institute for Strategic Studies, *Strategic Survey 1990–1991*, Brassey's, London, 1991. Paul Kennedy, *The Rise and Fall of the Great Powers: Economic Change and Military Conflict from 1500 to 2000*, Random House, New York, 1987, retains a good deal of its potency four years later. Useful and critical Australian comments on Kennedy's 'imperial over-stretch thesis' from David McLean, J. L. Richardson, Rodger Bell and Neville Meaney are in *Australian Journal of International Affairs*, Vol. 45, No. 1, 1991, pp. 60–97. Joseph S. Nye Jr, *Bound to Lead: The Changing Nature of American Power*, Basic Books, New York, 1990, is part of a growing American literature offering an alternative 'soft power' view of American capability. For a sharp American rebuttal of 'declinism', see Samuel P. Huntington, 'The US—Decline or Renewal?', *Foreign Affairs*, Vol. 67, No. 2, 1988/89, pp. 65–96. An early Australian comment on declining US hegemony was Andrew Mack, 'The Political Economy of Global Decline: America in the 1980s', *Australian Outlook*, Vol. 40, No. 4, 1986. While the debate about America's future persisted, the Soviet Union's decline became a reality and the success of the United States in the Gulf War brought a flood of 'triumphalist' journalism in the US. For a cautionary comment, see Owen Harries, 'Drift and Mastery, Bush-Style', *National Interest*, No. 23, 1991. Coral Bell's chapter, 'The Changing Central Balance and Australian Policy' in Bell (ed.), *Agenda for the Nineties*, Longman Cheshire, Melbourne, 1991, makes an argument for a concert of powers in the 1990s.

   Other commentaries include: Michael Howard, 'The Springtime of Nations', *Foreign Affairs*, Vol. 69, No. 1, pp. 17–32; S. B. Linder, *The Pacific Century: Economic and Political Consequences of Asian-Pacific Dynamism*, Stanford University Press, 1986; Andrew Linklater, 'New Directions in International Relations Theory', in Hugh V. Emy and Andrew Linklater (eds), *New Horizons in Politics: Essays with an Australian Focus*, Allen & Unwin, Sydney, 1990; Evan Luard, *The Globalization of Politics: The Changed Focus of Political Action in the Modern World*, New York University Press, 1990; Robert C. North, *War, Peace, Survival: Global Politics and Conceptual Synthesis*, Westview Press, Boulder, Co., 1986; John Zysman, 'U.S. Power, Trade and Technology', *International Affairs*, Vol. 67, No. 1, 1990, pp. 81–106; Owen Harries (ed.), *America's Purpose: New Visions Of U.S. Foreign Policy*, ICS Press, San Francisco, 1991.

2   THE EVOLUTION OF AN INDEPENDENT FOREIGN POLICY

[1] Parkes's speech to the Australasian Federation Conference, Melbourne, 1890. (C. M. H. Clark, *Select Documents from Australian History 1851–1900*, Angus and Robertson, Sydney, 1971, Doc. 41.)

[2] Sir Henry Parkes's speech at Wagga Wagga, 1888. (Neville Meaney, *Australia and the World: A Documentary History from the 1870s to the 1970s*, Longman Cheshire, Melbourne, 1985, Doc. 37.)

[3] Leader of the Opposition, Andrew Fisher, at an election meeting at Colac, 31 July 1914. (Ibid., Doc. 108.)

[4] In a speech on 26 April 1939, shortly after becoming Prime Minister. (Ibid., Doc. 233.)

[5] House of Representatives, *Debates*, 5 October 1938, pp. 392–7, 428–33.

[6] Menzies's announcement in Melbourne at 8.45 p.m., 3 September 1939. (Meaney, op. cit., Doc. 236.)

[7] Neville Meaney, *The Search for Security in the Pacific 1901–14*, Sydney University Press, 1976, argues that Australia did in fact come to possess the substance of a foreign policy during this period:

> Though in these years Australia was still constitutionally a dependent part of the British Empire and lacked all the forms and frills of a fully developed foreign policy, nevertheless it evolved a distinctive view of its own position in the world, a view based on its peculiar geographical position . . . it undertook diplomatic initiatives and defence programmes aimed at safeguarding the security of the nation in the Asian Pacific region. (p. viii)

But Meaney also acknowledges that 'Australia's defence and foreign policy in these early years of the Commonwealth was articulated in an indirect, almost clandestine manner'. (p. ix) It is a matter partly of judgment and partly of semantic taste as to whether a set of ill-articulated responses to particular events and pressures does in fact constitute the creation of a foreign policy: we are inclined to think not, but acknowledge that the contrary view for later periods as well as this earlier one is certainly arguable.

[8] See W. J. Hudson, *Casey*, Oxford University Press, Melbourne, 1986, pp. 134–5.

[9] Meaney, *Documentary History*, op. cit., Doc. 254.

[10] Precisely when Menzies first used the phrase is not clear, but an example is in the debate on West New Guinea in the Parliament on 29 March 1962. House of Representatives, *Debates*, pp. 1161–4.

[11] BBC broadcast reported in the *Age*, Melbourne, 15 August 1956.

[12] House of Representatives, *Debates*, 25 September 1956, p. 825.

[13] Announcement of further military commitment to ANZAM (British, New Zealand and Australian agreement for co-operation in suppressing insurgency movement in Malaya) April 1955. (Meaney, *Documentary History*, op. cit., Doc. 329.)

[14] Ibid., Doc. 402, 5 December 1972.

[15] Alan Renouf, *Malcolm Fraser and Australian Foreign Policy*, Australian Professional Publications, Sydney, 1986, p. 119.

[16] Ibid., p. 91.

Annotated Bibliography Useful general surveys of the history of Australian foreign policy include Alan Watt, *The Evolution of Australian Foreign Policy, 1938–65*, Cambridge University Press, London, 1967; T. B. Millar, *Australia in Peace and War: External Relations, 1788–1977*, Australian National University Press, Canberra, 1978; E. M. Andrews, *A History of Australian Foreign Policy: From Dependence to Independence*, Longman Cheshire, Melbourne, 1979; P. G. Edwards, *Prime Ministers and Diplomats: The Making of Australian Foreign Policy 1901–1949*, Oxford University /Australian Institute of International Affairs, Melbourne, 1983; Neville Meaney, *Australia and the World: A Documentary History from the 1870s to the 1970s*, Longman Cheshire, Melbourne, 1985, and 'Australian and the World' in Meaney (ed.), *Under New Heavens*, Heinemann, Melbourne, 1989; Joan Beaumont, *The Evolution of Australian Foreign Policy, 1901–1945*, Australian Institute of International Affairs, Victorian Branch, Occasional Paper No. 1, 1989. More specifically focused works which we have found useful include Bruce Grant, *The Crisis of Loyalty: A Study of Australian Foreign Policy*, Angus and Robertson, Sydney, 1972; Claire Clark (ed.), *Australia Foreign Policy: Towards a Reassessment*, Cassell, 1973; several works by the prolific American writer on Australian foreign policy, Professor Henry S. Albinski, including *Politics and Foreign Policy in Australia*, Duke University Press, North Carolina, 1970, *Australian External Policy under Labor*, University of Queensland Press, Brisbane, 1977, and *The Australian-American Security Relationship*, University of Queensland Press, Brisbane, 1982; Coral Bell, *Dependent Ally: A Study in Australian Foreign Policy*, Oxford University Press, Melbourne, 1988; P. Boyce and J. Angel (eds), *Independence and Alliance: Australia in World Affairs 1976–80*, Allen & Unwin, Sydney, 1983; Norman Harper, *A Great and Powerful Friend: A Study of Australia-America Relations Between 1900 and 1975*, University of Queensland Press, Brisbane, 1987; W. J. Hudson (ed.), *Australia in World Affairs 1971–1975*, Allen & Unwin, Sydney, 1980; Alan Renouf, *The Frightened Country*, Macmillan, London, 1979.

3 ELEMENTS IN FOREIGN POLICY MAKING

[1] *The Defence of Australia*, AGPS, Canberra, 1987, paras 1.10–11, 2.2.

[2] Hedley Bull in *Foreign Policy of Australia*, Proceedings of Australian Institute of Political Science Summer School, Angus and Robertson, Sydney, 1973, p. 137.

[3] The situation in Fiji is discussed further in Chapter 11.

[4] See Alan Oxley, *The Challenge of Free Trade*, Harvester Wheatsheaf, London, 1990.

[5] *Age*, Melbourne, editorial, 2 November 1990.

[6] Hans J. Morganthau, 'Another Great Debate: The National Interest of the United States', included in H. K. Jacobson (ed.), *America's Foreign Policy*, University of Michigan, 1965, p. 130.

[7] Nicolo Machiavelli, *The Prince* (1513), quoted in Lanyei and McWilliams (eds), *Crisis and Continuity in World Politics*, Random House, New York, 1966, p. 9.

Annotated Bibliography   For recent comprehensive accounts of Australian foreign policy, see Coral Bell (ed.), *Agenda for the Nineties: Australian Choices in Foreign and Defence Policy*, Longman Cheshire, Melbourne, 1991; F. A. Mediansky and A. C. Palfreeman (eds), *In Pursuit of National Interests: Australian Foreign Policy in the 1990s*, Pergamon Press, Sydney, 1988. One of the clearest examinations of a nation's capacity to pursue its interests is contained in Walter Lippmann's classic, *U.S. Foreign Policy*, Hamish Hamilton, London, 1943 (Aust. ed., 1944).

Other commentaries include: Hans J. Morganthau, 'Another Great Debate: The National Interest of the United States', *American Political Science Review*, Vol. 46, No. 4, 1952, pp. 961–88, and included in H. K. Jacobson (ed.), *America's Foreign Policy*, University of Michigan, 1965; Stanley Hoffman, 'Hans Morganthau: The Limits and Influences of "Realism"' in *From Janus to Minerva: Essays in the Theory and Practice of International Politics*, Westview Press, Boulder, Co., 1987; Thomas Cook and Malcolm Moos, 'The American Idea of International Interest', *American Political Science Review*, Vol 47, No. 1, 1953, pp. 28–44; Robert Keohane, *Neo-Realism and its Critics*, Westview Press, Boulder, Co., 1987; Richard Higgott, 'The State and International Politics: Of Territorial Boundaries and Intellectual Barriers' in Richard Higgott (ed.), *New Directions in International Relations: Australian Perspectives*, Canberra Studies in World Affairs No. 23, Department of International Relations, Australian National University, 1988, pp. 177–209.

4   THE POLITICS OF FOREIGN POLICY

[1] The expression 'second track' diplomacy is sometimes also used to describe less formal and sometimes secret ways of doing business between governments: the despatch, for example, of an envoy who is not a diplomat and who has no public personality but who is in essence a messenger from one side to another; or, again, the development of foreign policy ideas by asking academics to sound out their opposite numbers in other countries.

[2] Ministerial Statement by Senator Gareth Evans, Minister for Foreign Affairs and Trade, 6 December 1989.

[3] We would not, however, be so bold as to put the issue, in an Australian context, in quite the graphic terms of Harold Nicolson:

> I should go so far as to contend that whenever a State seeks to run two foreign policies concurrently—a temptation to which despots and Prime Ministers are specially liable—then diplomacy becomes immediately ineffective . . . (*The Evolution of the Diplomatic Method*, Constable, London, 1954, pp. 70–1.)

[4] 'Guidelines for Management of the Australian Government Presence Overseas', October 1985, reproduced in Stuart Harris, *Review of Australia's Overseas Representation*, AGPS, Canberra, 1986, p. 262.

[5] The one contentious resolution, an attack on the United States presence in Panama, was overwhelmingly defeated on the voices. A good deal of the consensus achieved was the product, as always in Labor Party affairs, of prior negotiation between Ministers and representatives of the factions—Right, Left

and Centre-Left. The language to emerge from this process is not always comfortable to a foreign minister, who is not obliged in practice to use it. In foreign affairs as elsewhere, the manner and speed with which a Labor government implements Conference resolutions is up to it: only prohibitory resolutions have a necessarily direct and immediate impact.

6 There is probably no clearer example in recent times of the Australian media uncritically embracing a 'diplomatic row' story, in circumstances crying out for closer analysis of the merits, than the reports of the Foreign Minister's visit to South Africa in June 1991. (See Sam Lipski, 'Off With Evans' Head', *Bulletin*, 2 July 1991, p. 78.)

7 Equally, there is no clearer recent example of a 'kowtow' reaction than the storm of Australian media criticism which accompanied a fence-mending visit to Malaysia by the Foreign Minister (aimed at un-freezing the situation described on p. 192) a month later in July 1991—while this book was in press. See, for example, Mark Day, 'Grotesque Grovelling', *Telegraph Mirror*, 24 July 1991; Geoffrey Barker, 'Evans Turns Values to Vices in the Attempt to Appease Mahathir', *Age*, 25 July 1991; Editorial, 'Kow-towing to Kuala Lumpur', *West Australian*, 25 July 1991. One of the few accurate and balanced accounts of the whole affair was Tony Parkinson, 'Gareth's Malaise', *Weekend Australian*, 3–4 August 1991.

Annotated Bibliography Historical background to the important role of prime ministers in Australian foreign policy is provided in P. G. Edwards, *Prime Ministers and Diplomats: The Making of Australian Foreign Policy 1901–1949*, Oxford University Press/Australian Institute of International Affairs, Melbourne, 1983. R. G. Menzies, *Afternoon Light: Some Memories of Men and Events*, Coward-McGam, New York, 1968, and Gough Whitlam, *The Whitlam Government*, Penguin, Melbourne, 1985, ch. 2, provide first-hand accounts, as do accounts by former Foreign Ministers, which include H. V. Evatt, *Foreign Policy of Australia: Speeches by H. V. Evatt (1941–44)*, Angus and Robertson, Sydney, 1945; R. G. (Lord) Casey, *Friends and Neighbours*, F. W. Cheshire, Melbourne, 1954, and *Australian Foreign Minister: The Diaries of R. G. Casey, 1951–60*, edited by T. B. Millar, London, Collins, 1972. Alan Renouf, *Malcolm Fraser and Australian Foreign Policy*, Australian Professional Publications, Sydney, 1986, is critical but appreciative. Chapters by W. J. Hudson, Hugh Smith and Nancy Viviani give a domestic perspective to foreign policy in F. A. Mediansky and A. C. Palfreeman (eds), *In Pursuit of National Interests: Australian Foreign Policy in the 1990s*, Pergamon Press, Sydney, 1988. Other commentaries include: Henry S. Albinski, 'Bipartisanship and Australian Foreign Policy', *Asian Pacific Review*, Vol. 2, 1986, pp. 2–16; A. Bergin, 'Pressure Groups and Australian Foreign Policy', *Dyason House Papers*, Vol, 9, No. 3, 1983, pp. 2–16; 'The Foreign Policy Process' in P. J. Boyce and J. R. Angel (eds), *Independence and Alliance: Australia in World Affairs 1976–80*, Allen & Unwin, Sydney, 1983; P. J. Boyce, 'The Influence of the United States on the Domestic Debate in Australia', *Australian Outlook*, Vol. 38, No. 3, 1984, pp. 159–62. An early critique of the Australian media's approach to foreign affairs is W. Macmahon Ball (ed.), *Press, Radio and World Affairs: Australia's Outlook*, Melbourne University Press, 1938. For a foreign correspondent's perspective, see Bruce Grant, 'Foreign Affairs and the Australian Press', Roy Milne Memorial Lecture for the Australian Institute of International Affairs, Sydney, 1969. Henry Mayer, *The Press in Australia*, Lansdowne Press, Melbourne, 1964, remains the most substantial work on the Australian press but does not deal particularly with international affairs. For a discussion of Australian reporting of the Asia Pacific region, see contributions by Dominic Nagle, Graeme Dobell, Sean Dorney, Julianne Schultz and Tom Krause in Annmaree O'Keeffe (ed.), *The Australian Media's Treatment of the Developing World*, Australian

International Development Assistance Bureau/AGPS, Canberra, 1989; Rodney Tiffen, 'The Australian Media and Australian–ASEAN Relations' in A. Broinowski (ed.), *ASEAN into the 1990s*, Macmillan, London, 1990, pp. 200–18; Errol Hodge, 'The Impact of the ABC on Australian-Indonesian Relations since Timor', *Australian Journal of International Affairs*, Vol. 45, No. 1, 1991.

5   THE PRACTICE OF FOREIGN POLICY

[1] Stuart Harris, *Review of Australia's Overseas Representation*, AGPS, Canberra, 1986, pp. xv–xvi.

[2] Ibid., p. xvi.

[3] The other Australian intelligence bodies, the Australian Security Intelligence Organisation (ASIO), the Defence Intelligence Organisation (DIO) and the Office of National Assessments (ONA) are responsible, respectively, to the Attorney-General, the Minister for Defence and the Prime Minister. The Australian intelligence community has been the subject of two major enquiries in 1974–77 and 1983–84 by Mr Justice R. M. Hope, resulting in a series of both published and unpublished reports (and subsequent organisational changes). See *Royal Commission on Intelligence and Security*, Government Printer, Canberra, 1978; *Royal Commission on Security and Intelligence Agencies*, AGPS, Canberra, 1985.

[4] See Austrade Media Release, 'Austrade Announces Major Re-allocation of International Resources', Sydney, 30 May 1991.

[5] Harris, op. cit., p. 19.

[6] Ibid., p. 20.

[7] Rawdon Dalrymple, The Australian Government's Role in the Relationship with Japan, unpublished address to the Australian Chamber of Commerce, Tokyo, 31 January 1991.

[8] House of Representatives, *Debates*, 13 March 1946, p. 192.

[9] Ross Garnaut, *Australia and the Northeast Asian Ascendancy*, AGPS, Canberra, 1989, Ch. 16.

Annotated Bibliography   The most substantial work available is Stuart Harris's comprehensive and thoughtful study of the Australian diplomatic service, *Review of Australia's Overseas Representation*, AGPS, Canberra, 1986. For an account of the Australian service by a diplomat and former 'permanent head', see Alan Watt, 'The Australian Diplomatic Service 1935–1965' in Gordon Greenwood and Norman Harper (eds), *Australia in World Affairs 1961–1965*, Australian Institute of International Affairs/F. W. Cheshire, Melbourne, 1968, pp. 134–81. Paul Hasluck, *Diplomatic Witness: Australian Foreign Affairs 1941–1947*, Melbourne University Press, 1980, offers insights from a departmental official who later became Minister. First-hand accounts of Australian foreign policy in action include Malcolm Booker, *The Last Domino*, Collins, Sydney, 1976; Walter Crocker, *Australian Ambassador: International Relations at First Hand*, Melbourne University Press, Melbourne, 1971; Bruce Grant, *Gods and Politicians*, Penguin, Melbourne, 1984; Alan Renouf, *The Champagne Trail: Experiences of a Diplomat*, Sun Books, Melbourne, 1980. Hugh Collins's theme paper is worth careful attention in *Australian Diplomacy: Challenges and Options for the Department of Foreign Affairs*, Occasional Paper No. 5, Australian Institute of International Affairs, Canberra, 1986.

Other commentaries include: Hugh Collins, 'The Coombs Report: Bureaucracy, Diplomacy and Australian Foreign Policy' *Australian Outlook*, Vol. 30, No. 3, 1976, pp. 387–413; Di Yerbury and Bronwyn Duncan on 'Cultural Diplomacy' and Wang

Gungwu on 'Cultural Interpreters' in *Australian Diplomacy* op. cit.; Ross Garnaut, *Australia and the Northeast Asian Ascendancy*, AGPS, Canberra, 1989, Ch. 16; *Patronage, Power and the Muse: An Inquiry into Commonwealth Assistance for the Arts*, Report of the House of Representatives Standing Committee on Expenditure, AGPS, Canberra, 1986; 'Australian Perceptions of Asia' in *Australia's Cultural History*, No. 9, University of New South Wales, 1990.

6 THE SEARCH FOR GLOBAL SECURITY

[1] The functions of these facilities were described in these terms in a Parliamentary Statement by Prime Minister Hawke on 22 November 1988 (House of Representatives, *Debates*, pp. 2937–9), and in a public statement on the same day by Defence Minister Kim Beazley; both spelt out new arrangements for the facilities, upgrading Australia's role in their day-to-day operation. On 12 March 1990, the Prime Minister announced negotiations for Australia to take over and wholly operate the North West Cape Naval Communications Station. On 17 October, the Minister for Defence Science and Personnel, Gordon Bilney, advised in answer to a parliamentary question that 'The handover will be phased and may extend over a period as long as seven years. The Minister for Defence expects that the arrangements will be finalised by the time of the next Ausmin talks, which are planned to be held in Australia next year'. (House of Representatives, *Debates*, 17 October 1990, p. 3057.)

[2] The most substantial contributions to that debate have been Desmond Ball's *A Suitable Piece of Real Estate: American Installations in Australia*, Hale & Iremonger, Sydney, 1980; *A Base for Debate: The US Satellite Station at Nurrungar*, Allen & Unwin, Sydney, 1987; *Pine Gap*, Allen & Unwin, Sydney, 1988.

[3] November 1988 Statement, op. cit.

[4] An unofficial account of this co-operation is Jeffrey T. Richelson and Desmond Ball, *The Ties that Bind: Intelligence Co-operation between the UKUSA Countries*, Allen & Unwin, Sydney, 1985.

[5] *Common Security: A Program for Disarmament*, Report of the Independent Commission on Disarmament and Security Issues under the Chairmanship of Olof Palme, Pan Books, London, 1982.

[6] Now thirty-nine, since Germany re-united.

[7] 'Fullscope' safeguards involve a commitment by suppliers to require, and non-nuclear-weapons states to accept, International Atomic Energy Agency (IAEA) safeguards on all existing and future nuclear activities and on material and technology, which safeguards in turn involve inspection and verification arrangements to ensure effective surveillance, containment and materials accountability.

[8] In what follows, we have drawn extensively on some excellent reporting and analysis from Dr Peter Wilenski, Australia's Permanent Representative to the United Nations in New York from 1989.

Annotated Bibliography The rapidity of events after 1989 made commentary on international security issues more ephemeral than usual. Events were ahead of debate. Publications of the International Institute for Strategic Studies, London, provided a handy running commentary in writing this chapter. *America's Role in a Changing World*, Adelphi Papers 256 and 257, Brassey's, London, 1990, are a summary of the IISS's annual conference held in September 1990. They include several non-American (including Soviet) contributions. *Survival*, Vol. 32, No. 2, 1990, is devoted to 'The Changing World Order'; No. 4 to 'Arms Control and the New

Strategic Environment'; and Vol. 33, No. 3, 1991, to 'The Gulf War'. Good Australian references are: Desmond Ball and Cathy Downes (eds), *Security and Defence: Pacific and Global Perspectives*, Allen & Unwin, Sydney, 1990; Jeffrey T. Richelson and Desmond Ball, *The Ties that Bind: Intelligence Co-operation between the UKUSA Countries: The United Kingdom, the United States of America, Canada, Australian and New Zealand*, 2nd edition, Allen & Unwin, Sydney, 1990; Joint Committee on Foreign Affairs and Defence, Parliament of Australia, *Disarmament and Arms Control in the Nuclear Age*, AGPS, Canberra, 1984; Department of Foreign Affairs, *An A to Z of Australian Disarmament and Arms Control Initiatives and Activities*, AGPS, Canberra, 1987; and four publications of the Peace Research Centre, Research School of Pacific Studies, Australian National University, Canberra: Richard Butler, *Australia and Disarmament*, Working Paper No. 64, 1989; Ron Huisken, *Strategic Defence: An Australian Perspective*, Working Paper No. 58, 1989; Peter Dunn, *Australian Diplomatic and Technical Inputs into the Control of Chemical Weapons*, Working Paper No. 65, 1989; Michael Hamel-Green, *The South Pacific Nuclear Free Zone Treaty: A Critical Assessment*, 1990. See also Jennifer Tuckman Mathews, 'Redefining Security', *Foreign Affairs*, Spring 1989; Theodore C. Sorensen, 'Rethinking National Security', *Foreign Affairs*, Summer 1990.

7 SECURITY IN THE ASIA PACIFIC REGION

[1] *The Defence of Australia*, AGPS, Canberra, 1987.

[2] *Australia's Regional Security*, Ministerial Statement by Senator Gareth Evans, Minister for Foreign Affairs and Trade, 6 December 1989.

[3] Paul Dibb, *A Review of Australia's Defence Capabilities: Report to the Minister for Defence*, AGPS, Canberra, 1986.

[4] House of Representatives, *Debates*, 21 August, 1990, p. 1191.

[5] Carl Ford, Deputy Assistant Secretary of Defence for International Security Affairs, speech to National Defence University Symposium, Honolulu, 2 March 1991.

[6] Greg Fry (ed.), *Australia's Regional Security*, Allen & Unwin, Sydney, 1991, comprises symposium papers which constitute an excellent and up-to-date treatment of all the issues.

[7] The full text of the relevant paragraph in the Ministerial Statement, op. cit., is as follows:

> 90. The use of military force may conceivably be appropriate, however, in unusual and extreme circumstances. While every situation needs to be treated on a case-by-case basis, there are certain cumulative criteria which suggest themselves, viz: the agreement of the recognised domestic authorities (except possibly in cases where an unfriendly government is supporting actions immediately detrimental to Australian nationals, e.g. hostage-taking); a manifestly direct threat to major Australian security interests; a finite time frame for the military operation; a clear and achievable operational objective; and consultation with, and if possible the co-operation and participation of, other states in the region.

For Senator Evans's response to criticisms, both of the over-reach and under-reach of this statement, see Fry, op. cit., pp. 148–9.

[8] R. J. L. Hawke, 'Australian Security in Asia', Inaugural Asia Lecture, Asia-Australia Institute, Sydney, 24 May 1991.

[9] See, for example, 'Security in Letter and Spirit', *Australian Financial Review*, 2 May 1991, p. 12.

10 Clear evidence of the momentum rapidly developing in favour of a dialogue process was the Manila Seminar on 'ASEAN and the Asia-Pacific Region: Prospects for Security Cooperation in the 1990s', hosted by the Philippines Government on 5–7 June 1991 and attended by officials and academics from fourteen countries including the United States, Soviet Union, Japan and Australia. Although 'informal' in character, attended by participants in their personal capacities and designed more to stimulate further discussion than to produce specific outcomes, this seminar—the first in a planned regional series—was described by a number of participants as a watershed in the dialogue process.

Annotated Bibliography   The most up-to-date source, from Australia's point of view, is Greg Fry (ed.), *Australia's Regional Security*, Allen & Unwin, Sydney, 1991; it includes the full text of the Ministerial Statement, critical comments by twelve specialists and a response to their comments by Senator Evans. A forward-looking analysis is provided by Peter Polomka 'Towards a "Pacific House"', *Survival*, Vol. 33, No. 2, 1991. For a general analysis, see Bruce Grant, *What Kind of Country?*, Penguin, Melbourne, 1988, pp. 68–85; Ross Babbage, *A Coast Too Long: Defending Australia Beyond the 1990s*, Allen & Unwin, Sydney, 1990; Henry Albinski, *The Australia-American Security Relationship: A Regional and International Perspective*, University of Queensland Press, Brisbane, 1982. For specific insights: Andrew Mack and Paul Keal (eds), *Security and Arms Control in the North Pacific*, Allen & Unwin, Sydney, 1988; Ross Babbage (ed.), *The Soviets in the Pacific in the 1990s*, Brassey's, Sydney, 1989; Gary Klintworth, 'China's Security', Harold Crouch 'Indonesia and the Security of Australia and Papua New Guinea' and David Hegarty, 'The South Pacific and Papua New Guinea', in Desmond Ball and Cathy Downes (eds), *Security and Defence: Pacific and Global Perspectives*, Allen & Unwin, Sydney, 1990.
  Other commentaries include: Ross Babbage 'Change in the North Pacific: Implications for Australia's Security', *Australian Outlook*, Vol. 43, No. 3, 1989, pp. 1–17; Graeme Cheeseman, 'Australia's Defence: White Paper in the Red', *Australian Journal of International Affairs*, Vol. 44, No. 2, 1990; Muthiah Alagappa, 'The Dynamics of International Security in Southeast Asia; Change and Continuity', *Australian Journal of International Affairs*, Vol. 45, No. 1, 1991, pp. 1–37; Joint Committee on Foreign Affairs, Defence and Trade, *Australia's Relations with the South Pacific*, AGPS, Canberra, 1989; David Hegarty and Peter Polomka (eds), *The Security of Oceania in the 1990s*, Volume 1, *Views from the Region*, and Volume 2, *Managing Change*, Canberra Papers on Strategy and Defence Nos 60 and 68, Strategic and Defence Studies Centre, Australian National University, Canberra, 1989; R. J. May and Matthew Spriggs (eds), *The Bouganville Crisis*, Monograph No. 12, Department of Political and Social Change, Australian National University, Canberra, 1991.

8 TRADE AND INVESTMENT IMPERATIVES

1 Daniel Bell, quoted by Samuel P. Huntington in *Survival*, Vol. 33, No. 1, 1991.
2 World Bank, *World Development Report 1991*, Oxford University Press, 1991, p. 205. Another measure, however, the Human Development Index, established by the United Nations Development Programme to take account not only of income but also of factors such as life expectancy and education, ranks Australia behind only six other countries, and ahead of the United States and Germany. (*Human Development Report 1990*, Oxford University Press, 1990, p. 129.)
3 *Australian Exports: Performance, Obstacles and Issues of Assistance*, Report of the

Committee for Review of Export Market Development Assistance (Hughes Committee Report), July 1989, p. xix.

4 *Building a Competitive Australia*, statements by Prime Minister Bob Hawke, Treasurer Paul Keating and Industry Minister John Button, 12 March 1991, AGPS, Canberra, 1991.

5 The nominal rate of assistance on the output of an industry measures the effect not only of tariffs on outputs but also of input quotas and bounties. The effective rate of assistance measures net assistance to value-added by taking account not only of output assistance but also of the penalties (e.g. from tariffs) and benefits (e.g. from import subsidies) on government intervention in the prices paid by the industry for its inputs.

6 Hughes Committee Report, op. cit., p. xviii.

7 The most up-to-date, and helpful, account of current issues in global trade policy generally, and the Uruguay Round in particular, is Alan Oxley, *The Challenge of Free Trade*, Harvester Wheatsheaf, London, 1990.

8 See Ross Garnaut, *Australia and the Northeast Asian Ascendancy*, AGPS, Canberra, 1989, p. 5.

9 See Summary Statement by the Chairman, Senator Gareth Evans, APEC Ministerial-Level Meeting, Canberra, 7 November 1989.

Annotated Bibliography For Australian perspectives on the international economic system, a good start is Stuart Harris, 'Economic Change in the International System: Implications for Australia's Prospects' in Carol Bell (ed.), *Agenda for the Nineties: Australian Choices in Foreign and Defence Policy*, Longman Cheshire, Melbourne, 1991, pp. 24–45. For a pungent, internationalist approach by an Australian businessman, see Arvi Parbo in *Company Director*, April 1991, pp. 17–21. See also Richard Higgott, *The Evolving World Economy: Some Alternative Questions for Australia*, Canberra Papers on Strategy and Defence No. 51, Strategic and Defence Centre, Australian National University, Canberra, 1989. A wide range of critics of deregulation and free trade is presented in *Quadrant*, May 1991. Alan Oxley, *The Challenge of Free Trade*, Harvester Wheatsheaf, London, 1990, is excellent on the Uruguay Round negotiations. See also 'Australia and Northeast Asia: The Garnaut Report', a collection of articles in *Australian Journal of International Affairs*, Vol 44, No. 1, 1990, pp. 1–51. For some international perspectives, the most probing and provocative is Robert B. Reich, *The Work of Nations: Preparing Ourselves for 21st Century Capitalism*, Knopf, New York, 1991. See also M. K. Hawes, 'Assessing the World Economy: The Rise and Fall of Bretton Woods' in D. G. Haglund and M. K. Hawes, *World Politics: Power, Interdependence and Dependence*, Harcourt Brace Jovanovich, Toronto, 1990, Chs 3, 5; Jagish Bhagwati, *Protectionism*, MIT Press, Cambridge, Mass., 1988, Ch. 1, and 'Multilateralism at Risk: The GATT is Dead: Long Live the GATT', *World Economy*, Vol. 13, No. 2, 1990, pp. 149–69; R. Gilpin, *The Political Economy of International Relations*, Princeton University Press, Princeton, NY, 1987, Chs 2, 3; Peter Drucker, 'The Changed World Economy', *Foreign Affairs*, Vol. 64, 1986; Samuel P. Huntington, 'The US—Decline or Renewal? *Foreign Affairs*, Vol. 67, No. 2, 1988/89. The growing Australian literature on Asia Pacific trade and economic co-operation includes: Ross Garnaut, *Australia and the Northeast Asian Ascendancy*, AGPS, Canberra, 1989; Peter Drysdale, 'Australia's Asia-Pacific Economic Diplomacy', *Current Affairs Bulletin*, Vol. 66, No. 10, 1990, pp. 14–21; Peter Drysdale, *International Economic Pluralism: Economic Policy in East Asia and the Pacific*, Allen & Unwin, Sydney, with the Australia-Japan Research Centre, Australian National University, Canberra, 1988; Gavan McCormack (ed.), *Bonsai Australia Banzai*, Pluto Press, Sydney, 1991; Robin Burnett 'Regional Trading Groupings: Legal Issues for Australia in the Pacific Region', *Australian Journal of*

International Affairs, Vol. 44, No. 1, 1990, pp. 63–82. Some other perspectives: Robert A. Scalapino, Seizaburo Sato, Jusuf Wanandi and Sung-joo Han (eds), *Pacific Asian Economic Policies and Regional Interdependence*, Institute of East Asian Studies, University of California, Berkeley, 1988; Steve Chan, *East Asian Dynamism: Growth, Order and Security in the Pacific Region*, Westview Press, Boulder, Co., 1990; Bernard K. Gordon, *Politics and Protectionism in the Pacific*, Adelphi Paper 228, Brassey's, London, 1988.

9   DEVELOPMENT ASSISTANCE RESPONSIBILITIES

[1] R. Gordon Jackson, *Report of the Committee to Review the Australian Overseas Aid Program*, AGPS, Canberra, March 1984.

[2] This was the view expressed by the Joint Committee of Foreign Affairs, Defence and Trade in their most recent review of Australia's aid program, *A Review of the Australian International Development Assistance Bureau*, tabled in Parliament on 9 March 1989. The Government response was tabled on 20 December 1989.

Annotated Bibliography   The Jackson Report, op. cit., is a useful starting point. Four articles on the Jackson Report are in *Australian Outlook*, Vol. 39, No. 1, 1985. See also Joint Committee on Foreign Affairs, Defence and Trade, *A Review of the Australian International Development Assistance Bureau*, AGPS, Canberra, 1989; Gareth Evans in *Australian Foreign Affairs and Trade, the Monthly Record*, Vol. 61, No. 8, pp. 495–502, 1990; Philip Eldrige, Dean Forbes and Doug Porter (eds), *Australian Overseas Aid: Future Directions*, Croom Helm, Sydney, 1986; Derek E. Tribe, *Doing Well by Doing Good*, Pluto Press/Crawford Foundation for International Agriculture Research, Sydney, 1991. For North-South issues: Ben Jackson, *Poverty and the Planet: A Question of Survival*, Penguin, 1990; Paul Harrison, *Inside the Third World*, rev. 2nd edition, Penguin, 1990; Doug Porter, Bryant Allen and Gaye Thompson, *Development in Practice: Paved with Good Intentions*, Routledge, New York, 1991; Stephen Krasner, *Structural Conflict: The Third World Against Global Liberalism*, University of California, Berkeley, 1985; S. Gill and D. Law, 'North-South Relations' in *The Global Political Economy*, Harvester Wheatsheaf, New York, 1988. The UN's 1991 Human Development Report takes up several current issues in what is described as a challenge to the World Bank's dominance of the international debate about development; see Peter McCawley, 'A Challenge to the World Bank', *Backgrounder*, Department of Foreign Affairs and Trade, Canberra, Vol. 2, No. 8, 1991.

10   THE NEW INTERNATIONAL AGENDA

[1] *A Review of the Australian International Development Assistance Bureau and Australia's Overseas Aid Program*, Canberra, 1989, esp. pp. 101–4, 139; *Australia's Relations with the South Pacific*, Canberra, 1989, esp. pp. 215–17.

[2] *Report of the World Commission on Environment and Development* (Brundtland Report), Oxford University Press, 1990, p. 8.

Annotated Bibliography   For a rounded discussion of human rights and foreign policy, see R. J. Vincent, *Human Rights and International Relations*, Cambridge University Press, 1986; R. J. Vincent, 'Human Rights in Foreign Policy', *Australian Outlook*, Vol. 36, No. 3, 1982, pp. 1–5. A legal context is provided by Paul Sieghart,

The Lawful Rights of Mankind: An Introduction to the International Legal Code of Human Rights, Oxford University Press, 1985. The philosophical issues are explored by Michael Smith, 'Ethics and Intervention', *Ethics and International Affairs*, Vol. 3, 1989; C. Melakopides, 'Ethics and International Relations' in D. G. Haglund and M. K. Hawes (eds), *World Politics: Power, Interdependence and Dependence*, Harcourt Brace Jovanovich, Toronto, 1990; Stanley Hoffman, 'Ethics and International Affairs' in *Duties Beyond Borders: On the Limits of Ethical International Politics*, Syracuse University Press, 1981. For recent official Australian statements, see speech by the former Minister for Foreign Affairs, Bill Hayden, to the Australian Parliamentary Group of Amnesty International, 28 May 1987, *Australian Foreign Affairs Record*, Vol. 58, No. 5, 1987, pp. 240–3; Dr Stuart Harris, former Secretary of the Department of Foreign Affairs and Trade, address to H. V. Evatt Memorial Foundation, 14 November 1987, *Australian Foreign Affairs Record*, Vol. 58, No. 5, 1987, pp. 569–75. A critical comment on Australia's performance is made by Gough Whitlam, 'Australia and the UN Commission on Human Rights', *Australian Journal of International Affairs*, Vol. 45, No. 1, 1991, pp. 51–9. The best general source on the environment as an issue is World Commission on Environment and the Future, *Our Common Future*, Oxford University Press, 1987; but for a more recent analysis see Alan Burnett, 'Defence of the Environment: The New Issue in International Relations' in Coral Bell (ed.), *Agenda for the Nineties: Australian Choices in Foreign and Defence Policy*, Longman Cheshire, London, 1991, pp. 46–70. Other commentaries include: Robert Goodin, 'International Ethics and the Environmental Crisis', *Ethics and International Affairs*, Vol. 4, 1990; Richard Elliot Benedick, *Ozone Diplomacy: New Directions in Safeguarding the Planet*, Harvard University Press, Cambridge, 1990; R. A. Herr, H. R. Hall and M. G. Haward (eds), *Antarctica's Future: Continuity or Change?*, Australian Institute of International Affairs, Canberra, 1990. Robert Boardman, *Global Regimes and Nation-States: Environmental Issues in Australian Politics*, Carleton University Press, Ottawa, 1990, provides a scholarly background to Australia's emergence as an innovator in environmental politics.

11   THE SOUTH PACIFIC

[1] Compare John Ravenhill (ed.), *No Longer an American Lake?*, Allen & Unwin, Sydney, 1989.

[2] Senator Gareth Evans, 'Australia in the South Pacific', address to the Foreign Correspondents Association, Sydney, 23 September 1988. The policy theme was further spelt out in the Ministerial Statement on *Australia's Regional Security* on 6 December 1989, paras 177–80.

[3] Quoted in C. M. H. Clark, *A History of Australia*, Melbourne University Press, 1981, Vol. V, p. 72.

[4] Ibid., p. 36.

[5] *Australia's Regional Security*, op. cit.

[6] Senator Gareth Evans, Senate, *Debates*, 6 December 1989, p. 4024.

[7] For an evocative account of the 'time of the master', see Hank Nelson, *Taim Bilong Masta: The Australian Involvement with Papua New Guinea*, ABC, Sydney, 1982 and the ABC Radio Series produced by Tim Bowden on which this book was based.

[8] Joint Statement by Prime Ministers Malcolm Fraser and Michael Somare on the Defence Relationship between Papua New Guinea and Australia, 11 February 1977.

[9] 'The Parties will consult together whenever in the opinion of any of them the territorial integrity, political independence or security of any of the Parties is

threatened in the Pacific.' (Article III) 'Each Party recognises that an armed attack in the Pacific Area on any of the Parties would be dangerous to its own peace and safety and would act to meet the common danger in accordance with its constitutional processes.' (Article IV) (ANZUS Treaty, 1951, in Neville Meaney, *Australia and the World: A Documentary History from the 1870s to the 1970s*, Longman Cheshire, Melbourne, 1985, Doc. 312.)

10 'The Ministers also declared, in relation to the external defence of Malaysia and Singapore, that in the event of any form of armed attack externally organised or supported, or the threat of such attack against Malaysia or Singapore, their Governments would immediately consult together for the purpose of deciding what measures should be taken jointly or separately in relation to such attack or threat.' (Communique of Five Power Ministers' Meeting, London, 16 April 1971.)

11 See John Piper 'Pacific Challenges: The Islands and New Zealand', in Coral Bell (ed.), *Agenda for the Nineties*, Longman Cheshire, Melbourne, 1991, p. 214.

12 See, for example, Rowan Callick, 'Many Headaches in Way of Fiji Dream', *Australian Financial Review*, 5 April 1991.

Annotated Bibliography   For general background, the best source is the Report of the Joint Committee on Foreign Affairs, Defence and Trade of the Parliament, *Australia's Relations with the South Pacific*, AGPS, Canberra, March 1989. A good set of papers, even if dated, is contained in Robert Kisle and Richard Herr, (eds), *The Pacific Islands in the Year 2000*, University of Hawaii/Pacific Islands Development Program, 1985. See also papers from the H. V. Evatt Memorial Foundation conference on Australia and the Pacific, 18–19 October 1986, published by the Foundation, Sydney, 1986. John Piper's chapter, 'Pacific Challenges: The Islands and New Zealand', is a balanced, up-to-date account in Coral Bell (ed.), *Agenda for the Nineties*, Longman Cheshire, Melbourne, 1991. Greg Fry's introduction and chapter, ' "Constructive Commitment" with South Pacific: Monroe Doctrine or New "Partnership"?', in Fry (ed.), *Australia's Regional Security*, Allen & Unwin, Sydney, 1991, offer a critical assessment of the Ministerial Statement on regional security of December 1989. Two articles by Rowan Callick in *Australian Society* (May and August 1989) provide a regional perspective. Other commentaries include: John Ravenhill (ed.), *No Longer an American Lake ?*, Allen & Unwin, Sydney, 1989; P. Polomka and D. Hegarty (eds), *The Security of Oceania in the 1990s, Volume 1, Views from the Region*, Canberra Papers on Strategy and Defence, No. 60, Strategic and Defence Studies Centre, Australian National University, Canberra, 1989; R. A. Herr, 'Regionalism, Strategic Denial and South Pacific Security', *Journal of Pacific History*, Vol. 23, No. 3, 1986; F. Mediansky, 'The Security Outlook in the Southwest Pacific', *Australian Quarterly*, Vol. 59, Nos 3, 4, 1987; Senator John Button, 'Australia's Partnership in the South Pacific: Trade Opportunities and Constraints in the 1990s', *Social Alternatives*, Vol. 8, No. 2, 1989; D. Hegarty, 'Small State Security in the South Pacific', and 'Stability and Turbulence in South Pacific Politics', Working Papers Nos 126 and 185, Strategic and Defence Centre, Research School of Pacific Studies, Australian National University, Canberra, 1989 and Owen Harries, *Strategy and the Southwest Pacific: An Australian Perspective*, Pacific Security Research Institute, Sydney, 1989. New Zealand background and perspective is given in *New Zealand Foreign Affairs Review*, Vol. 37, Nos 2, 3, 1987 and Vol. 38, Nos 1–4, 1988; *New Zealand External Relations Review*, Vol. 39, Nos 1–4, 1989; Report of the South Pacific Policy Review Group, 'Towards a Pacific Island Community', Wellington, May 1990. See also H. Albinski, *ANZUS: The U.S. and Pacific Security*, University Press of America/Asia Society, New York, 1987; D. Ball (ed.), *The Anzac Connection*, Allen & Unwin, Sydney, 1985 and A. Burnett, *The Anzus Triangle*, Strategic and

Defence Studies Centre, Australian National University, Canberra, 1988; Coral Bell, 'The ANZUS Alliance: The Case For', and Gary Brown, 'The ANZUS Alliance: The Case Against', in Des Ball and Cathy Downes (eds), *Security and Defence: Pacific and Global Perspectives*, Allen & Unwin, Sydney, 1990. On Papua New Guinea, the World Bank Country Report, *PNG: Policies and Prospects for Sustained and Broad-based Growth*, Washington DC, 1988, is comprehensive. A sharp analysis is provided by Utula Samana, 'The Choice for PNG: Self Reliance or Mutual Destruction', *Social Alternatives*, Vol. 8, No. 2, 1989. A balance is given in David Anderson (ed.), *The PNG–Australia Relationship: Problems and Prospects*, Pacific Security Research Institute, Sydney, 1990. See also Peter Hastings, 'Australia, Indonesia, Papua New Guinea and the South West Pacific' in *Proceedings of the Third Australia–Indonesia Conference, Griffith University*, Research Paper No. 31, Centre for the Study of Australian–Asian Relations, July 1984; Peter Polomka (ed.), *Bougainville: Perspectives on a Crisis*, Canberra Paper No. 66, Strategic and Defence Centre, Research School of Pacific Studies, Australian National University, 1990; R. J. May and Matthew Spriggs (eds), *The Bougainville Crisis*, Monograph No. 12, Department of Political and Social Change, Australian National University, 1991.

12   SOUTH-EAST ASIA

[1] 'Comprehensive engagement' was first used to describe Australia's policy approach towards South-East Asia (in juxtaposition with 'constructive commitment' in the South Pacific) in the Ministerial Statement by Senator Gareth Evans, *Australia's Regional Security*, 6 December 1989, paras 173–6.

[2] Ibid., para. 176.

[3] Bangkok Declaration 1967. (See Alison Broinowski (ed.), *ASEAN into the 1990s*, Macmillan, London, 1990, esp. chs 1, 4.

[4] Op. cit., esp. ch. 3.

[5] 'Australia's Relations with Indonesia', speech to the Australian–Indonesian Business Co-operation Committee, Bali, 24 October 1988.

[6] The change in name from Burma to Myanmar (and from Rangoon to Yangon) was decreed by the State Law and Order Restoration Council in June 1989. Although normal practice is to accept the English language version of the name a country gives to itself, occasionally some variations are justified. Here the new name has not commanded universal acceptance in international usage, or by Burmese expatriates, or by the opposition NLD. For these reasons the Australian Government uses the new names only in formal communications with the SLORC Government, and for other purposes reverts to the more familiar usage: see Senator Gareth Evans, Senate, *Debates*, 13 November 1990, p. 3975.

[7] See Senator Gareth Evans, Senate *Debates*, 16 May 1991, pp. 3519–20.

Annotated Bibliography   A good general history is Milton Osborne, *South-East Asia: An Illustrated Introductory History*, Allen & Unwin, Sydney, 1990. For current issues, the *Far Eastern Economic Review*'s annual *Year Book*, published by Review Publishing Co., Hong Kong, can be a useful reference. For an ASEAN overview, Alison Broinowski (ed.), *Asean into the 1990s*, Macmillan, Sydney, 1990; Michael Leifer, *ASEAN and the Security of South-East Asia*, Routledge, London, 1988; Leszek Buszynski, 'ASEAN and its Orbits' in Coral Bell (ed.), *Agenda for the Nineties: Australian Choices in Foreign and Defence Policy*, Longman Cheshire, Melbourne, 1991. See also David Jenkins, 'The South-east Asia Dimension' and Andrew MacIntyre, ' "Comprehensive engagement" and Australia's Security Interests in South-east

Asia' in Greg Fry (ed.), *Australia's Regional Security*, Allen & Unwin, Sydney, 1991; Harold Crouch, 'Coups, Democracy and Human Rights: Australia and her Neighbours', in R. J. May and William J. O'Malley (eds), *Observing Change in Asia: Essays in Honour of J. A. C. Mackie*, Crawford House, Bathurst, 1989. Two issues of *Asian Studies Review*, No. 2, 1990, pp. 101–3 and No. 3, 1991, pp. 1–42, present a range of current opinions on Australian business in Asia. See also Anne Booth 'The Economic Development of South-East Asia', Centre for South-East Asian Studies, Monash University, Working Paper No. 63, 1990. Australian scholarly writing on Indonesia is prolific. Topical commentaries are included in Desmond Ball and Helen Wilson (eds), *Strange Neighbours: The Australia–Indonesia Relationship*, Allen & Unwin, Sydney, 1991; Hal Hill and Terry Hull (eds), *Indonesian Assessment 1990: Proceedings of the Indonesia Update Conference, October 1990*, Department of Political and Social Change, Australian National University, 1990. For the interaction of government and business, see Richard Robison, *Indonesia: The Rise of Capital*, Allen & Unwin, Sydney, 1986; Andrew MacIntyre, *Business and Politics in Indonesia*, Allen & Unwin, Sydney, 1991. Critical studies of particular issues include Margaret George, *Australia and the Indonesian Revolution*, Melbourne University Press, 1980 (which canvasses some of the reasons, including Australian ambiguity on the West New Guinea question, which may have contributed to relations drifting apart from the late 1940s); R. J. May (ed.), *Between Two Nations: The Indonesia–Papua New Guinea Border and West Papua Nationalism*, Robert Brown and Assoc., Bathurst, 1986; Robin Osborne, *Indonesia's Secret War: The Guerrilla Struggle in Irian Jaya*, Allen & Unwin, Sydney, 1991; James Dunn, *Timor: A People Betrayed*, Jacaranda, Queensland, 1983.

13   INDO-CHINA

[1] *A Strategic Basis of Australian Defence Policy*, 18 December 1952, quoted in Frank Frost, *Australia's War in Vietnam*, Allen & Unwin, Sydney, 1987, p. 5.

[2] House of Representatives, *Debates*, vol. 45, 29 April 1965, p. 1061. While Menzies's rhetoric was certainly full-blown, it was not well grounded. As Peter Edwards has noted, his statement to Parliament, drafted in the Department of External Affairs, would appear to contradict the 1964 Strategic Basis paper which expected China to act cautiously for the next ten years. ('Vietnam—How the Menzies Bullets Backfired', *Sydney Morning Herald*, 6 June 1989.)

[3] Histories of the war abound: for example, Stanley Karnow, *Vietnam*, New York, Viking Press, 1983 (also Middlesex, Penguin, 1984). Very helpful from an Australian perspective is Frost, op. cit., esp. ch. 1.

[4] Cable sent by the Minister-Counsellor, Alan Renouf, 11 May 1964, quoted in Frost, op. cit., p. 16.

[5] Sir Anthony Eden, *Full Circle*, London, 1960, p. 102, quoted in Alan Watt, *Vietnam: An Australian Analysis*, F. W. Cheshire/Australian Institute for International Affairs, Melbourne, 1968, p. 51.

[6] The point has been made succinctly by Frost, op. cit., p. 12:

> The Australian Army combat force which entered the conflict from 1965 did not simply face in South Vietnam an external aggressor without an internal base of support. Rather, it faced a political movement directed from the north but conducting a struggle in South Vietnam the origins of which extended back to the anti-colonial struggle against the French and the impetus of which was, to a large extent, derived from the errors of the RVN and from social inequalities in South Vietnam.

See also Greg Lockhart, *Nation in Arms: The Origins of the People's Army of*

Vietnam, Allen & Unwin, Sydney, 1989; Carlyle A. Thayer, *A War by Other Means: National Liberation and Revolution in Viet-Nam 1954–60*, Allen & Unwin, Sydney, 1989.

[7] W. MacMahon Ball, published as *Australia's Role in Asia*, 18th Roy Milne Lecture, Australian Institute of International Affairs, 1967.

[8] Prince Sihanouk's deposition by Lon Nol and the events which followed were themselves the product of a complex interplay of currents, but one powerfully argued view is that secret United States bombing of the Cambodian border zone in 1969, effectively bringing the country into the Vietnam War for the first time, was the most important precipitant. (William Shawcross, *Sideshow: Kissinger, Nixon and Destruction of Cambodia*, Deutsch, London, 1979.)

[9] Elizabeth Becker, *When the War was Over: Cambodia's Revolution and the Voices of its People*, Simon and Schuster, New York, 1987, p. 322.

[10] This position was maintained after 1982, when the Khmer Rouge joined in coalition with Prince Sihanouk and Son Sann's KPLNF to form the CGDK. For the remainder of the Fraser Government's term, and subsequently under the Hawke Government, Australia abstained on the credentialing of the CGDK to the Cambodian UN seat whenever that issue arose. The fact that we were no more willing to accept the claim of the Vietnamese-backed SOC Government to the seat did not entirely soothe ASEAN, although the recognition issue did not, in itself, remain an irritant between Australia and ASEAN for very long.

[11] *Cambodia: An Australian Peace Proposal*, Working Papers prepared for the Informal Meeting on Cambodia, Jakarta, 26–28 February 1990, AGPS, Canberra, 1990.

[12] See, for example, the Prime Minister's keynote speech to the Bangkok Conference organised by *Nation* and the *Asia Wall Street Journal* on 28 April 1989, 'Indo-China: From War Zone to Trade Zone'.

Annotated Bibliography   Frank Frost, *Australia's War in Vietnam*, Allen & Unwin, Sydney, 1987, is a good single source for an understanding of Australia's military commitment to Vietnam. For an official account, see Department of Foreign Affairs, *Australia's Military Commitment to Vietnam*, AGPS, Canberra, 1975. Other useful studies include Gregory Pemberton, *All the Way: Australia's Road to Vietnam*, Allen & Unwin, Sydney, 1987; Kenneth Maddock and Barry Wright (eds), *War: Australia and Vietnam*, Harper & Row, Sydney 1987; Michael Sexton, *War for the Asking: Australia's Vietnam Secrets*, Penguin, Melbourne, 1981; Glen St. J. Barclay, *A Very Small Insurance Policy*, University of Queensland Press, Brisbane, 1988. For Australia's initiative on Cambodia, see *Cambodia: An Australian Peace proposal: Working Papers prepared for the Informal Meeting on Cambodia, Jakarta, 26–28 February, 1990*, AGPS, Canberra, 1990; Gareth Evans, 'Australia, Indo-China and the Cambodian Peace Plan', address to the Sydney Institute, *Australian Foreign Affairs and Trade, Monthly Record*, Vol. 61, No. 3, pp. 142–8, March 1990 and Ministerial Statement, Senate, *Debates*, 6 December 1990, pp. 5164–75. Also Colin Mackerras, Robert Cribb and Allan Healy (eds), *Contemporary Vietnam: Perspectives from Australia*, University of Wollongong Press, 1988. Other commentaries on Cambodia include: Gary Klintworth, *Vietnam's Intervention in Cambodia in International Law*, AGPS, Canberra, 1990; Grant Evans and Kelvin Rowley, *Red Brotherhood at War: Vietnam, Cambodia and Laos since 1975*, rev. ed., Verso, London, 1990; Michael Vickery, *Kampuchea: Politics, Economics and Society*, Allen & Unwin, Sydney, 1986. Further reading: Greg Lockhart, *Nation in Arms: The Origins of the People's Army of Vietnam*, Allen & Unwin, Sydney, 1989; Carlyle A. Thayer, *War By Other Means: National Liberation and Revolution in Viet-Nam, 1954–60*, Allen & Unwin, Sydney,

1989; Nancy Viviani, *The Long Journey: Vietnamese Migration and Settlement in Australia*, Melbourne University Press, 1984.

14   NORTH-EAST ASIA

1 See Ross Garnaut, *Australia and the Northeast Asian Ascendancy*, Report to the Prime Minister and the Minister for Foreign Affairs and Trade, AGPS, Canberra, 1989, ch. 2.
2 Ibid., p. 2.
3 Ibid., pp. 6–7. These and other aspects of the Garnaut Report are usefully discussed in J. L. Richardson (ed.), *Northeast Asian Challenge: Debating The Garnaut Report*, Australian National University, Canberra, 1991.
4 Garnaut Report, op. cit., ch. 16. We discussed in detail the role of public diplomacy in Chapter 5.
5 Speech to the Japan–Australia Dietmembers Friendship League, Tokyo, 19 September 1990.
6 'Joint Communique of the Australian Government and the Government of the People's Republic of China Concerning the Establishment of Diplomatic Relations between Australia and China', Paris, 21 December 1972.

Annotated Bibliography   The basic document for this chapter is Ross Garnaut, *Australia and the Northeast Asian Ascendancy*, AGPS, Canberra, 1989. Useful comments on the Garnaut Report are J. L. Richardson (ed.), *Northeast Asian Challenge: Debating the Garnaut Report*, Australian National University, Canberra, 1991; 'Australia and Northeast Asia: The Garnaut Report', *Australian Journal of International Affairs*, No. 44, Vol. 1, pp. 1–51, 1990. For reservations about Australia's relations with the region, especially Japan, see Coral Bell (ed.), *Agenda for the Nineties*, Longman Cheshire, Melbourne, 1991; Gavan McCormack, *Bonsai Australia Banzai: Multifunction Polis and the Making of a Special Relationship with Japan*, Pluto, Sydney, 1991; Yukio Sugimoto and Ross E. Mouer, *The MFP Debate*, La Trobe University Press, Melbourne, 1990. Shintaro Ishihara, *The Japan That Can Say No: Why Japan Will Be First Among Equals*, Simon and Schuster, New York, 1991, is a controversial, best-selling Japanese response to US criticism. Other commentaries include: Ian Inkster, *The Clever City: Japan, Australia and the Multifunction Polis*, Sydney University Press/Oxford University Press, Sydney, 1991; Peter Drysdale (ed.), *The Australia–Japan Relationship: Towards the year 2000*, Australia–Japan Research Centre, Canberra, 1989; Peter Drysdale (ed.), *The Soviets and the Pacific Challenge*, Allen & Unwin/Australia–Japan Research Centre, Canberra, 1991. See also Alan Rix, *Japan's Aid Program: A New Global Agenda*, International Development Issues, No. 12, AGPS, Canberra, 1990. On China–Australia relations, E. M. Andrews, *Australia and China: The Ambiguous Relationship*, Melbourne University Press, 1985 and Edmund S. K. Fung and Colin Mackerras, *From Fear to Friendship, Australia's Policies towards the People's Republic of China, 1966–1982*, University of Queensland Press, 1985, provide historical background. For recent comments, see Stephen FitzGerald, 'Australia's China', *Australian Journal of Chinese Affairs*, No. 24, pp. 315–35, 1990; Colin Mackerras, Kevin Bucknall and Russell Trood, *The Beijing Tragedy: Implications for China and Australia*, Centre for the Study of Asian–Australia Relations, Research Paper No. 51, Griffith University, Queensland, 1989; Gary Klintworth (ed.), *China's Crisis: The International Implications*, Strategic and Defence Studies Centre, Research School of Pacific Studies, Australian National University, Canberra, 1989. See also Joan Grant, *Worm-eaten Hinges: Tensions and*

Turmoil in Shanghai in 1988–9, Hyland House/Institute for Contemporary Asian Studies, Monash University, 1991; and two publications from the Legislative Research Service, Department of the Parliamentary Library, Canberra: Ann Kent, *Human Rights in the People's Republic of China*, Discussion Paper No. 3, 1989–90 and Brian G Martin, China in Crisis: The Events of April–June 1989, Current Issues Paper No. 1, 1989–90.

15   SOUTH ASIA AND THE INDIAN OCEAN

[1] Quoted in T. B. Millar, *Australia in Peace and War: External Relations 1788–1977*, Australian National University Press, Canberra, 1978, p. 367.

[2] The Station's functions are described in the White Paper, *The Defence of Australia 1987*, presented to Parliament by Kim Beazley, Minister for Defence, AGPS, Canberra, 1987, paras 2.5–8.

[3] World Bank, *World Development Report 1991*, Oxford University Press, New York, 1991, p. 209. Indian GDP is US$235.2 billion, and Australia's US$281.9 billion. The ten larger economies are the United States, Japan, Germany, France, Italy, United Kingdom, Canada, China, Spain and Brazil.

[4] Francis Fukuyama makes the point, to reinforce his thesis in 'The End of History?', *National Interest*, Summer 1989, pp. 3–18, that 'in the two hundred years or so that modern liberal democracies have existed, there is not a single instance of one liberal democracy fighting another'. (Speech to Frost on 'Sunday Lunch', London, 6 September 1990, citing political scientist Michael Doyle.)

[5] See Senate Standing Committee on Foreign Affairs, Defence and Trade, *Report on Australia–India Relations: Trade and Security*, Canberra, July 1990, paras 6.51–6.55, and the Government Response to the report, presented to Parliament by Senator Gareth Evans, Minister for Foreign Affairs and Trade, Senate, *Debates*, 21 December 1990, pp. 6309–20.

[6] Figures (from Dr Michael McKinley) cited in Senate Standing Committee, *Report*, op. cit., para 5.2.

[7] See ibid., ch. 5, esp. para 5.52ff.

[8] India continues nonetheless to be extremely sensitive on questions of relative capability. Australia found this when a decision in 1988 to sell 50 elderly Mirage fighter aircraft to Pakistan unfortunately coincided, in its subsequent implementation in 1990, with heightened tension between India and Pakistan over Kashmir. The Indians reacted with genuine concern, although our explanation (that the timing of the sale was simply a function of protracted commercial negotiations, that it would be rescinded if hostilities commenced, that it manifestly did not alter the balance of military power and was not intended to send a political signal to either Islamabad *or* New Delhi) eventually settled the matter down.

[9] Government Response to Senate Standing Committee, *Report*, op. cit., p. 6318.

[10] Ibid., p. 6311.

[11] Pakistan rejoined the Commonwealth in 1989, having left in 1972 over the question of Bangladesh's membership.

[12] A Commonwealth role along these lines had also been strongly advocated publicly by Opposition Foreign Affairs spokesman, Senator Robert Hill.

Annotated Bibliography   A good beginning is the Senate Standing Committee on Foreign Affairs, Defence and Trade, *Report on Australia–India Relations: Trade and Security*, AGPS, Canberra, 1990, and the Government's response, Senate, *Debates*,

21 December 1990, pp. 6309–20. For a well-sourced, up-to-date commentary which takes account of India's point of view, see Sandy Gordon, 'India and South Asia: Australia's "Other Asia"', *Current Affairs Bulletin*, Vol. 67, No. 12, 1991. Although dated in some aspects, Robert H. Bruce (ed.), *Australia and the Indian Ocean: Strategic Dimensions of Increasing Naval Involvement*, Centre for Indian Ocean Regional Studies, Curtin University, Perth, 1988, contains several valuable conference papers and commentaries, including the former Defence Minister Kim Beazley on Australia's two-ocean navy. See also Trevor Findlay, *Regional Maritime Arms Control: The Pacific and Indian Ocean Cases*, Working Paper No. 47, Peace Research Centre, Australian National University, 1988; Michael McKinley, 'Australia and the Indian Ocean' in F. A. Mediansky and A. C. Palfreeman (eds), *In Pursuit of National Interests: Australian Foreign Policy in the 1990s*, Pergamon Press, Sydney, 1988. An insight into South Asian politics as well as Soviet foreign policy and its armed forces is provided by an array of specialists in Amin Saikal and Willian Maley (eds), *The Soviet Withdrawal from Afghanistan*, Cambridge University Press, 1989. For an historical perspective, see J. D. B. Miller, 'Australia and the Indian Ocean Area' in Gordon Greenwood and Norman Harper (eds), *Australia in World Affairs, 1961–65*, F. W. Cheshire, Melbourne, 1968; T. B. Millar, 'Australia and the Indian Ocean Area', in Greenwood and Harper (eds), *Australia in World Affairs, 1966–70*, F. W. Cheshire, Melbourne, 1974; Bruce Grant, *Gods and Politicians*, Allen Lane, Melbourne, 1982. Further reading: Jonathan Spencer (ed.), *Sri Lanka: History and the Roots of Conflict*, Routledge, London, 1990; Rafiq Zakaria, *The Struggle within Islam: The Conflict between Religion and Politics*, Penguin, London, 1989.

16   THE MIDDLE EAST AND AFRICA

[1] The figures for East Europe were 1 per cent and for South America 1.1 per cent; for Africa, just 0.4 per cent. For these and all other trade figures cited, see *Composition of Trade, Australia, 1990*, Central Statistics Section, Department of Foreign Affairs and Trade, 1991.

[2] The summary which follows is drawn from a very useful Department of Foreign Affairs and Trade reference document published in May 1991: *Middle East: Trade and Economic Overview*, Research and Policy Discussion Paper, No 8. AGPS, Canberra, 1991.

[3] The Arab League, formed in 1945, had in mid-1991 twenty-one members, consisting of all the countries mentioned in the text (except Iran and Israel), together with the countries of the Maghreb (Libya, Tunisia, Algeria, Morocco and Mauritania); Sudan, Djibouti and Somalia on the Red Sea and Gulf of Aden; and Palestine. The Gulf Co-operation Council was formed in 1981; it has six members (Saudi Arabia, Kuwait, Bahrain, Qatar, the United Arab Emirates and Oman) and its principal objectives are co-ordination, integration and co-operation in economic, social and cultural—and defence—affairs.

[4] United States commitment to such an approach was announced by President Bush on 29 May 1991. For a summary and assessment of these proposals, see Senator Gareth Evans, Senate, *Debates*, 30 May 1991, pp. 3947–8.

[5] See 'Middle East: Policy Review', Statement by Acting Foreign Minister Lionel Bowen, 30 September 1983.

[6] Thomas Friedman, *From Beirut to Jerusalem*, Farrar, Straus and Giroux, New York, 1989, p. 253.

[7] Ibid., pp. 438–9.

[8] Ibid., p. 485.

[9] The first four 'Frontline States' to designate themselves and meet as such were

Botswana, Mozambique, Tanzania and Zambia in 1974. The number expanded as new states in the region became independent, but there remains no formal institutional structure for the group.

10 Both the self-defeating and the externally imposed economic consequences of apartheid are brilliantly described in Keith Ovenden and Tony Cole, *Apartheid and International Finance*, Penguin, Melbourne, 1989. (This book, commissioned by the Australian Government and launched at the Commonwealth Foreign Ministers Committee on Southern Africa meeting in Canberra in August 1989, built upon an earlier report by a Commonwealth committee headed by Tony Cole, now Secretary of the Australian Treasury.)

11 See Phyllis Johnson and David Martin, *Apartheid Terrorism: The Destabilisation Report*, Commonwealth Secretariat/James Currey/Indiana University Press, London, 1989, p. 52.

12 Ibid., p. 161

13 Angola, Botswana, Lesotho, Malawi, Mozambique, Namibia, Swaziland, Tanzania, Zambia and Zimbabwe. SADCC—most of whose members are economically very dependent on South Africa—was formed in 1980 with the central objective of reducing that dependence. An active debate is now occurring as to how post-apartheid South Africa might fit into this structure and act as an engine of growth for the whole region.

14 The first five years of operation of this program—which initially applied to Namibians as well as South Africans—is fully described and reviewed in *Special Assistance Program for South Africans and Namibians* (SAPSAN), AIDAB Review 1991, No. 1.

15 Under the Gleneagles Agreement, heads of government
accepted it as the urgent duty of each of their Governments vigorously to combat the evil of apartheid by withholding any form of support for, and by taking every practical step to discourage, contact or competition by their nationals with sporting organisations, teams or sportsmen from South Africa or from any other country where sports are organised on the basis of race, colour or ethnic origin.

16 The elements of this were: no South African teams allowed entry to Australia; applications from individual South African athletes who represent South Africa to be refused; Australians to be actively discouraged from competing in South Africa; contact between Australian and South African sportspersons in third countries to be opposed; government to encourage Australian sporting bodies to exert pressure to have South Africans expelled from international competitions; government to encourage other governments not to permit South Africans to participate in sporting events in their country; and applications from South African officials or administrators to visit Australia in their official capacity to be refused. In relation to the 'individual athletes' part of this package, the practice applied that individual amateurs, who usually come under the authority of South African national sporting organisations, were regarded as prima facie representative, and individual professionals as prima facie non-representative, but with in each case proof to the contrary overturning the presumption.

17 See *South Africa: The Sanctions Report*, Penguin/James Currey, London, 1989, p. 38. (The report of an Independent Group of Experts prepared for the Commonwealth Committee of Foreign Ministers on Southern Africa, this is the third of a trilogy of books on apartheid commissioned by or on behalf of the Commonwealth and published in 1989: see also Ovenden and Cole, and Johnson and Martin, op. cit.)

18 The EPG was an Australian proposal to the Nassau CHOGM in October 1985. It involved a Commonwealth team, co-chaired by Malcolm Fraser, visiting South Africa in the first half of 1986 and producing an excellent report recommending a

'Possible Negotiating Concept' involving a phased series of actions and commitments by the South African Government, and the ANC and others respectively: see *Mission to South Africa: the Commonwealth Report*, Penguin/Commonwealth Secretariat, London, 1986. The details of the negotiating concept are set out at pp. 103–4.

19 *The Sanctions Report*, op. cit., p. 38.

20 Published as *Banking on Apartheid: The Financial Links Report*, Commonwealth Secretariat/James Currey, London, 1989.

21 Ovenden and Cole, op. cit.

Annotated Bibliography Thomas Friedman, *From Beirut to Jerusalem*, Farrar Straus Giroux, New York, 1989 (Fontana, 1990), can be read for both pleasure and instruction: the best introduction to the imbroglio of Middle East politics currently available. *Strategic Survey 1990–91*, published by Brassey's, London, for the International Institute for Strategic Studies has a section (pp. 49–102) on the Gulf War and its impact on the Middle East generally. See also Shahram Chubin, 'Post-war Gulf Security', *Survival*, Vol. 43, No. 2, 1991; Ze've Schiff, 'Israel after the War', *Foreign Affairs*, Vol. 70, No. 2, pp. 19–33, 1991; David Bar-Illan, 'Israel after the Gulf War', *Commentary*, Vol. 91, No. 5, pp. 35–40, 1991; Robert Springborg, 'Origins of the Gulf Crisis' and Amin Saikal 'The Persian Gulf Crisis: Regional Implications', *Australian Journal of International Affairs*, Vol. 33, No. 3, pp. 221–45, 1991. On the issue of South Africa and apartheid, Commonwealth Committee of Foreign Ministers on Southern Africa, *South Africa: The Sanctions Report*, Penguin/James Currey, London, 1989 and Commonwealth Group of Eminent Persons, *Mission to South Africa: The Commonwealth Report*, Penguin/Commonwealth Secretariat, London, 1986, provide a starting point. See also Keith Ovenden and Tony Cole, *Apartheid and International Finance: A Program for Change*, Penguin, Melbourne, 1989; Joseph Hanlon (ed.), *South Africa: The Sanctions Report, Documents and Statistics*, Commonwealth Secretariat/James Currey, London, 1990. *Survival*, Vol. 30, No. 1, 1988 has a section on 'Regional Security in Southern Africa' with articles on Angola, Mozambique and Zimbabwe. See also Robert S. Jaster, *The 1988 Peace Accords and the Future of South-western Africa*, Adelphi Papers, No. 253, Brassey's/International Institute for Strategic Studies, 1991; Chester A. Crocker, 'Southern African Peace-Making', *Survival*, Vol. 42, No. 2, 1990; Paul Nursey-Bray, 'South Africa: Retrospect and Prospect', *Current Affairs Bulletin*, Vol. 68, No. 2, pp. 4–11, 1991; Paul Johnstone, 'Resolution in Namibia?', *Melbourne University Law Review*, Vol. 17, No. 2, pp. 243–74, 1989. Further reading: Parliament of the Commonwealth of Australia, *Report of the Australian Parliamentary Delegations to Ethiopia, Tanzania, Mozambique and Zimbabwe, June–July 1988*, AGPS, Canberra, 1989.

17 EUROPE

1 The twelve EC countries are Belgium, Denmark, France, Germany, Greece, Ireland, Italy, Luxembourg, the Netherlands, Portugal, Spain and the United Kingdom. Strictly, the term is 'European Communities' not 'Community', embracing as it does the European Coal and Steel Community (ECSC) established by the Treaty of Paris in 1951, and the European Economic Community (EEC) and European Atomic Energy Community (EAEC or Euratom) established by the Treaties of Rome in 1957. But since 1967 the institutional arrangements of the Communities have been amalgamated into a single structure, the most important elements of which are the European Commission, the various ministerial

Councils (including the European Council involving heads of government, the Council of Ministers involving foreign ministers, and specialist Councils e.g. the Agriculture Council), the European Parliament, and the European Court of Justice. The institutional integration of the 'Community' was further strengthened by the European Single Market Act of 1987.

[2] The six EFTA countries are Austria, Finland, Iceland, Norway, Sweden and Switzerland. The Stockholm Convention establishing the Association dates from 1960.

[3] Albania, Bulgaria, Czechoslovakia, Hungary, Poland, Romania and Yugoslavia.

[4] 'Today Program', BBC Radio 4, 19 June 1991.

[5] Ibid.

[6] The sixteen NATO members are Belgium, Canada, Denmark, France, Germany, Greece, Iceland, Italy, Luxembourg, the Netherlands, Norway, Portugal, Spain, Turkey, the United Kingdom and the United States. The NATO Treaty was signed in 1949 by twelve of the present parties: Greece and Turkey were admitted in 1952, the Federal Republic of Germany in 1955 and Spain in 1982. The Key NATO bodies are the North Atlantic Council (which meets at ministerial or ambassadorial level), and the Defence Planning and Military Committees (on which France does not sit—but through the latter of which it liaises).

[7] See, e.g., Secretary of State James Baker in his address to the Aspen Institute on 18 June 1991, in which he emphasised also the need to 'reach out' to the Soviet military and let them 'know about NATO's strategy, doctrine and defensive nature'. Baker described US objectives as extending to 'both a Europe whole and free, and a Euro–Atlantic Community that extends east from Vancouver to Vladivostok'.

[8] The thirty-five states participating in the CSCE are the sixteen NATO members (see above, n. 6); the six former Warsaw Pact countries—Bulgaria, Czechoslovakia, Hungary, Poland, Romania and the Soviet Union; the twelve neutral or non-aligned countries—Austria, Cyprus, Finland, the Holy See, Ireland, Liechtenstein, Malta, Monaco, San Marino, Sweden, Switzerland and Yugoslavia; and —since June 1991—Albania.

[9] Quoted in 'Z', 'To The Stalin Mausoleum', *Daedalus* Vol. 119, No. 1, 1990, p. 295.

[10] Michael Mandelbaum, 'The Soviet Economy in Crisis', *Critical Issues*, No. 4, 1991, Council on Foreign Relations, New York, p. 5.

[11] *Perestroika: Implications for Australia–USSR Relations*, Report of the Senate Standing Committee on Foreign Affairs, Defence and Trade, AGPS, Canberra, 1991, tabled in the Senate on 21 December 1990; see also Government Response presented by Senator Gareth Evans, Minister for Foreign Affairs and Trade, 17 April 1991, Senate, *Debates*, pp. 2613–30.

[12] 'Stability and Change in Central and Eastern Europe', Address to Royal Institute of International Affairs (Chatham House), London, 16 April 1991.

[13] We are indebted for his kind assistance in the compilation of the immigrant population figures in this chapter to Dr James Jupp, Director of the Centre for Immigration and Multicultural Studies, Australian National University.

Annotated Bibliography   The speed and the complexity of events in Europe has left commentary behind. Grahame Cook (ed.), *Australia and 1992: The Nature and Implications of a Single European Market*, AGPS, Canberra, 1989, brings together papers from a conference at the Sir Robert Menzies Centre for Australian Studies, London; the London perspective is noticeable but the issues are broadly covered.

Chapters by Coral Bell, Robert Miller and Richard Higgott in Coral Bell (ed.), *Agenda for the Nineties: Australian Choices in Foreign and Defence Policy*, Longman Cheshire, Melbourne, 1991, are useful. As European background, the following are recommended: William Wallace (ed.), *The Dynamic of European Integration*, Royal Institute of International Affairs/Pinter, London, 1990; Nicholas Colchester and David Buchan, *Europe Relaunched: Truths and Illusions on the Way to 1992*, Economist Books, London, 1990; Barry Buzan et al., *Remaking the European Security Order: Scenarios for the Post-Cold War Era*, Pinter, London, 1990; Ralf Dahrendorf, *Reflections on the Revolution in Europe*, Chatto and Windus, London, 1990; Neill Nugent, *The Government and Politics of the European Community*, Macmillan, London, 1989. See also Marc Bentinck, *Nato Out-of-Area Problem*, and Ian Gambles, *Prospects for West European Security Co-operation*, Adelphi Papers, Nos 211 and 244, International Institute for Strategic Studies, London, 1986, 1989. A starting point for an Australian perspective on events in the Soviet Union and East Europe is Senate Standing Committee on Foreign Affairs, Defence and Trade, *Perestroika: Implications for Australia–USSR Relations*, AGPS, Canberra, 1990. See also John E. Tedstrom (ed.), *Socialism, Perestroika and the Dilemmas of Soviet Economic Reform*, Westview Press, Boulder, Co., 1990; Stephen White, Alex Pravda and Zvi Gitelman (eds), *Developments in Soviet Politics*, Macmillan, London, 1990. Other commentaries include: *The Strategic Implications of Change in the Soviet Union*, Adelphi Papers, Nos 247 and 248, 1989/90; Renee de Nevers, *The Soviet Union and Eastern Europe: The End of An Era*, Adelphi Papers, No. 249, 1990; Timothy Garton Ash, 'Angry New Eastern Europe', *New York Review*, 16 August, 1990; Harry Gelman, *Gorbachev and the Future of the Soviet Military Institution*, Adelphi Papers, No. 258, 1991; and Vol. 43, No. 4, 1991 of *Survival*, which is devoted to European security issues.

18 THE AMERICAS

[1] For the purposes of this Chapter, the 35 countries are aggregated as follows: *North America* (2), the United States and Canada; *the Caribbean* (16), made up of 13 independent island states (Cuba, Haiti and the Dominican Republic plus CARICOM members Antigua and Barbuda, Bahamas, Barbados, Dominica, Grenada, Jamaica, St Kitts-Nevis, St Lucia, St Vincent and the Grenadines, and Trinidad and Tobago), and three mainland states (Belize, Guyana and Suriname); and *Latin America* (17), made up of Mexico, the central American republics (Costa Rica, El Salvador, Guatemala, Honduras and Nicaragua—plus Panama), and the ten mainland republics (Argentina, Bolivia, Brazil, Chile, Columbia, Ecuador, Paraguay, Peru, Uruguay and Venezuela). These categories are by no means universally applicable—e.g. for a number of purposes, including in a number of multilateral organisations, Cuba and the three mainland states of Belize, Guyana and Suriname (along with the French Département of French Guiana) are treated as part of Latin America. For the purposes of the Charts in this book, Mexico is grouped with Canada and the United States as part of 'North America' and all the other countries are treated together as 'South America'.

[2] George Washington, Farewell Address on leaving the Presidency, 1796.

[3] Owen Harries (ed.), *America's Purpose: New Visions of U.S. Foreign Policy*, ICS Press, San Francisco, 1991, p. 3.

[4] The role of the joint facilities, and Australia's contribution to global security, are further discussed in Chapter 6.

[5] Letter from President Bush to Prime Minister Hawke, 25 March 1991.

[6] R. B. Byers, *Canadian Security and Defence: The Legacy and the Challenges*, Adelphi Papers, No. 214, International Institute for Strategic Studies, London, 1986.

[7] The CARICOM members are the twelve Commonwealth members in the region (Antigua and Barbuda, Bahamas, Barbados, Belize, Dominica, Grenada, Guyana, Jamaica, St Kitts-Nevis, Saint Lucia, St Vincent and the Grenadines, and Trinidad and Tobago), plus—rather oddly—the British colony, Montserrat.

[8] Britain retains control over five territories (Montserrat, Anguilla, the Turks and Caicos Islands, British Virgin Islands and Cayman Islands); the Netherlands over the six islands of the Netherlands Antilles (including Curacao) and the three islands of St Maarten in the Leewards; the French over the three 'Départments' of Martinique, Guadelope, and French Guiana on the mainland; and the United States over the US Virgin Islands as well as the Commonwealth of Puerto Rico.

[9] The Commonwealth members in the Caribbean are Antigua and Barbuda, Bahamas, Barbados, Belize, Dominica, Grenada, Guyana, Jamaica, St Lucia, St Kitts-Nevis, St Vincent and the Grenadines, and Trinidad and Tobago.

[10] See, for example, Tim Duncan and John Fogarty, *Australia and Argentina: On Parallel Paths*, Melbourne University Press, 1984.

[11] Recent economic integration initiatives, at varying stages of development or implementation, include: President Bush's 'Enterprise for the Americas', a comprehensive free trade agreement for all of Latin America and the Caribbean; the North America Free Trade Agreement (US, Canada and Mexico) targeted for 1992; Southern Cone Common Market (MERCOSUR), which proposes a free trade zone and common market for Argentina, Brazil, Uruguay and Paraguay by 1995; the Southern Cone Agricultural Co-operation Council (CONASUR), formed in 1990 between Argentina, Brazil, Chile and Uruguay; the Mexico Central America Economic Complementary Agreement, signed in 1991 by Mexico, Costa Rica, El Salvador, Guatemala, Honduras and Nicaragua, for a free trade zone by 1996; the Group of Three Energy Basin Initiative (COMEVEN) agreement in 1990 by three major fossil fuel exporters, Mexico, Colombia and Venezuela; and the Chile–Venezuela Free Trade Agreement, to begin in 1994.

Annotated Bibliography 'America's Role in a Changing World' was the topic of the 32nd annual conference of the International Institute for Strategic Studies in 1990. The papers, wide-ranging (although lacking an Asia Pacific dimension) and at best timeless are printed in *Adelphi Papers* Nos 256 and 257, International Institute for Strategic Studies, London, 1990/91. For two contrasting American views of what the end of the Cold War means for American foreign policy, see Theodore C. Sorensen, 'Rethinking National Security', *Foreign Affairs*, Vol. 69, No. 2, 1990; and Samuel P. Huntington, 'America's Changing Strategic Interests', *Survival*, Vol. 43, No. 1, 1991. An Australian perspective is given in Ross Babbage, 'The Australia–United States Alliance: The Stresses of Change' in Coral Bell (ed.), *Agenda for the Nineties: Australian Choices in Foreign and Defence Policy*, Longman Cheshire, Melbourne, 1991. See also Richard W. Baker (ed.), *Australia, New Zealand and the United States: Internal Change and Alliance Relations in the ANZUS States*, Praeger, New York, 1991; Richard Higgott, 'The Ascendancy of the Economic Dimension in Australian–American Relations' in John Ravenhill (ed.), *No Longer an American Lake?*, Allen & Unwin, Sydney, 1989; Coral Bell, 'The ANZUS Alliance: The Case For' and Gary Brown, 'The ANZUS Alliance: The Case Against' in Desmond Ball and Cathy Downes (eds), *Security and Defence: Pacific and Global Perspectives*, Allen & Unwin, Sydney, 1990. On Canada, some useful insights are provided by Bruce Hodgins, 'Canada and Australia: Some Future Directions from Historical Perspectives', *Australian–Canadian Studies*, Vol. 4, pp. 29–49, 1986; R. B.

Byers, *Canadian Security and Defence: The Legacy and the Challenges*, Adelphi Papers, No. 214, 1986. An up-to-date and comprehensive account of developments in Latin America is given in the review article, Peter H. Smith, 'Crisis and Democracy in Latin America', *World Politics*, Vol. 43, 1991. For a scholarly analysis, see Larry Diamond, Juan J. Linz and Seymour Martin Lipset (eds), *Democracy in Developing Countries, Volume 4: Latin America*, Lynne Riemer, Boulder, Co., 1989. Other commentaries include: Michael J. Dziedzic, *Mexico: Converging Challenges*, Adelphi Papers, No. 242, 1989; United Nations Commission for Latin America and the Caribbean, *Changing Production Patterns with Equity*, Santiago, 1990; James M. Malloy and Mitchell A. Seligson (eds), *Authoritarians and Democrats: Regime Transitions in Latin America*, University of Pittsburgh Press, 1987; Tim Duncan and John Fogarty, *Australia and Argentina: On Parallel Paths*, Melbourne University Press, 1984.

19   AUSTRALIA'S ROLE IN THE WORLD OF THE 1990s

[1] In his study *Middle Powers in International Politics*, Macmillan, London, 1984, Carsten Holbraad identifies eighteen middle powers, based on size of economy and population: Japan, West Germany, China, France, United Kingdom, Canada, Italy, Brazil, Spain, Poland, India, Australia, Mexico, Iran, Argentina, South Africa, Indonesia and Nigeria. Our own preference is for a reduction at the top end—China, France and the UK have special status as former 'great powers' who are now permanent members of the UN Security Council, and we would describe them, these days, along with Japan, Germany and India, as being at least 'major' powers. Ranked purely by latest GDP figures (in US$ million), today's list of eighteen (excluding the United States and the Soviet Union) is, according to the *World Development Report 1991*, Oxford University Press, New York, 1991, p. 209:

Country	$m	Country	$m
Japan	2 818 520	Australia	281 940
Germany	1 189 100	India	235 220
France	955 790	Netherlands	221 680
Italy	865 720	Republic of Korea	211 880
United Kingdom	717 870	Mexico	200 730
Canada	488 590	Switzerland	174 960
China	417 830	Sweden	166 520
Spain	379 360	Belgium	156 830
Brazil	319 150	Iran	150 250

[2] Earlier discussions include Annette Baker Fox, *The Politics of Attraction: Four Middle Powers and the United States*, New York, Columbia University Press, 1977; 'The Range of Choice for Middle Powers: Australia and Canada Compared', *Australian Journal of Politics and History*, Vol. 26, No. 2, 1980, pp. 193–3. Some recent accounts include Bernard Wood, 'Canada and Southern Africa: A Return to Middle Power Activism', *Round Table*, No. 315, 1990, pp. 280–90; Richard A. Higgott and Andrew Fenton Cooper, 'Middle Power Leadership and Coalition Building: Australia, the Cairns Group and Uruguay Round of Trade Negotiations', *International Organisations*, Vol. 44, No. 4, 1990, pp. 589–632. Again, in a recent speech to the Hoover Institution (Palo Alto, 29 June 1991), President Roh Tae Woo of the Republic of Korea stated that his country would in the 1990s 'seek new roles as a middle power—between the advanced and developing countries'. He saw Korea as a catalyst in the promotion of economic co-operation and exchanges of technology, capital, market resources and information in an era of

globalisation. We are indebted to David Hegarty for drawing our attention to some of this material.

3 For example, John Gorton's opening speech at the Higgins by-election on 14 February 1968, in which he spoke of Australians as having 'the same approach to life' as Britons and Americans. Gough Whitlam's speeches in the 1969 election campaign also persistently referred to 'comparable countries'—especially Canada, the Scandinavians and West Europeans. On foreign models generally, see also Stuart Harris, *Review of Australia's Overseas Representation*, AGPS, Canberra, 1986, p. 21.

4 Stephen FitzGerald, 'Australia: Lazy Country; Lovely Country', speech originally delivered to the Hong Kong Press Club in September 1990, and published in edited form in the Melbourne *Sunday Herald*, 4 November 1990.

5 'In Australia now in the field of education there is an attention to teaching, research and training in relation to Asia which is not matched in the education systems in any other country in the region. There are also plans in place for the widespread introduction, in general education and not in specialist schools, of the teaching of six Asian languages (and a seventh to a lesser degree), not just in university, where it happens in some countries, but in secondary and primary schools. No other government in the region has anything like this in contemplation. It shows Australia to be ahead of the field in reaching for the Asia consciousness that is the precondition for an Asian community'. (Ibid.) For details of the evolving national government strategy on Asian language teaching see Department of Employment, Education and Training, *Australia's Language: The Australian Language and Literacy Policy*, AGPS, Canberra, August 1991.

6 Bernard Kouchner, French Junior Minister attached to the Minister for Foreign Affairs, responsible for Humanitarian Policy, quoted in the Editorial, *Le Monde*, 7/8 April 1991, reprinted in *Guardian Weekly*, 14 April 1991.

7 These matters are more fully developed in Chapter 3, pp. 41–3; see also Chapter 10, p. 144ff.

8 Modern commentary on the search for an Australian identity seems to have begun with the publication of three books in the 1950s—Vance Palmer, *The Legend of the Nineties*, Melbourne University Press, 1954; Russel Ward, *The Australian Legend*, Oxford University Press, Melbourne, 1958; A. A. Phillips, *The Australian Tradition: Studies in a Colonial Culture*, F. W. Cheshire, Melbourne, 1958. The titles of two later books—Donald Horne, *The Lucky Country*, Penguin, Melbourne, 1964 and Geoffrey Blainey, *The Tyranny of Distance*, Sun Books, Melbourne, 1966—became household phrases. Robin Boyd, *The Australian Ugliness*, Penguin, Melbourne, 1963, used evidence from our highly urbanised society to attack the artificial culture of modern Australia. An excellent source, especially because it includes the contribution of painters to Australia's sense of national identity is Geoffrey Serle, *From Deserts the Prophets Come: The Creative Spirit in Australia 1788–1972*, Heinemann, Melbourne, 1973. Today, film and television are increasingly important in establishing 'images' of Australia but the result so far is inconclusive: the images tumble out in profusion, but none (not even Crocodile Dundee) is definitive. For an attempt to re-assess the imagery of the Australian 'digger', see Peter Pierce, Jeffrey Grey and Jeff Doyle, *Vietnam Days: Australia and the Impact of Vietnam*, Penguin, Melbourne, 1991. For some sensible comments on 'opening' and 'closing' tendencies in Asia and their effect on Australian culture, see Nancy Viviani, 'Australia's Future in Asia: People, Politics and Culture', *Australian Perceptions of Asia*, Australian Cultural History No. 9, University of New South Wales, 1990. For an international Australian identity, see Bruce Grant, *What Kind of Country?*, Penguin, Melbourne, 1988, pp. 87–104.

Index

compiled by
Dorothy F. Prescott